The Art Gallery on Stage

Methuen Drama Engage offers original reflections about key practitioners, movements and genres in the fields of modern theatre and performance. Each volume in the series seeks to challenge mainstream critical thought through original and interdisciplinary perspectives on the body of work under examination. By questioning existing critical paradigms, it is hoped that each volume will open up fresh approaches and suggest avenues for further exploration.

Series Editors

Mark Taylor-Batty
University of Leeds, UK
Enoch Brater
University of Michigan, USA

Titles in the series include:

Contemporary Drag Practices and Performers: Drag in a Changing Scene Volume 1
Edited by Mark Edward and Stephen Farrier
ISBN 978-1-3500-8294-6

Performing the Unstageable: Success, Imagination, Failure
Karen Quigley
ISBN 978-1-3500-5545-2

Drama and Digital Arts Cultures
David Cameron, Michael Anderson and Rebecca Wotzko
ISBN 978-1-472-59219-4

Social and Political Theatre in 21st-Century Britain: Staging Crisis
Vicky Angelaki
ISBN 978-1-474-21316-5

Watching War on the Twenty-First-Century Stage: Spectacles of Conflict
Clare Finburgh
ISBN 978-1-472-59866-0

Fiery Temporalities in Theatre and Performance: The Initiation of History
Maurya Wickstrom
ISBN 978-1-4742-8169-0

Ecologies of Precarity in Twenty-First Century Theatre: Politics, Affect, Responsibility
Marissia Fragkou
ISBN 978-1-4742-6714-4

Robert Lepage/Ex Machina: Revolutions in Theatrical Space
James Reynolds
ISBN 978-1-4742-7609-2

Social Housing in Performance: The English Council Estate on and off Stage
Katie Beswick
ISBN 978-1-4742-8521-6

Postdramatic Theatre and Form
Edited by Michael Shane Boyle, Matt Cornish and Brandon Woolf
ISBN 978-1-3500-4316-9

Sarah Kane's Theatre of Psychic Life: Theatre, Thought and Mental Suffering
Leah Sidi
ISBN 978-1-3502-8312-1

For a complete listing, please visit
https://www.bloomsbury.com/series/methuen-drama-engage/

The Art Gallery on Stage

New Vistas on Contemporary British Playwriting

Mariacristina Cavecchi

methuen | drama

LONDON • NEW YORK • OXFORD • NEW DELHI • SYDNEY

METHUEN DRAMA
Bloomsbury Publishing Plc, 50 Bedford Square, London, WC1B 3DP, UK
Bloomsbury Publishing Inc, 1359 Broadway, New York, NY 10018, USA
Bloomsbury Publishing Ireland, 29 Earlsfort Terrace, Dublin 2, D02 AY28, Ireland

BLOOMSBURY, METHUEN DRAMA and the Methuen Drama logo
are trademarks of Bloomsbury Publishing Plc

First published in Great Britain 2024
Paperback edition published 2025

Copyright © Mariacristina Cavecchi, 2024

Mariacristina Cavecchi has asserted her right under the Copyright, Designs and
Patents Act, 1988, to be identified as Author of this work.

For legal purposes the Acknowledgements on pp. xiii–xiv constitute an
extension of this copyright page.

Series design by Louise Dugdale
Cover image © Donald Cooper

All rights reserved. No part of this publication may be: i) reproduced or transmitted in any form, electronic or mechanical, including photocopying, recording or by means of any information storage or retrieval system without prior permission in writing from the publishers; or ii) used or reproduced in any way for the training, development or operation of artificial intelligence (AI) technologies, including generative AI technologies. The rights holders expressly reserve this publication from the text and data mining exception as per Article 4(3) of the Digital Single Market Directive (EU) 2019/790.

Bloomsbury Publishing Plc does not have any control over, or responsibility for, any third-party websites referred to or in this book. All internet addresses given in this book were correct at the time of going to press. The author and publisher regret any inconvenience caused if addresses have changed or sites have ceased to exist, but can accept no responsibility for any such changes.

A catalogue record for this book is available from the British Library.

Library of Congress Cataloging-in-Publication Data
Names: Cavecchi, Mariacristina, author.
Title: The art gallery on stage : new vistas on contemporary British
playwriting / Mariacristina Cavecchi.
Description: London ; New York : Methuen Drama, 2024. |
Series: Methuen Drama engage | Includes bibliographical references and index.
Identifiers: LCCN 2023033738 (print) | LCCN 2023033739 (ebook) |
ISBN 9781350330702 (hardback) | ISBN 9781350330726 (epub) |
ISBN 9781350330719 (pdf)
Subjects: LCSH: Art museums in literature. | English drama–20th
century–History and criticism. | English drama–21st century–History
and criticism. | Theater–Great Britain–History–20th century. |
Theater–Great Britain–History–21st century. | Theaters–Stage-setting
and scenery–Great Britain.
Classification: LCC PR739.A77 C38 2024 (print) | LCC PR739.A77 (ebook) |
DDC 822/.9209357–dc23/eng/20231115
LC record available at https://lccn.loc.gov/2023033738
LC ebook record available at https://lccn.loc.gov/2023033739

ISBN: HB: 978-1-3503-3070-2
PB: 978-1-3503-3073-3
ePDF: 978-1-3503-3071-9
eBook: 978-1-3503-3072-6

Series: Methuen Drama Engage

Typeset by Newgen KnowledgeWorks Pvt. Ltd., Chennai, India

For product safety related questions contact productsafety@bloomsbury.com.

To find out more about our authors and books visit www.bloomsbury.com
and sign up for our newsletters.

To Yaripza and Martina, masterpieces in my heart's gallery

Contents

List of figures		xi
Acknowledgements		xiii
List of abbreviations		xv
Introduction: The art gallery as muse		1
1	How the art gallery came to the stage	17
	The seduction of the art gallery	17
	Beckett's museum fever and performative turn	20
	The art gallery experience on stage	25
	Fatal attraction	41
	The eighties: Towards something new	41
	The drama of Young British Artists	57
	Theatricalizing the art gallery: The Tate	75
	Plays for galleries, plays in galleries	82
2	The drama of authenticity, connoisseurship and identity	93
	Forgeries, copyrights and Polaroids	96
	Questions of attribution	104
	Restoration or conservation?	124
	True stories about fakes: Towards a meta-modern experience?	138
	'Counterfeit … meets … conceptual!'	150
3	Staging the art gallery	155
	Black boxes and white cubes: From Beckett to Crouch	155
	This stage is a gallery	156
	An art gallery for all	163
	To exhibit or not to exhibit?	171
	The artist's studio	180
	'Making' the art gallery on stage	195
	Displaying the absence: Martin Crimp's *Attempts on Her Life*	198
	Transplanting the white cube: Tim Crouch's *ENGLAND*	204

	A choreographed collection: Mark Ravenhill and Frantic Assembly's *pool (no water)*	211
4	The price of everything	223
	Art is money-sexy	223
	All the beauty and the bloodshed	234
Bibliography		245
Index		263

Figures

1.1	*Closer* written by Patrick Marber and directed by David Leveaux	37
1.2	*Closer* written and directed by Patrick Marber	39
1.3	*A Number* written by Caryl Churchill and directed by Lyndsey Turner	42
1.4	*Three Birds Alighting on a Field* written by Timberlake Wertenbaker and directed by Max Stafford-Clark	49
1.5	*The Line* written by Timberlake Wertenbaker and directed by Matthew Lloyd	56
1.6	*My Arm* written by and with Tim Crouch. Co-directed by Tim Crouch, Karl James, Hettie Macdonald	73
2.1	*Bay at Nice* written and directed by David Hare	107
2.2	*Pentecost* written by David Edgar and directed by Michael Attenborough	128
2.3	*Pentecost* written by David Edgar and directed by Michael Attenborough	131
3.1	*Sunday in the Park with George*. Music and lyrics by Stephen Sondheim. Book by James Lapine	158
3.2	*The Pitmen Painters* written by Lee Hall and directed by Max Roberts	165
3.3	*The Pitmen Painters* written by Lee Hall and directed by Max Roberts	168
3.4	*Scenes from an Execution* written by Howard Brenton and directed by Ian McDiarmid	174

3.5	*Scenes from an Execution* written by and directed by Howard Barker	175
3.6	*Scenes from an Execution* written by Howard Barker and directed by Tom Cairns	178
3.7	*Red* written by John Logan and directed by Michael Grandage	184
3.8	*Red* written by John Logan and directed by Michael Grandage	187
3.9	*ENGLAND* written by Tim Crouch, and directed by Karl James and a smith	206
3.10	*pool (no water)* written by Mark Ravenhill. A production by Frantic Assembly	215
4.1	*Long Live the Little Knife* written and directed by David Leddy	232

Acknowledgements

My heartfelt gratitude is due to Caroline Patey, Maggie Rose and Sara Soncini, colleagues and dear friends, for sharing a life in the theatre and for their help before and during the writing and revisions of the present volume. Special thanks to my companion of many theatrical adventures, Sara, alias Guildenstern (or is it Rosencrantz?), whose observations were invariably helpful, as was her reading of some parts of the present work.

I would like to say a sincere thank you to my colleagues at the Centro di Ricerca Coordinata 'AltreScene', University of Milan, a lively centre of discussion and exchange, and to colleagues at the Department of Languages, Literatures, Culture and Mediation, University of Milan. The latter Department very kindly funded the illustrations.

I am most grateful to the Series Editors at Bloomsbury, Enoch Brater and Mark Taylor-Batty, for their prompt acceptance of my proposal in the Methuen Drama Engage series, as well as to Anna Brewer, Elizabeth Kellingley, Aanchal Vij, and Dhanujha Harikrishna at Newgen for their valuable editorial help.

Many thanks to Ale, Claudio, Fede, Marti, Viola and Yari, my lively companions on visits to many exhibitions and theatre performances, whose youthful, spontaneous perception and startling insight have enriched my perspective on several paintings and plays in the present work.

Finally, a special acknowledgement to the students who have attended my course on History of British Theatre, whose contribution in class discussions has inspired the analysis of some of the plays in this book.

Earlier versions of material used in some of the chapters have appeared in the following book chapters and articles:

'From Playwriting to Curatorship. An Investigation into the Status of Beckett's Stage Objects'. In *The Exhibit in the Text. The Museological Practices of Literature*, edited by C. Patey, L. Scuriatti, 161–82. London: Peter Lang, 2009.

'Hogarth's progress in Nick Dear's *The Art of Success*'. In *Enduring Presence: The Afterlives of William Hogarth*, edited by G. Letissier, C. Patey and C. Roman, vol. 1, 183–204. Bern: Peter Lang, 2021.

'Il museo in scena. I Seagram Murals di Rothko sul palco di John Logan', *Acme*, LXXI, 2018, 191–207.

'Quando il teatro va al museo. Una storia di oggi', *Altre Modernità/Otras Modernidades/Autre Modernités/Other Modernities*, 5 (2011), 26–44.

'The Museum is the Thing. Treading New Ground on British Stage', *Letteratura e Letterature*, 13, 2019, 119–38.

'The New Art Galleries on the Contemporary British Stage'. In *The Museal Turn*, edited by S. Coelsch-Foisner, D. Brown, 299-313. Heidelberg: Universitätsverlag Winter, 2012.

'Tim Crouch's "Transplant": Performing Narrative in Art Galleries', *TEXTUS. English Studies in Italy*, vol. XXXII (2018), 131–44.

Abbreviations

Art	Dear, Nick, *The Art of Success*.
Attempts	Crimp, Martin, *Attempts on Her Life*.
Bay	Hare, David, *Bay at Nice*.
E	Crouch, Tim. *ENGLAND*.
Line	Wertenbaker, Timberlake, *The Line*.
Long	Leddy, David, *Long Live the Little Knife*.
Magritte	Stoppard, Tom, *After Magritte*.
Masters	Gray, Simon, *The Old Masters*.
Museum	Khalil, Hannah, *A Museum in Baghdad*.
Oak	Crouch, Tim, *An Oak Tree*.
Painter	Lenkiewicz, Rebecca, *The Painter*.
Pitmen	Hall, Lee, *The Pitmen Painters*.
Poltergeist	Ridley, Philip, *The Poltergeist*.
pool	Ravenhill, Mark, *pool (no water)*.
Question	Bennett, Alan, *A Question of Attribution*.
RoB	Bridgemont, Andrew, *Red on Black*.
Scenes	Barker, Howard, *Scenes from an Execution*.
Shoreditch	Lenkiewicz, Rebecca, *Shoreditch Madonna*.
True	Breach, *It's True, It's True, It's True*.
3 Birds	Wertenbaker, Timberlake, *Three Birds Alighting on a Field*.

Introduction

The art gallery as muse

The Art Gallery on Stage investigates the representation of the art gallery on the contemporary British stage and discusses how issues and practices relating to the art world have intrigued and engaged playwrights with growing intensity over the past four decades. Indeed, since the 1980s, an ever increasing number of playwrights and theatre-makers have started to regard the art gallery as a muse in itself rather than simply the home of the muses, 'an independent locus of artistic inspiration and activity', to quote Kynaston McShine, the curator of the 1999 exhibition at the New York Museum of Modern Art, *The Museum as Muse*.[1] Just like the artists in the MoMa exhibition, British playwrights have turned the art gallery into a recurrent subject for their plays, questioning and challenging its space and function.

The Art Gallery on Stage contends that since the 1980s, the British stage has become a place for 'encounters' with the art gallery. But which art gallery? The choice of the title requires clarification, given the somewhat slippery meaning of an art gallery and its close and complicated relationship with the art museum. The terms 'art gallery' and 'art museum' are often used interchangeably to describe institutions that display art, and, in the United Kingdom, most public art museums are called galleries. Perhaps the most prominent examples of such institutions are the National Gallery, inaugurated with the aim of establishing and preserving public heritage, and the Tate Gallery, which is a public-private institution. However, even if both the art museum and the art gallery fulfil the essential task of exhibiting art and are both concerned with questions of acquisition, collection and displaying, they generally serve different purposes and cater to different audiences.

Variously defined as a storehouse, a repository of memory, a history book and a place for the collections that are at the core of cultural and national identities as well as aesthetic values, museums are constantly engaged in a conversation with knowledge, tradition, memory and the past. Even if

---

[1] Kynaston McShine, *The Museum as Muse: Artists Reflect* (New York: The Museum of Modern Art, 1999), 6.

museums have been increasingly positioned as for-profit enterprises governed by market-oriented cultural policies and addressing the visitor as a client with identifiable, manipulable needs, we nonetheless see this older, more public-oriented function evidenced in plays such as David Edgar's *Pentecost* (1994) or Hannah Khalil's *A Museum in Baghdad* (2019). On the other hand, an art gallery, whether commercial or public funded, tends to have more adventurous and entrepreneurial aims, showcasing the latest (and often 'cutting-edge') work by emerging artists, as well as a range of new and diverse artistic languages and narratives. One remark by a character in Alan Bennett's *A Question of Attribution* (1988) is somewhat telling: 'Museums I know where I am. An art gallery, I always come out feeling restless and dissatisfied. Troubled. [...] In a museum I'm informed, instructed. But with art ... I don't know' (*Question* 317). This comment on the informative and educational nature of art museums versus the more enigmatic space of art galleries might succinctly sum up one of the main differences between the two institutions regarding both their motives and their relationships with visitors. As centres of avant-gardist experiment, galleries (propelled by their often audacious curators) set their sights on the future. While is certainly the case in respect of the fictional gallery, 'The Gallery', at the centre of Timberlake Wertenbaker's *Three Birds Alighting on a Field* (1991), a number of actual galleries, such as Jay Joplin's White Cube or the Saatchi Gallery, to name the most famous, have also worked as the driving force behind the launch of emerging artists, successfully disseminating modern and contemporary art in London. The recognition of the complex interaction between museums and art galleries underpins the fascinating relationship between theatre and the art gallery, which this book explores. Their mutual influence on strategies for displaying artworks, endorsement and investments in branded artists, and attempts to engage visitors resonates through all the plays analysed in the present book, which, with a few exceptions, are mostly about art galleries, whether public or private.

The boom in dramaturgy dealing with the art gallery and the art world exploded in the 1990s and the first two decades of the twenty-first century in response to the altered role of the art gallery, the growing importance of London as the capital of contemporary art, and the major changes and developments within British theatre. While it is undeniable that since the 1980s an unprecedented body of research and discussion has focused on art galleries and museums and their social, cultural and institutional significance, the extraordinary conjunction of historical and cultural circumstances that led to London becoming the world contemporary art capital, snatching the title from New York, has played an equally indisputable role in bringing art galleries to the forefront as objects of cultural and dramaturgical attraction. Indeed, 1988 might be regarded as a turning point in the history of the fascinating affair between British theatre and the art gallery. This same year Sir Nicholas Serota became director of the Tate Gallery and began exerting a profound influence on the changing attitudes to the way contemporary galleries and museums present art. It was also the year that saw *Freeze*, the Young British Artists' (YBAs) first exhibition, an age-defining show that triggered a process of change in the British art world. A decade later, in 1997, it was the turn of super-collector Charles Saatchi's *Sensation* exhibition, one of the most significant cultural events of so-called Cool Britannia; both controversial and highly theatrical, this exhibition started a new chapter in the 'dramatization' of the art gallery, bringing to the Royal Academy crowds of enthusiastic visitors eager to take part in the great art spectacle offered by the thought-provoking installations of artists such as Mark Quinn, Damien Hirst, Tracey Emin or Rachel Whiteread.

Furthermore, the opening of the Tate Modern in 2000 brought art and galleries closer to the general public and to those who had hitherto felt the art world was not for them. It should also be noted that under Serota's direction, from 1988 to 2017, the Tate Modern abandoned sequentiality – that is, requiring the organization of displays in a series of particular historical stages with a range of more or less obvious underlying teleological agendas – which had been until then the dominant structuring principle of public and national museums. As Serota noted in his seminal book, *Experience or Interpretation* (1996), in the 1990s, it became a common trend to dismiss the encyclopaedic and dictionary functions of the museum and the system of categorization, used to classify art into periods and movements, in favour of 'a new, now even dominant convention for the presentation of twentieth-century and contemporary art'. He wrote that the best museums of the future would seek 'to promote different modes and levels of "interpretations" by subtle juxtapositions of "experience"'. In the new museum, 'each of us, curators and visitors alike, will have to become more willing to chart our own path, redrawing the map of modern art, rather than following a single path laid down by a curator'.[2]

There is considerable agreement among specialists and commentators from various fields that recent years have witnessed a shift in museum practice from the 'quiet contemplation of authoritative interpretation' to a more 'active participation that implies the collaborative production of meaning(s)'.[3] This shift towards the 'experiential museum' challenges the idea that collections include 'an orderly arrangement of things past' and promotes instead 'a performative present that might make history anew'.[4] As a matter of

---

[2] Nicholas Serota, *Experience or Interpretation. The Dilemma of Museums of Modern Art* (London: Thames and Hudson, [1996] 2000), 15, 54–5.
[3] Susan Bennett, *Theatre & Museums* (Basingstoke: Palgrave Macmillan, 2013), 60.
[4] Ibid.

fact, the Tate Modern on Bankside, Serota's central project, has accepted the challenge posed by artists and historians to rethink the canon of art history and the museum's relation to it, to replace one history with 'many stories of the twentieth and twentieth-first centuries, understood through a shifting and multifaceted perspective',[5] and, last but not least, to generate a condition in which visitors can 'experience a sense of discovery' by looking at particular pictures, sculptures or installations in a particular space at a particular moment, rather than finding themselves 'on the conveyor belt of history'.[6] Furthermore, as is well known, Serota has also welcomed collaborations with living artists, and the Tate Modern has hosted highly successful installations that have challenged the widespread notion of the museum experience, transforming it into an exciting form of engagement that encourages active visitor participation and the production of multiplicitous and unconventional modes of meaning.

In the light of such a fertile period of change, it is no wonder that playwrights have captured the possibilities of this encounter between exhibition and performance and embarked on radical onstage explorations. The paradigmatic change both in the way art galleries and museums display their collections and the ways visitors perceive them has had a demonstrable impact on theatrical form and presentation, to the extent that a hitherto unexplored connection needs to be investigated between modes of representation on stage and modes of exhibiting in galleries. Indeed, it seems possible to establish a connection, or at least to identify a parallel development, between those forms of theatre-making that have been variously referred to as post-dramatic or meta-modern and what is commonly known as the post-museum, a new concept of the museum that has radically changed the way it presents its exhibits by offering 'more possibility for mental and physical interaction'.[7] Without pushing the point too far, one might be tempted to consider the shift in the way art gallery-related plays represent the art gallery – that is, from the mimetic plays of the 1980s to the more experimental plays of the 1990s and 2000s – in the light of the aforementioned parallel shift in the gallery world from exhibition to experience. Since the 1990s, audiences have encountered forms of theatre-making that require more open and active participation, undermining the

---

[5] Iwona Blazwick and Frances Morris, 'Showing the Twentieth Century', in Iwona Blazwick and Simon Wilson (eds), *Tate Modern the Handbook* (London: Tate Publishing, 2000), 28–39, 39.
[6] Serota, *Experience or Interpretation*, 55.
[7] Eilean Hooper-Greenhill, *Museum and the Interpretation of Visual Culture* (London: Routledge, 2000), 6.

authority of the playwright, and art gallery visitors have been experiencing the work of art in less predetermined ways that challenge the traditional role of the curator 'as the person who exercises discriminating judgement over selection and display in the museum'.[8] Increasingly, in both theatre and art gallery, spectators and visitors have become active meaning makers, active participants in an exercise geared to build new meaning collaboratively.

In this light, *The Art Gallery on Stage* explores the ways in which, over the past four decades, several British playwrights have interacted with the art gallery, whether as inspiration, location, focus or theme, as part of an ever more intense process of cross-fertilization. Some of them have looked with interest at the art world and have moved between theatre and art in the course of their careers, albeit for different reasons and with different aims. Playwrights Samuel Beckett and Brian McAvera are also art connoisseurs, Howard Barker and Philip Ridley are painters, Tom Stoppard and Tim Crouch are particularly interested in the relationships between the verbal and the visual. For others, the encounter with the art world is limited to a single play. Sometimes, very personal events in the life of a playwright inspire her or him to write a play about a gallery or an exhibition. Some art gallery-related plays concern fictional characters and galleries, while others are based on real historical figures and galleries. As already noted, theatre in Britain has increasingly become host to famous artists. These plays lure audiences with the promise of spending a few hours with celebrities who have achieved fame.[9] They include William Hogarth, Vincent van Gogh, Stanley Spencer, Edouard Monet, Edgar Degas, Suzanne Valadon, Pablo Picasso, Marc Chagall, William Turner and Artemisia Gentileschi. Other figures such as gallerist owners, art dealers and historians are brought to life in a surprising number of plays set in art galleries, museums and artist's studios, exploring questions of attribution, curatorship or display. Sometimes playwrights speculate on a crucial moment, such as the explosive final meeting and attribution dispute between Joseph Duveen and Bernard Berenson (BB) in Simon Gray's *The Old Masters* (2004). On other occasions they offer a chronological view of longer periods, as in Lee Hall's *The Pitmen Painters*, in which the playwright leads the audience from gallery to gallery over a period from 1934 to the nationalization of the mines in 1947. Significantly, in addition to biographical plays with largely mimetic settings, auto-fictional narrative has increasingly found its way into works where the liminal sense of being suspended between fiction and fact prevails, transforming the role of the audience into

---

[8] Serota, *Experience or Interpretation*, 15.
[9] Ursula Canton, *Biographical Theatre. Re-Presenting Real People?* (Basingstoke: Palgrave Macmillan, 2011).

a co-creator of the theatre experience, as in Tim Crouch's *My Arm* (2003), *An Oak Tree* (2005) and *ENGLAND* (2007), or Mark Ravenhill's *pool (no water)* (2006).

It is worth saying that most of the playwrights addressed in this study are white and thus cannot be said to represent the broader ethnic diversity of contemporary British theatre. There are a number of possible reasons for this. The first one is the criteria for my selection. Although the material examined is mainly textual, I have generally preferred to discuss plays that I have been able to see performed, attending productions whenever possible, but often also watching video recordings. The V&A National Video Archive of Performance (before it was closed for refurbishment), the National Theatre Archive and the Drama and Literature Recordings collection at the British Library likewise helped me gain a deeper understanding of the plays and their performance possibilities. Inevitably, however, the direction of my study has been influenced by the selectivity of these collections, which focuses almost exclusively on productions staged in major venues in and around London. Indeed, one could examine the reasons why it is only recently that plays offering a multicultural insight into how the museum relates to national identity have been conceived and staged in major theatres. Telling examples in this respect are Hannah Khalil's *A Museum in Baghdad,* which opened at the RSC's Swan Theatre, Stratford-upon-Avon, on 11 October 2019, and Winsome Pinnock's *Rockets and Blue Lights*, which opened at Manchester's Royal Exchange Theatre on 13 March 2020. It is only recently, in fact, that art galleries have been widely and urgently called upon to provide a platform for under-represented histories and narratives.[10] One might also take into account the fact that there are still only a relatively small number of multi-ethnic voices on stage and backstage in the British theatre, as suggested by Young Vic's Black artistic director and champion of diversity, Kwame Kwei-Armah. It is perhaps significant that it was the Young Vic who produced and staged *The Collaboration* (2022), the acclaimed play by the London-based New Zealand writer Anthony McCarten about the working relationship, racial tensions and cultural collision between Black street artist Jean Michel-Basquiat and Andy Warhol, the doyen of Pop Art, 'two pugilists in art'.[11] Significantly, even before the play begins, Kwei-Armah invites the audience to view and compare their works, transforming the theatre into an art gallery, with reproductions of Warhol and Basquiat's works hanging on the walls around the perimeter of the theatre, thus confirming the art gallery as an

---

[10] John H. Falk and Lynn D. Dierking, 'Why Do People NOT Visit Museums?' in *The Museum Experience* (London: Routledge, [1986] 2013), 52–61.

[11] Anthony McCarten, *The Collaboration* (London: Methuen Drama, 2022), 41.

interpretive tool and medium for the audience to engage with and reflect on their own past and cultural background and the contiguity and overlap between theatre and art gallery. It is reasonable to assume that there may have been many other plays in addition to these better-known ones, such as *Whose Sari Now* by Malaysian-born Rani Moorthy, playwright, actress, and artistic director of Manchester's Rasa Productions, which deals with the subject at hand through its portrayal of a character who has the expertise to curate an exhibition on saris yet is not allowed to publicly take the credit for it because 'she is just too brown'.[12]

It is also worth noting that in their attempt to imagine and stage art galleries and museums, the playwrights and theatre-makers discussed in this book are bent on engaging in a self-reflexive inquiry into the limits and possibilities of theatre itself, considering the ways in which it addresses, instructs and confronts its audiences, all the while questioning their own roles and responsibilities as playwrights and theatre-makers. Some of them, like David Hare, express frustration when comparing their means of expression with those of visual artists:

> I remember visiting a Lucien Freud exhibition and experiencing blind jealousy that a painter could achieve precisely the kind of dramatic portraiture I sought in the theatre but with an infinitely more effective economy of means. Plays are so much labour compared with paintings.[13]

Almost a decade later, Hare maintains that painting gives the artist ultimate responsibility for every aspect of the work, with all the creative decisions determined solely by the artist's own vision and style. However, he presents himself as a playwright/painter whose written text is fixed and hierarchical, constrained by the needs of his authorial intent, immune to directorial or performative intervention and fundamentally resistant to devising and/or collaboration practices:

> It would be truer to say that every single thing [...] feels right or doesn't feel right in exactly the same way that a painter says something feels right or doesn't feel right. [...] And, similarly, if an actor paraphrases a line, I say, 'I'm sorry. That is not the line. The line is that.' And they say to you, 'Well, it's exactly the same. It means exactly the same. Why does

---

[12] Shaidi Ramsurrun, 'Review of *Whose Sari Now?*', *LondonTheatre1*, 27 November 2016. https://www.londontheatre1.com/reviews/review-of-whose-sari-now-rani-moorthy/ (accessed 26 May 2023).
[13] David Hare, *David Hare. Plays 2* (London: Faber and Faber, 1997), xiii–xiv.

it have to be the way you want it?' And I say, 'Well, it's style. And the mystery of style is precisely that: it's a mystery. But I know that it pleases me if you say my line, and it doesn't please me if you paraphrase my line. And I can't explain to you why it sounds better or more perfectly expresses what I want. I can't tell you why. I can only tell you, you have to do it. Because you are in my painting. I am the writer, and you have to be in my painting, and you have to behave like a character in my style. And you can't behave in another style.' And that doesn't mean the actor can't bring something incredibly creative, but they have to accept the discipline of belonging in my picture.[14]

Hare's reverence for the playwright, whose text demands obedience from those directors, actors and designers charged with bringing it to life as faithfully as possible, perhaps epitomizes an attitude that has been largely shared in the British theatre for decades. It is precisely this attitude that a writer such as Tim Crouch has sought to challenge by shifting the emphasis from text and plot to design and spectacle. Crouch emerges as a key figure in each chapter – hardly a surprise since no other playwright has been as interested in the world of art galleries as Crouch. His plays demonstrate not only his interest in understanding and challenging the dynamics behind theatre performance and visual art exhibitions but also his political engagement, which places questions of the economic exploitation of art, individual agency and collective responsibility at the heart of all his work in both thematic and structural terms. Rather than simply importing and appropriating the motifs of the art gallery, Crouch, in the wake of Beckett, uses the art gallery as a site of interaction (or 'transplantation', as he defines it in his introduction to *ENGLAND*) between different visual and verbal grammars, as well as a place to experiment with and question the mode of storytelling and its intertwining with cultural capital and collective responsibility. The comparison between the visual arts and theatre seems to be the petrol that powers the engine of Crouch's theatre, with plays like *My Arm* (2003), *An Oak Tree* (2005) and *ENGLAND* (2007) acting as its roadmap. Realizing that, as an actor, he has 'often worked far too hard "to host" an audience's journey through a play', as a playwright, Crouch attempts 'to provoke questions about the qualitative distinctions between viewing theatre and viewing visual art', between 'the social nature of watching a play and the private, stand-alone

---

[14] David Hare in Simon Stephens, 'David Hare Talks to Simon Stephens', *Royal Court Theatre Playwright's Podcast*, season 1, episode 5, 6 January 2017. https://royalcourttheatre.com/podcast/episode-5-david-hare-talks-to-simon-stephens (accessed 7 May 2023).

nature of looking at a painting'.[15] Inspired by the visual arts, where the viewer is expected 'to work hard', Crouch seeks fully to engage audience members, giving them a greater sense of authority over what they see,[16] while inviting them to question their own role and the underlying ontology of theatre itself.

In discussing how theatre, and art in general, relates to their audiences, *The Art Gallery on Stage* seeks to unpick the intersections between theatre and performance art, even if it does not cover the heterogeneous world of performing art. Borrowing conceptual framing strategies from performance artists, several playwrights and theatre-makers have undoubtedly begun to focus more on the creative process of making rather than on the finished text itself. They have also adopted ensemble modes of working that, as Duška Radosavljević claims, 'have challenged and altered the previously held hierarchies of text over performance in the Anglo-American context'.[17] While Crouch, in his 'play for galleries', *ENGLAND*, is indebted to conceptual art and Fluxus and uses the blank slate of the white cube in a gallery to deconstruct the elements of the theatre, Mark Ravenhill pushes the boundaries of theatre in the play *pool (no water)* by collaborating with Frantic Assembly, a company that specializes in devising and favouring the physical over the verbal text.

While some playwrights seem more inclined than others to explore the world of art galleries, some venues are more suited than others to stage plays dealing with the creation and display of works of art. Hackney's Arcola Theatre is a fine example. Founded in 2000 by Turkish-born Mehmet Ergen and Leyla Nazli, in 2011 it made its home at the former Reeves and Sons paint factory on Ashwin Street in Dalston, where J.M.W. Turner and John Constable used to buy their blocks of paint. As such, it perhaps comes as no surprise that the venue opened with Rebecca Lenkiewicz's play about Turner, *The Painter*. Between 2009 and 2014 the Arcola Theatre went on to host the premieres of three other shows about three artists,[18] two of which explored spaces and places for the making and exhibiting of art. Wertenbaker's *The Line* (2009) focuses on the artist's studio as the arena for the troubled relationship between Edgar Degas and his ambitious protégée Suzanne Valadon, while Tom Wainwright's highly successful one-man show *Banksy: The Room in the*

---

[15] Tim Crouch, 'Introduction', in *My Arm* (London: Faber and Faber, 2003), 9–11, 10.
[16] Ibid.
[17] Duška Radosavljević, *Theatre-Making. Interplay between Text and Performance in the 21st Century* (New York: Palgrave Macmillan, 2013), 23.
[18] In 2010, Snoo Wilson's play about the trial of the painter Egon Schiele for allegedly seducing his young model, *Reclining Nude with Black Stockings*, opened at the tiny Studio 2 at East London's Arcola Theatre with direction by Alexander Gilmour. The script is available online: http://www.snoowilson.co.uk/Reclining%20Nude.pdf (accessed 15 January 2023).

Elephant (2014) analyses how narrative is framed and shaped through the story of a man left homeless when the Los Angeles water tank he was living in is transformed into a Banksy artwork.[19] Philip Ridley has acknowledged the Arcola, where *The Pitchfork Disney* was successfully revived in 2012, as a 'raw and more earthy place' and one of the few theatres where the atmosphere of the place influences the performance:

> The new Arcola is a great space. The thing that's become more important to me over the years is the space in which the plays are done and it's interesting because that was always vitally important to me when I was showing artwork and it took me a while to realise that the atmosphere of a place was part of what contributed to whether it worked or not. There are certain venues in London at the moment that are exciting me beyond belief. The Arcola does.[20]

No wonder, then, that ten years later, his award-winning *The Poltergeist*, a one-man show about a struggling artist who was hailed as an *enfant prodige* for his large-scale murals as a teenager and is now a bitter unknown, made its stage debut at the Arcola Theatre, after an acclaimed streamed run at the Southwark Playhouse during the Covid-19 pandemic.

Since the late 1980s, playwrights' radical re-imagining of the stage mediated by visual arts has also raised questions around British identity in ways this book aims to trace and analyse. From Alan Bennett's perspective on British foreign policy in relation to the rise of Nazism and Thatcher's Falklands War to David Edgard's rethinking of refugee rights after the break-up of Yugoslavia, from David Leddy's play about what is 'real' on the eve of Brexit to Crouch's examination of the dynamics between the Western world and others, for several of the playwrights in this book, the art gallery, as a site for constructing narratives and the self,[21] seems the ideal place to explore and discuss individual and national, past and present identity, and to challenge the notion of 'identity' as bounded and coherent. The visual and the theatrical, the museum and the playhouse, have increasingly interacted in provocative and sometimes enigmatic ways, blurring the specificities of

---

[19] Originally commissioned by Bristol's Tobacco Factory Theatres and a Play, a Pie and a Pint at Òran Mór, it was a sell out at the 2013 Edinburgh Fringe Festival. The script is still unpublished.

[20] Ridley interviewed by Theo Bosanquet, 'Philip Ridley on … Revisiting *The Pitchfork Disney*', *WhatsOnStage*, 30 January 2012. https://www.whatsonstage.com/west-end-theatre/news/philip-ridley-on-revisiting-the-pitchfork-disney_5566.html (accessed 7 May 2023).

[21] Hooper-Greenhill, *Museum*, 76.

each idiom – artistic and theatrical – and of the physical spaces traditionally allotted to them.

The Art Gallery on Stage charts the motives and interests that playwrights have brought to the subject, highlights their approaches, and explores the range of their formal strategies. It thus reconstructs how art gallery-related plays were initially performed in traditional theatres, requiring playwrights and set, costume and light designers to endeavour to re-create the art gallery in mimetic terms, and how they later moved to site-specific venues where playwrights have instead attempted to challenge the naturalistic conceptions of theatrical structure. However, as a coda to this brief introduction to the book, it is worth saying that, although this is the first monograph devoted to a systematic investigation of the full range and significance of the mutual relationship between the art gallery and British playwriting, a comprehensive and exhaustive review of art gallery/museum-related plays is beyond the scope of this volume. Instead, the present text seeks to provide an analysis of some important formal responses to the new aesthetic questions raised by the changing role and function of art galleries and museums over the past four decades. The number of plays about art galleries written and/or performed in Britain during this time is both impressive and growing, so it has been necessary to narrow down the selection to a more manageable corpus for closer analysis. The plays included in the book have been chosen primarily for their paradigmatic value as examples of trends, both old and new, and as demonstrations of the formal developments stimulated by the emergence of a new paradigm of the art gallery. This approach combines chronological and typological analysis with close readings of a number of individual and exemplary plays, while also gesturing more broadly to a range of other plays that can be said to have contributed to the overall movement in question. Although most of the plays considered in *The Art Gallery on Stage* are by British playwrights, there are some notable exceptions, including a few by American writers that were first staged in the UK, such as John Logan's *Red*, which had its world premiere at the Donmar Warehouse (2009).

Chapter 1, 'How the Art gallery Came to Stage', shows how the art gallery became an important issue in contemporary playwriting and provides a preliminary discussion of some crucial issues when considering the history of the interplay between British theatre and art galleries. It argues that drama's interest in questions of art display and exhibition, which can be traced back to early modern drama, was rekindled in the late 1980s after a long history not only of setbacks but also of glimpses of successful partnership (e.g. in the wake of the artistic and cultural experimentation of the 1960s). The chapter describes the reasons behind the increasingly frequent crossings between modes of exhibiting in art galleries and modes of representing in theatre in a country that, despite sixteenth-century iconoclasm and a long-standing historical mistrust of the visual, is nonetheless eager to assert itself on the global contemporary art world. In particular, the chapter offers a preliminary incursion into the work of Samuel Beckett and Tom Stoppard, whose dramas, although for very different reasons, may be regarded as milestones in the liaison between theatre and art gallery. Beckett's understanding of collecting, ordering and re-presenting images, objects, and characters on stage bears affinities to that of a museum curator, and indeed, over time, his work has increasingly cross-fertilized theatre and the visual arts. If Beckett is a major visual artist who has turned the stage into an art gallery, Stoppard is the first British playwright to consider and accurately describe the experience of visiting an art gallery, before the boom of academic interest in the 1980s and 1990s in the nature, quality and impact of 'museum experiences'.

The chapter also provides a chronological framework, exploring some of the critical moments and events that have shaped the dialogue between theatre and art galleries, including the emergence of the heritage industry in the 1980s and the accompanying oppositional attempts to challenge Thatcherite nostalgia and break new ground in both the art world and the theatre (as exemplified by Dear's *The Art of Success* (1987) and Wertenbaker's *Three Birds Alighting on a Field*); the YBAs' first age-defining exhibition, *Freeze*; Charles Saatchi's *Sensation* exhibition at the Royal Academy in 1997, which helped to consecrate the 1990s as a golden age for the arts but whose more troubling sides have been explored in more or less explicit ways by many YBAs themselves as well as by playwrights, from Philip Ridley and Lee Hall to Tim Crouch and David Leddy; and, finally, the opening of the Tate Modern in 2000, which has also played a driving role in bringing art museums and art galleries to the forefront of a significant cultural debate, not only in the elite circles of intellectuals, curators, museum directors, trendsetters and playwrights but also among the general public and those who had thus far shown little interest in the art world. With a career-long interest in visual arts and art galleries, Crouch does not just devise a play to be performed in art galleries (e.g. *ENGLAND*) but sets up a form of engagement that encourages active audience participation and the free production of meaning. In this way, he somehow challenges both the playwright and the curator's authority, paralleling or mirroring what is happening in many art galleries, including the Tate Modern, where director Sir Nicholas Serota has rejected the sequential order in the display artworks, challenging the common notion of the museum experience as the contemplation of an exhibition designed by a curator's authoritative interpretation. Finally, the chapter charts the rise to prominence of a growing exchange between theatre and gallery spaces, which seems to have intensified over the past two decades. Indeed, it is important to note that the dynamic between theatre and the visual arts has also been reshaped by an increasing number of performances staged in art galleries and museums, sometimes in conjunction with specific exhibitions and/or specific and pressing sociopolitical issues. In the wake of the #MeToo movement, to take one prominent example, issues of sexual violence have invaded both art galleries and theatres.

Chapter 2, 'The Drama of Authenticity, Connoisseurship and Identity', sets out to show how debates around connoisseurship and authorship, differences between originals and copies, and questions of conservation and restoration have been appropriated by playwrights both to re-negotiate long-standing tensions and to question their own political and aesthetic strategies and aims. An early indication of these museological concerns on stage is the presence in many plays of prominent artists and figures from the art world, from William Hogarth to Tracey Emin or Joseph Duveen to Anthony Blunt. David Hare's *The Bay at Nice* (1986), Nick Dear's *The Art of Success* (1987), Alan Bennett's *A Question of Attribution* (1988), David Edgar's *Pentecost* (1994) and Simon Gray's *The Old Masters* (2004) are all plays set in or around art museums or galleries, focusing on the biographies of people in the art world, and entertaining audiences with sophisticated questions of attribution and debates about the best methods of examining a painting.

On stage, the mysteries surrounding a work of art, including questions of its authorship and provenance, contribute to the development of dramatic plots while reeling in spectators by means of suspense, trepidation, and coup de théâtre; furthermore, the attribution process works as a catalyst for other and perhaps more important aesthetic and political issues. By bringing onstage the long tradition of hostility between connoisseurship as the subjective talent of the trained and experienced eye and the 'objective' expertise of science, which was fuelled in 1920 by the cause célèbre of Andrée and Harry Han's disputed version of Leonardo's *La Belle Ferronnière*, these playwrights have rekindled a critical debate in the art world. While inviting their audiences to enlarge and strengthen their gaze, they have also brought to the fore crucial political issues. Indeed, even though written in different years and with different intentions, these plays focus on the power and limits of the eye before either a painting or a performance, thus mobilizing questions about the act of spectating as a source of action and a site of agency. The questions of expertise and authenticity that have haunted the work of David Hare and Alan Bennett and fed their stage explorations of the politics of art and the art of politics in the Thatcher era have grown and changed over the years.

A theme rich in dramatic potential, the question of attribution also provides metaphoric suggestions for playwrights. Interestingly, not only does it encourage a questioning and reassessment of the problem of identity, both individual and national, but it also offers a unique opportunity to address in more experimental ways the ontological relationship between lying and acting. In *Long Live the Little Knife* (2013), David Leddy acknowledges the crucial role of fakes and forgeries and their exhibition in triggering discussion on the connection between reality and its representation, and, in particular, on verbatim theatre. In *An Oak Tree*, Crouch grapples even more radically with the precarious balance between true and false as well as with multiple and sometimes contradictory layers of representation in an attempt to liberate the authority of the audience.

Chapter 3, 'Staging the Art Gallery', examines modes of representing artworks, collections and art galleries. It traces a trajectory from plays that engage in fierce competition with the spectacle of art to plays that shatter all familiar dramaturgical conventions in favour of a radical reconfiguration of visual representation. Drawing (after Beckett) on the grammar of the visual arts, playwrights have challenged both the conventions of naturalistic theatre and the playwright's traditional authorial role in guiding audiences through a predetermined and closed dramatic experience. Increasingly, they have made the stage a significant forum for discussing the relation between representation and performance and have experimented with new dramatic forms.

On the one hand, in some plays where the core of the action, dialogue and lectures is the process of art making as well as art exhibiting, from Lee Hall's *The Pitmen Painters* (2008) to John Logan's *Red* (2009), playwrights seem to be inviting theatre directors and set designers to compete with curators in conceiving onstage art galleries or artists' studios. In biographical plays, in particular, the need to present the life and work of the artists as 'authentic' leads directors and set designers to adopt the model of dioramic representation, which is used by museums to re-create the studios of deceased artists, often as permanent installations to be gazed at with voyeuristic wonder. The chapter also shows how the theatre has rivalled the art gallery in that, by capitalizing on the mythology of the artist, stage designers and directors have been able not only to convey the aura of famous masterpieces but also to offer audiences the thrilling privilege of being allowed to witness the artistic process of creation, and to be taught how to look at works of art while their creators passionately discuss them.

On the other hand, the stage has increasingly become a laboratory in which to experiment with the interaction between display, performing and storytelling, and to engage both the director and the audience in a different way, as in Breach's *It's True, It's True, It's True* (2018). Having abandoned any attempt at naturalism, some playwrights or, rather theatre-makers, conceive (post-dramatic) plays, in which the reduction of explicit stage directions is a theatrical (textual) challenge that contributes to the openness of the plays, requiring both a creative intervention in staging and an active participation of the audience in the process of meaning-making. By intersecting the grammars of theatre, visual arts and performing arts, Martin Crimp, Mark Ravenhill and Tim Crouch have adopted the kind of conceptual framing strategies developed by performance artists, emphasizing the creative process of making, rather than on the text, as discussed in Duška Radosavljević's *Theatre Making* (2013).

While redefining the role of the text in theatre, very different but equally engaging plays such as Crimp's *Attempts on Her Life* (1997), Ravenhill's *pool (no water)* and Crouch's *ENGLAND* invite directors, actors and audiences to participate directly in the process of imagining, or, better, 'theatre-making' of art galleries and artworks, thus outlining a new post-Beckett theatre of absence. While making their audiences aware of the artificial mechanisms deployed in the construction of the imaginary worlds they conjure up through words and images, they induce a visceral, unmediated understanding and experience of the performance. But while Crimp's *Attempts on Her Life* seems to be written with the vocabulary of postmodern critique, the other two plays, oscillating between sincerity and irony, deconstruction and construction, apathy and affect,[22] and encouraging generative collaboration in collective activities, seem to embrace, albeit differently, that structure of feeling and dramaturgy defined as meta-modern.

The fourth and final chapter, 'The Price of Everything', charts the rise of a growing body of plays by authors who, after witnessing the shift from welfare state to the art market and the increasing hybridization of state support and corporate patronage, have directed attention to such phenomena as the commercialization, marketing and consumption of art and denounced the damaging and interconnected implications of philistinism and commodification for the art world. Suffice it to mention *The Art of Success*, in which Dear discusses the rise of the globalized art market and the political manipulation of aesthetics by establishing a close correspondence between William Hogarth's historical context and the 1980s debate on the complex identity of British art. It was this debate that paved

---

[22] Timotheus Vermeulen and Robin van den Akker, 'Notes on Metamodernism', *Journal of Aesthetics & Culture*, 2 (2010): 5–6.

the way for the impressive success of YBA and other playwrights determined to investigate a world of contemporary art that had been made so suddenly and conspicuously spectacular by globalization, financialization, the appeal of scandal and a range of other factors which can be seen to interact with aesthetics, craftsmanship and talent. Wertenbaker's *Three Birds Alighting on a Field* – to take just one example – revives the long-running debate about national taste, raises questions about art as a rewarding financial investment and ponders the issue of what constitutes legitimation in the contemporary art world as well as the dangers of private funding in both the art and theatre worlds. Controversial issues such as commission prices, fierce competition between artists, auctions and processes of endorsement to determine which works are worthy of a potential place in art history urge playwrights not only to explore the difference between the intrinsic and exchange value of the artwork but also to question the relationship of visual arts and theatre to the market and the public bodies that are financially and medially involved in their management. Even if some of these plays highlight the more mysterious and troubling entanglements of art with more or less serious crimes, from intellectual property theft to paedophilia and the global black market in human organs, what ultimately emerges is our need for art. Both art galleries and theatres are places where we question our assumptions about the past, ourselves, our present and our value system, but above all where we actively cultivate hope and plan for a better and more ethically engaged future.

By exploring contemporary British theatre at its intersection with the art gallery, *The Art Gallery on Stage* re-evaluates existing paradigms and points to a new connection between the distinct and yet related fields of theatre and museum studies. It does so, however, in recognition of the fact that this is only a first attempt to map and critically analyse a phenomenon that has been largely neglected, despite its potential to offer meaningful contributions to the understanding of the mechanisms behind the cultural, social and political construction of art and our value system. I hope that *The Art Gallery on Stage*, with its focus on contemporary playwriting, will inspire further research and theoretical and social reflection on this fruitful theatre/art gallery bond.

1

How the art gallery came to the stage

The seduction of the art gallery

Since the 1990s, art historians and curators have often revived the old-standing idea of a connection between museums and theatre when writing about the representational challenges posed by recent changes in the language and concept of the museum in general. At the end of the past millennium, performance studies specialist Barbara Kirschenblatt-Gimblett wrote that the museum is 'a theatre, a memory place, a stage for the enactment of other times and places, a space of transport, fantasy, dreams'.[1] She even suggested that exhibitions are fundamentally theatrical, 'for they are how museums perform the knowledge they create'.[2] Roughly at the same time, Carol Duncan, a professor in religion and cultural studies who considers museums as symbolic, social spaces that convey beliefs and ideas about identity, regarded 'the totality of the museum as a stage setting that prompts visitors to enact a performance of some kind, whether or not actual visitors would describe it as such (and whether or not they are prepared to do so)'. She concluded that, 'the museum's sequenced spaces and arrangements of objects, its lighting and architectural details constitute a dramatic field – a combination of stage set and script – that both structures and invites a performance'.[3] Ten years later, American art historian Donald Preziosi underlined that all museums 'use theatrical effects to enhance a belief in the historicity of the objects they collect',[4] in his own way confirming a growing trend towards an increasing interaction between collections/exhibitions and artists/performers.

If, on the one hand, then, art galleries and museums seem to be intrinsically theatrical, on the other hand British playwrights and theatre practitioners have increasingly recognized the art gallery as an inspiring place in plays that have

---

[1] Barbara Kirschenblatt-Gimblett, *Destination Culture: Tourism, Museums and Heritage* (Berkeley: University of California Press, 1998), 139.
[2] Ibid., 3.
[3] Carol Duncan, *Civilizing Rituals: Inside Public Art Museums* (London: Routledge, 1995), 1–2, 12.
[4] Donald Preziosi and Claire Farago, 'Introduction: Creating Historical Effects', in *Grasping the World: The Idea of the Museum* (Aldershot, VT: Ashgate), 13.

been frequently hailed as among the best of their respective seasons, from Alan Bennett's *A Question of Attribution* to David Edgar's *Pentecost*; from Patrick Marber's *Closer* (1997) to Lee Hall's *The Pitmen Painters* (2008). Whether private or public, big or small, family-owned or corporate-run, the art gallery provides a place for encounters, emotions and stories. From the Tate Gallery in Pimlico to the Tate Modern on Bankside; from London's National Gallery to the Hermitage in Saint Petersburg or the posh fictional The Gallery off Cork Street, placing an art gallery or an art museum on stage sets in motion a narrative full of potential, museological inquiry and unpredictable consequences.

Tracing the long historical trajectory of the fascinating affair between the British theatre and the art gallery is beyond the scope of this volume. However, it is worth turning back briefly to the Elizabethan times[5] and recalling both Frances A. Yates' classic study *The Art of Memory* (1966), which relates the art of memory and Robert Fludd's theatre memory system to the Globe Theatre, and Shakespeare's *The Winter's Tale* (5.3). The 'statue scene' in Shakespeare's romance is one of the most famous representations of both an art gallery and a patron of the visual arts in early modern English drama, notoriously interpreted as Shakespeare's will to confirm his status as visual artist and to legitimize 'a way of knowing asserted against the humanist claims for an exclusive, or near-exclusive, truth in language.'[6] There is no need to delve into the maze of iconoclasm with its connection to Elizabethan anti-theatricalism and its many consequences. Undoubtedly, the war on icons and the destruction of images have left an indelible mark on the history of the country. They are, in a sense, the primary scenario of a museology that, though wounded by dissolution and dispersion, was born and grew, as elsewhere in Europe, between the end of the seventeenth and the nineteenth centuries, but also the seeds of what director Peter Hall calls 'a recurrent national neurosis', that, he argues, still makes the English 'suspicious of the visual delights of the theatre'.[7]

Despite this distrust of visual representation, the liaison between the theatre and the art gallery has seen various vicissitudes and fruitful partnerships: the

---

[5] Paula Findlen, 'The Modern Muses. Renaissance Collecting and the Cult of Remembrance', in Susan A. Crane (ed.), *Museum and Memory* (Stanford: Stanford University Press, 2000), 161–78.

[6] Michael O'Connell, *The Idolatrous Eye. Iconoclasm and Theater in Early-Modern England* (Oxford: Oxford University Press, 2000), 144. See also Diehl Huston, '"Does Not the Stone Rebuke Me?": The Paulina Rebuke and Paulina's Lawful Magic in *The Winter's Tale*', in Paul Yachnin and Patricia Badir (eds), *Shakespeare and the Cultures of Performance* (London: Routledge, 2008), 69–82; Michael O'Connell, 'The Idolatrous Eye: Iconoclasm, Anti-Theatricalism, and the Image of the Elizabethan Theater', *ELH*, 52, 2 (Summer, 1985): 279–310.

[7] Peter Hall quoted in Dennis Kennedy, *Looking at Shakespeare. A Visual History of Twentieth-Century Performance* (Cambridge: Cambridge University Press, 1993), 6.

exploitation of the visual potentialities coming from continental stage design with the reopening of theatres in 1661; the Victorian theatre's growing interest in creating pictorial stage re-renderings, whose mimetic reconstructions of the environments and atmospheres of the past aimed at historical (and almost museological) authenticity; the experiments of the avant-gardes, challenging both naturalistic theatre and the traditional museum, often regarded as antiquated, aristocratic and authoritarian institutions.

The 1960s marked a turning point. Boundaries between theatre, art and performance were variously breached by pioneering playwrights and theatre-makers experimenting with cross-fertilizations of languages, codes and grammars. Happenings and performances inspired by Body art, Fluxus and Environmental and Conceptual Art contributed to a consolidation of the relationship between British theatre and art galleries.[8] Visual artists began to explore participatory forms of entertainment and to encourage spectator participation, while many developments in theatre sought to reduce the distance between actor and audience, favouring 'a paradigm of physical involvement'[9] in the tradition of Antonin Artaud's *Theatre of Cruelty*.

In this inevitably sketchy survey, it is also worth mentioning the so-called Fun Palace, perhaps one of the most interesting projects of the 1960s (it was never actually built). Designed by actress and theatre director Joan Littlewood and British architect Cedric Price as an innovative alternative to both mainstream theatre and conventional architecture, the Fun Palace was intended as a utopian agent of change for the individual, community and environment that would provide a provisional stage to be continuously set and reset, sited and re-sited. Above all, it was to offer 'a democratic space that opened itself up for negotiation by the user, a deliberate attempt to redefine the standard relationship between people and institutions. Movement between different zones was to be part of the overall experience of freedom and the activation of individual agency'.[10] Never realized but nonetheless a source of inspiration in the following decades – not least for The Tanks, Tate Modern's new space opened in 2016 as a permanent gallery for live art, performance, installation and film –[11] the Fun Palace seemingly embodied

---

[8] Gunter Berghaus, 'Happening in Europe: Trends, Events, and Leading Figures', in Mariellen R. Sandford (ed.), *Happenings and other Acts* (London: Routledge, 1995), 368–71.
[9] Claire Bishop (ed.), *Participation. Documents of Contemporary Art* (London: Co-published by Whitechapel Gallery and the MIT Press, 2006), 11.
[10] Nadine Holdsworth, *Joan Littlewood's Theatre* (Cambridge: Cambridge University Press, 2011), 225.
[11] Nicholas Serota, 'The 21st-Century Tate Is a Commonwealth of Ideas', *The Art Newspaper*, 1 July 2016. https://mefsite.wordpress.com/2016/07/01/the-art-newspaper-the-21st-century-tate-is-a-commonwealth-of-ideas/ (accessed 7 May 2023).

the zeitgeist of the 1960s, the growing fluidity of the boundaries between art forms and the desire for artists to create events rather than works of art.

Samuel Beckett is a milestone in the history of the liaison between the theatre and the art gallery. He has played a remarkably rich and groundbreaking role and has remained a constant reference and influence in the development of British playwriting, all the way from the revolutionary 'performative turn' of the 1960s[12] to the post-dramatic and meta-dramatic experiments of the twenty-first century. However, his fascinating movements between theatre and art museums and galleries, to which many pages have been devoted and many more should be, can only necessarily be confined to a short section.

Beckett's museum fever and performative turn

Samuel Beckett's *That Time*, a short one-act play, first performed at the Royal Court on 20 May 1976, features one of the first theatrical characters in the British theatre to enter an art gallery. The play imagines that C, one of the three voices that come out of the dark as aspects of the Listener's past, belongs to a broken man, who takes refuge in London National Portrait Gallery. Surprisingly, C is only interested in the gallery as a shelter from the rain and cold:

> C   when you went in out of the rain always a winter then always raining that time in the Portrait Gallery in off the street out of the cold and rain slipped in when no one was looking and through the rooms shivering and dripping till you found a seat marble slab and sat down to rest and dry off and on to hell out of there when was that.[13]

Unlike C, Beckett was an assiduous visitor of art galleries and a connoisseur of the highest order. His art gallery fever, nurtured by a lifelong passion born in the National Galleries in Dublin and London, pursued during the uneasy 1930s from Dresden to Erfurt, Berlin, Hamburg and Munich, and then in the United States, New York especially, has a manifold articulation: it echoes the

---

[12] Erica Fisher-Lichte, *The Transformative Power of Performance: A New Aesthetics* (London: Routledge, 2008).

[13] Samuel Beckett, 'That Time', in *The Complete Dramatic Works* (London: Faber and Faber, 1986), 388. Written in English between June 1974 and August 1975. First published by Grove Press, New York, in 1976.

familiarity he had with many public and private collections; it illuminates the visual world deployed in texts and on stage; it gives shape and significance to the stage as a theatre of (defective) memory, a space that stores fragile memories triggered by a few objects; and it works to clear the stage and bring theatre closer to performing arts.

In her memoir, Anne Atik wrote that Beckett's visual memory was 'striking' and that 'he remembered paintings of Old Masters which he'd seen in his travels through museums in Germany, France and Italy, those in Ireland, and England, their composition and colour, the impact each one had had'.[14] His intimate knowledge of art and personal friendship with artists, obscure and famous, is now part of the critical lore as is the fact that he was a collector. His own collection consisted, as it happened, almost exclusively of the works of his friends: the van Velde brothers, Jack Yeats, Henri Hayden and Jean-Paul Riopelle – artists whom Beckett wrote about and who shared his personal struggle towards a form of expression free from the tyranny of representation. In fact, he used his art criticism as an opportunity to explore his own ideas about art, the 'crucible in which he could forge his aesthetic ideas'.[15]

Beckett had the eye of a *connoisseur*, whom, he joked (winking at Hamlet), 'can just separate Uccello from a handsaw'.[16] In the 1930s, he exchanged ideas on attributions with his friend Thomas McGreevy, the director of Dublin's National Gallery of Ireland from 1950 to 1963, and sometimes rightly doubted what curators and official catalogues said about an artist. He even seriously considered a career in museums, when, in 1933, 'in a moment of gush', he applied for an assistant position at the National Gallery in Trafalgar Square.[17] Indeed, the correspondence with McGreevy reveals Beckett's expertise in art as well as his peculiar sensitivity to issues of curatorship and display, which will also be found in his plays. Thus, his complaint about the display of Perugino's *Pietà*, just purchased at the National Gallery of Ireland, 'buried behind a formidable barrage of shining glass, so that one is obliged to take cognisance of it progressively, square inch by square inch',[18] reappears later in *That Time*. C speaks of a similar obstacle to a clear view when he describes the

---

[14] Anne Atik, *How It Was. A Memoir of Samuel Beckett* (London: Faber and Faber, 2001), 4.
[15] Riann Coulter, in Fionnuala Croke (ed.), *Samuel Beckett: A Passion for Paintings* (Dublin: National Gallery of Ireland, 2006), 26. See also David Lloyd, *Beckett's Thing. Painting and Theatre* (Edinburgh: Edinburgh University Press, [2016] 2018), 5.
[16] Samuel Beckett, 'Letter to Thomas McGreevy', 9 October 1933, in Martha Dow Fehsenfeld and Lois More Overbeck (eds), *The Letters of Samuel Beckett. 1929-1940* (Cambridge: Cambridge University Press, 2009), 166, 167.
[17] Ibid.
[18] Beckett wrote to McGreevy:

Portrait Gallery portraits as 'black with dirt and antiquity' and recalls 'a vast oil black with age and dirt [...] black behind the glass', where 'he experiences the shock of a ghost-like face emerging from an oil black with age':[19]

> C   till you hoisted your head and there before your eyes when they opened a vast oil black with age and dirt someone famous in his time some famous man or woman or even child such as a young prince or princess some young some young prince or princess of the blood black with age behind the glass where gradually as you peered trying to make it out gradually of all things a face appeared had you swivel on the slab to see who it was there at your elbow. (*That Time* 389)

Undoubtedly, Beckett's understanding of displaying and lighting as well as his focus on the relationship between viewer and object are rooted in his early interest in curatorship, which would later fuel his theatre.[20] Significantly, Atik recalls that in his art catalogues he used to write 'scattered annotations which bear witness to an attentive, passionate viewer, and in his work he referred, sometimes indirectly, sometimes directly, to these paintings, positioning his actors and actresses accordingly'.[21] His connoisseurship as well as his ongoing exposure to and engagement with the world of visual arts played an important role in determining much of his textual and theatrical practice, leading him to use the visual resources of the stage – depth and foreground, lighting and darkness, movement and stillness, colour and gesture – to conceive his plays as a visual artist. Increasingly, Beckett moved further away from writing plays with any trace of the conventions of drama.

As with all museums,[22] Beckett's stage entails concerns with the retrieval and conservation of memory, which, however flawed and fragmented, is

> I've been several times to look at the new Perugino Pietà in National Gallery here. It's buried behind a formidable barrage of shining glass, so that one is obliged to take cognisance of it progressively, square inch by square inch. It's all messed up by restorers, but the Xist and the women are lovely [...] Rottenly hung in a rotten light behind this thick shop window, so that a total view of it is impossible, and full of grotesque amendments. (*Letter to Thomas McGreevy*, 20 December 1931, 100)

---

[19] Chris J. Ackerley and Stanley E. Gontarski, *The Faber Companion to Samuel Beckett* (London: Faber & Faber, 2004), 569.

[20] Mariacristina Cavecchi, 'From Playwriting to Curatorship. An Investigation into the Status of Beckett's Stage Objects', in Caroline Patey and Laura Scuriatti (eds), *The Exhibit in the Text. The Museological Practices of Literature* (London: Peter Lang, 2009), 161–82.

[21] Atik, *How It Was*, 2.

[22] Crane, *Museums and Memory*, 12; Marvin Carlson, *The Haunted Stage: The Theatre as Memory Machine* (Ann Arbor: University of Michigan Press, 2001), 11.

triggered by a few objects endowed with intertextual stories.[23] Through his art galleries onstage – both empty and yet full of echoes and images – Beckett leads us to the heart of the tormented modernist memory: an unresolved site both void and inhabited. Such is also the result of an artistic process of 'shrinking' that, by winking at both visual arts and media, liberates the stage from all excess and goes beyond text to use the stage as a multimedia space crossed by a continuous contradictory rhythm of showing and hiding, adding and subtracting, which would later inspire several (post-dramatic) playwrights, including Martin Crimp and Mark Ravenhill.

Last but not least, the grammar of contemporary art gallery influences Beckett's theatre in another and perhaps more important way. Undeniably, his texts and performances developed in the context of the major changes in the art world of the 1960s, the period of the interlinked evolution of both the minimalist and modernist paradigms.[24] As the boundaries between art, drama, performing arts and music were broken down, Beckett's plays became more and more like art installations, taking place on a stage that was also very much like a gallery space, as Billie Whitelaw suggested in an interview with Jonathan Kalb:

> I do not think he just writes a play. I think he's a writer, a painter, a musician, and his works seem to me all these things rolled into one. I remember once he said to me in my home, 'I don't know whether the theater is the right place for me anymore.' He was getting further and further away from writing conventional plays. And I know what he meant. I thought, well perhaps he should be in an art gallery or something. Perhaps I should be pacing up and down in the Tate Gallery, I don't know, because the way the thing looks and the way he paints with light it is just as important as what comes out from my mouth. [...] Now, perhaps I'm being silly, perhaps I shouldn't do that, but I feel that the shape my body makes is just as important as the sound that comes out of my mouth. And that's the shape my body wants to take, of somebody who's spiraling inward.[25]

---

[23] Suffice it to consider his gallery of chairs, which, before becoming part of his highly personal dramatic and visual idiom, were nurtured by countless encounters with paintings that often deeply impressed him. However uncomfortable, ordinary or dilapidated, the seats recall the Rembrandts and Giorgiones, the van Goghs and Francis Bacons, that the playwright encountered in his beloved museums. (Mariacristina Cavecchi, 'Samuel Beckett, Visual Artist', in Daniela Guardamagna and Rossana M. Sebellin (eds), *The Tragic Comedy of Samuel Beckett. 'Beckett in Rome'* (Rome: Laterza-Tor Vergata University Press, 2009), 122–42.

[24] Enoch Brater, *Beyond Minimalism. Beckett's Late Style in the Theater* (New York: Oxford University Press, 1987), 3–17.

[25] Billie Whitelaw in Jonathan Kalb, *Beckett in Performance* (Cambridge: Cambridge University Press, 1989), 235, 236.

What kind of play is *Not I* (1972), where the stage is 'in darkness but for MOUTH upstage audience right, about 8 feet above stage level, faintly lit from close-up and below, rest of face in shadow' (*Not I* 376)? Is it a play? Is it a piece of performing art, as the actresses who have interpreted Mouth seem to suggest when they make clear how the characteristics of performance art practice such as endurance, physical restraint and athletic rather than intellectual engagement are central to a successful performance?[26] Should Beckett's plays still be considered as pieces of theatre or rather as manifestations in the tradition of what would be called performance art some years later? Or, as Gerhard Hauck claims, is the proximity of Beckett's theatre to the visual arts a purely accidental by-product of the generally 'reductive process' of playwriting?[27] As a result of this process of reduction, or rather, subtraction, Beckett not only created a series of multimedia images and living sculptures as striking and memorable as those of the greatest visual artists,[28] but he also challenged the boundaries between theatrical performance and purely visual representation, paving the way for generations of playwrights, who would join him in this exploration of new ways of performing. One might mention how Martin Crimp's Anne in *Attempts on Her Life* winks at Beckett's MOUTH: two entities not only without bodies but also victims of a performance, which, though in different ways, both restrains and liberates them. Or we might even consider the similarity between the swimming pool in Mark Ravenhill's *pool (no water)* and the urns in Beckett's *Play*, as both generate stories of infidelity and jealousy from fragments of lines spoken by actors who do not relate to each other and who address the audience directly.

How should the black box of Beckett's stage be interpreted? As a space in a theatre or as an art gallery? Without venturing further into the debate about the nature of Beckett's theatre, it is possible to assert that more and more, reduced to their most essential elements – the body in space, light and darkness, the word, the breath – his plays exist somewhere between visual art and theatre.

---

[26] Derval Tubridy, 'Samuel Beckett and Performance Art', *Journal of Beckett Studies*, 23, 1 (2014): 47.
[27] Gerhard Hauck, *Reductionism in Drama and the Theatre. The Case of Samuel Beckett* (Potomac, MD: Scripta Humanistica, 1992), 176.
[28] See Lois Oppenheim, *The Painted Word. Samuel Beckett's Dialogue with Art* (Ann Arbor: University of Michigan Press, 2000).

The art gallery experience on stage

A visit to an art gallery is one of the primary sources of inspiration for playwrights, who often conceived their plays in the wake of great exhibitions. This is the case with Tom Stoppard. His farce *After Magritte* followed the great success of René Magritte's exhibition at the Tate Gallery in Pimlico, in 1969, while his 1972 radio play *Artist Descending a Staircase* was perhaps prompted by the first major retrospective exhibition of Marcel Duchamp's work held in Europe, in 1966, which showed *Nude Descending a Staircase (No 2)*.[29] Not surprisingly, the first stage production of *Artist Descending a Staircase*, at the Old Red Lion in 2009, was probably boosted by Tate Modern's major 2009 exhibition 'Duchamp, Man Ray, Picabia', which explored the fascinating connections between the three pioneering figures and included Duchamp's iconic painting.

The first British play openly revolving around an art exhibition, Tom Stoppard's *After Magritte* premiered in April 1970 at the Ambience Lunch-Hour Theatre Club, which was founded by American playwright and producer Ed Berman and located in the Green Banana/Ambiance Restaurant basement in Queensway. 'Mildly and humbly a homage to the Belgian artist', as Stoppard declared in an interview,[30] the play dramatizes the (surreal) consequences for the Harris family deriving from their visit to 'an exhibition of surrealistic art at the Tate Gallery' (*Magritte* 35). It is also notable for focusing on and staging the experience of visiting an art gallery.

Appropriately, the title of this farce, *After Magritte*, is a pun on both the iconological inspiration, as Stoppard borrows Magritte's iconography for his set design, and the chronological time of the play, which is set after the Harris family's visit to the Magritte exhibition. The Belgian artist's *L'assassin menacé*,[31] exhibited at the Tate in 1969, inspires the compelling stage image that opens the play, where the characters seem to have stepped straight out of the painting, the female figure lying on an ironing board, the woman in a ball gown crawling on the floor and the man in rubber waders and black evening dress trousers blowing in a lampshade:

---

[29] Arts Council, *The Almost Complete Works of Marcel Duchamp. At the Tate Gallery 18 June-31 July 1966* (London: Arts Council, 1966).
[30] Tom Stoppard in Mel Gussow, *Conversation with Stoppard* (London: Nick Hern Books, 1995), 7.
[31] René Magritte, *L'assassin menacé*, 1926–7; oil on canvas, 150.4 × 195.2 cm, Museum of Modern Art, New York.

A room. Early evening. The only light is that which comes through the large window which is facing the audience. The street door is in the same upstage wall. There is another door on each side of the stage, leading to the rest of the flat. The central ceiling light hangs from a long flex which disappears up into the flies. The lampshade itself is a heavy metal hemisphere, opaque, poised about eight feet from the floor. A yard or more to one side (Stage L), and similarly hanging from the flies, is a fruit basket attractively overflowing with apples, oranges, bananas, pineapples, and grapes. The cord or flex is tied round the handle of the basket. It will become apparent that the light fixture is on a counterweight system; it can be raised or lowered, or kept in any vertical position, by means of counterbalance, which in this case is a basket of fruit. Most of the furniture is stacked up against the street door in a sort of barricade. An essential item is a long low bench-type table, about eight feet long, but the pile also includes a settee, two comfortable chairs, a TV set, a cupboard, and a wind-up gramophone with an old-fashioned horn. The cupboard is probably the item on which stand the telephone and a deep-shaded table lamp, unlit but connected to a wall plug. Directly under the central light is a wooden chair. Hanging over the back of the chair is a black tailcoat, a white dress shirt and a white bowtie. Towards Stage R, in profile, is an ironing board with its iron upended on the asbestos mat at the centre-stage end of the board. There is no other furniture. There are three people in the room.

Mother *is lying on her back on the ironing board, her head to Stage R, her downstage foot up against the flat of the iron. A white bath towel covers her from ankle to chin. Her head and part of her face are concealed in a tight-fitting black rubber bathing cap. A black bowler hat reposes on her stomach. She could be dead; but is not.*

Thelma Harris *is dressed in a full-length ballgown, and her hair is expensively 'up'. She looks as though she is ready to go out to a dance, which she is. Her silver shoes, however, are not on her feet: they have been discarded somewhere on the floor.* **Thelma** *is discovered on her hands and knees, in profile to the audience, staring at the floor ahead and giving vent to an occasional sniff.*

Reginald Harris *is standing on the wooden chair. His torso is bare, but underneath his thigh-length green rubber fishing waders he wears his black evening dress trousers. His hands are at his sides. His head is tilted back directly below the lampshade, which hangs a foot or two above him and he is blowing slowly and deliberately up into the recess of the shade. Gazing at this scene through the window is a uniformed Police Constable (***Holmes***). Only his shoulders, his face and his helmet are visible above the* sill. He stands absolutely motionless and might be a cut-out figure but is not. (*Magritte* 9–11)

Opening with a 'bizarre spectacle' (*Magritte* 24) that re-stages the unknown and mysterious world of Magritte, Stoppard challenges the audience's preconditioned perceptions of reality in the manner of the Belgian artist and sets in motion a surreal and farcical plot of police investigations, misunderstandings, bizarre spectacles and faulty logic and perceptions.

What is particularly interesting in a play conceived in the 1960s is the focus on the Harrises' experience as museum goers: their reasons for going, their tastes, the way the visit influenced their lives. Despite its farcical tone, the play seems to anticipate a serious interest in the figure of the visitor within the art gallery and museum space, which would become the subject of critical and theoretical investigation from the 1980s onwards.[32]

Stoppard seems more interested in amusing his audience with Magritte's paradoxes and aporia than in instructing them directly about Magritte's aesthetic aims through lectures or explanations by some of the characters onstage. In the same spirit, the Harrises visit the Tate Gallery for reasons not entirely consistent with the gallery's public service mission to educate that became a priority in the early 1970s.[33] In fact, Mother visits the Tate Gallery motivated by what Falk and Dierking define as a 'desire to satisfy a specific content-related objective'.[34] As Mr Harris tells inspector Foot, his mother brought the whole family to the exhibition when she learnt that 'among the canvases on view were several depicting the instrument of her chief and indeed obsessional interest', as she was 'an accomplished performer and passionate admirer in all its aspects, of the tuba' (*Magritte* 36). Indeed, in the light of Falk and Dierking's taxonomy of museum visitors, Stoppard's character of Mother would fall into the category of 'visitors who feel a close tie

---

[32] Suffice it to mention John H. Falk and Lynn D. Dierking's seminal volume *The Museum Experience* (1986) or *Museum Visitor Studies in the 90s* (1993), a collection of essays on the new concepts of the visitor written by leading museum scholars, edited by Sandra Bicknell and Graham Farmelo and published by the Science Museum in London.

[33] At its inception, and through the 1950s and 1960s, the Tate was characterized by collection-centred museology. In the early 1970s it embraced a curator-centred museology, which began to recognize the potential role of the museum as an educator and the potential role of the visitor as a pupil. Thus, in the early 1970s the Tate acted as an institution that complemented school and adult education, thus supporting the perception of museums as responsive to public needs. Seph Rodney, *The Personalization of the Museum Visit: Art Museums, Discourse, and Visitors* (London: Routledge, 2019), 48–9, 56–9.

[34] John H. Falk and Lynn D. Dierking, *The Museum Experience Revisited* (London: Routledge, 2013), 48.

between the museum content and their professional or hobbyist passions'.[35] With great irony, however, Stoppard has Mother leave disappointed, for her experience as visitor is far from that 'enjoyable and satisfying experience' that Falk and Dierking, decades later, would advise museums to offer their visitors.[36] In fact, Mother dismisses her experience as a 'disappointment' or, even worse, 'rubbish' (*Magritte* 36), as she explains in a highly comic passage:

> **Mother** Tubas on fire, tubas stuck to lions and naked women, tubas hanging in the sky – there was one woman with a tuba with a sack over her head as far as I could make out. I doubt he'd ever tried to play one; in fact, if you ask me the man must have been some kind of lunatic. (*Magritte* 37)

Unexpectedly, however, despite their inability to understand the meaning of Magritte's paintings such as *La Découverte du feu, Le domaine enchanté (VI), Le Temps Menaçant* and *L'Histoire Centrale*, once they leave the Tate, the Harrises themselves experience the deceptive traps of perception of Magritte's paintings and begin to doubt what they see in the real world. In fact, they cannot even agree on the description of an alleged burglar and murderer they would have passed just outside of the gallery, thus demonstrating how the experience of the exhibition has somehow mirrored the surreal chaos of their real lives and even significantly affected them (*Magritte* 38–41).

After Magritte paved the way to a series of plays that, starting in the mid-1980s, have staged stories about people whose lives change after visiting an art gallery. One could compile a catalogue of the various motivations that drive the characters on stage to visit art museums and galleries and the impact of these visits on their lives. Indeed, it could be argued that, somehow, many plays seem to answer (albeit unintentionally) the German photographer Thomas Struth's question as to whether a museum/gallery can influence visitors 'in their public lives, in their activity, in their family, with their friends'.[37] This question was central to his 1990 exhibition 'Museum Photographs' at the New York's Marian Goodman Gallery, which immortalized the variety of attitudes and expressions of visitors to major art museums.

Can change come from a visit to a museum or art gallery? Several playwrights show that entering an art gallery or museum is always an activity

---

[35] Ibid.
[36] Ibid., 34.
[37] Thomas Struth in Kynaston McShine, *The Museum as Muse: Artists Reflect* (New York: The Museum of Modern Art, 1999), 116.

fraught with risk and a range of potential consequences for the characters' behaviour and lives.

That a painting can change a life (and perhaps many lives) is the absolute belief of Galactia, the fictional painter of Renaissance Venice in *Scenes from an Execution*, probably Howard Barker's best known and most accessible play, first broadcast on BBC Radio 3 on 14 October 1984 and then presented at the Almeida Theatre in Islington in 1990, directed by Ian McDiarmid and with Glenda Jackson as the painter. Commissioned by the Venetian Republic to create a painting celebrating the triumph over the Turks at the Battle of Lepanto in 1571, Galactia produces a work that instead seethes with the violence of the massacre, infuriating the Doge Urgentino and jeopardizing the painting's exhibition. When, at the end of her tug-of-war with the Doge, Galactia's controversial one hundred feet canvas is finally on display in St. Mark's, the exhibition is, as she hoped, a triumph. People 'flock' in droves to see her painting, although it does not provoke any 'mutiny down the docks', as Galactia herself would have expected: 'And then God help us, it's blood and mayhem down the cold museum' (*Scenes* 270). People interpret the painting to their own liking, as the art critic Rivera predicted (*Scenes* 304). In art, Rivera argues, 'Nothing is what it seems to be, but everything can be claimed. The painting is not independent, even if the artist is. The picture is retrievable, even when the painter is lost ...' (*Scenes* 299). Galactia's huge canvas, which, in defiance of the Doge's commission to 'celebrate' the battle of Lepanto, depicts war as a 'butchery', thus insulting the State, can therefore be 'absorbed' by the State authorities who, in deciding to show it, demonstrate their 'greater majesty'. Rivera herself contributes to the process of 'absorbing' the provocative painting in the (anachronistic) catalogue she dedicates to the exhibition, as she indulges in Galactia's artistic skill and interest in anatomy – 'some people say they can touch the flesh, such is the realism of it' (*Scenes* 304) – and completely ignores the artist's subversive political message.

Paradoxically, even Prodo, the Man with the Crossbow Bolt in his Head and one of the victims of the war whose grief Galactia wanted to express with his portrait on the right side of the painting, distorts and even reverses the meaning of the painting when, improvising as a spontaneous and naïve Cicero, he emphasizes the patriotic note of the painting. Whether out of ineptitude or self-interest, he completely ignores the revolutionary potential of the painting and invites the viewers to notice the bolt in his head, which he claims to be heroically enduring for the cause of his nation: 'You see I shudder in an ecstasy of patriotic fervour ...!' (*Scenes* 302).

Similarly, the two artists Sordo and Lasagna twist the meaning of the painting with their male chauvinist interpretation, dubbing it 'The Slag's Revenge', as they believe that several of the corpses in the painting look like

Galactia's secret lover: 'If it had been painted by a man, it would have been an indictment of the war, but as it is, painted by the most promiscuous female within a hundred miles of the Lagoon, I think we are entitled to a different speculation' (*Scenes* 302). They therefore allude to Galactia's promiscuity and the personal reasons that justify her aggressive style, borrowing a range of hackneyed critical arguments designed to refute and defuse female agency while at the same time enabling an interpretation of the works of women artists, from Artemisia Gentileschi onwards, according to simplistic schemes. There is no need to recall how the work of Artemisia, a possible source of inspiration for Galactia, has until recently been interpreted in the light of her biography and taken as her vindication against her rapist.

However, the painting is powerful and, for reasons unknown, it touches one particular visitor above all, as the Doge himself cannot help noticing:

> **Urgentino** The queue is fifty metres long and the man there has return eight times, ask him, it is a fact, he kneels there, and he weeps. Look, you have drawn tears from him, wrung water from his coarse imagination! Do you feel powerful? I have such power, but no such power. I can make men weep, but only by torturing them, while you – don't resent me. In a hundred years no one will weep for your painting, only respect it. Cold, dull respect. Enjoy your peculiar authority! (*Scenes* 305)

By the end of the play, as the Doge himself acknowledges when he invites her to dinner, Galactia, against her own expectations, is no longer a rebel artist but a celebrity: 'I hate to miss a celebrity from my table' (*Scenes* 305).

Surprisingly, and not without a certain amount of irony, Barker assigns several tasks to Prodo, a character unfamiliar with the art world but who tries to cash in on his war-deformed body as a freak attraction (*Scenes* 255) and poses as a model for Galactia. First of all, Prodo describes the impact of the pictorial epic on the visitors, naively (or mockingly?) summarizing the two relatively standard modes and attitudes of artistic reception through a concise emotional language of 'gasp' and 'mmm': a one-to-one relationship with the painting, culminating in a 'gasp', expressing surprise or even pain, or an exchange mediated by an anachronistic catalogue providing context and perhaps other didactic materials, which leads either to perplexity or quiet consideration:

> **Galactia** What do they say, you know more than any critic, what do they say? Trash, do they say?
> **Prodo** Unfortunately, I am obliged by the custodian to perch here at the right end of the picture, so they pass me as they enter, and they have no opinion. It is at the other end, the exit, you should listen. One

hundred feet later, a man might change his mind about many things. Some have catalogues, but most can't read. The ones who can't read gasp, the ones with catalogues go 'mmm'. So, it's either gasp or mumm. Take your pick. (*Scenes* 304)

In addition, Prodo reveals that people do not always go to museums and art galleries to look at pictures. So, instead of thanking Galactia for the brave and honest portrayal of the war that turned him 'from a man into a monkey' (*Scenes* 257), he thanks her because the exhibition offers him a shelter from the winter cold (*Scenes* 304), prompting Galactia's bitter reflection on the meaning of his art and galleries: 'Nothing's in vain! Nothing is wasted! If one beggar is kept from starving, no effort is too extreme!' (*Scenes* 304). Perhaps Alan Bennett had Prodo in mind when he wrote that some people enter art galleries 'just to take the weight off their feet or to get out of the rain, to look at the pictures perhaps, or to look at other people looking at the pictures'.[38] Surely, he is thinking of Beckett's C in *That Time*, when he concludes that he hopes that 'the paintings will somehow get to them and take away something they weren't expecting and couldn't predict'.[39]

Indeed, Beckett's broken man, who, while sheltering from the rain in the National Portrait Gallery, experiences the shock of recognizing his own ghostly face emerging from 'a vast oil black with age and dirt' (*That Time* 389), could not fail to attract the attention of Bennett and many other playwrights who would write about similar gallery visits. Despite Bennett's warning that 'the experience of someone in front of a painting cannot be assessed and remains a mystery even, very often, to them',[40] the jolt of recognition felt by Beckett's C is undeniable and shared by other characters in other plays. Among them is surely Biddy, the insecure and self-deprecating upper-class protagonist of Timberlake Wertenbaker's witty *Three Birds Alighting on a Field*, which was first performed at the Royal Court on 5 September 1991.

Written towards the end of the Thatcher government, which sought to stifle the arts by forcing many organizations and artists into potentially compromising sponsorship deals, *Three Birds Alighting on a Field* is a satire of the contemporary art world of dealers, collectors and patrons. The protagonist, Biddy, is an English 'Sloaney' who turns to art collecting to help her wealthy Greek husband buy a place in high society, and eventually finds solace in Stephen, a working-class artist who abandoned the avant-garde to

---

[38] Alan Bennett, 'Going to the Pictures', in *Untold Stories* (London: Faber and Faber, [2005] 2006), 476.
[39] Ibid. See also Alan Bennett, 'Portrait or Bust', in *Untold Stories*, 494–514.
[40] Bennett, *Going to the Pictures*, 476.

paint traditional landscapes. At the beginning of the play, while stalking a woman she suspects of having an affair with her husband, Biddy enters a Francis Bacon exhibition where, instead of discovering more about the rival threatening her marriage, she unexpectedly discovers something about herself:

> **Biddy** [...] Those men isolated – in their circles, so uncomfortable and smudged, well, I felt like that. It was so sad, but I left the exhibition feeling, I don't know, recognized, better. (*3 Birds* 20)

Significantly, a visit to the exhibition allows Biddy to step back from the social relationships of her everyday life and look at herself and her world with a different set of thoughts and feelings. This epiphany and her growing love of painting help her to break free from the constraints of her upbringing and become an artist's muse and art lecturer.

The analysis of art's effects on viewers is an evolving field of research, and visceral reactions like Biddy's to Bacon's art have been theorized by many art professionals, including art historian and curator Sir Nicholas Serota, who was director of the Tate from 1988 to 2017:

> You enter a Richard Serra sculpture and your body changes. Its feeling and its shape and its form. It makes you aware of yourself, but it also makes you aware of the persona who has made it. And then you understand more about the way in which other people's minds work and their emotions and their experiences. [Art] is about encountering other people's experiences, other people's language, other people's view of the world.[41]

While Wertenbaker's *Three Birds Alighting on a Field* shows the difference between the price and value of art and focuses on the psychological effects of art and exhibitions on visitors and artists alike, Andrew Bridgemont's play *Red on Black*, which premiered at the Hen & Chickens Theatre in 2003,[42] shows a different kind of impact on the visitor's emotions. In this play inspired by the art and life of Mark Rothko, the protagonist, Joe, is a young journalist

---

[41] Nicolas Serota in Charlotte Higgins, 'How Nicholas Serota's Tate Changed Britain', *The Guardian*, 22 June 2017. https://www.theguardian.com/artanddesign/2017/jun/22/how-nicholas-serota-tate-changed-britain (accessed 7 May 2023).

[42] Winner of the International Playwriting Festival in 2000, *Red on Black* is still unpublished, while a low-quality video recording of Katie Read's 2003 production at the Hens & Chicken is still available online: https://www.youtube.com/watch?v=q6FahHUHvww (accessed 1 May 2023).

whose indifference towards art has been overcome by Rothko's 'wonderful paintings' in the gallery where he casually enters, seeking protection from the heat. Whether his words are authentic or not, Joe claims to have been so seduced, even enraptured, by these 'miracle paintings' that he decides to meet the abstract American painter to express to him his admiration:

> I went into the gallery. Not because I was interested in art at the time, but to get out of the sun. Looked at some art. Big stuff. Brash. Like it knew it belonged there. Cruel, that's how it seemed to me that day. I was ready to go back to the hotel. Pack. Go back to … 'Sorry' to outstay my welcome. (*Pause.*) Your painting was to the right. On the way out. Like a window. I liked that. To look through. And beyond it, hot country. Behind smoke. Then I saw the others. All around me. They seemed to appear. Pushing through the half-light. The place was full of them. This glow. I thought they were angels. Miracle paintings. True. And so fucking sad. That's how they seemed to me, and I loved them for that. I could feel water pouring down my face. It was an embarrassment. I hadn't cried since I was a kid. Not in public. Nowhere. I heard this sound come out of my throat, like a … (*He touches his throat.*). People getting edgy. I could tell. They started to sort of shift around me. Moving away. So, I found a bathroom. Cleaned myself up. I was shaky but okay. I felt good. (*Pause.*) The people seemed different now. Altered. I wanted to tell them what had happened to me. What I had found. These wonderful paintings. For us. They belonged to us. Not to the city or the traffic, but to the citizens. Us. (*Pause.*) One day I would meet their creator. The man who told me I had a right to be there. (*RoB* 14)

Although this is probably mere coincidence, it is nonetheless significant that in *Going to Pictures* Bennett himself speaks of 'glow' in terms similar to Joe's when trying to express what attracts him to a painting:

> If as a young man I'd had to put into words what my response was to pictures, I'd have said I like paintings that had what I thought of as a glow to them. That is what drew me across a room to a picture and (*I say this slightly shamefacedly*) made me want to take the picture home.[43]

Joe's fervent depiction of Rothko's works as 'miracle paintings', or 'angels' 'appearing' with a 'glow' echoes one of the most traditional ways of describing

---

[43] Bennett, *Going to the Pictures*, 457.

the art gallery as 'a sacred space' that declares that its objects 'possess an aura that offers spiritual enlightenment as it inspires Platonic values of beauty and morality'.[44] As Sir Kenneth Clark, director of the National Gallery from 1934 to 1945 and presenter of the popular 1970s BBC television series *Civilization*, recalled in his essay *The Ideal Museum*, works of art were first gathered together as objects or accessories of worship and the first great exhibitions of painting and sculpture in ancient Greece took place in temples and were made in honour of the gods. As he argued, 'It was in the great cathedrals that men became conscious of the power of works of art to quicken their spirits and give dignity and order to their lives.'[45] He even warned the art curator of the danger of confusing the Platonic nature of the modern gallery, which is concerned with 'essences and ideas' with the museum's 'Aristotelian interests with facts and its encyclopaedic, documentary character', to conclude:

> The only reason for bringing together works of art in a public space is that for which they were brought together first, that they produce in us a kind of exalted happiness. For a moment there is a clearing in the jungle; we pass on refreshed, with our capacity for life increased and with some memory of the sky.[46]

Recently, scholars and practitioners have recognized the healing potential of the art gallery, while they have, unsurprisingly, attacked the idea of the art gallery as a shrine or sanctuary, as it requires passive visitors, and advocated a more experiential art gallery and museum practice. Tim Crouch's post-dramatic *ENGLAND* (2007) is an exception in this regard. Indeed, the play, which is designed to be experienced as a visit to a gallery, invites the audience to contemplate art in architecturally distinctive spaces that enhance the individual's emotional and psychic well-being, while at the same time giving them new authority (we will have the opportunity to describe and develop such a dynamic more fully in the pages that follow).

A social and political recognition is experienced by the group of the pitmen painters in front of van Gogh's masterpieces in Lee Hall's *The Pitmen Painters* (2008), the successful play based on art critic William Feaver's 1988

---

[44] Janet Marstine (ed.), *New Museum Theory and Practice. An Introduction* (Oxford: Blackwell, 2006), 9.
[45] Kenneth Clark, 'The Ideal Museum', *ARTnews*, 52, 9 (January 1954): 28–31, re-published as 'The Ideal Museum: Art Historian Kenneth Clark on the Formation of Western Institutions, in 1954', *ARTnews*, 19 March 2021. https://www.artnews.com/art-news/retrospective/kenneth-clark-the-ideal-museum-1234587297/ (accessed 8 May 2023).
[46] Ibid.

book,[47] which opened at the Live Theatre, Newcastle upon Tyne in 2007, and then at the National Theatre Cottesloe in May 2008. The play presents the true story of the so-called Pitmen Painters, or 'Ashington Group' as they chose to call themselves: a group of (mostly) Northumbrian miners from Ashington, a Northumberland colliery town, who in 1934 engaged Robert Lyon, Master of Painting at Armstrong College, Newcastle, to teach 'Art appreciation' as part of their continuing studies with the Workers' Educational Association (WEA). Focusing on the Group's most prolific years (1933–47), the play shows how the pitmen painters soon began to paint themselves, creating a remarkable body of work that attracted the interest of the art world and the media in the 1930s, while raising questions about the social and political impact of art on the lives of the working-class, access to education, the transformation of heavy industry sites into heritage sites and the loss of traditional leftist values in the British Labour Party.

It is therefore significant that when Hall imagines the Ashington Group visiting the Tate Gallery, the portrayal of the pitmen painters implies a social and political self-awareness of themselves as working-class people who rarely visit museums or art galleries. Unsurprisingly, it is the van Gogh Room that impresses them most, for it is when they are confronted with the Dutch painter and his early drawings of miners that they finally realize their strength as a working-class group and their ability to 'transform things and make something beautiful through their art' (*Pitmen* 74):

George   But the main thing to impress us –
Oliver   – the main thing –
Young Lad   – was the Van Gogh.
[…]
Oliver   Even when we walked into the room. You could feel that this was special.
Harry   It might have been the mining connection.
Oliver   He used to live in a mining village.
George   Before he was a painter.
[…]
Oliver   He was a trainee vicar. Trying to look after the well-being of the miners.
Harry   And that's where he learned to draw.
[…]

---

[47] William Feaver, *Pitmen Painters. The Ashington Group 1934–1984* (Newcastle-upon-Tyne: Northumbria Press in association with Ashington Group Trustees, 2010).

More slides of Van Gogh.

George   And the first things he actually drew were miners –

Slides of the early drawings of miners.

Oliver   But what seemed overwhelming – was the intensity.
George   When you see this room, it's not just like you were in it having a look round –
Harry   – it's like you were inside his heed when he was in it.

The slides start coming thick and fast – much more quickly than in any realistic lecture.

George   'I don't paint pictures. I paint experience.' That's what he used to say.
[…]
Harry   And really, I think it was at that moment –
Jimmy   – when we saw the Van Gogh. Something happened.
Oliver   When we saw the Van Gogh I think –
George   – we became a group. (*Pitmen* 71–2)

It is in this room that they finally understand that art is 'communal and active', and should not be something to be bought and sold, but 'the intellectual and emotional air we breathe', as Lee writes in the play's introduction.[48]

But onstage, the art gallery is not always a place of epiphanies, intellectual recognition or spiritual regeneration. In many plays, the art gallery has become one of the most mundane places for socializing and meeting people beyond the encounter with art and artists, even though these meetings are always full of consequences and reveal that encountering the other is always potentially threatening, as in Patrick Marber's *Closer*, one of the most successful plays of the 1990s.

In Marber's sexual comedy, which was first presented at the Lyttelton, National Theatre, in 1997, two contemporary couples, who switch partners several times, meet, love and betray each other in many urban locations, including a commercial art gallery. In a play concerned with the bitter fact that honesty is as brutal as deception when it comes to matters of the heart, a vernissage becomes the occasion for Alice, the subject of Anna's huge photographic portrait (Figure 1.1), to meet the man who would become her

[48] Lee Hall, *The Pitmen Painters* (London: Faber and Faber, 2008), viii.

Figure 1.1 *Closer* written by Patrick Marber and directed by David Leveaux. With Rachel Redford and Oliver Chris. The Donmar Warehouse, London, February 2015.

Source: Courtesy Johan Persson / ArenaPAL.

lover while exposing the photographer's (and therefore art's) untruthfulness and hypocrisy:

> **Larry** I know it's *vulgar* to discuss 'The Work' at an opening of 'The Work' but *someone*'s got to do it. Serious, what d'you think?
> **Alice** It's a lie.
> It's a bunch of sad strangers photographed beautifully and all rich fuckers who appreciate *art* say it's beautiful because that's what they want to see. But the people in the photos are sad and alone but the pictures make the word seem beautiful. So, the exhibition is reassuring, which makes it a lie, and everyone loves a Big Fat Lie.
> **Larry** I'm the Big Fat Liar's boyfriend.
> **Alice** Bastard! (*Closer* 38)

Alice exposes the art gallery as a place of fiction and lies. The exhibition, entitled 'Strangers', which features photographs of many anonymous people, 'a bunch of sad strangers photographed beautifully', and the photo of Alice, captioned as 'Young Woman, London', is the perfect setting for the four characters' intricate quadrille of deceptions. Looking at her own image, Alice sees her portrait as a reassuring lie, which has nothing to do with the feelings of despair she felt when the picture was taken, immediately after realizing she had been betrayed by her boyfriend. Alice's portrait and the whole exhibition of beautifully photographed sad strangers is a 'big fat lie' because of the discrepancy between the sadness and loneliness of the people in the portraits and their representation as beautiful, pleasant and consumable. This exploration of the objectification and appropriation of the other by the gaze of the artist and the art gallery visitor, which is at the heart of many other plays, in which the characters who are the subjects of portraits denounce how their existence has been stolen and commodified by presenting it in a pleasurable form, is also part of the playwright's interest in memory and the past. How do we remember things? How do we remember old love affairs or the terrible scars of the mind?

The meeting at the exhibition is also an opportunity for Alice to remind Larry that they have met before and to refer to Postman's Park, the small park near where he used to go for a smoke. As the play develops, the audience understands that the reference to Postman's Park is not accidental. No wonder, in Vicky Mortimer's minimal and versatile set design for the Lyttleton theatre, a series of mysterious rectangles are hung up and down the back wall like faceless paintings in an art gallery (Figure 1.2).

Figure 1.2 *Closer* written and directed by Patrick Marber. With Sally Dexter as Anna and Ciaran Hinds as Larry. Cottesloe Theatre at The Royal National Theatre, London, October 1997.

Source: Courtesy Geraint Lewis / ArenaPAL.

Perhaps they draw a metaphorical background for the characters' many shifting identities until they reveal themselves as the plaques commemorating ordinary people who died saving others on the wall of the Watts Memorial of Heroic Self-Sacrifice in Postman's Park. They also serve, therefore, as a visual trigger for the many questions about memory and the way the past is narrated and represented, together with a set design that has been visually transformed into a Christian Boltanski-like installation, in which the accumulation of objects and furniture belonging to the characters visually evokes the memory and trauma of troubled lives full of regrets.

The art gallery (in this case an art museum) is a place where connections are made both with people and with memory even in Rebecca Lenkiewicz's *Shoreditch Madonna*, a play that was first presented at the Soho Theatre, on 6 July 2005, and that deals with a group of young artists who run an exhibition space in the hip art scene of Shoreditch, in London's East End, far from the posh commercial art galleries of the city centre. In this case, Devlin, a shrewd and sex-obsessed bohemian artist, suggests to his former lover Martha, the mother of his child, that he meet his new-found twelve-year-old son at the National Gallery: 'Perhaps we could all meet there once. I could walk him round the National Gallery and explain the paintings?' (*Shoreditch* 194). Presented almost a decade after *Closer*, while confirming the art gallery/museum as a place of encounters, Lenkiewicz's play also shows a significant change not only in the social background of art gallery visitors, who now seem to come from diverse social classes, but also in the function of the gallery, which has become more accessible and seems to have a role in the daily life of a family.[49] Thus, Devlin recognizes the National Gallery, which, by its very nature is steeped in memories, as the appropriate place for such an emotionally charged meeting that is an opportunity to rethink the past and start planning a future with his son. In addition, he understands that the art gallery will offer him the opportunity not only to entertain his son but also to teach him, considering his poor knowledge of art history: 'He'd never heard of Giotto. What have you been teaching him?' (*Shoreditch* 200).

Without going into detail, it is worth noting that, although with very different ethical and philosophical implications, Lyndsey Turner's recent production of Caryl Churchill's *A Number* at the Old Vic (February 2022) similarly celebrates the art gallery as a site of encounters, using it as one of the settings where the middle-aged Salter meets Michael Black, one of the clones of his sons, played by Paapa Essiedu. Turner contradicts Churchill's stage directions, which suggest that the scene should be the same for all five parts and that it should be where Salter lives. In fact, designer Es Devlin not

---

[49] Falk and Dierking, *Museum Experience Revisited*, 67.

only traps the characters 'in a red box of a home, where the fixtures and fittings have become featureless – a kind of nightmarish nowheresville'[50] but also sets the final scene in an art gallery. Painted entirely in a monochromatic, womb-like red and only hinted at by an empty frame in the same red (Figure 1.3), Devlin's art gallery is a perfect metaphorical setting for this noirish thriller of shifting realities, multiple identities and clones, which Churchill wrote in 2002, at a time when ethical debates over Dolly the sheep were raging, using the concept of cloning to explore identity, inheritance and the essence of our individuality. While suggesting an obvious connection between cloning and Walter Benjamin's mechanical reproduction of artworks, the empty frame also seems to reflect Michael Black's lack of introspection, which stands in cruelly ironic contrast to his tormented brothers. When Salter asks him what makes him unique, he says: 'I like blue socks. Banana ice cream.'[51]

The art gallery has become an increasingly popular setting in contemporary British theatre, where it is a place of encounter (literal and metaphorical), entertainment and education, but also of mystery, memory and lies, rarely a safe place. It has proved an evocative site of confrontation and revelation, where characters explore some fundamental questions about themselves, art and the world.

Fatal attraction

The eighties: Towards something new

In the 1980s and early 1990s, questions of heritage, memory and conservation inspired and informed the work of many playwrights, who developed new formal strategies in response to the 'museal sensibility' that was beginning to permeate the culture,[52] by appropriating museal motifs and vocabulary to question and challenge the art gallery and museum as sites for storing memories and constructing national identity.

Like many other commentators, the cultural historian Robert Hewison has suggested that British culture itself was inherently nostalgic in the 1980s, and that 'the heritage industry' (of which museums were only one part) was born as an attempt 'to dispel the climate of decline' by exploiting the economic potential of culture: 'Instead of manufacturing goods, we are

---

[50] Sarah Hemming, 'Variation on a cloning classic', *Financial Times*, 3 February 2022: 18.
[51] Caryl Churchill, *A Number* (London: Nick Hern Books, 2002), 59.
[52] Andreas Huyssen, *Twilight Memories: Marking Time in a Culture of Amnesia* (London: Routledge, 1995), 32–5.

Figure 1.3 *A Number* written by Caryl Churchill and directed by Lyndsey Turner. With Lennie James as Salter. Old Vic Theatre, London, January 2022.

Source: Courtesy Manuel Harlan / ArenaPAL.

manufacturing *heritage*, a commodity which nobody seems able to define, but which everybody is eager to sell, in particular those cultural institutions that can no longer rely on government funds as they did in the past' (emphasis in original).[53] The simultaneous boom in artists' biographies, then, is surely no coincidence. As part of this broader cultural phenomenon, Nick Dear's *The Art of Success* (1987) and Timberlake Wertenbaker's *Three Birds Alighting on a Field* (1991), two plays based on artist biographies – Dear's on the historical figure of William Hogarth,[54] Wertenbaker's on the fictional Stephen Ryle – seem crucial to an understanding of the decade, as both aim, albeit in different ways, to challenge the cultivated nostalgia that characterized Thatcher's years, and to insist on the need to break new grounds both in the art world and the theatre.

Both Dear's interest in William Hogarth's battle for the birth of English art and Wertenbaker's satire of the London art scene of the late 1980s may find their roots in the cultural atmosphere of the mid-1980s, when the time appears to have been ripe for redefining a specifically British identity in art, and when London was on the verge of becoming the cool metropolis of the 1990s and the undisputed centre for the practice and display of contemporary art in the wake of the huge success of the *Freeze* exhibition staged by Damien Hirst in July 1988. Indeed, many commentators have suggested that *Freeze* started an inexorable process of change and 'entered modern art history as a cataclysmic happening on a par with the Cabaret Voltaire and the Salon des Refusés'.[55]

Nick Dear's Olivier Award-winning *The Art of Success*, first presented in 1986 by the Royal Shakespeare Company at The Other Place Theatre in Stratford-upon-Avon,[56] demonstrates how vibrantly William Hogarth's staged biography

---

[53] Robert Hewison, *The Heritage Industry. Britain in a Climate of Decline* (London: Methuen, 1987), 9.
[54] Significantly, William Hogarth is also the subject of both Timberlake Wertenbaker's *The Grace of Mary Traverse* (1985) and Mark Ravenhill's *Mother Clap's Molly House* (2001). See Sara Soncini, 'Hogarth in drag. Acts of Transvestism in *The Grace of Mary Traverse* and *Mother Clap's Molly House*', in Caroline Patey, Cynthis E. Roman and George Letissier (eds), *Enduring Presence. William Hogarth's British and European Afterlives*. Book 1: *Aesthetic, Visual and Performative Cultures* (Oxford: Peter Lang, 2021).
[55] Jessica Berenza, 'Freeze: 20 Years on', *The Guardian*, 1 June 2008. https://www.theguardian.com/artanddesign/2008/jun/01/art (accessed 8 May 2023).
[56] The play transferred to the Pit Theatre at the Barbican on 13 August 1987. It was later reprised at the Rose in Kingston (29 September–21 October) in a double-bill entitled *The Hogarth Plays* with the premiere of Dear's newly written sequel, *The Taste of the Town*. *The Art of Success*, first published by Mehuen in 1986, revised and reprinted in 1994 by Methuen Drama and in 2000 by Faber and Faber, was therefore later included in a two-play edition published in 2018 as *The Hogarth Plays*. All the quotations in this essay are from the 2000 edition, abbreviated as '*Art*'.

engaged in mid-1980s cultural issues and how urgently his impudent challenges to the fine art establishment and the print market practices caught the 1980s' rampant spirit. His inter-textual dialogue with the past provides therefore the opportunity for addressing political issues and for coming to terms with one's difficult and even contradictory role as an artist working in late twentieth-century society. Thus, in his introduction to the published script, Dear warns his readers that the historical setting is 'purely a matter of convenience'.[57] As evidence of the play's relevance to contemporary concerns, it is perhaps worth recalling that when Pip Broughton and Paines Plough successfully revived it at The Place, London, in November 1989, Hewson observed that 'the lewd and cynical London of the 1730s' was 'clearly intended to parallel' the 1980s, where 'money, power and art are woven into an eternal triangle', and where political authority 'approves art as an embellishing investment, but is wary of its potentially subversive influence on public opinion'.[58] It is perhaps on the grounds of such similarity that Dear acted freely with his sources, exacerbating, for instance, both Hogarth's unconventional sexual tastes and his entrepreneurial talents in a budding and profitable mass-market.

By drawing inspiration from the series *A Rake's Progress*, Dear represents his main character as a rake himself, who 'progresses' across ten years of English history as the play boldly encompasses the political rise of Robert Walpole, the advent of the 1734 Engraving Copyrights Act, also known as Hogarth's Act, and Walpole's Licensing Act of 1737, which established the Lord Chamberlain as theatre censor and which drove playwright Henry Fielding – among others – away from the London stage. Compressing ten years of Hogarth's life (1727–37), *The Art of Success* rushes through various episodes taking place in a single night in the 1730s: the artist paints the portrait of the murderess Sarah Sprackling prior to her execution; cheats on his wife Jane Thornhill with a prostitute; runs around in drag; discusses the relation between art and censorship with Henry Fielding, and the copyright law for printed images; and attempts to analyse his castration nightmares two hundred years before Freud.

By means of the drunken exchange at the Beefsteak Club which opens the play, *The Art of Success* loses no time in leading the audience into the very gist of the debate that was inflaming London in the eighteenth century:

> **Oliver** A great artist? Willy Hogarth a great artist? Let us assess his curriculum vitae. What cathedrals has he done? What frescos of what

---

[57] Nick Dear, *Nick Dear. Plays One* (London: Faber and Faber, 2000), vii.
[58] Robert Hewison, 'A Rake and a Rebel in a Morality Play That Mirrors Our Time', *Sunday Times*, 19 November 1989.

battles? What mansion walls adorned with Roman heroes? [...] a great artist – Let me remind you one has toured the Continent and one has *seen* great art, I mean the originals, vast canvases in gold leaf frames, huge blocks of stone chipped up to holiness, Annunciation, Pietà, and in the damp palaces of Venice spent my inheritance, spent money like water building my collection of Madonnas –
William   Dead Christs, Holy Families, flying fucking angels, and shiploads no doubt of similar dismal, dark subjects.
Oliver   Historical allegories, mainly, drawn from the well of antique myth.
William   Which no one can understand.
Oliver   Not open to the common heard, I grant you.
William   Which I can't understand. (*Art* 10, 11)

What is at stake here is Hogarth's endeavour to impose his own work in an art world dominated by connoisseurs, dealers and auctioneers.[59] As to the historical Hogarth, one knows how strenuously he challenged the awe in which tradition and Old Masters were held by the moderns, and, specifically, by the connoisseurs who saw the birth of modern English art as dependent on the imitation of the grand foreign models of the past. On stage, Dear's Hogarth vividly marks his distance from the artistic establishment of his time and its consolidated practices. As the son of a school teacher who was imprisoned for debt, he does not accompany connoisseurs on their tours around Italy advising them and copying works of the Old Masters, and moreover, he prefers working on 'original subjects conceived as comments on contemporary events'.[60] If the historical Hogarth engages in a dialectical relation with the past, Dear's artist appears less sophisticated in his aesthetic thought and fiercely demolishes classical and Renaissance ideals and their supporters, the connoisseurs: 'I have no patron, no office, no inheritance, but what I do have is this body of work behind me, built from nothing' (*Art* 15).

This professional dispute, both on stage and in actual life, is inscribed in the larger cultural war initiated with the battle of the books at the beginning of the century, starring Alexander Pope and Jonathan Swift among others, and ready to re-erupt in the late 1750s around the identity and aesthetics of British art, with, of course, William Hogarth and Joshua Reynolds championing different causes. On the one side was an artist whose

---

[59] Carolina Brook and Valter Curzi (eds), *Hogarth Reynolds Turner: British Painting and the Rise of Modernity* (Milan: Skira, 2014), 20.
[60] Ilaria Bignamini, 'William Hogarth: From *The Battle of the Pictures* to *Industry and Idleness*', in *William Hogarth: Nationalism, Mass Media and the Artist* (Vancouver: The Vancouver Art Gallery, 1980), 12.

pronouncedly middle-class art, in Bindman's words, 'contained the germ of an idea of a British school of painting owing nothing, or very little, to the idealism associated with the art of antiquity and the Italian Renaissance'.[61] But, on the other side of the fence, antagonism was rife and Hogarth was becoming increasingly isolated as, in the 1740s and 1750s, more and more English artists, including Reynolds, were beginning to travel to Rome and to place their emphasis on learning rather than observation, and the 'ideal' rather than imperfect nature.

As Nick Dear well knew when writing his play, another ruthless battle of the pictures was ready to be waged, entailing issues strangely redolent of the ones debated centuries before: the weight of the past, continuity, tradition, commodification, identity, rules and transgression. The first battle took place at the 1981 Royal Academy exhibition *A New Spirit in Painting*, curated by Christos M. Joachimides, Norman Rosenthal and Nicholas Serota. The exhibition displayed the work of thirty-eight painters belonging 'roughly speaking to three generations' that better represented the state of painting at the onset of the 1980s and paradoxically argued for a look backwards:

> Our times, wherever you look, are pervaded by a reassessment of traditional values. [...] The exhibition presents a position in art which conspicuously asserts traditional values, such as individual creativity, accountability, quality, which throw light on the condition of contemporary art and, by association, on the society in which it is produced. Thus for all its apparent conservatism the art on show here is, in the true sense, progressive. Consciously or instinctively, then, painters are turning back to traditional concerns.[62]

In Britain, during the late 1970s and the early 1980s, many artists who chose to confront traditional concerns with painting the human figure and the physical and social world moved into prominence, reinforcing the sense of a national 'resurgence'. In 1987 Michael Peppiatt curated the touring exhibition *A School of London: Six Figurative Painters* that presented Michael Andrews, Frank Auerbach, Francis Bacon, Lucien Freud, R. B. Kitaj and Leon Kossoff as a group to a European audience. Tradition was also at the core of the exhibition held at the Tate Gallery in mid-1984, *The Hard-Won Image. Traditional Method and Subject in Recent British Art*, whose contention was

---

[61] David Bindman, *Hogarth and His Times* (London: British Museum Press, 1997), 15.
[62] Christos M. Joachimides, Norman Rosenthal and Nicholas Serota (eds), *A New Spirit in Painting* (London: Royal Academy of Arts, 1981), 15.

likewise that 'the finest art of a more traditional and less self-consciously innovatory kind not only has a place in the heart of its period but that, even if not alone, it lies actually at its centre'.[63]

Young British Artists (YBA) was perhaps born, among other reasons, as a completely new and radical attitude towards realism, or rather towards reality and real life itself. It was a radical reaction to tradition, provincialism and even boredom. As Matthew Collings writes: 'When you think about the older artists going around in their suits and being in biennales and giving the same interviews all the time about their concerns and being a bit gratingly half-intellectual, you feel refreshed by this frankly abject juvenile style, even if it's only for a moment.' Indeed, as he argues, 'Part of the mythology of the Young British Artists is that they were oppressed by Thatcher's Britain and rebelled against the dominant culture.'[64]

Hogarth's onstage concerns with experience, the transgression of rules and the observation of life give voice to the *Zeitgeist* of the 1980s and convey the anger and new appetites shared by a new generation of spectators and artists waiting for something newly meaningful not hetero-directed by American 'masters' but instead steeped in British identity. One battle of the paintings mirrors another, in a to-and-fro movement from then to now, making Hogarth the contemporary of Damien Hirst. No wonder the actor James Allen, who was cast as Hogarth in Gillian King's revival at the Man in the Moon Pub in 1996, had a face 'reminiscent of Damien Hirst'.[65] No wonder, too, that Rachel Halliburton, reviewing Amelia Nicholson's production at the Arcola Theatre in 2002, wrote that Hogarth's reputation as one of Britain's most provocative artists was reminiscent of YBAs Chris Ofili and Tracey Emin, 'still remorselessly on the ascent'.[66]

That British art needed a shake was also Alex's view in *Three Birds Alighting on a Field*, another 'savage critique of the Thatcherite legacy in Britain, figuratively represented through the art world'.[67] Both a biting satire of the ultra-rich art world, and an earnest discussion of the nature and purpose of art, it was first presented in 1991 at the Royal Court, a 'chronically

---

[63] Richard Morphet, *The Hard-Won Image. Traditional Method and Subject in Recent British Art* (London: Tate Gallery Publications, 1984), 10.
[64] Matthew Collings, *Blimey! From Bohemia to Britpop: The London Artworld from Francis Bacon to Damien Hirst* (London: 21 Publishing, 1997), 15, 21.
[65] Craig Higginson, 'The Art of Success', *Time Out*, 29 May 1996, reprinted in *Theatre Record 6–19 May 1996*, 615.
[66] Rachel Halliburton, 'The Art of Success', *Evening Standard*, 17 June 2002, reprinted in *Theatre Record 4–17 June 2002*, 808.
[67] Elaine Aston, *Feminist Views on the English Stage. Women Playwrights, 1990–2000* (Cambridge Books Online: Cambridge University Press, 2009), 151.

underfunded' venue which many reviewers felt was the perfect stage for a play dealing with the value of art in a commercial world.[68]

Three Birds Alighting on a Field is a hilarious guide to both the anthropology and the economics of London's contemporary art market, much like Caryl Churchill's satire of international finance in *Serious Money* (1987). In the best tradition of Royal Court's established style, Wertenbaker and director Max Stafford-Clark sent actors to interview artists and art dealers in the glamorous but recession-hit galleries of Cork Street, where the 1987–90 boom brought exorbitant prices after art collecting became a vibrant social scene for the rich. The play is therefore the result of workshops in which the playwright, director and actors carried out field research and developed the subject. Art dealer Bernard Jacobson, whose Clifford Street gallery represents artists such as Maggie Hambling, Leon Kossoff, Frank Auerbach and William Tillyer, acted as a consultant on the script. William Tillyer, an artist living in an old farmhouse in Yorkshire at the time and specializing in abstract paintings inspired by the landscape, painted a huge thirteen-foot canvas that served as Stephen's painting in scene nineteen. The idea supported in the play, that the recession of the 1990s called for a different kind of art, also emerged from the group's research.

On stage, the future of British art is debated in Jeremy Bertrand's commercial art gallery, 'The Gallery', which the playwright imagines not far from the galleries of Cork Street in Mayfair, the spiritual home of modern and contemporary art in London, and which designer Sally Jacob conjures up in plexiglass and matt white (Figure 1.4). In this exclusive art gallery, Wertenbaker stages the complex process of endorsement that determines which works are worthy of a potential place in art history. Gallery owners buy and sell on the market, curators select works for exhibitions and critics write about works of art, all 'with a view to finding a last place in the history of visual culture', as Louisa Buck would write a decade later in her report on the dynamics of art market.[69]

Wertenbaker captures the late 1980s debate about the need to redefine a British art identity that had until then been subordinated to the New York market and explores the dynamics behind creating and promoting 'branded' artists, 'the Picassos of tomorrow' (*3 Birds* 16) at the dawn of what would become the impressive YBA movement and the growing popularity of artists such as Damien Hirst and Tracey Emin.

[68] Ian Dodd, 'Three Birds Alighting on a Field', *Tribune*, 20 September 1991, reprinted in *Theatre Record 10–23 September 1991*, 1116.
[69] Louisa Buck, *Matters. The Dynamics of the Contemporary Art Market* (London: British Council, 2004), 12.

Figure 1.4 *Three Birds Alighting on a Field* written by Timberlake Wertenbaker and directed by Max Stafford-Clark. Royal Court Theatre, London, September 1991. Painting by William Tillyer.

Source: Courtesy Mark Douet / ArenaPAL.

American commodity-broker dealer Alex Brandel, who works for 'The Gallery' and enters onstage 'storming around' in 'labelled power cloths' (*3 Birds* 4), expresses the need to find alternatives to New York art. It is time to react against the dominant contemporary art movements, Minimalism, Conceptualism and Abstract Expressionism. It is time to forget Rothko, even though his retrospective at the Tate Gallery in 1987 deeply impressed her boss, Jeremy: 'I remember the American shows at the Tate, we were dazzled. The scale, the daring. Rothko's colours' (*3 Birds* 5). It is also time to forget the American art, which London celebrated with the exhibition 'New York Art Now' (September 1987–April 1988) at the Saatchi Gallery in St John's Wood, an exclusive space that through the 1980s showed much of US and European art rarely seen in Britain, reinforcing the feeling that the artistic avant-garde was elsewhere:

> **Alex** This stuff is New York. And this is neo-New York. New York is finished. Mary Boone is in trouble. Castelli's showing Old Masters. Basically New York is closing down. My company was too late to save New York, but we can save England. Do you want to save England or don't you? […] Now what you've gotta do is get rid of New York. (*3 Birds* 5)

The need for something new is particularly evident in Alex's argument. While she acknowledges the closure of many galleries both in New York and London, she (and Wertenbaker) seems to predict the surprising and growing relevance throughout the 1990s and the 2000s of the private art galleries as a significant aesthetic, cultural and commercial site. Surely, Alex's thoughtful marketing plan could have inspired the future launch of emerging artists, not least the young British artists: first of all, 'go national' and then 'make it international' (*3 Birds* 6), but also find the right artist, a label and finally an art critic who can promote the work and make it appeal:

> **Alex** […] Well, Jeremy, you'll have to go out there and find some English landscapes. Trees, a dark piece of water, a windmill, but new, now. […] The school of new English landscape, no, the English Garden School, you'll think of something. Better, invite Morris [an art critic], he'll think of something. I don't think he understands art, but he sure has a way with words. (*3 Birds* 7)

Perhaps inspired by the Hayward Gallery's 1983 exhibition *Landscape in Britain 1850–1950*, Alex's proposal to reassess and revive the English landscape tradition is the starting point for the plot to try and bring Stephen Ryle back into the gallery: 'I'm not saying Constable, I'm saying England, but as it looks now' (*3 Birds* 6). The fictional artist imagined by Wertenbaker, Stephen Ryle is a working-class painter who used to exhibit at the Serpentine Gallery (*3 Birds* 29), teach at the Slade School of Fine Arts and even sell some paintings to the Tate Gallery, and who has turned his back on the avant-garde in order to paint landscapes, instead. The artist fell out of favour when he abandoned the brilliant works of his early period, ironically represented by *Door Handles* (*3 Birds* 18). According to Jeremy, who was his art gallerist at the time, his mistake was refusing to bow to the demands of the art market by continuing to paint landscapes when the demand was for more conceptual and abstract art: 'It was the beginning of the Eighties, Thatcher, no one wanted to look at watercolours' (*3 Birds* 37). Significantly and also perhaps ironically, Stephen's artistic and commercial success was ultimately derailed by Charles's disapproval of his art (*3 Birds* 34). Charles stands perhaps for Charles Saatchi, the controversial prototype of the modern brand collector who sees art as a speculative investment, one of the few 'supercollectors' to exert a significant influence on the contemporary art market,[70] who would soon launch the YBA. The fact is that 'these days it's not enough to have talent' (*3 Birds* 17).

---

[70] Rita Hatton and John A. Walker, *Supercollector. A Critique of Charles Saatchi* (London: Ellipsis, 2000).

In the turbulent world of contemporary art, talent often goes hand in hand with profitability and branding replaces critical judgement, so that dealers are sometimes unable to identify or define what will become million-dollar art, as Jeremy cynically explains to an American investor who wants to return the Basquiat-like graffiti whose value has not increased as expected:

> **Jeremy** Odd about this painter. He had everything going for him: young, black, new, there wasn't much else that year, he even died young, very good of him, in a business sense, but …
> **Mr Boreman** But?
> **Jeremy** It's so difficult … His paintings should be selling for three-quarters of a million by now. But they're not. Why? Sometimes you make a mistake. The value of the stock goes down. I suppose it's loss of confidence. We may have sold his paintings to the wrong people. I mean, he's not in the most famous collections. Some of the people who bought his paintings are now in prison. All those stock-market scandals. It's not good. People change. And then some critics laid into him. Mmm. We're all slave to fashion.
> […]
> He wasn't much of a painter, but he might have become one, or a media star, like Warhol, it's just as good, so we all valued his potential. But potential itself lost value. What can I do? (*3 Birds* 48–9)

It is impossible to predict whether a given art purchase will really be a good long-term investment. However, while no one can predict what will happen to artists who seem to be promising or artworks in the hands of investors, a branded artist needs a combination of 'talent, luck, and particularly, marketing and branding' to rise to the top, as the economist and contemporary art collector Don Thompson would write a decade later in his ground-breaking analysis of the economics of the contemporary art market, *The $12 Million Stuffed Shark* (2008).[71]

As the plot develops it becomes clear that the gallery space plays a crucial role in the process of endorsement. In fact, the gallery is the space of legitimation. By opening her play with two canvases being auctioned for a fortune, Wertenbaker shows from the beginning that the gallery is the space where meaning can develop and the price of a work of art increase. 'Totally flat, authentically white' (*3 Birds* 1), like the one that would later be at the

---

[71] Don Thompson, *The $12 Million Stuffed Shark: The Curious Economics of Contemporary Art* (Basingstoke: Palgrave Macmillan, 2008), 60.

centre of Yasmina Reza's successful play *Art*, which premiered in London in 1996, the first painting shows how the gallery can transform the flatness and emptiness of a canvas and turn its emptiness into money.

The art critic seems to be equally crucial in the endorsement of art. It is, therefore, no coincidence that in the play the art critic Jean is portrayed as egocentric and self-absorbed, perhaps even as the humorous embodiment of the tyranny of the art critic that Tom Wolfe denounced in his entertaining volume, *The Painted Word* (1975). Take, for example, the following conversation with Stephen:

> **Jean** Everybody reads my magazine. I determine style. I tell people what's important.
> **Stephen** Why don't you just tell them to look?
> **Jean** It's not enough to look with modern art. You have to understand. Good modern art must be difficult. And so it needs us – the interpreters. Art criticism is undervalued in this country, the English are so amateur about everything. In America you'll soon be able to get a degree in it.
> **Stephen** What exactly do you explain: how to match the recipes to the paintings?
> **Jean** The fact is the critic these days is the equal of the artist and without the critic to point out significance and deconstruct it, the artist's work is incomplete. Every artist needs a good critic and if you don't have one, you are nothing. […] And I'm going to lecture to the Patrons of New Art. They want my advice for the Turner Prize. I certainly couldn't nominate any of the stuff here. (*3 Birds* 35)

Similarly allusive and emblematic, the second work of art to be auctioned is an illuminated billboard highlighting the intricate and often contradictory relationship between art, money and social status: 'Art is sexy, art is money, art is money-sexy, art is money-sexy-social-climbing-fantastic' (*3 Birds* 2). This is a quotation of Thomas Hoving, director of the Metropolitan Museum of Art from 1967 to 1977, who recognized art's intersection with wealth and power and recalled that art patronage in general, and that of museums and art galleries in particular, had become a way of acquiring social distinction. It is 'a marriage of business and art', 'one of the most successful marriages ever', Lady Lelouche suggests in the play when she publicly thanks for his £1 million donation to the Opera House the rich social-climbing Greek, Yoyo Andreas, himself desperate to be assimilated into the English upper-class and welcomed into London exclusive clubs:

Lady Lelouche   Whenever I look at a businessman I think of marriage.

(*Some polite titters.*)

I think, that is, of the marriage of business and art. It could be one of the most successful marriages ever. What better partnership than art – fine, delicate and often wayward – looked after by powerful and hard-headed business. Yes, let us wish this marriage long and lasting happiness. (*3 Birds* 9)

Since the 1980s, in line with a broader shift from welfare state to art market and an increasing hybridization of state support with corporate patronage, art galleries, museums, opera houses and theatres have been consistently encouraged to function in accordance with the neoliberal imperatives of a globalized economy: 'you can buy cheap and sell at great prices. Moral questions have been out of fashion for ten years' (*3 Birds* 44). A cynical but knowledgeable art dealer, Jeremy shares Stephen Ryle's understanding of the difference between price and value and challenges the audience:

Jeremy   (*to the audience*)   I wonder if the Medicis had to put up with these antics. I like my painters. I only want to help them. Most of them are whores. Occasionally you get an angry virgin. I think I prefer the whores. We all have to live. Great art … great art happens two or three times a century. But there's a fair amount of beauty around. Why should beauty be cheap? I know, people come and buy paintings because they want status, but they get beauty thrown in. That's a good deal, at any price. (*3 Birds* 40–1)

Jeremy interrogates the status of the contemporary art gallery, asking questions that are about to come to the fore as Damien Hirst's iconic formaldehyde-soaked tiger shark entitled *The Physical Impossibility of Death in the Mind of Someone Living* (1991) became a global symbol of British art, auctioned for $12 million: 'If we had an invasion here, what would I save? Would I save this painting? Would I save it because it is worth half a million, or was, yesterday, or would I save it because I was convinced humanity would be the poorer without it?' (*3 Birds* 20).

Wertenbaker invites the audience to question the role that private but also public contemporary art galleries play in influencing the reception and evaluation of a work of art. She also asks them to reflect on the excessively tight knot between art (any form of art, from the visual arts to the theatre) and the economy and to imagine possible alternatives to an ethics that seems both materialistic and male.

Perhaps unsurprisingly, then, it is Julia, the Anglo-Indian art dealer working for Jeremy, who proposes a different idea of a gallery, far from Jame's elitist branded art gallery, conceived as a cold, unwelcoming place for visitors, an exclusive space evoked by Jacobs' antiseptic Perspex screens, which does not even 'bother to show any picture'.[72] Julia's gallery, by contrast, will be a 'warm' place, 'where people don't feel intimidated', because 'people are friendly, the paintings are there to be looked at, not always sold to someone rich' (*3 Birds* 62). Contrary to the rapacious 1980s, Julia, Biddy and Wertenbaker herself, all suggest that visual art is not just a commodity but something that can be morally and spiritually enriching. Despite its strong satirical drive, *Three Birds Alighting on a Field* wants to suggest that 'art is wonderful and important, but it got perverted by the consumerism of the market and became risible'.[73] In Michael Billington's words, the play is 'a bracing antidote to a culture that views art in terms of style, status and money rather than aesthetic pleasure or moral improvement'.[74] It is driven by a utopian impulse that Stafford-Clark himself sought to describe in the programme: 'Theatre without a picture of Utopia is scarcely worth working for'.[75]

Written at the end of a Thatcherite government that still forced many organizations and artists into potentially compromising sponsorship, the play is also a stand against the Royal Court decision, in 1991, to approach private sponsors to support its commissioning fund. The scene in *Three Birds Alighting on a Field* in which Yoyo is invited to 'state a preference for tunes' in the Opera House his money will fund, and not allow himself to be intimidated 'with all this artistic independence nonsense' (*3 Birds* 11), epitomizes Wertenbaker's great concern for private sponsorship. 'Horrified by this prospect',[76] she wrote to the Royal Court's associate director Lindsay Posner:

> If I know that a contributor to the commissioning fund is a company I have worries about, I feel I am accepting a commission I am not comfortable

---

[72] Charles Spencer, 'Three Birds Alighting on a Field', *Daily Telegraph*, 12 September 1991, reprinted in *Theatre Record 10–23 September 1991*, 1119.
[73] Wertenbaker in Sophie Bush, *The Theatre of Timberlake Wertenbaker* (London: Bloomsbury, 2013), 263.
[74] Michael Billington, 'Three Birds Alighting on a Field', The *Guardian*, 11 September 1991, reprinted in *Theatre Record 10–23 September 1991*, 1119.
[75] Max Stafford-Clark, 'Artistic Director's Statement', programme for *Three Birds Alighting on a Field* at the Royal Court, 1991, Timberlake Wertenbaker Archive (TWA), British Library Manuscripts Collection (BLMC), Add 79386.
[76] Bush, *Theatre of Timberlake Wertenbaker*, 254.

with and at the very least I will have to waste a lot of time finding out what the company does exactly [...] [I]t is [my responsibility] to know who might be paying directly for my play. [...] How can you guarantee that the theatre will not try to 'please' its sponsors by commissioning certain writers rather than others? Or that sponsors won't exercise discreet pressure to see more of some writers, less of others, by threatening to stop supporting the fund? [...] Surely, the Royal Court should be in the forefront of those asking new and important questions about sponsorship, not finding new ways to get it.[77]

Wertenbaker eventually resigned from the Royal Court Board over the theatre's move towards private sponsorship.[78] In her play, *The Line*, first presented at the Arcola Theatre in 2009 and dealing with the Pygmalion-like relationship between Edgar Degas and his talented, indomitable protégée Suzanne Valadon, Wertenbaker again expressed the fear of new funding cuts that threatened the arts as much as those of the 1980s,[79] and continued to explore a possible alternative path for art, challenging the 'masculine mystique' that had reinforced 'the historical association of masculinity with production and femininity with passivity and consumption' (Figure 1.5).[80]

Crucially, throughout the play, the studio emerges as a place where artists (mostly male) taught their (mostly male) pupils, entertained friends or clients or engaged in in-depth discussions about their work, as Degas explains to her talented, self-taught pupil, Suzanne Valadon (who had herself grown up on the streets of Montmartre, first as an acrobat in a circus and then as a model in the studios of artists such as Pierre-Auguste Renoir and Pierre Puvis de Chavannes). It is in his studio that Degas, a man from a wealthy

---

[77] Wertenbaker, draft/copy of letter to Lindsay Posner, 14 January 1991, TWA, BLMC, Add 79217.

[78] As she said to Michael Billington, 'I also resigned from the Royal Court board because I was deeply unhappy. It was partly because of the increasing encroachment of private sponsorship, which I passionately believe is dangerous for new writing – partly because of seemingly trivial things like the new leather seats. Every time I took up a cause, it was lost; and I began to feel like Don Quixote, still talking about the age of chivalry. I don't want to open up a lot of old wounds, but as the only playwright on the board, after Winsome Pinnock left, I began to feel anachronistic'. Michael Billington, 'Men Judge the Plays, Put on the Plays and Run the Theatres', *The Guardian*, 25 November 1999, 10.

[79] Rachel Segal Hamilton, 'This Week's Art Funding News', *The Guardian*, 13 May 2011. https://www.theguardian.com/culture/culture-cuts-blog/2011/may/13/arts-funding-news+(8 (accessed 8 May 2023).

[80] Mary Bergstein, 'The Artist in His Studio: Photography, Art and the Masculine Mystique', *Oxford Art Journal 18*, 2 (1995): 45–58, in Mary Jane Jacob and Michelle Grabner (eds), *The Studio Reader: On the Space of Artists* (Chicago: University of Chicago Press, 2010), 208.

Figure 1.5 *The Line* written by Timberlake Wertenbaker and directed by Matthew Lloyd. With Henry Goodman as Edgar Degas and Sarah Smart as Suzanne Valadon. Arcola Theatre, London, November 2009.

Source: Courtesy Marilyn Kingwill / ArenaPAL.

Parisian family who had received a first-class education at the prestigious École des Beaux-Arts, copied Old Masters in the Louvre and spent years studying in Italy, teaches his anarchic working-class pupil Suzanne how to become a real artist: he shows her how to make a soft ground etching; he lectures her on the importance of hard work, concentration, repetition, tradition; he debates with her about the superiority of art over life. He even tries to impose his idea of the artist's life as 'an austere life, full of pleasures not taken' (*Line* 19). Wertenbaker presents the studio as the gendered arena in which a new 'battle of the picture', not dissimilar to that in Dear's *The Art of Success*, is fought, and in which Suzanne, a woman full of youthful vitality and with a hectic love life, desperately claims her right to paint in her own personal way, heralding new values and challenging both tradition and gender hierarchy:

> **Suzanne**   And I'm going to make great big canvases full of colour, and maybe they won't be Degas but they'll be Valadons. They'll be new and shocking and me! And the twentieth century is coming, and we'll sweep tradition out the door like the dust it is. (*Line* 39)

Suzanne refuses to bow down in order to 'integrate' herself 'in the line of history', and thus, according to her Maître Degas, risks 'being forgotten' because 'no one will know how to judge her work' (*Line* 59). On the contrary, as art critic Patricia Mathews argues, the artist's marginalized position allowed her not only the freedom to use a genre otherwise dominated by male artists but also to mediate that genre through many other discourses, including her gender, her position as an artist's model and her class. Her nudes pose numerous problems and raise questions about constructed femininity and 'the potential role of diverse female gazes in slipping through the construction'.[81] Mathews prises Valadon's disruption of the conventions of the nude and, against Degas' argument in the play, invites us to regard precisely 'the resistances to conventional interpretations present in her art, those contradictions for which no deciphering tools exist' as 'the most fruitful and obvious places to begin an investigation of the nature and relevance of the alternative models of representation developed by women artists of the past'.[82]

Significantly, Wertenbaker shows how Suzanne refuses to submit to the authoritarianism of her Maître, who, although he is the one who most encourages her as an artist, buys some of her work and gives her the ultimate accolade, demands obedience from her: 'You have a master to teach you. I am that master. […] I decide what is good for you' (*Line* 38). It is not surprising that she decides to escape from his studio, 'a room of privilege, a domain of male authorship that is determinedly undomestic',[83] to move to 12 Rue Cortot in Montmartre, where, in 1914, at the end of the play, an old Degas comes to meet her, now become 'the best woman painter of the century' (*Line* 61).

The drama of Young British Artists

The use of the art gallery and museum as a subject for theatre accelerated in the 1990s in response both to the huge success of the YBA, which, whatever its inherent qualities, transformed the British art world, and to the changing social role of the art gallery and museum, which created a broad public interest in the world of contemporary arts. Young British Artists attracted and engaged the new playwrights who were paving the way for a revolutionary and unique theatrical sensibility, especially, but not exclusively, the group that made up the Royal Court's seasons of the mid-1990s. Many

---

[81] Patricia Mathews, 'Returning the Gaze: Diverse Representations of the Nude in the Art of Suzanne Valadon', *The Art Bulletin*, 73, 3 (September 1991): 430.
[82] Ibid.
[83] Grabner, 'Introduction', in Jacob and Grabner (eds), *Studio Reader*, 2.

playwrights reacted to these young artists' provocative conceptual challenges by staging plays that borrowed their modes of expression and/or taboo themes, or, conversely, denounced the meaninglessness of a market-driven and celebrity-driven art.

In March 2007, Tony Blair decided to give his farewell speech to the most influential people in Britain's cultural establishment in the highly symbolic Turbine Hall of Tate Modern, which he had officially opened seven years earlier at the height of his political career. While many political commentators saw his speech as a last-ditch attempt to conceal his real legacy of failure, it was instead intended to celebrate his decade in office as 'a golden age for the arts'.[84] Interestingly, the examples that he cited as successful results of his recipe for a mixed economy combining public funding with private enterprise, subsidy and box office, were mainly drawn from the art world and the theatre, thereby acknowledging the primacy and perhaps even the connection between the two.

There is no doubt that the British cultural scene of the 1990s touted itself as 'Cool Britannia', a country with a thriving culture industry with London as the capital of cool. Indeed, Stryker McGuire's famous cover story 'London rules', published in *Newsweek* (4 November 1996), was a celebration of the hipness of London and of Prime Minister Tony Blair's attempt to appropriate the pop-cultural badge of 'Cool Britannia' for specifically personal and political purposes. In the decade 1997–2007, cultural policy became part of economic policy, although many commentators have denounced New Labour's jubilant rhetoric as an act of cultural capitalism on a grand scale. John Tulsa, director of the Barbican Arts Centre and former head of the BBC World Service, defined Blair as 'the true son of Margaret Thatcher',[85] combining neoliberalism with neoconservative moralism. Equally critically, Robert Hewison denounced the process of urban de-industrialization and the invention of the Heritage Industry, which culminated in the transformation of an abandoned power station into one of the world's most visited tourist attractions and of the once oppositional art of the avant-garde into the capital driving the international art market. But despite his scepticism about New Labour neoliberal agenda, even Hewison had to admit that government spending on the arts had almost doubled, and that after years of neglect, regional museums had received significant help; the nation's cultural infrastructure had been renovated and expanded; the National Lottery had been transformed into 'an engine of urban regeneration', which had made regional theatres, the Royal Shakespeare Company and the National

---

[84] Tony Blair, 'Blair's Speech on the Arts in Full', *The Guardian*, 6 March 2007. https://www.theguardian.com/politics/2007/mar/06/politicsandthearts.uk1 (accessed 20 August 2023).

[85] John Tulsa, *Art Matters: Reflecting on Culture* (London: Methuen, 1999), 77–8.

Theatre 'adventurous and their theatres full'; and, finally, that the abolition of admission charges to all national museums and galleries had helped to double annual attendance.[86] In 1996, he wrote enthusiastically of what he described as a 'rebirth of a nation', a cultural renaissance, based on a new generation of young talent whose creative upsurge was regenerating both the world of contemporary art and the world of theatre.[87]

Undeniably, whether cool or cruel, as the new theatre dubbed it, the 1990s London was both the cradle of the resurgence of theatre with a new wave of angry young playwrights at the forefront and the navel of contemporary art in the wake of the 1988 'Freeze' exhibition. The new and extreme theatre of the 1990s found favour with younger audiences, who responded enthusiastically to a new way of experiencing theatre. They gave Philip Ridley's *The Pitchfork Disney* standing ovations and considered Martin Crimp, Sarah Kane and Mark Ravenhill the coolest playwrights. Similarly, YBA played a significant role in bringing contemporary art to the attention of young, often ordinary people, both as a source of inspiration and as a target of criticism. Consecrated by Charles Saatchi's exhibition *Sensation* at a major British public gallery, the Royal Academy, in 1997, YBA heralded a radical change in the interaction between the art gallery and the stage.

Sensation was undoubtedly a landmark show. It brought together an extraordinary number of works and visitors. It marked an intensification of the alliances between public spaces, collectors and commercial interests. It demonstrated the power of mass communication and marketing in turning contemporary art exhibitions into a major box-office event. A total of 350,000 visitors during the three-month exhibition, many of whom had never been to a gallery before, were attracted by controversial works like Tracey Emin's tent appliquéd with the names of everyone she had slept with, Marcus Harvey's portrait of the infamous Moors murderer Myra Hindley painted with the aid of a group of children's fingerprints or Christ Ofili's Holy Virgin Mary decorated with resin-covered elephant dung and surrounded by collage cut-outs of female genitalia from pornographic magazines acting as putti. Lured by the press controversy that Saatchi's PR machine deliberately sought to generate by whipping up the anticipation with tantalizing hints of scandalous works and promises of outrage to come, visitors were also likely to have been excited by art that seemed and felt new. Young British Artists made their work accessible to those without an art background, often using materials drawn from mass culture to present conceptual works that seemed visually

---

[86] Robert Hewison, *Cultural Capital. The Rise and Fall of Creative Britain* (London: Verso, 2014), 2.
[87] Robert Hewison, 'Rebirth of a Nation', *The Times*, 19 May 1993.

accessible and spectacular, or selling merchandizing items that quickly became cult objects, such as Sarah Lucas' socks decorated with fried eggs, Mona Hatoum's badges and Jake and Dinos Chapman's phone cards.

As a result, the huge public response to the provocative installations by artists like the Chapman brothers, Damien Hirst, Tracey Emin and Rachel Whiteread brought to the Royal Academy enthusiastic masses of spectators, willing to participate in the grand show of art, despite their often untrained eyes, and thus fulfilling the intention of Norman Rosenthal, the co-curator of the exhibition, together with Charles Saatchi, the owner of the collection displayed:

> It [*Sensation*] should act as a platform that will open a large public's eyes to a scene in which all are welcome to participate if they wish, as artists first and foremost, but also as collectors, promoters and, equally importantly, as enthusiastic supporters and observers. Contemporary art is a club well worth joining.[88]

Although it included artists with very different aims and methods, the 'gang' of YBAs, according to Rosenthal, had a public resonance that was 'unparalleled' in the United Kingdom since the arrival of the Pop generation. Indeed, looking back, playwright Philip Ridley acknowledged how contemporary art entered the lives of ordinary people literally 'overnight':

> I remember when I was studying painting at St Martins School of Art, the conception there was that nobody in England knows any artists. It's like nobody. They might know Constable, and Turner. But the concept that you could be alive and a painter, and people would be generally interested and go and see it. In the space of two years over the 1990s that changed. My mum knows who Tracey Emin is, and Damian Hirst is, and the Chapman Brothers. You go to Tate Modern its packed, absolutely packed. I went to see the David Hockney show at the Royal Academy and you're in there like this *sucks in cheeks*, you cannot move. For a seventy-five year old man's paintings of the English countryside. It's more popular than a football match. It's incredible, almost overnight in kind of artistic terms. So something can change, and I don't know it is that will change. But I've got a feeling that something is out there, rumbling, of a new audience working to find for themselves the kind of

---

[88] Norman Rosenthal, 'The Blood Must Continue to Flow', in Brooks Adams, Lisa Jardine, Martin Maloney, Norman Rosenthal and Richard Shone (eds), *Sensation. Young British Artists from the Saatchi Collection* (London: Thames & Hudson in association with the Royal Academy of Arts, 1997), 11.

plays that they want to go and see. And not just receiving it, taken for granted.[89]

Highly theatrical in its display and apparently easy to understand, *Sensation* became itself a play for the theatre of London, which triggered a new chapter in the dramatization of the art gallery as a stage. No wonder playwrights should wish to capture the possibilities of this encounter in radical explorations where the stage is mediated, or rather short-circuited, by art. It is an encounter that points to the deep heart of British identity, with an increasing number of playwrights starting to place art galleries at the centre of their plays and to experiment with new ways to engage audiences who, like the visitors at the *Sensation* exhibition, seemed ready not to take what they saw for granted.

The proliferation of new plays dealing with issues relating to the nature of art and exhibiting spaces confirms a concern in the art world and a concomitant interest and sometimes fascination for the rapid rise of entrepreneurial young British artists. The YBA's popularity and the related process of 'brandization' somewhat foreshadowed in Wertenbaker's *Three Birds Alighting on a Field* affected British theatre in ways that have yet to be fully explored.

First of all, it is important to note that Philip Ridley, one of the youth idols of the time, describes himself as a *Sensation* artist working in a linguistic medium, complaining that theatre critics failed to realize how much his plays owe to YBA in terms of imagery and shock and scandal. A playwright whose plays combine the visual and the verbal, Ridley explains: 'A lot of the stuff they [*Sensation* artists] are dealing with I am dealing with. Birds, insects, crocodiles, dinosaurs, dolphins – there's a menagerie that keeps coming back in my work.'[90] Significantly, on the occasion of the 2012 revival at the Arcola Theatre, he even attempted to write (or rewrite) the history of the theatre in the 1990s, presenting *The Pitchfork Disney* as the play that introduced a 'new in-yer-face' sensibility to theatre, ahead of the new wave of Royal Court plays:

> I think I brought in a complete outsider voice because I hadn't trained in theatre and hadn't studied theatre or gone to drama school. I was a visual artist, so what I was bringing to it was an art school, performance-art

---

[89] Philip Ridley, 'Philip Ridley Q&A', *Exeunt Magazine*, 23 April 2012. https://exeuntmagazine.com/features/exeunt-philip-ridley-qa/3/ (accessed 8 May 2023).

[90] Philip Ridley quoted in Hermione Eyre, 'Philip Ridley: The Savage Prophet', *Independent*, 18 September 2011. https://www.independent.co.uk/arts-entertainment/films/features/philip-ridley-the-savage-prophet-395320.html (accessed 8 May 2023).

sensibility, which is what a lot of 'in-yer-face' theatre started to feed from. I guess in hindsight it all kind of fits in and makes a narrative, but it didn't feel like it at the time. I had done my first three plays – *The Pitchfork Disney*, *The Fastest Clock in the Universe*, and *Ghost from a Perfect Place* – by 1994, and that's the year that most people say the 'in-yer-face' thing started. All those seeds were laid before that, but it didn't feel that I was doing that, and no one said I was doing that until many years after the event. Because many theatre commentaries tend to be National Theatre and Royal Court-centric, it often seems that the story started there.[91]

Although not giving him the attention Ridley himself felt he would have deserved, Alek Sierz, in his volume *In-Yer-Face Theatre*, had nevertheless quoted the playwright's words as follows:

I was part of the London art scene at a very exciting time. I knew most of the people that went on to be in the controversial *Sensation* show at the Royal Academy in 1997. […] All my plays have the *Sensation* sensibility; their images and set pieces are garish and brash. For me the visual side of drama has always been vital. I've always seen images as engines of emotion. I've always sought that one icon-like image that will convey a wordless meaning, an image-aria, if you like.[92]

It is equally significant that Ridley's fierce attack on the hypocritical moralism of theatre critics led him to draw a parallel between theatre and the visual arts, and to refer to Tracey Emin and her iconic work *My Bed* (1998).[93] Controversially exhibited at the 1998 Turner Prize, this piece consisted of a wooden bed, with wrinkled sheets, pillows, twisted blankets, tangled nylon stockings, crumpled towels and clutter of personal effects (empty vodka bottles, slippers and underwear, crushed cigarette packs, a snuffed-out candle, condoms and contraceptives, a cuddly toy and several Polaroid self-portraits), which the artist presented as her bed exactly as it had looked like during a difficult period in her life:

---

[91] Ridley interviewed by Theo Bosanquet, 'Philip Ridley On … Revisiting *The Pitchfork Disney*', *WhatsOnStage*, 30 January 2012. https://www.whatsonstage.com/west-end-theatre/news/philip-ridley-on-revisiting-the-pitchfork-disney_5566.html (accessed 8 May 2023).

[92] Aleks Sierz, *In-Yer-Face Theatre. British Drama Today* (London: Faber and Faber, 2001), 42, 43.

[93] Tracey Emin, *My Bed*, 1998, mattress, linen, pillows, rope, various memorabilia (dirty knickers, used condoms, empty vodka bottles, cigarette butts, slippers, etc.), 79×211×234cm.

> The last vestige of Victorian criticism exists in critics who see it as their moral duty to tell the audience what they think is morally correct. They will do a review and, in effect, say, 'In terms of subject matter, we feel that you shouldn't see this play.' But it's not their job to say that. As if you would get a visual art critic saying about the work of Tracey Emin: 'There's used knickers and spunky condoms on the bed. Morally we feel that you shouldn't see this work.' No, they judge it as an aesthetic piece of work.[94]

It can easily be argued that while Ridley rightly acknowledges the sensation caused when his and some other playwrights' provocative plays were first staged, causing astonishment and disgust, he fails to recognize the wave of outrage produced by many of the artworks exhibited at the Royal Academy. Indeed, both in-yer-face plays and YBA's works of art seemed to be at the centre of contentious arguments. Somewhat representative of the ambivalent feelings towards the new art is Sarah Kane's attitude. On the one hand, she expresses her admiration for Mona Hatoum's work, which manages to speak directly to the audience's experience in a way that rarely happens in theatre. She seems to appreciate the discomfiting and compelling sense of invasion and invitation evoked by Hatoum's video installation, *Corps étranger*, which used an endoscopic camera to film both the surface and the interior of her body to investigate the meaning of surveillance and trespass:

> I found myself longing for a theatre that could speak so directly to an audience's experience. It rarely happens. […] It also happened at the Mona Hatoum exhibition at the Scottish National Gallery of Modern Art. In a tiny cylindrical room I watched a projection of a surgical camera disappearing into every orifice of the artist. True, few people could stay in the room as long as me, but I found that the voyage up Mona Hatoum's arse put me in powerful and direct contact with my feelings about my own mortality. I can't ask for much more.[95]

No wonder some theatre critics have drawn links between Kane's work and the YBA,[96] and others have promoted her as a full member of the 'Britpack',

---

[94] Philip Ridley in conversation with Aleks Sierz, '"Putting a New Lens on the World": The Art of Theatrical Alchemy', *New Theatre Quarterly*, 25, 2 (May 2009): 113.

[95] Sarah Kane, 'Sarah Kane: Why Can't Theatre Be as Gripping as Footie?', *The Guardian*, [From *The Guardian* Archive, 1998] 12 January 2015. https://www.theguardian.com/stage/2015/jan/12/sarah-kane-theatre-football-blasted (accessed 8 May 2023).

[96] Dan Rebellato noted how the aggressive, confrontational and provocative 'in-yer-face-theatre' of the 1990s resonates with YBA's work, where bodies were 'distended, preserved,

preoccupied with sex and death like Hirst and Emin, and convinced, like them, of the need to deliver extreme shocks to the audience.[97]

On the other hand, Kane herself, despite being portrayed as a controversial in-yer-face playwright whose tales of rape, anthropophagy and sodomy have provoked outrage and protest, was critical of some YBA works, and in particular of Marcus Harvey's *Myra*, which was part of the *Sensation* exhibition, advancing the suspicion that the face of Moors murderer Myra Hindley, drawn with children's fingerprints, was simply an unfair and gratuitous stunt to gain a bit of scandal and publicity:

> I didn't see it [Marcus Harvey's *Myra*], I had a very mixed feeling about it. Because on the one hand I suppose I would defend anyone's right to create a piece of art out of anything they want, and yet somehow with the Myra Hindley picture – without having seen it – I suspect that the artist's intentions were not entirely honest ... What I wouldn't want to do is upset someone by reference to someone like Myra Hindley or a specific situation ... Because then you are being cynical, you are using people's pain in order to justify your own work which I don't think is acceptable. As I've said I haven't seen it so I don't know whether the Myra Hindley picture has any resonance outside of the specifics of those children that were killed. And if it doesn't then it isn't justifiable because then you are tapping in on a group of people who have lost their kids.[98]

The 1990s was a heated decade indeed, with aesthetic experimentation and ethical issues jumping from art galleries to theatres and back again. It is particularly significant that in Martin Crimp's *Attempts on Her Life*,

---

miniaturised, parodied, punctured and transplanted'. According to the theatre critic, 'There were continuities between "Sensation" imagery and that unfolding on [our] stages' and gives one example, citing Sarah Kane's *Cleansed* as a play that 'seemed to pick up – perhaps unconsciously – on the show's images of bodily distortion and dismemberment'. (Dan Rebellato, ' "Because It Feels Fucking Amazing": Recent British Drama and Bodily Mutilation', in Rebecca D'Monté and Graham Saunders (eds), *Cool Britannia? British Political Drama in the 1990s* (Basingstoke: Palgrave Macmillan, 2008), 194). Christopher Innes also wrote that there are clear connections between *Blasted* or *Cleansed* and the radical modern British artists like Damien Hirst assembled by Saatchi for the notorious 'Sensation' exhibition (Christopher Innes, *Modern British Drama. The Twentieth Century* (Cambridge: Cambridge University Press, 2002), 530).

[97] Mary Luckhurst, 'Infamy and Dying Young: Sarah Kane, 1971–1999', in Mary Luckhurst and Jane Moody (eds), *Theatre and Celebrity in Britain, 1660-2000* (Basingstoke: Palgrave Macmillan, 2005), 114.

[98] Sarah Kane, 'Interview with Nils Tabert, "Gespräch mit Sarah Kane"', in Nils Tabert (ed.), *Playspotting: Die Londoner Theaterszene der 90er* (Rowohlt: Reinbeck, 1998), 8–21, quoted in Graham Saunders, *'Love Me or Kill Me': Sarah Kane and the Theatre of Extremes* (Manchester: Manchester University Press, 2002), 28.

first presented at the Royal Court Upstairs in 1997 and arguably the most influential play of the decade, the art installation of the suicidal artist Anne in Scenario 11, 'Untitled (100 words)', one of the seventeen scenarios that make up the play, emerges in the mind of the audience through different kinds of images creating an ongoing conversation between the stage and the art gallery. As is discussed in Chapter 3, in Crimp's scenario, the response to the art installation and the artist who had conceived it was inspired by the response to Kane's *Blasted* (1995), a play that overnight became the Royal Court's biggest controversy since Edward Bond's *Saved* in 1965. Kane became the target of personal attacks, and 'the level of critical brouhaha' was so extreme that director James MacDonald felt he owed some explanation about the process by which the play came to be produced.[99] The infamous words in Jack Tinker's review – 'some will undoubtedly say the money might have been better spent on a course of remedial therapy'[100] – are echoed in the reaction to Anne's installation by one of the speakers/art critics: 'Because what we see here is the work of a girl who quite clearly should've been admitted not to an art school but to a psychiatric unit' (*Attempts* 47). But the art installation in *Attempts on Her Life* was also the inspiration for *4:48 Psychosis* (2000), the play Kane completed one week before hanging herself in a hospital where she was being treated for depression, from which she had suffered recurrently. 'Where are the boundaries? What is acceptable …?' '… Where does the 'life' – literally in this case – end, and the 'work' begin?' (*Attempts* 46). There is no doubt that the questions raised by Anne's installation intercept a similar set of debates in both the contemporary art world and theatre, primarily regarding the relationship between representation, lived experience and the construction of the self. In this two-way conversation between theatre and art galleries, 'Mad Tracey from Margate'[101] also comes to mind. Like Anne's installation and Sarah Kane's plays, Tracey's work, which repeatedly traces her own presence and unfilteredly reveals her psychological suffering, has often been criticized and dismissed as overly emotional, as if it had been put together in a fit with no regard for artistic value. This link between Anne and Emin is further consolidated by Katie Mitchell in her production of the play in 2007, as described in Chapter 3.

Over the decades that have followed, the theatrical responses to the YBA wave have made the stage a significant forum for exploring the role of art,

---

[99] James MacDonald, 'Review of *Blasted*', *Observer*, 22 January 1995, reprinted in *Theatre Record 1–28 January 1995*, 43.

[100] Jack Tinker, 'The Disgusting Feast of Filth', *Daily Mail*, 19 January 1995, reprinted in *Theatre Record 1–28 January 1995*, 42.

[101] As she titled herself in her textile work *Mad Tracey from Margate. Everyone's Been There*, 1997. Appliqué blanket fabric from clothing provided by friends. 215 × 267cm.

the rapid rise of some of the group's artists and the meaning and nature of art venues.

It is perhaps no coincidence that the YBA artists most famous among ordinary people for their spectacular and attention-grabbing fusion of art and personality, Damien Hirst and Tracey Emin, are also those most referenced or alluded to by playwrights.

Surprisingly, given his political and social commitment and the glamorous media aura of Hirst and Emin, Lee Hall refers to them in the introduction to *The Pitmen Painters* (2008). Without making any aesthetic judgement of their works, he shows interest in Damien Hirst as a foul-mouthed, working-class boy from Leeds, and in Tracey Emin as a half-Cypriot and working-class woman, who succeeded as artists despite their disadvantaged backgrounds. Like the pitmen painters in the play, Emin and Hirst are thus presented as exceptions within an unequal cultural system where the uneven distribution of cultural assets and access to education keep art out of deprived communities:

> Despite an occasional Damien Hirst or Tracey Emin, the art world remains disproportionately cluttered with the sons and daughters of the middle classes.
>
> When I was growing up in the sixties and seventies, the first generation to benefit from the boldness of the Labour Government of 1945, especially in education, had come of age understanding that the arts were fundamental to a life fully lived. The roots of Live Theatre lie in this moment, when there was a huge urgency, an almost missional zeal to take art to 'deprived' communities. I was hooked by their efforts and drawn into a richly rewarding life. But like so many in my profession, I find those advances are now being reversed. The globalisation of capital, the monopolisation of the media, and the deregulation of TV have produced a situation where we get less culture but pay more for it. It's both a joke and a tragedy as the working classes who are denuded of political power and spiritual succour are also excluded from the system of culture so ravenously enjoyed by their exploiters.[102]

As proof that Tracey Emin and her work continue to hold a wider cultural resonance, Philip Ridley refers to her, albeit incidentally and quickly, in his recent play *The Poltergeist*, first performed at Southwark Playhouse in 2020, where the protagonist regards her iconic *Bed* as a pillar in art history: 'There's

---

[102] Hall, *Pitmen Painters*, vii.

the library! It used to have this huge book in the reference section. *The Complete History of Art*. I could barely lift it. There were photos on every page. From cave paintings to Tracey Emin's bed' (*Poltergeist* 19).

Other playwrights are less kind to Emin and Hirst and the art they represent. Some of them are even suspicious and critical of their celebrity status, which would be a cover for the lack of meaning in their art. They became objects of ridicule and parody in plays such as Simon Smith's *You Be Ted and I'll Be Sylvia* (1999), Rebecca Lenkiewicz's *Shoreditch Madonna* (2005) and David Leddy's *Long Live the Little Knife* (2013). First performed at the Hampstead Theatre in 1999, directed by Jonathan Church, *You Be Ted and I'll Be Sylvia* was reviewed as 'an ironic comment on the Damien Hirst school of modern art' that 'also smacks of sensationalism'.[103] It pokes fun at the excesses of art through the protagonist, a feminist conceptualist who made her name with a series of works painted with a mixture of her father's cremated ashes and her own menstrual blood, challenging audiences with 'crazed intellectual wrangles and plans for conceptual works of art beyond Damien Hirst's wildest dreams'.[104] While *Shoreditch Madonna*, a play about sex and suicide, drug addiction and redemption in London's YBAs-beloved East End art scene, mocks 'the likes of the White Cube gallery, Damien Hirst, elephant-dung paintings',[105] David Leddy's *Long Live the Little Knife* (Traverse Theatre, Edinburgh, 2013), Liz and Jim's seventy-five-minute double monologue, mocks the contemporary art market while offering a sharp and tongue-in-cheek investigation into the veracity of contemporary art itself. The protagonist, Liz, one of the two shape-shifting, voice-changing, tackily glamorous con artists, poses as conceptual artist Tracey Moomin, whose life and art are obviously inspired by Tracey Emin. Liz/Moomin mocks Emin's controversial art and celebrated media persona in a 'harsh Margate-ish accent', confirming critics' claim that the artist herself has become a focus of curiosity as a celebrity:

> **Liz** (*impersonates Tracey Emin – harsh Margate-ish accent*) I'm working on a neon artwork above an unmade bed. It's called *Every Toilet Where I Ever Had a Dump*. I'm going to get drunk on television and do a turd on the Pollock painting to represent the Freudian oedipal moment when

[103] Carole Woddis, 'You Be Ted & I'll Be Sylvia', *Jewish Chronicle*, 17 September 1999, reprinted in *Theatre Record 10–23 September 1999*, 1194.
[104] John Gross, 'You be Ted & I'll be Sylvia', *Sunday Telegraph*, 19 September 1999, reprinted in *Theatre Record 10–23 September 1999*, 1194.
[105] Mark Cook, 'Shoreditch Madonna', *What's on*, 20 July 2005, reprinted in *Theatre Record 2–15 July 2005*, 949; Lloyd Evans, 'Shoreditch Madonna', *The Spectator*, 23 July 2005. Reprinted in *Theatre Record 2–15 July 2005*, 949.

one artistic movement is subsumed by the next. My name is Tracey Moomin.[106]

Firstly, the title of Tracey Moomin's work, *Every Toilet Where I Ever Had a Dump*, is a blatant parody conflating allusions to several of Emin's works: the famous *Everyone I Have Ever Slept With 1963–1995* (1995), a tent appliquéd with the names of everyone the artist has ever shared a bed with, displayed in the *Sensation* exhibition; her neon artworks, spelling out her intimate confessions; and the iconic installation *My Bed*, exhibited at the 1998 Turner Prize. Like the bad-girl artist who inspires her, Liz/Moomin goes so far as to mention one episode in Emin's overexposed life, when, drunk after attending the 1997 Turner Prize awards dinner, she participated in a live television art debate, causing much outcry. It is perhaps important to remember that the Tate's annual Turner Prize for New Art, launched in 1984 with the intention of creating a climate of understanding of modern and contemporary art and relaunched by Serota, who restricted eligibility to artists under fifty and based in the UK, by the mid-1990s had become a major annual event. This was, in large part, thanks to the appeal of the young British artists shortlisted and Channel 4's broadcasting of gala dinners and award ceremonies hosted by the likes of Madonna, giving the general public a chance to see contemporary art and to get to know the artists.

In Tim Crouch's site-generic play *ENGLAND*, which was first presented at the Edinburgh Fruitmarket Gallery in 2007, co-directed by Karl James and a smith, and has been consistently performed since by Tim Crouch and Hannah Ringham, the reference to contemporary art, including YBA, is so ingrained that it could be argued that it is not just an occasional allusion but a major source of inspiration. Most of the works referred to are by painters of the YBA generation who contributed to *Sensation*, such as Marc Quinn, Gary Hume and Tacita Dean (*E* 17–8).[107] While the connection with Saatchi feeds into Crouch's questioning of the problematic status of art within a free-market economy, this explicit name-dropping seems an invitation to compare and connect the work of YBAs with the story of illness and death that is told in the play, and to rethink the play in the light of these artists' engagement with the apparently extreme fragility of the body, or what Norman Rosenthal has called 'metaphors of sensations'.[108] Indeed, signs of decay and death permeate the lives and words of the two characters far beyond the symptoms of the protagonist's heart disease, and creep into the two guides' story of illness,

---

[106] David Leddy, 'Deleted Scenes', in *Long Live the Little Knife* (Fire Exit: Glasgow, 2013), 104.
[107] Tim Crouch, *ENGLAND. A Play for Galleries* (London: Oberon, 2007).
[108] Adams, Jardine, Maloney, Rosenthal and Stone, *Sensation*, 11.

mainly through allusions to the YBA in ways that will be explored in the following pages.

YBA and contemporary art in general have also deeply influenced Crouch's *My Arm*, first presented at the Traverse Theatre, Edinburgh, on 31 July 2003. On one level, while exploring the contemporary art world, Crouch's plays seem to address the excesses and pointlessness of some works of art and reveal the dark side of the marriage between art and the market. On another level, the confrontation with the visual arts – including the YBA – and the awareness of the qualitative differences between watching theatre and viewing visual art, have led him to find new ways of giving his audiences a greater sense of their own authority over what they see. As he writes in the introduction to *My Arm*:

> *My Arm* attempts to provoke questions about the qualitative distinctions between viewing theatre and viewing visual art. The visual arts have stolen a march on theatre in their ability to handle progressive forms; the state of modern British art is one of the main engines of the story. While I was developing the play, I ran a series of classes looking at the division between the social nature of watching a play and the private, stand-alone nature of looking at a painting. The narrative drive behind *My Arm* is from a clear theatrical tradition; the accompanying visual focus, however, requires a different frame of approach. As an actor, I've often worked far too hard to 'host' an audience's journey through a play; something visual art rarely does. Visual art expects its viewers to work hard. *My Arm* attempts to let the audience be by itself for periods of time, and for me as the actor to feel all right about that.[109]

My Arm is a monologue-based performance that tells the story of a boy whose casual 'artless gesture' of holding his arm raised above his head 'is mythologised ('morphologised') into a cultural icon',[110] although instead of becoming a living work of art, he is slowly and tragically transformed into a decaying work of art, rotting and 'composting from the fingers down' (*My Arm* 36). The story is told by the adult self of the protagonist (the armed boy), played by Crouch, whose retrospective view of his pointless gesture

---

[109] Tim Crouch, 'Introduction', in *My Arm* (London: Faber and Faber, 2003), 9–10. *My Arm* had its first reading with the Franklin Stage Company, New York, in September 2002. Tim Crouch performed preview showings of *My Arm* at the Hayward Gallery (February 2003), Battersea Arts Centre (2003) and the ICA (2009) in London. It has been performed worldwide in numerous venues, from the Andy Warhol Museum in Pittsburgh (2006) to the Metropolitan Arts Space in Tokyo (2010).
[110] Ibid., 10.

suggests criticism of both modern commercial art and consumerist celebrity culture, which perhaps also includes YBA's excesses, morbidity and penchant for provocation.

Indeed, the body-oriented art of many YBAs, not least Damien Hirst, seems to be a source of inspiration for the armed boy's friend, Simon, who confronts the audience with the disturbing way in which bodies become mere objects or raw materials when he attempts to transform the carcass of a horse from the slaughterhouse into art:

> When I arrived, Simon had got hold of the carcass of a horse from an abattoir, and he and Carla were busy stripping the remains of the sinews and bleaching the bones. They had no idea what they were doing with it, but it had only cost ten quid. The project was ditched, but the house smelt of rotting horse for – well, for as long as we were there, which was nearly five years. (*My Arm* 27)

Such territories were notoriously the preserve of visual artists such as Hirst, who brought dead animals, whole or dismembered, into the gallery in his uncompromising exploration of the fragility of existence. The artistic failure of Simon and his girlfriend Carla, both lacking in skill and purpose, results in a scathing satire on the futility of much contemporary art. Crouch mocks, but at the same time acknowledges what Hirst could do with carcasses in his controversial and ostensibly artistic exploration of the 'the nature of our cultural and physiological disgust reaction'.[111] One thinks of Hirst's uncomfortable works, which are based on a fascination with the physical presence of death: the cow's head and countless swarming flies of *A Thousand Years*; the formaldehyde-suspended lamb of *Away from the Flock*, one of the most famous works in Britain after it was vandalized during the group exhibition 'Some Went Mad, Some Ran Away' at the Serpentine Gallery in 1994; or *The Physical Impossibility of Death in the Mind of Someone Living* (1991), the most iconic image of late-twentieth-century art, whose conceptual title is perhaps evoked in the title, 'Death in Life', which, in the play, Simon not coincidentally gives to one of the huge lithographic reproductions of the texture of the Boy's arm and hand in the 'Man-i(n)festation' exhibition:

> When Simon came back from Berlin, he asked me if I would work with him on an exhibition that he was planning. It was called Man-i(n)festation, with a hyphen after the 'Man' and brackets around the 'n' of

[111] Brian Dillon, 'Ugly Feelings', in Ann Gallagher, *Damien Hirst* (London: Tate Publishing, 2012), 25.

'in'. [...] And it was all about me. I was even in it. I went along with it all out of – out of nothingness really. Simon's idea was – would you like to explain it yourself? Simon's idea was, I think, that I was a bit of an oddity. He took photographs of me, naked. Naked sitting on my bed. Naked in the bath. Naked by the stump of a tree [...] He photographed me clothed and out and about, signing on, outside a newsagent. By each photograph which was displayed in the exhibition were descriptions of social and military injustices made to look like my medical records. One room contained huge lithographic reproductions of the texture of my arm and hand, with titles such as 'Death in Life'. Another had a smaller collection of double-exposure Polaroids with healthy arms superimposed on images of me sleeping, as though I was dreaming about the arms. The centrepiece of Man-i(n)festation was me, sitting in a cradle for three two-hour shifts each day, watching television through earphones. Bulgarian chants were piped through the gallery. I should have enjoyed the attention but didn't feel able. The exhibition was a great success. (*My Arm* 30)

It is not only Hirst's art or certain experiences of other performing artists that are brought to mind by the exhibition curated by Simon, 'Man-i(n)festation'. Many other YBAs' works from *Sensation* exhibition seem to be parading in it: from the life-size flesh-coloured wax cast of Sarah Lucas' finger, *Receptacle of Lurid Things* (1991) to Mat Collishaw's *Bullet Hole* (1988–93), an eight-by-twelve-foot backlit transparency in fifteen frames of a bloody head wound, whose image was taken from a pathology textbook; from Tracey Emin's Polaroids to Ron Mueck's hyper-realistic sculptures of humans, such as *Dead Dad* (1996), cast in silicone and acrylic.

As if all that were not enough, Simon capitalizes on the exhibition of his dead friend's rotting arm, which looks less like a sculpture than a high-tech gothic horror, perhaps contained in a Perspex box and mounted on a refrigeration unit, like Marc Quinn's frozen head called *Self* (1991), one of the most visceral self-portraits in sculpture:

> At the most, I had a couple of years. I had rotten. [...] In addition to a one-off fee of 250,000, the dealer offered to pay all my medical and living expenses until I died. [...] In return I would sell him my arm. Of course, he wouldn't take it whilst I was alive, but he would have unrestricted access to my terminal decay – documentary-makers, photographers, visual artists. Then, after my death, he would have global rights to display my arm in an aesthetic context to be determined between him, Simon and me. Any display would be accompanied by an exhibition of

my life, including family photographs, cine film, school, and medical reports. (*My Arm* 36)

Whether it is Quinn's frozen bust, Hirst's carcasses or Crouch's rotting arm, the use of images of dead bodies or parts of bodies raises questions not so much about the choice of using mortal remains but about the kind of emotional and aesthetic responses these works evoke. Thus, while Hirst's real-life corpses or Quinn's bust are displayed in the traditional manner of fine art, to restore the gallery to its almost forgotten function as a place of wonder or, in the case of Hirst' work, to emphasize the viewer's readings of otherwise meaningless works, as sceptics such as Julian Stallabrass argue,[112] Crouch's arm is only in the mind of the audience.

The inspiration of visual arts, particularly conceptual art, leads Crouch to try something new in the early 2000s. As a theatre-maker he is interested in enhancing the visual focus of his performances. Therefore, he conceives a play where the narrative drive is 'from a clear theatrical tradition' but 'the accompanying visual focus […] requires a different frame of approach'.[113] Indeed, in *My Arm*, the narrator never raises his arm above his head, because his focus is on the spectators' experience of imagination and 'transformation', not on sight. Similarly, Crouch/narrator presents to the camera objects and pictures that he has borrowed from the audience at the beginning of the play to refer to other characters and objects within the story. As Crouch explains in the introduction to the play, these objects are 'randomly selected to become icons in the story', so that ordinary things such as the 'lucky charms, key rings, badges, toys' take on 'extraordinary significance'[114] and become characters.

With the sole exception of one doll, 'which represents the performer' and whose arm the narrator raises up above its head (*My Arm* 19) (Figure 1.6), all these objects and images are 'in no way representational' so that an earring could be the father, a lipstick could be a car and a voice recorder the mother. As Crouch himself explains in an interview with Seda Ilter,

[112] Julian Stallabrass writes:

> Beyond this amazement, though, Hirst's works often seem empty. He plays on this, of course, telling interviewers that he wants to call some piece, "I sometimes feel I have nothing to say, I often want to communicate this." This emptiness is a product of the simple collage of ready-made elements, brought together not to build meaning but to throw opposed ingredients into unresolved opposition.

High Art Lite. The Rise and Fall of Young British Art. London: Verso (1999), revised and expanded edition, 2006, 27.
[113] Crouch, *Introduction*, 10.
[114] Ibid., 11.

How the Art Gallery Came to the Stage 73

Figure 1.6 *My Arm* written by and with Tim Crouch. Co-directed by Tim Crouch, Karl James, Hettie Macdonald. Traverse Theatre, Edinburgh Festival, August 2003.
Source: Courtesy Geraint Lewis / ArenaPAL.

The central philosophical tenet of the play is that the person should not put his/her arm above their head. That is fundamental to my conception of the play. In terms of the objects, it is important that they are not cast in a traditional way. I try not to look at them before selecting them. I don't try to find a feminine object to 'be' my mother or a traditionally masculine object to 'be' my father because that's not the point. I want to play against it. [...] this object here [*showing the voice recorder*] is my mother; this object cannot perform my mother. In performance, I think there is a dynamic to transform that comes from the audience. So I can say that I am Hamlet, and I look like Tim Crouch. And so I can say that this is my mother, but it looks like a voice recorder. I am just playing with that space between what we say something is and what it actually is, which happens in theatre all the time. It is not a problem for me as an audience member, I can contain both those ideas in one thing, and I am excited about the audience containing those ideas at the same time, the idea of mother and the idea of recorder. And this gives an audience a more active role in transformation. Transformation happens in theatre all the time.[115]

The performance unfolds on several levels, not only through Crouch's storytelling but also through his use of objects, thus involving the audience in the theatrical process by means of the lingering significance and resonance that the objects hold for each audience member, and that seem to resist any notion of a dramatic world isolated from the real. Intriguingly, the functions and meaning of fictional characters (father, mother, Simon) and objects for the protagonist are unchangeable, but they are simultaneously unique and fluid for each spectator, and their representation changes from night to night. Thus, the audience not only actively contributes to the script's dramaturgy but also experientially shares the armed boy's concerns about displacement, ownership, meaning and value.

Whatever its intentions, its intrinsic qualities or its future developments, it is undeniable that the YBA has transformed the British art world but, above all, it has brought about a change in the social role of art galleries, invested by an entirely new and wider public interest. With genuine curiosity or, more often, with a critical attitude and irony, British playwrights found a rich source of inspiration in both the YBA and its eccentric and media-savvy personalities.

---

[115] Tim Crouch interviewed by Seda Ilter, ' "A Process of Transformation": Tim Crouch on *My Arm*', *Contemporary Theatre Review*, 21, 4 (2011): 400, 401.

Theatricalizing the art gallery: The Tate

The opening in 2000 of Tate Modern, that great popularizing contemporary art engine, also undoubtedly played a role in bringing the art gallery to the forefront of cultural debate. In fact, the success of its exhibitions and its new ways of presenting art have sparked the interest not only of elite circles of intellectuals, curators, art gallery directors or trendsetters but also of the general public and of those who had hitherto been disinterested in or distanced from the art world. This is how Rose Aidin, a freelance journalist who covered art for the mainstream press in the late 1990s, comments retrospectively on its opening and its winning association with YBA:

> When Tate Modern […] opened in London in May 2000, its launch party for 4,000 people was the hottest ticket in town and broadcast live on the BBC. Invitations were said to be changing hands for up to £1,000 and some left town rather than admit they were not on the list. 'Everyone' was there, yet it was the Young British Artists who had done so much with their talent, energy, and glamour to bring the art world's focus to London for the first time in centuries (and to create a climate of acceptance for contemporary art), who provided the stardust. The YBAs ensured that Tate Modern's opening party was the place to be, and the museum was an instant success, with visitor numbers vastly higher than anticipated.
>
> As the artistic duo Gilbert & George said as they opened the building earlier that day in front of the Queen of England, 'Art is power.' The YBAs ruled the establishment: the artists were celebrities, and everyone wanted to know more about them. And that, for a while, was how I made my living. Then it all suddenly came to an end, with 9/11 as a marker. Shortly after the twin tower attacks, Charles Saatchi closed the private gallery that had done so much to incubate the YBA movement, and there was a sense of moving on. I went into teaching and now teach the work of many of the artists I interviewed. The young adults I teach are consistently fascinated by the YBAs' work, which speaks very strongly to them, and convinces me that even now – long after the parties and the scene have faded – the work itself will endure and stand the test of time.[116]

For all its glamour and media attention, Tate Modern has played a central role in accelerating the boom in playwriting about art galleries. Indeed,

---

[116] Rose Aidin, 'The YBAs: The London-Based Young British Artists', *Smarthistory*, 7 September 2018. https://smarthistory.org/YBA-3/ (accessed 8 May 2023).

beginning with Stoppard's *After Magritte* in 1970, there is no denying that British playwrights have chronicled both the changing nature and function of Tate Gallery and the rise of the Tate Modern as one of the most influential art galleries in the international art world. Indeed, it has forever changed the way people view art in the wake of that momentous shift which, from the mid-1980s, transformed many art galleries and museums from institutions primarily focused on collection and preservation of works of art and objects to their current emphasis on the visitor experience.

The Tate Gallery depicted by Stoppard in *After Magritte* is the art museum in Pimlico, on Millbank, which opened in 1897 as the National Gallery of British Art, even though from the start it was known by the name of its founder Sir Henry Tate. It is perhaps interesting to note that according to Stoppard's Inspector Foot, the Tate was a place where ordinary people did not usually go, as confirmed by his derisive reaction to the alibi story of the Harrises, who say they were at the Tate at the time of the alleged crime they are suspected of: 'I must say that in a lifetime of off-the-cuff alibis I have seldom been moved closer to open derision' (*Magritte* 35).

Thirty-seven years later, in 2007, the Tate that Crouch refers to in *ENGLAND* is the Tate Modern, the mecca of contemporary art that director Nicholas Serota so desperately wanted, which opened on 11 May 2000 in the former Bankside Power Station converted by Herzog & de Meuron and welcomed over 5 million visitors in its first year alone. Tate Modern is embedded in Crouch's *ENGLAND* on a number of levels.

First and foremost, *ENGLAND* is a play for galleries intended to be actualized as a gallery visit in which the two performers, one man (often Tim Crouch himself) and one woman (often Hannah Ringham), who take turns speaking while sharing the same narrative voice (leaving us uncertain as to whether this is female or male, straight or gay), are cast as guides who take the audience on a tour of the gallery, alternating between describing the art gallery they are in for that specific performance and a story of love, money, illness and heart transplant.

Significantly, as the focus shifts from the real art works on display in the gallery to the fictional places and fragments of a story about a severe heart condition that strains the love relationship between an Englishman/Englishwoman and a brilliant art dealer, the two art gallery guides/performers declare their affection for the Tate Modern. They explain how much they enjoy spending quiet moments contemplating art in its architecturally distinctive spaces. They even establish a kind of continuity between Tate Modern and the nearby Southwark Cathedral, somehow embracing the idea of the art gallery as a shrine or sanctuary:

> This is Southwark Cathedral. I like to come here when I've been to the doctors. Here or to the Tate Modern gallery, which is only about just a stone's throw from here. From Southwark Cathedral.
> […]
> I enjoy the peace. I enjoy the clean lines and the feel and look of the stone. Everyone talks so quietly.
> It's beautiful.
> It's like heaven.
> Look. (*E* 26–7)

Here, they are openly winking at art critic Brian O'Doherty's well-known description of the 'White Cube', the modern art gallery space built according to laws as rigorous as those for building a medieval church. It is no coincidence that, as a provocation, O'Doherty's words from his influential three-part essay *Inside the White Cube. The Ideology of the Gallery Space*, first published in *Artforum* (1976), are reported both in the epigraph of *ENGLAND*'s published script – 'One has to have died already to be there' – and in the programme at London's Whitechapel Gallery (8 May–16 June 2009):

> The ideal gallery subtracts from the artwork all clues that interfere with the fact that it is 'art' … A gallery is constructed along laws as rigorous as those for building a medieval church. The outside world must not come in, so windows are usually sealed off. Walls are painted white … In this context a standing ashtray becomes almost a sacred object … Modernism's transposition of perception from life to formal values is complete. This, of course, is one of modernism's fatal diseases. Art exists in a kind of eternity of display … This eternity gives the gallery a limbo like status; one has to have died already to be there. Indeed the presence of that odd piece of furniture, your own body, seems superfluous, an intrusion. The space offers the thought that while eyes and minds are welcome, space-occupying bodies are not – or are tolerated only as kinesthetic mannequins for further study.[117]

In the play, echoes of such sanitized art sanctuaries, suffused with a limbo-like status and normatively requiring the body to disappear, collide with the narrative fragments about the protagonist's heart illness that the audience

---

[117] Brian O'Doherty's essays, first published in *Artforum* between 1976 and 1981, were then gathered under the collective title *Inside the White Cube. The Ideology of the Gallery Space*

becomes gradually aware of. Crouch challenges the image of the art gallery as a 'shrine' inspiring values of beauty and morality and contaminates its sanctity and otherworldliness by 'transplanting' dirty, pulsating life (which is the mortal essence of theatre) into its centre. *ENGLAND* is therefore a piece of theatre transplanted into a gallery, as Crouch explains in the *foreward* to the programme at London's Whitechapel Gallery (8 May–16 June 2009):

> In *ENGLAND* I place the dynamics of visual art and theatre up against each other. The materialised world of visual art against the de-materialised word of theatre. I have not attempted to create a hybrid work. Instead, I have simply taken what I consider to be the mortal essence of theatre and transplanted it into a gallery.[118]

Crucially, Tate Modern is a constant reference in a text as unstable as *ENGLAND*, designed as a site-generic play to be represented in different art galleries all over the world and to be modified accordingly. Is perhaps Crouch's tale of mortality and decay inspired by Tate Modern's architecture itself, which avoids London's 'neutered domain of white walls and glass by revelling in its scars, in the traces of history and industry, machinery and power'?[119] Far from the antiseptic, otherworldly, white and clean space of the white cube gallery described by O'Doherty and challenged by Crouch, Tate Modern, with its architectural diversity of spaces ranging from the secluded purity of the white cube to spaces overlooking London, like Crouch's theatre, seems open to the mortal and infected mayhem of everyday life.

As a matter of fact, Serota's Tate Modern has opened itself up to both the mortal essence of the performing arts and the chaos of ordinary people. No wonder that the Tate Gallery's new approach to display and new ways of engaging with the visitors inspired Crouch. The theatre-maker's challenge to both the sacredness of the art gallery and the implicit authority of the director/curator/connoisseur, a patriarchal figure who ensures that museum objects are 'authentic' masterpieces expressing universal truths in an established canon, parallels his challenge to the role of the author in theatre through a process of signification that is inseparable from the performance's dynamics and the complex relationships between performer, art and audience.

(Berkeley: University of California Press, [1976] 1999), 14–15. Quoted in Tim Crouch, *foreward* in the 2009 programme at London's Whitechapel Gallery.

[118] Crouch, *foreward*.

[119] Edwin Heathcote quoted in Lars Nittve, 'How Tate Modern Transformed London – and Beyond', *Apollo. The International Art Magazine*, 31 May 2016. https://www.apollo-magazine.com/how-tate-modern-transformed-london-and-beyond/ (accessed 8 May 2023).

ENGLAND encourages the removal of authority from both the gallery and the stage and the granting of new authority to the spectator/viewer, following in the footsteps of a process that began in the late 1980s and which the Tate Modern has fully embraced since its opening.

Indeed, the Turbine Hall, Tate Modern's vast and iconic entrance area with ramped access and exhibition space for large-scale sculptural projects and site-specific installation art, has become a display space for making contemporary art accessible to many people who have never been to an art gallery before, or never thought of it, and who are invited to be part of the artwork, leaving behind all the deference usually associated with art exhibits. To understand the impact of these artworks in which, as has been noted, the spectacularity of the theme park encroaches on the art installation, it is enough to mention Louise Bourgeois' spiral staircases and twisting towers of *I Do, I Undo, I Redo* (12 May–26 November 2000), Anish Kapoor's enigmatic sculptural *Marsyas* (9 October 2002–6 April 2003), Olafur Eliasson's *The Weather Project* (16 October 2003–21 March 2004) or Carsten Höller's five spiral tubular slides, which whisked visitors from the museum's upper floors to the lower floors of the grand hall in *Test Site* (10 October 2006–15 April 2007). By incorporating viewer interaction and viewer's agency, all these installations transformed the art gallery into a space for metamorphic experiences and demanded a rethinking of what art and exhibitions could be. One might give special mention to Eliasson's *The Weather Project*, the legendary site-specific installation that is indelibly etched into the memory of London and its citizens. Using semi-circular screens, a mirrored ceiling and artificial mist to create the illusion of an indoor sunset, the installation produced what art critic Jonathan Jones called 'an almost psychotropic transformation of human social behaviour', turning art into a mass event and the Turbine Hall into a literally mystical site:

> Olafur Eliasson's *The Weather Project* only opened a couple of weeks ago, but it is already a legend. Visitors seem to think they are at some storied 60s festival – barriers are melting, frosty politeness traded at the door for cockeyed mysticism and love, love, love. Under a vast blazing sun, in clouds of dry ice, revellers lie, looking up at what must surely be the biggest mirrored ceiling in the world, and conclude that, hey, maybe we really are all made of stars. The scale is so excessive, it is hard to experience Eliasson's artwork as art – it is more like nature itself, and we, down below, make the art. [...] It all feels rather pleasantly regressive. We are reconnecting with our roots, with the communal, with the origins of art. [...] It is Stonehenge most of all that the Eliasson project reminds you of – in fact, what you most think of, seeing all these people

lying down, their minds blown, witnessing a synthetic sun, is an illegal modern druidic gathering.[120]

The response to Eliasson's installation revealed an unexpected interest in works whose meaning is not at all determined by the artist, a far cry from the aggressively individualist and iconic conceptual art of the 1990s, 'towards a reengagement with materiality, affect and the sublime', which is the expression of a new meta-modern sensibility.[121] Furthermore, people taking over the space of the Turbine Hall and using it as an arena for their own experiences not only clearly demonstrated their desire for more active engagement with the art but also gave the work an unanticipated performative aspect. Increasingly, in fact, art galleries are inviting their visitors to experience the exhibition as a place of aggregation, engagement and debate in which one participates – in a word, as a drama. Museum theorist Eilean Hooper-Greenhill coined the expression 'post-museum' to describe those institutions that recognize that visitors are not passive consumers and, in fact, encourage them to become active participants. Art historian Chris Bruce, director of the Washington State University Museum of Art and curatorial and collections director of the Experience Music Project in Seattle from 1999 to 2002, defined the post-museum as 'a utopian display institution' that rejects patriarchal authority to become a flexible, ever-changing social space that prioritizes interactivity, audience choice and pleasure.[122]

It is then more than likely that the paradigmatic shift in the way art galleries and museums, particularly the Tate Modern, display their collections, and the way they are perceived, has had a profound impact on dramatic form and theatrical presentation, to the extent that it may be possible to establish a hitherto unexplored connection between post-museum modes of exhibit and the modes of performance of those forms of theatre-making, variously defined as post-dramatic or meta-modern, that cannot be categorized as either solely theatre or solely performance. Crouch might therefore be regarded one of those theatrical reformers who have increased the pressure on spectators in order to draw them out of their passive attitude and transform them into active participants in a shared world. With a nod also

---

[120] Jonathan Jones, 'Reflected Glory. G2's Human Logo Project at Tate Modern', *The Guardian*, 30 October 2003. https://www.theguardian.com/culture/2003/oct/30/1 (accessed 8 May 2023).
[121] Luke Turner, 'Metamodernism: A Brief Introduction', *Notes on Metamodernism*, 12 January 2015. https://www.metamodernism.com/2015/01/12/metamodernism-a-brief-introduction/ (accessed 8 May 2023).
[122] Chris Bruce, 'Spectacle and Democracy: Experience Music Project as a Post-Museum', in Janet Marstine (ed.), *New Museum Theory and Practice*, 129–51.

to the post-museum dynamic, he challenges materialist individuality and reformulates subjectivity not only thematically through the plot but, more importantly, through the construction of the audience's experience in the performance. Significantly, at the opening of *ENGLAND*, the audience is warmly welcomed as a group of visitors who are accorded the essential role of the saviours of the exhibition/performance:

> Thank you.
> Thanks very much.
> Thanks.
> Ladies and gentlemen.
> Thank you.
> If it weren't for you, I wouldn't be here. You saved my life!
> Welcome to the Fruitmarket Gallery here in Edinburgh.
> World class contemporary art at the heart of the city.
> (We'll be here for around twenty-five minutes and then we'll go to another room.
> Where we can sit down). (*E* 13)

At the centre of a complex intertextual experience, audiences are invited to position themselves within the performance taking place in a gallery (watching, commenting, moving), and within the neocolonial and neoliberal world of transplantation and emigration represented in *ENGLAND* (as we will describe in further detail in Chapter 4).

But Tate Modern also inspires *ENGLAND* in other ways. In this play intertwining art and commercial transactions, Crouch, unsurprisingly, mentions the gallery's gift shop, café and bookshop (*E* 20, 31), confirming the increasing merging of culture and commerce, the further blurring of the line between high culture and popular culture, and the transformation of the museum into a consumer playground. The shop and the café are at the heart of the museums and art galleries and are no longer an after-visit accessory to the aesthetic experience, but a primary site of consumption in itself. Accordingly, Sir Serota claimed that 'it is easy to be cynical about the impact of café, restaurant or shop spaces on the culture and character of museums, but such facilities have made museums less daunting, more welcoming, and more open to general visitors', while being well aware that such openness ('democratization' he calls it) 'needs to go deeper than the provisions of opportunities to purchase or to consume'.[123] Consumerism is

---

[123] Nicholas Serota quoted in M. H. Miller, 'Nicholas Serota: 'The Concept of the Museum Is in constant Evolution', *ARTnews*, 1 July 2016. http://www.artnews.com/2016/01/07/

not just a correlate but a significant factor of what the museum has become, as evidenced by Saatchi and Saatchi's 1990s advertising campaign for the Victoria and Albert Museum, which promoted the institution as 'an ace caff with quite a nice museum attached'.[124] Art galleries and museums have grown massively to accommodate different levels of entertainment. It is, therefore, a telling sign of the times that in Ridley's solo play *The Poltergeist* the protagonist, Sasha, an unsuccessful artist who had been dubbed as a prodigy as a teenager for his large-scale murals and who has become instead a bitter unknown, tells Mrs Kulkarni that he met his partner Chet in the bookshop of the Whitechapel Art Gallery where he was working and where they began talking about a postcard reproduction of Louise Bourgeois' *Maman*, the monumental steel spider commissioned for the opening of Tate Modern:

> 'So where did you two meet?' 'In Whitechapel Art Gallery, Mrs Kulkarni.' 'I had a part time job in the gallery bookshop.' [...] 'And you two just … started talking …?' 'Sasha bought a postcard, Mrs Kulkarni.' 'Of a Louise Bourgeois sculpture. 'A giant spider!' 'And Chet said how much he liked that piece too.' 'And so we talked.' 'And we wanted to talk more but –' 'It was tricky because I was at work and so –' 'I waited two hours for him to finish.' (*Poltergeist* 19)

It is now commonplace for a visit to an art gallery or museum to include a browse in the gift shop and, in the case of the Tate Modern, a break in the cafeteria, a lunch in the restaurant or a trip up to the viewing platform to admire the panorama of London. It is an experience of 'being there', which somehow means absorbing the aura of its brand. Tate Modern is so social, fun and cool that among the British visitors, an afternoon spent looking at Rachel Whiteread's mattress cast or Tracey Emin's unmade bed has become less an act of ostentatious rebellion than a respectable family outing.

Plays for galleries, plays in galleries

Given such a rich production of plays exploring art world issues and spaces and engaging more or less explicitly with artists, gallery curators, art

---

nicholas-serota-the-concept-of-the-museum-is-in-constant-evolution/ (accessed 8 May 2023).

[124] Nick Prior, 'Having One's Tate and Eating It: Transformations of the Museum in a Hypermodern Era', in Andrew McClellan (ed.), *Art and Its Publics: Museum Studies at the Millennium* (Malden, MA: Blackwell, 2003), 55.

historians and art dealers, whether fictional or historical, past or present, one might speak of a 'transplantation' – as Crouch calls it – of art gallery motifs onto the British stage, and of a growing exchange between theatre and gallery spaces that seems to have intensified over the past two decades. In fact, it is important to note that the dynamic between theatre and the visual arts has also been reshaped by an increasing number of plays being staged in art galleries and museum spaces, sometimes in conjunction with specific exhibitions.

Co-ventures between theatres and art galleries are the most obvious forms of connection. The collaboration of playwright Timberlake Wertenbaker and director Max Stafford-Clark with the Bernard Jacobson Gallery on *Three Birds Alighting on a Field* (1991), in the best tradition of the Royal Court, with the art dealer Bernard Jacobson as script consultant and William Tillyer's painting on loan to the production, paved the way for those synergistic relationships between theatres and galleries that would become increasingly common in the decades to come.

If the stage exhibits artworks and imports art gallery issues, the reverse is equally true. Following twentieth-century movements, from Dada to Conceptual art, many museums and art galleries in recent decades have commissioned artists' interventions to help these institutions renegotiate their relationship with their publics, confirming a convergent trajectory between British theatre and the visual arts.

Edinburgh's Fruitmarket Gallery has been particularly active and significant in this regard. Two events need only be mentioned: Crouch's aforementioned *ENGLAND* (2007) and the presentation of the fifty-minute film *Event for a Stage* (2018) by Tacita Dean, one of Britain's most compelling international visual artists who was associated with the YBAs early in her career. Interestingly, the art gallery has become a critical vantage point for examining the nature of theatre for both a playwright and a visual artist.

Commissioned by Traverse Theatre and Fruitmarket Gallery, *ENGLAND* is 'a play for galleries' that emerged after a long gestation, as Crouch explains:

> I spent a long time thinking about creating a hybrid piece that would be a visual art, or a Janet Cardiff, or a Graeme Miller, or an earpiece-guided tour, and then I realized that that was not my strength. My strength was to tell a story and think about theatre because I think that that's probably what I should be fighting for. All my work is about narrative – *ENGLAND* is a really key example of that. So there was the idea of placing a piece of theatre inside a gallery without altering the structure of the gallery whatsoever, and it was that formal consideration that led to a narrative consideration of transplantation: we placed one thing inside something

else. What happens to the thing? What happens to the host of the thing? So the narrative of *ENGLAND* is about transplantation.[125]

Significantly, the theatrical performance and the gallery situation overlap and come to coincide with the two performers/guides leading the audience for a gallery tour, while the audience is cast as gallery-goers, standing, watching and walking around following the performers as they move around the space and engage them in multiple layers of viewing, sometimes inviting them to 'look' at the works on the walls, at other times to imagine the works of art they are only referring to in their story. It is a multiple and complex vision that leads the audience to have both a vision of visual art and a vision of theatre, looking at the art and also at the two performers and the other viewers. Placing a play inside a gallery undermines the neutrality of those white walls, making it site-specific in a place that is, by very nature, unspecific. The performance changes radically each night as the audience moves freely around the gallery and the actors attempt to accommodate and contain them with their body movements. In fact, the rhythm of the performance changes according to the space, too, and it is altered as they move around the Fruitmarket Gallery, which is hosting the solo exhibition of British artist Alex Hartley, or between the huge, monumental sculptures of Arnaldo Pomodoro, as in the Italian production at the Fondazione Pomodoro in Milan in 2008, directed by Carlo Cerciello, or through Isa Genzken's mirrors and reflective surfaces, which refract the viewer's body into the artist's work at the Whitechapel Gallery, where *ENGLAND* was presented in collaboration with the National Theatre in 2009.[126]

Finally, setting the play in a gallery means that each and every visitor may feel encouraged to question the possible links between the performance and the artworks exhibited, according to their own prior experience, interests, values and background knowledge. Each particular location gives rise to an immediate dialogue with the gallery collections and displays as well as modifies the dynamics of the performance by affecting the spectator's perception, as Crouch himself explains in an unpublished interview with Stephen Bottoms:

> In Pittsburgh, at the Andy Warhol Museum, the energy of Warhol was infusing the show – the notion of commodity, of reproduction, of

---

[125] Tim Crouch interviewed by Duška Radosavljević, 'Appendix 3: Tim Crouch – Interview', *Theatre-Making. Interplay between Text and Performance in the 21st Century* (London: Palgrave, 2013), 221.

[126] Mariacristina Cavecchi, 'Quando il teatro va al museo. Una storia di oggi', *Altre Modernità*, 5 (2011): 26–44. https://riviste.unimi.it/index.php/AMonline/article/view/1027 (accessed 8 May 2023).

commercial value. In Yale, we were at the Yale Center for British Art, with Turners and Constables, and in the second act was a room full of Stubbs. Horses and lions! So there was a huge weight of establishment and imperialism which is ideal for the second act of the show. We're not wanting to force these associations or connections but hoping that people will get them in the nature of the space.[127]

Meanings slide. At the play's premiere at the Fruitmarket Gallery, spectators might have supposed a sort of connection between the post-heart-operation new life described in the play and the name of 'new world' that Alex Hartley (whose work, by the way, was included in the *Sensation* exhibition) gave to the new Arctic Island off Norway he discovered in 2004 (*E* 32–3). Spectators might have connected Crouch's investigation of the architectural structure of art galleries, hospitals and churches with Hartley's new ways of physically experiencing and thinking about constructed surroundings. In a similar way, at Naples Donnaregina Contemporary Art Museum, where the play was directed by Carlo Cerciello in 2008, one might think that Georg Baselitz's paintings on the walls, in which the German artist unconventionally disrupts the space and represents his subjects upside-down, appropriately hold a mirror up to Crouch's unconventional theatre. Interestingly, when the play was performed at the Henry Art Gallery in Seattle in 2008, the gallery blog promoted *ENGLAND* as a transformative experience, where the tour of the exhibition turns into a '"tour to the end of the world", spinning into an intensely personal narrative that resonates beautifully with *The Violet Hour*', the exhibition hosted at the time.

By locating his play in a gallery and reshuffling the relationship between stage and audience, Crouch somehow displaces and undermines certainties about both – theatre and gallery – and by holding up a mirror to the gallery space, invites the audience to question the nature of the theatre space itself. The same invitation comes from Tacita Dean's film *Event for a Stage*, which was screened during the *Woman with a Red Hat* exhibition at the Fruitmarket Gallery from 26 July to 26 August 2018 as a part of the Edinburgh Art Festival. Originally commissioned for the 2014 Sydney Biennale as a live theatre piece, *Event for a Stage* was Dean's first foray into theatre and her first collaboration with an actor. The film focuses on the intense interaction

---

[127] Crouch, unpublished interview with Stephen Bottoms, Leeds, 6 November 2008, quoted in Stephen Bottoms, 'Materialising the Audience: Tim Crouch's Sight Specifics in *England* and *The Author*', *Contemporary Theatre Review*, 21, 4 (2011): 448; Mariacristina Cavecchi, 'The New Art Galleries on the Contemporary British Stage', in S. Coelsch-Foisner and D. Brown (eds), *The Museal Turn* (Heidelberg: Winter, 2011), 299–313.

between Dean and actor Stephen Dillane as they struggle to understand and revel in their respective art forms, with Dillane performing from a script written for him and handed to him, page by page, by Dean herself. A compelling and complex exploration of the balance between reality and illusion in both visual arts and theatre, it continues the artist's inspirational investigations into the imaginary worlds of art and the artifice of theatrical invention, producing an undeniably compelling contribution to the evolving history of collaboration between gallery and theatre.

Indeed, in recent years, collaboration with external creative partners has become increasingly common in United Kingdom's art galleries and museums, and in the wider heritage sector. Although the plays are often not conceived as site-specific plays to be performed in art galleries, like *ENGLAND*, they take on new significance when they are performed in the evocative, charged space of the art gallery.

Brian McAvera's *Picasso's Women*, which premiered at the National Theatre in London in 2000, is also a fascinating case study, not only because McAvera is an art curator and historian as well as a playwright and director but also because the monologues that make up the play have often been performed in art galleries, which have, in turn, worked somehow to amplify their significance. Indeed, the play has had an equally successful following in both art galleries and theatres.

Conceived as a stand against Picasso as a man who 'could be a total bastard, using people and discarding them like spent condoms',[128] *Picasso's Women* consists of eight monologues that should ideally be performed one after the other, in chronological order, although each can stand alone, and is meant to design a cubist portrait of Picasso through the different voices of eight women who were central to his life and art: Fernand Olivier, Eva Gouel, Gaby Lespinasse, Olga Khokhlova, Marie-Thérèse Walter, Dora Maar, Françoise Gilot and Jacqueline Roque. Significantly, when it was revived as part of Flying Elephant Productions' 2018 project 'Picasso's Women', it was presented both in theatres and in contemporary art spaces at the Edinburgh Fringe Festival and in London. Beyond any obvious connection to the art world, according to director Collette Redgrave, who also took on the role of ballet dancer Olga Khokhlova in one of the three out of eight confessional monologues presented at the Fruitmarket Gallery, the limbo-like nature of the gallery's white space seemed an appropriate backdrop for a triptych in which a trio of the artist's lovers are destined to be trapped forever. Significantly, Redgrave also invited the audience to consider McAvera's play

---

[128] Brian McAvera, 'Introduction', in *Picasso's Women* (London: Oberon, 1999), 15.

at the Fruitmarket Gallery, which showed the victims and sacrifices behind Picasso's art, as an alternative perspective on the Spanish artist that was meant to counterbalance the EY Exhibition at the Tate Modern, *Picasso 1932 – Love, Fame, Tragedy*, in 2018:

> The current EY Exhibition at the Tate features works from 1932, one of Picasso's most prolific periods of work. The title poster features *Le Rêve* or *The Dream* which many people will be familiar with – Marie-Therese sits asleep with her famous blonde-haired head tilted to one side. What is she dreaming, what is she thinking, why did she later go on to kill herself? Since the project was conceived in 2016, many significant movements have occurred in terms of the recognition of the treatment of female actresses, artists, models, performers, and the question of equality in creative industries.[129]

Unsurprisingly, after a critically acclaimed sell-out run at the Edinburgh Fringe Festival, and coinciding with the EY exhibition at the Tate, a re-imagined production of *Picasso's Women* moved to London's Gallery Different, on Percy Street, while the gallery was hosting the exhibition *Muse, Model or Mistress?* in September 2018. The interplay between the performance in such an intimate space and the works of twenty artists inspired by both Picasso's art and McAvera's play, from Patsy Whiting's *Demoiselles after Picasso* to Irene Lees' *Lady in Waiting (Marie Therese Walter)* and *Me Too (Dora Maar)*, added a whole extra dimension to the dramatic experience. Indeed, both the play and the exhibition revisited Duchamp's commentary on the restrictive role of women in the Surrealist movement and art in general while somehow being at the forefront of the cultural aftershock of the #MeToo movement.

With #MeToo shining a global spotlight on the role of women in society and how they are portrayed and perceived, theatres and art galleries alike have invested in plays and exhibitions dedicated to female artists whose importance had been eclipsed by husbands and lovers, writing a new and important chapter in the history of synergy between theatre and gallery. Suffice it here to mention the 2020 exhibition *Dora Maar* at the Tate Modern, exploring the breadth of the long artistic career of a woman still best known today as Picasso's lover and the muse for *Weeping Woman*, and Breach

---

[129] Colette Redgrave interviewed by Nathalie O'Donoghue, 'Edinburgh 2018: BWW Q&A – Picasso's Women', *Broadway World*, 2 July 2018. https://www.broadwayworld.com/westend/article/EDINBURGH-2018-BWW-QA--Picassos-Women-20180702 (accessed 8 May 2023).

Theatre's 'seicento #MeToo' play[130] *It's True, it's true, it's true*, the undisputed hit of the 2018 Edinburgh Fringe Festival.

It's True, it's true, it's true is a politically committed play dealing with the issues of sexual harassment, gender inequities, abuses of power and the inadequacy of the legal system when it comes to cases of rape. In the play, the multimedia performance theatre company Breach Theatre cleverly re-stages the 1612 rape trial in which Artemisia Gentileschi, a survivor of abuse, confronted her rapist Agostino Tassi in court. Conceived as an all-female, multi-roling three-hander, the play 'was created using verbatim material and a devising process with the cast'.[131] Through a formally inventive performance that draws the audience into the inner workings of a theatrical experience, Breach Theatre addresses the question of truth (legal, artistic and theatrical), perhaps over-emphatically announcing it with the triple repetition in the title *It's True, It's true, It's true*. These words, spoken by the seventeen-year-old Artemisia Gentileschi, have come down to us in a 1612 trial transcript which is held in the State Archives in Rome and was displayed at the National Gallery in the first major exhibition of Artemisia's work in the United Kingdom (3 October 2020–24 January 2021). Indeed, the quest for truth invests equally in the courtroom, where Artemisia is on trial, and with her the countless women who've come forward with accounts of rape before and after her; the art world; and the theatre itself. The trial inquiry, with the few characters summoned to give evidence as witnesses, is strictly intertwined with both tribunal theatre's and art history's attempt at historical accuracy. As is written in the 'Notes on the Text',

> So, is it true? Yes and no. We've always thought of this show's title as both a statement of solidarity – an 'I believe her' for Artemisia and the countless women who've come forward with accounts of rape before and after her – and a provocation: how much of what we're hearing is historically accurate? What does 'verbatim theatre' – which typically aspires to truth – actually mean when dealing with a four-hundred-year-old court transcript, like the one we set out to re-voice? Hand-written by notaries whilst the testimonies were given, it was later discovered, patched together, transcribed and translated several times before reaching our rehearsal room.[132]

---

[130] Laura Freeman, 'Painting: The Extraordinary Life and Art of Artemisia Gentileschi', *The Spectator*, 11 April 2020.
[131] Breach, *It's True, It's True, It's True* (London: Oberon Books, 2008), unnumbered.
[132] Breach, 'Notes on the Text', in *It's True*, unnumbered.

Thus, the play disrupts the specific performance and *mise-en-scène* techniques of the tribunal theatre and challenges the traditional notion of the studio as a masculine, largely private space where the lone male genius works and where the female model is the object of his gaze. The play blurs the spaces of the courtroom and artist's studio to give voice to Artemisia Gentileschi, both the woman and the artist, thus counter-balancing her silence in the 1612 trial and making her speak directly to the twenty-first-century audience, in ways that we will consider in more detail in Chapter 3.

Beyond its overarching themes, however, *It's True, It's True, It's True* is one of the most recent significant examples of a successful synergetic collaboration between theatre and the art world.

Firstly, it was conceived at the National Gallery when director Billy Barrett, visiting the *Beyond Caravaggio* exhibition (12 October 2016 – 15 January 2017), stumbled upon Artemisia Gentileschi and discovered not only her art but the existence of the record of Agostino Tassi rape trial. Also at the National Gallery, Barrett and Ellice Steven, the actress who plays Artemisia in the courtroom drama, discuss Artemisia's work in a conversation with Letizia Treves, the curator of the National Gallery's *Artemisia* exhibition. Meanwhile, Steven stars as Artemisia in a series of video clips produced by the National Gallery as part of its in-depth offering, entitled *Following Artemisia*, which retrace her footsteps and encounter some of her most important works. Both the video clip of this conversation, with a presentation of their play, and the *Following Artemisia* clips are published on the National Gallery website, strengthening the ongoing dialogue between art and theatre.

As a footnote to this overview of the increasingly common art/theatre short-circuit, it is worth mentioning two other plays and collaborations which reveal how London has become a fertile ground for plays about contemporary art. American playwrights Neil Labute and John Logan staged their plays, *The Shape of Things* and *Red*, respectively, in London before bringing them to New York, perhaps thinking that they would reach audiences more interested in contemporary art. Labute's corrosive play, exploring art and identity and debating about the use an artist makes of her or his life, was successfully first presented at the Almeida Theatre in 2004. When Tom Attenborough revived it at the chic The Gallery Soho of London in 2011 (1 February–6 March) with the site-specific theatre company Rhapsody of Words, the gallery's clean white walls provided a blank canvas in perfect harmony with the key theme of the play, the 'metamorphosis' in art and love. Logan, who decided to present *Red* at the London's Donmar Warehouse in 2009 (3 December 2009–6 February 2010) – just after the great exhibition that the Tate Modern devoted to Mark Rothko's late series (26 September 2008–1 February 2009) and before it went on to Broadway, where it won six Tony Awards – discovered the Rothko's

Seagram murals at the Tate Modern, where contemplating them inspired him the 'shape of the play':

> The Seagram murals […] They had a very powerful effect on me. I knew very little about Mark Rothko, very little about Abstract Expressionism, but I found the paintings themselves profoundly moving and kinetic in a strange way. I went to the wall and read a little description about how he painted them originally for the Seagram Building and then decided to keep them and give the money back. And I thought, 'Well, this is an interesting story.' So, I decided that I would read a little more about it, and the more I read the more I thought that it was a play. And I almost immediately thought it was a two-hander play with Rothko and a young assistant. The shape of the play came to me very early in the contemplation of the work.[133]

The connection between the play and the Tate Modern was further strengthened when a new production opened at Wyndham's Theatre in London's West End in 2018. The gallery's director Frances Morris took the play's director, Michael Grandage, and the cast on a tour of the Rothko Room, telling the story behind the Seagram paintings and discussing with them what it was like to bring Rothko's painting process to the stage. Conveniently, the video of the tour and discussion is available as part of the educational tools on the Tate's website.[134]

Significantly, *Red*'s audience is taken through an experience that is comparable to the entertaining and at the same time educational experience of a visit to a public art gallery. The stage functions like 'a book of history', to cite Serota's definition of most public art galleries in the world, which until the 1980s exhibited according to the principle of historical grouping by schools. Indeed, the playwright instructs the audience about the precise collocation of Rothko's work in the line of art history, and the inevitable generational shift, through a Socratic dialogue between Rothko and his young (and fictional) assistant Ken:

> **Ken** 'The child must banish the father. Respect him, but kill him' … Isn't that what you said? … You guys went after the Cubists and

---

[133] John Logan in Richard J. Roberts (ed.), 'Study Guide for *Red* by John Logan', *Indiana Repertory Theatre*, 2014, 3. https://d1fl2pbib0u1tq.cloudfront.net/pdf/Study%20Guides/20142015/IRT%20Study%20Guide%20for%20Red.pdf (accessed May 20023).

[134] Tate, 'In the Gallery. Rothko on Stage', *Tate*. https://www.tate.org.uk/art/artists/mark-rothko-1875/rothko-on-stage (accessed 8 May 2023).

> Surrealists and, boy, did you love it. And now your time has come, and you don't want to go. Well, exit stage left, Rothko. Because Pop Art has banished Abstract Expressionism… (*Red* 52)

Is it a coincidence that Ken describes the art world as a stage on which artists, like actors, are in the spotlight until they lose the interest of the public, gallery owners, art dealers and connoisseurs and are asked to leave? In addition, for the set of *Red*, designer Christopher Oram commissioned the reproduction of Rothko's *Seagram Murals*, so that copies of those in the Tate Modern's permanent collection were on display at the Donmar Warehouse, whose stage was literally transformed into an art gallery, which had the unparalleled privilege of being inhabited by two men – an artist and his assistant, father and son – who paint, discuss art and its meaning, argue and eventually learn to respect each other.

Exploring the encounter between theatre and art galleries is no easy affair. But beyond the intricacies of the dense traffic between the two places and between verbal and visual, what remains compelling is the extraordinary vividness of the interconnected stories and the voices to which they play host, and which seem, often, to have an immediacy unscathed by the complications of hermeneutics.

2

The drama of authenticity, connoisseurship and identity

In his volume *Authenticity in Contemporary Theatre and Performance* (2017), Daniel Schulze argues that 'it is no exaggeration to claim that for the past two or three decades a feeling of fakeness and deception in almost all areas of cultural production has surfaced' and that 'authenticity has been a major factor in theatre and the performing arts for the past decade or so'.[1] Not surprisingly, then, the concepts of fakeness and authenticity play a major role in both the art world and the theatre, epitomizing a trend that proclaimed fraud 'the growth industry of the eighties'.[2] While the growing interest in and fascination with forgeries led to the ground-breaking exhibition *Fake? The Art of Deception* at the British Museum in 1989,[3] and again to the exhibition *Close Examination: Fakes, Mistakes and Discoveries* at the London National Gallery in 2010,[4] there has been a boom in British playwrights transforming the stage into a gallery, a museum or a lecture room, where ideas of authenticity and forgery in the art world can be at once debated and exploited.

---

[1] Daniel Schulze, *Authenticity in Contemporary Theatre and Performance. Make It Real* (London: Methuen, 2017), 253.

[2] Mihir Bose and Cathy Gunn, *Fraud: The Growth Industry of the Eighties* (New York: HarperCollins, 1989).

[3] This exhibition followed the 1961 *An Exhibition of Forgeries and Deceptive Copies* held in the Department of Prints and Drawings, the first exhibition dealing with forgeries ever held at the British Museum. (Edward Croft-Murray, 'An Exhibition of Forgeries and Deceptive Copies: Held in the Department of Prints and Drawings from 9 February 1961', *The British Museum Quarterly*, 24, 1/2 (August 1961): 29–30). In London, the first exhibition on the subject had been at the Burlington Fine Arts Club in 1924, *Counterfeits, Imitations and Copies of Works of Art*.

[4] Small but significant, the museum focused on the advanced techniques in the scientific examination, conservation and art historical research that the National Gallery's Scientific Department had employed to investigate paintings' physical properties since it opened in 1934.

Significantly, by offering the experience of 'an anti-museum, a history of art written through the inauthentic',[5] the 1989 exhibition sought to reassess what curator Mark Jones defined as the 'unjustly neglected' fakes: all those works that are 'scorned or passed over in embarrassed silence by scholar, dealer, and collector alike', while instead providing 'unrivalled evidence of the values and perceptions of those who made them, and of those for whom they were made'.[6] Just as art historians and museum curators debate what constitutes a fake and how to detect it, contemporary playwrights have raised questions about how authenticity is to be viewed in the art world, on stage and in life, while at the same time doubting that it has any definite meaning or relevance.

David Hare's *The Bay at Nice* (1986), Nick Dear's *The Art of Success* (1987), Alan Bennett's *A Question of Attribution* (1988), David Edgar's *Pentecost* (1994) and, later, Simon Gray's *The Old Masters* (2004) are particularly interesting plays that take place in art galleries or museums, entertaining the audience with sophisticated discussions on questions of attribution, methods of studying a painting and the uneasy relationships between originals, 'counterfeits, imitations and copies', to quote the title of the 1924 exhibition of the London Burlington Fine Arts Club, the first in London on the subject.

Onstage, the mysteries surrounding a work of art, its authorship and provenance contribute to the development of the plots as well as helping to reel in spectators through suspense, apprehension and coup de théâtre; furthermore, the attribution process works as a catalyst for other and perhaps more critical aesthetic and political issues. In various ways, this theatrical trend questions and challenges the art museum as a place that stores memories, constructs national identity and cultivates nostalgia for a past nurtured by the growing heritage culture that began to be valued as an essential economic enterprise in the Thatcher decade. Tapping into a national love affair with the past, entrepreneurial artists such as William Hogarth, connoisseurs, art historians and prominent art world figures, such as Bernard Berenson, aka BB, Joseph Duveen, Kenneth Clark, Anthony Blunt, or forgers such as Shaun Greenhalgh, with their flamboyant personalities and buried secrets, materialize on stage to interrogate and demolish conventional assumptions about authenticity, authorship, creativity and originality. In the end, they all

---

[5] Wendy Steiner, 'Art; In London, A Catalogue of Fakes', *New York Times*, 29 April 1990, 37. https://www.nytimes.com/1990/04/29/arts/art-in-london-a-catalogue-of-fakes.html (accessed 8 May 2023).

[6] Mark Jones, 'Why Fakes?' in *Fake? The Art of Deception* (London: British Museum Publications, 1990), 11.

reveal that none of these concepts are uncontroversial or straightforward, challenging a past that is too-often domesticated and made safe.

A theme rich in dramatic potential, the question of attribution offers playwrights a range of metaphoric suggestions. Interestingly, it not only encourages the exploration and reassessment of the problem of identity, both individual and national, as in Bennett's *A Question of Attribution* and Edgard's *Pentecost*, but also offers a unique opportunity to address in a more practical way the ontological connection between lying and acting as well as the power and limits of the gaze in front of a painting or performance, thus mobilising questions, also, about the act of spectating as a source of action and a site of agency. Echoing Jean Baudrillard's theory of simulacra, Forced Entertainment's artistic director Tim Etchells has proposed that the fake is 'more pertinent than the real' and suggested that since theatre is 'so inherently bound up in fakery' it is the ideal medium in which to explore contemporary observations and concerns about the status of 'truth' and its relationship to representation.[7] Thus, the playwrights of the new millennium have taken up the questions of fakeness and authenticity that haunted playwrights like Bennett, Dear, Edgar and Hare and fuelled their stage explorations of the politics of art and the art of politics in the Thatcher era in order to renegotiate the relationship between experience and representation in the light of new cultural urgencies and theatrical practices.

Since the turn of the millennium, the visual and the scenic, the art gallery and the theatre, have increasingly interacted in new, provocative, and sometimes mysterious and paradoxical ways, hybridizing their specific logics and challenging the very concept of representation. It is no coincidence that Tim Crouch and David Leddy turn to the two great cultural icons of the mythology of 'cool Britannia', the art gallery and the stage, to explore and represent the fabric of contemporary anxieties and turbulences by focusing on the stories of people trying to overcome a particular set of challenges. In *An Oak Tree* (2005, Traverse Theatre),[8] Crouch draws inspiration from a conceptual work of visual art to grapple radically with the precarious balance between truth and falsehood and the multiple and sometimes contradictory layers of representation, while exploiting the risks and challenges of live performance. A few years later, in a similar vein, Leddy explores fakes and forgeries in *Long Live the Little Knife* (2013), showing that they are 'a response to demand, an ever-changing portrait of human desires'[9] and therefore crucial 'keys to understanding the changing

---

[7] Tim Etchells, *Certain Fragments*. London: Routledge, 1999, 35.
[8] Tim Crouch, *An Oak Tree* (London: Oberon Books, 2005).
[9] Jones, *Why Fakes?*, 13.

nature of our vision of the past'.[10] Even more interestingly, fakes and forgeries open up a discussion about the limits of verbatim theatre and the complex relationships between reality and its representation.

It is important to note that the biography (or pseudo-biography) of an artist, a connoisseur or a forger who speculates on originals and copies in art and other areas, which was a trend in the theatre of the 1980s and 1990s, has been replaced in both *Long Live the Little Knife* and *An Oak Tree* by the narration of performers, who expose the mechanics of theatrical representation and meaning-making and the paradox of being both and off scene and, in Crouch's case, exploit the possibilities (and risks) of live performance. This is a dramaturgy that 'makes us aware of the mechanisms of communication and the artificial construction of the imaginary (real) worlds, even while we are moved and engaged by them'.[11] It is precisely because of this declared artificiality and fakeness of the dramatic situation, together with the audiences' awareness of their performative selves, that both *Long Live the Little Knife* and *An Oak Tree* induce a visceral and unmediated understanding and experience of performance.

Forgeries, copyrights and Polaroids

Nick Dear dissects notions of authoriality and piracy and questions the political manipulation of aesthetics in *The Art of Success*. As mentioned in the previous chapter, the play shows William Hogarth discussing the relation between original and copy, art and censorship, and the copyright law for printed images: all concerns which project a bridge towards the art scene of the 1980s in London, indeed towards Nick Dear himself, for embedded in the play is Dear's provocative, self-reflexive questioning of his role and responsibility as a playwright.

It is perhaps on the grounds of such similarity that Dear acts freely with his sources, exacerbating, for instance, both Hogarth's entrepreneurial talents in a budding and profitable mass-market and his unconventional sexual tastes. Indeed, in staging Hogarth's life Dear has taken 'lots of liberties', persuaded as he is that 'all history is speculating and liberty-taking anyway, dressed up with fancy clothes'.[12] The play 'is set in the past,

---

[10] Ibid., 16.
[11] Cathy Turner and Synne Behrndt, *Dramaturgy and Performance* (Basingstoke: Palgrave Macmillan, 2008), 193.
[12] Nick Dear, 'Play Notes' in the programme for the first production at The Other Place – Stratford upon Avon, which opened July 9, 1986 (Victoria & Albert Archive), unnumbered.

but [it] is not a history play'[13] and Dear's portrait of the 'father' of English painting as 'a drunken, riotous, chauvinist misogynist'[14] is poised both between centuries and between history, fiction, performance and narration of the present. *The Art of Success* is thus a 'rather lurid comedy of sexual manners',[15] funny, passionate, sexy and, at times, like much of Hogarth's work, surreal and grotesque, where centuries are thus given the opportunity to intermingle and overlap.

At The Other Place, the actors wore eighteenth-century costumes along with today's sneakers; John Gromada's original music was electronic and the language was contemporary, 'a classless Cockney'.[16] Director Adrian Noble and designer Ultz conceived 'a theatrical limbo' of compressed tomes where all levels of society 'meet on a huge blank sheet of drawing paper suspended on steel hawsers like the lines of an engraver's perspective'.[17] On the one hand, the striking design presented a space of extraordinary minimalism and modernity as The Other Place was dominated by a huge blank canvas stretched out across a platform that 'becomes both an acting area and something to be drawn on, scribbled over, desecrated and ripped as the evening progresses'.[18] The white canvas was also reminiscent of Locke's metaphor of 'white paper, void of all characters, without any ideas' that is 'to be furnished [...] with an almost endless variety',[19] this last word being notoriously the keystone of Hogarth's *The Analysis of Beauty*. On the other hand, the stripes of pseudo-Hogarthian caricatures, visible on the backdrop, echo Hogarth's cartoons, such as *The Laughing Audience* (1733–7) or *A Church Choir* (1736); they are, however, mere piracies, in tune indeed with the endless process of piracy/appropriation which took place at the time,[20] and centrally relevant to the play's focus on copies and originals. History and stage connive in blaming 'the double annoyance of seeing large sums of money [Hogarth] felt rightly his still going to other parties, and of seeing wretched copies made of the works he had laboured over with such care'.[21] The question of copyright, much discussed throughout the play, is also comically hinted at when, in

---

[13] Ibid.
[14] Michael Coveney, '*The Art of Success*/The Other Place', *Financial Times*, 10 July 1986, 25.
[15] Dear, *Play Notes*.
[16] Irving Wardle, 'The Gap between Life and Dreams', *The Times*, 10 July 1986, 19.
[17] Michael Ratcliffe, 'Review of *The Art of Success*', *Observer*, 13 July 1986. In *Theatre Record 2–15 July 1986*, 754.
[18] Michael Billington, 'The Moralist's Lewd Progress', *The Guardian*, 11 July 1986, 18.
[19] Ronald Paulson, *Hogarth. High Art and Low. 1732–1750*, vol. 2 (New Brunswick, NJ: Rutgers University Press, 1992), 334.
[20] Ibid., 55.
[21] Ibid., 36.

prison, the painter explains to the ignorant Sarah that 'the squiggle at the bottom' of his sketch is his signature, 'so people know it's authentic' (*Art* 36).²²

The issue of authenticity comes to the fore when Hogarth, in a nightmare, dreams he is making a variety of pornographic Polaroid portraits:

> *A Stage-hand enters, crosses the stage, gives William a Polaroid camera and exits.* [...] *William examines the camera with great interest.* [...] *Jane enters, seductively dressed.* [...] *Jane embraces Oliver, and leads him aside. They make love. She calls out to her husband.* [...] *William sees them now, and starts to take photographs of them. Harry enters.* [...] *Harry kisses William passionately on the mouth.* [...] *Walpole enters.* [...] *Frank goes to Jane and joins in.* [...] *Harry goes to Jane and joins in. William photographs the proceedings.*
> [...] *Photographs rain from the camera.* (*Art* 86–9)

In the wake of this scene, when the play was staged at the Manhattan Theatre Club in New York in 1989, the American critic Frank Rich defined Dear's Hogarth as 'the Warhol of the eighteenth century'.²³ Andy Warhol's huge collection of Polaroid pictures and his artistic engagement with the practices of popular culture and commercial processes can indeed be seen to reverberate in Dear's artist. Moreover, the New York context made reviewers especially sensitive to the intertwined issues of rough or scabrous (when not sadomasochistic) sex, patronage, the merchandizing of art and scatological language, many of which had been reactivated in the autumn of 1989 by the death of Robert Mapplethorpe, the author and lover of provocative and often homoerotic Polaroid photos not unlike the ones enacted in Dear's play:

> *Four men advance on William.* [...] *They chase him and strip him of his clothes. He tries to scrabble away but he is surrounded. The drumbeat drives into his brain. Each of the men produces a camera, all with flash.* [...] *They all photograph a naked and terrified man crouching on the floor.* (*Art* 89)

Last but not least, the artist's nightmare in Dear's play charts and visualizes Hogarth's concerns about the question of reproducibility, which was at the

---

[22] Nick Dear, 'The Art of Success', in *Plays One* (London: Faber and Faber, 2000), 1–98.
[23] Frank Rich, '*Art of Success* Makes Hogarth the Warhol of the 18th Century', *The New York Times*, 21 December 1989. https://www.nytimes.com/1989/12/21/theater/review-theater-art-of-success-makes-hogarth-the-warhol-of-the-18th-century.html (accessed 20 August 2023).

heart of his career and preoccupation as an engraver and would one day be forcefully reactivated in the context of pop art and pop culture:

> **Oliver** Oh, prints, well, prints, absolutely, naturally one shall have a set of prints oneself, but one is talking about paintings, canvases, one is talking about art. Art rests in the original, not the copy. […] Anyone can own a copy. Genius is not shared around like a bag of peppermints. […]
> **William** … But what if every bloke in the street can own a masterpiece for sixpence? Then where are your connoisseurs? Your gentlemen collectors? (*Art* 12–3)

Hogarth naturally contests Oliver's trust in the value of originals and their implicit aura – to use Benjamin's words in his famous essay on mechanical reproduction. On the contrary, he acknowledges something that would become even truer almost three centuries later – namely that a copy can be as good as the original. Intended to protect both the copyright of engravings, by conferring it on the artists rather than the print sellers, and the quality of the image by preventing cheap copies, the 'Act for the Encouragement of the Arts of Designing, Engraving, Etching & co.' became the foundation for copyright protection in the Western world.[24] The partnership between reproductive engraving and the mass-market was ready to flourish; and there is little wonder, therefore, if Rich associates Hogarth with Warhol and Mapplethorpe among the many who have explored and exploited the aesthetics of reproduction.

But Dear's play also resonates with the artistic landscape of London, and with David Hockney in particular, who, at the time, was experimenting with Polaroid photo collages. As a matter of fact, *The Art of Success* opened after Hockney's 1983 lecture 'On Photography' at the Victoria and Albert Museum, where he argued for a multi-viewpoint and multi-temporal approach to photography.[25] And the play also engages with questions raised by the artist's two solo exhibitions: *Moving Focus Print from Tyler Graphics Ltd* at the Tate Gallery and *Still Lives and Landscapes* at the London Knoedler Gallery, both in 1986. This is without mentioning Hockney's own kinship with Hogarth: as a kind of contemporary Hogarth himself, Hockney replicated his first trip to America 'as a modern version of the Grand Tour in the suite of sixteen

---

[24] Jonathon Keats, *Forged. Why Fakes Are the Great Art of Our Age* (Oxford: Oxford University Press, 2012), 17.
[25] Website of 'The David Hockney Foundation', https://www.thedavidhockneyfoundation.org/chronology/1983 (accessed 20 August 2023).

etchings *A Rake's Progress* (1961–3)'.²⁶ In the wake of the etchings, Hockney was also notoriously commissioned to design the set for Stravinsky's opera *The Rake's Progress*, staged for the first time in 1975.

Not surprisingly, then, issues of authenticity and piracy/forgery are tightly interwoven in Dear's play with the construction and performing of identity, perhaps paving the path for a number of later works, including Bennett's *A Question of Attribution* and Gray's *The Old Masters*. When Dear's Hogarth describes 'the bastard pirates of print', he reinforces the connection between art forgery and acting – a connection further explored and exploited in Leddy's *Long Live the Little Knife*. Indeed, it is not coincidental that the forger 'poses as a buyer':

> **William** [...] Some geezer will come around my place posing as a buyer for the original painting, and the next thing you know there'll be a shoddy bloody copy of it in the shops before I've even got the acid off my etching, and then they'll knock down my payments because the market's flooded with imitations – it makes you weep! (*Art* 14–5)

The playwright is thus following in the painter's footprints – that is, if what Paulson suggests is true, that as early as *A Harlot's Progress*, Hogarth 'had detected the analogy between the emulation of upper-class behaviour and the copying of art' as they 'both assume that the copy is as good as the original'.²⁷ While he was striving for the Engravers' Copyright Act, 'Hogarth thematized copying in *A Rake's Progress*, which is about genuine versus imitation, original versus copy in the story of the merchant's son who tries to be an aristocratic rake'.²⁸ Even more provocatively, in *The Art of Success*, discussions about copies and originals go hand in hand with the protagonist's extraordinary metamorphoses and multiple lives. Dear engages defiantly with what Bindman describes as 'the different and sometimes contradictory *personae* attributed to Hogarth by himself, by his contemporaries and by posterity'²⁹ and offers a prismatic characterization of the rake-husband-intellectual-craftsman and moralist-cum-debauchee.

The issues of copying, misrepresentation and performance coalesce in the emotional prison scene featuring Sarah Sprackling's portrait, which is

---

[26] Nikos Stangos (ed.), *David Hockney by David Hockey: My Early Years* (London: Thames and Hudson, 1976), 91.
[27] Paulson, *Hogarth*, 36–7.
[28] Ibid.
[29] David Bindman, *Hogarth and His Times: Serious Comedy* (London: British Museum Press, 1997), 1.

obviously inspired by Hogarth's portrait of the murderess Sarah Malcolm. Interestingly, Hogarth's obsession with the piracy and merchandizing of his works – on punch bowls or snuffboxes – finds a dramatic parallel in Sarah's obsession with her own image and Hogarth's distortion of it. Thus, Sarah is repeatedly mirroring herself in reflecting surfaces such as a metal spoon or the water in a bowl:

> *When finished [washing], she looks into the water with distaste. She arranges her filthy clothes as neatly as she can. She has a silver spoon concealed in a pocket. She polishes it up and checks her reflection. […] Sarah takes out her spoon, polishes it, stares at the picture, stares at her reflection, stares at the picture again.*
>
> **Sarah** It's warped.
> **William** No, the spoon's warped, the spoon distorts.
> **Sarah** That's a good silver spoon! Are you telling me I look like that?
> **William** I'm not completely useless with a stick of chalk.
> **Sarah** Liar! (*Art* 24–5, 35)

In engaging so intently with problems related to likeness and representation, the scene brings into focus the larger debates on portraiture that marked both the route towards the foundation of the Royal Academy of Arts and the dispute on figuration and realism in the London of the 1980s, largely triggered by the group of figurative painters (Lucian Freud, Francis Bacon, Frank Auerbach) who had migrated to Bohemian Soho, as 'guardians of the Great Tradition of "British" figurative oil painting' that traces its line back to William Hogarth.[30]

Hogarth's portrait of Sarah Malcolm, one of 'the lowest denizens of the London Underworld',[31] painted at a time when Hogarth was 'poised uneasily between the world of high society and the lowest depths',[32] hovers of course over the artist's visit to Newgate and conversation with the other Sarah. With Malcolm's portrait, Hogarth reasserted forcefully his choice to find his 'subject matter not in the Bible or epic literature but in real life and even in the streets of London',[33] making for an episode in which genuine curiosity and interest in physiognomy are possibly not exempt

---

[30] Sue Malvern, 'The Spaces of British Art: Patronage, Institutions, Audiences', in Chris Stephens (ed.), *The History of British Art* (London: Tate Publishing, 2008), 224.
[31] Paulson, *Hogarth*, 7.
[32] Ibid., 10.
[33] Bindman, *Hogarth and His Times*, 15.

from a shade of exploitative cynicism.[34] Dear speculates that Sarah, dissatisfied with the artist's portrait, reclaims it, since, she believes, it fails to capture her true 'essence' (*Art* 36), thus touching upon one of the most contentious issues in art history: the relation between a subject and their representation and the freedom of the artist. Even on stage, artists often leave their sitters unsatisfied with portraits that the latter find deceiving: we might recall HMQ (Queen Elizabeth II) in *A Question of Attribution*, for example, lamenting the failure of many portraitists and declaring that some of them were guilty of misrepresenting not only her but also her horse (*Question* 338). She confides her dislike of 'avant-garde' artists, the Picassos or Bacons, who would probably portray her 'with two noses' or as 'the Screaming Queen' (*Question* 338-9), while she declares that she likes her Annigoni portrait because it 'does look like a photograph' (although she does not say which one, among those painted by the artist between 1954 and 1972). Meanwhile, in Howard Barker's *Scenes from an Execution*, the Doge of Venice is yet more displeased, standing ready to send to prison the brilliant but impudent painter Galactia who dared not to celebrate his brother enough and failed to give him 'a prominent enough position' in her painting of the Battle of Lepanto (*Scenes* 261).

In *The Art of Success*, Sarah would like to appear 'as a proper lady' (*Art* 34) while holding on to her identity as a murderess (*Art* 38) and invites the artist to imagine her in the scenario of a conversation piece, with 'the lapdog and the velvet and the negro feller with the studded silver collar' (*Art* 30). The reference to *Marriage à la mode* and *A Harlot's Progress* is transparent, emphasized moreover by the allusion to a Black subject. Many portrait-related issues are dramatized in the Newgate scene. First of all, the whole episode must be framed in relation to the perennial aesthetic argument of the century between Reynold's grand style and the imitation of nature, rule and variety, tradition and observation.[35] But, beyond the discussion of form, what is crucially at stake is Sarah's body. As a sitter, she takes offence at having been portrayed as a common prostitute:

Sarah   Are you telling me I look like that?

Liar! … Look at her with the little pout and the sparkle in the corner of her eye. The face is hard. But! Do I ever sit like that with my damn knees apart? I do not. You give me desire. I have none!

---

[34] Paulson, *Hogarth*, 7-11.
[35] Bindman, *Hogarth and His Times*, 15-18.

[...] The whole blasted reason I'm in here in the first place is that I would not whore! And you gone and made me one!
[...] I have a reputation like anyone else! [...] You have made me some creation of your own. Warped what you see sitting here. You assumed. You are a prick.
[...] Give me my likeness back, you are stealing it, you are taking my soul. (*Art* 36–7)

Sarah's virulence is primarily a reminder of the feminine bodies on sale in London, of all the 'fallen' women who eventually came to be captured in so many Hogarthian pictures and engravings. Dear's treatment of Sarah Sprackling poignantly conflates both the roguish search for commodified bodies in the streets and the artist's eye selecting the more titillating details for his work. Sarah complains bitterly about her portrait, which she believes has little to do with her: 'How does he expect to put the whole of me, all my doings, all my dreams and disappointments in a few small dollops of paint?' (*Art* 73). The two Sarahs were never to be represented in a carefree or cheerful note. As a matter of fact, they are members of a large community of women visually captured on the edge of crime, as if to signify once more the perverse erotic attraction attached to the image of criminal women, from Judith's archetypal killing of Holofernes, which would meaningfully reappear in Breach's play *It's True, It's True, It's True* (2019), to Marcus Harvey's *Myra*, his portrait of the serial child killer Myra Hindley, famously and chillingly painted with children's handprints, and shown in the 1997 *Sensation* exhibition discussed in Chapter 1.

If the process of portraiture interrogates the identity of both artist and sitter, it is also closely embroiled in the question of property. Because – as per the question that is so central to Dear's Hogarth – who owns the picture and the person represented? Appropriating Sarah's image and bending it to a vision of his own, Dear's Hogarth cruelly reminds her that the painting belongs to him, something which entails both legal ownership and the projection of the artist's will and perception: 'I'm truly sorry, Sarah, but it's mine, I own it, I hold a thing called copyright, you see' (*Art* 37). The artist is indeed the master of his sitter's destiny: if he gives the portrait up, 'the world will never hear of Sarah Sprackling, she will never have existed, she will be a ghost, who stalks the landscape of my brain' (*Art* 86). But properties, especially artistic ones, are subject to piracy, as William Hogarth knew all too well, having been the victim of so many. In this context, it is worth recalling the famous adaptation of Hogarth's picture, *Sarah Malcolm in Prison Writing Her Note*, a copy engraved for Boydell in 1791 by an unknown artist, in which Malcolm's 'original' features were manipulated to give her a more 'feminine' look, depriving her one more time of her identity.[36] Nick Dear's emphasis on the interrelated processes of appropriation, piracy and duplication, legal or illegal, is a double-sided mirror held to the practices of the eighteenth century and simultaneously to their revival in late-twentieth-century visual and performative culture.

Questions of attribution

Hare's *The Bay at Nice* (1986), Bennett's *A Question of Attribution* (1988) and, later, Gray's *The Old Masters* (2004): these three plays seem to respond to the number of remarkable studies that appeared in the 1980s and 1990s dealing with the past and the contemporary fascination with heritage.[37] For a number of different reasons, the three playwrights bring controversial figures and historical periods to life by wrestling with history and documents. Each, in their own way, focuses on the question of authenticity in art and life in plays that mimetically stage well-developed stories without explicitly questioning their authorial appropriation (and manipulation) of 'real' material, although Bennett's ironic and detached deconstruction of history/story indirectly alludes to problems related to the creative process.

Viewed together, the three plays provide an engaging guide to issues surrounding the process of art attribution and the implied 'war' between the 'critical eye of the connoisseur' and the 'emerging array of scientific and forensic tests' promising 'objectivity and reliability'.[38] This was an increasingly important issue in the growing art world and market and had earlier been fuelled in the 1920s by the cause célèbre of Andrée and Harry Han's controversial version of Leonardo's *La Belle Ferronnière*.

The Bay at Nice[39] brings the issues of art authenticity and curatorship to the theatre in an unprecedented way that has paved the way for new theatre

---

[36] Elizabeth Einberg, *William Hogarth. A Complete Catalogue of the Paintings* (New Haven: Yale University Press, 2016), 68.
[37] David Lowenthal, *The Past Is a Foreign Country* (Cambridge: Cambridge University Press, 1985); Raphael Samuel (ed.), *Patriotism: The Making and Unmaking of British National Identity* (London: Routledge, 1987); Kevin Walsh, *The Representation of the Past: Museums and Heritage in Post-Modern World* (New York: Routledge, 1992).
[38] John Brewer, *The American Leonardo. A Tale of Obsession, Art and Money* (Oxford: Oxford University Press, 2009), 2.
[39] David Hare, 'The Bay at Nice', in *Plays: 2* (London: Faber and Faber, [1986] 1997, 301–60). The 75-minute play was performed at the National's Cottesloe Theatre on 9 September 1986 as the first half of a double bill that contrasts the stark repression of Khrushchev's Russia (*The Bay at Nice*) with the post-war opulence of Eisenhower's Baby Boomers (*Wrecked Eggs*).

openings. It is perhaps the first play to revolve around the authenticity of a work of art – Matisse's eponymous painting, bequeathed to the nation by a Russian émigré.

The action is set in the Hermitage Museum in Leningrad in 1956, where an unnamed assistant curator, unwilling to risk exhibiting a fake, seeks the opinion of someone who 'understands' Matisse's 'spirit', even though the painting has already been authenticated by 'scientific methods', designed to test 'dating, pigment, brushwork' (*Bay* 312, 313). Indeed, Hare offers his audience a brief lesson in the limitations of scientific methods in the analysis of recent paintings:

> **Assistant** […] The scientific experts are used to handling older paintings. […] We know a great deal about pigment chronology. We have radiocarbon. We have X-ray crystallography. We have wet chemistry. All these are invaluable if the painting is old enough. Because dating is what usually gives the forger away. (*Bay* 311)

Hare even refers to Matisse as a 'fanatic' vigilant enough 'to check the works being sold under his name' (*Bay* 313) and the complicated problem of his certificates of authenticity. To verify the touch of the French master's hand in the unsigned painting, the politically cautious curator summons Valentina Nrovka, a student of Matisse when she was a bohemian expatriate in Paris in her youth in the early 1920s. Valentina, who gives an onstage lecture on Matisse's study of the model and his use of colour, quoting the *Notes* of Sarah Stein, a close friend of Matisse who studied at his school (*Bay* 336–7),[40] is regarded as someone who knew him well enough to be able to correctly attribute an otherwise unverifiable painting. As the Assistant points out,

> There are tests. But these are all negative by nature. They tell you if it cannot be Matisse. Dating, pigment, brushwork, so on. If the negative tests are all passed you are forced to conclude the work must be real. The absence of disproof is finally proof. No one ever says 'Oh yes, this is his …' Except … […] Except when there's someone. I don't know … when there's someone who knew him quite well. (*Bay* 314)

---

[40] Sarah Stein, 'Sarah Stein's Notes, 1908', in Jack D. Flam, *Matisse on Art* (Oxford: Phaidon, [1973] 1978), 41–6. Carol Homden, *The Plays of David Hare* (Cambridge: Cambridge University Press, 1995), 145.

Valentina's opinion is important because she understands 'what's called his handwriting', an 'indefinable' painting term that 'it's not quite even signature. It's more than that. It's spirit' (*Bay* 341). By bringing to the stage the long tradition of hostility between connoisseurship as the personal talent of the trained and experienced eye and the 'objective' expertise of science, David Hare imports onto the stage the critical debate in the wider art world about how attribution is made and what effect it has on the status and value of paintings. By inviting his audience to widen and intensify their gaze, Hare also brings crucial political issues to the fore. On a stage that has come to represent an art museum, issues of family life intersect with political and aesthetic questions about display and exhibition.

A veteran of political theatre as he is, Hare sets these art-historical questions against the political, social and cultural situation in Communist Russia in the 1950s, which he defines as one of 'the deadliest moments of Soviet conformity',[41] when propaganda aimed to promote duty, moral integrity and renunciation. Showing how 'political ideologies infuse personal and family relationships',[42] Hare conceives of a chamber piece, or rather an 'art museum piece', that deals with issues of identity by focusing on the social and political constraints at work in the confrontation between Valentina and her thirty-six-year-old daughter, Sophia. On the one hand, the artist who chose responsibility over hedonism and gave up her painting career when she could not allow herself to conform to the Party's restrictive ideology and aesthetics; on the other, the angry revolutionary Sophia, whose only act of rebellion is to divorce her ambitious Party member husband to marry a gentle sixty-three-year-old worker. Public and private worlds blend in the play, as Valentina is called upon to judge the validity of both a painting and a passion.

As he writes in his stage notes, Hare imagines the Hermitage Museum in Leningrad in 1956 as a large room, 'airy and decaying', with 'a gilt ceiling and a beautiful parquet floor', in which, 'at the back hangs Guérin's huge oil painting of *Iris and Morpheus*' (*Bay* 303), 'a triumphant nude sitting on a cloud over the body of the King of Sleep' (Figure 2.1).[43] Fittingly, in a room that Valentina dismisses as a 'graveyard' run by 'old idiots' (*Bay* 303), the graceful classical nudes sitting on a cloud above the body of the King of Sleep seem to mock the socialist realism of Soviet art, which she also strongly criticizes. The woman is so disappointed by what she defines as 'whirlpools

[41] Hare, *David Hare*, xiv.
[42] Richard Boon, *The Cambridge Companion to David Hare* (Cambridge: Cambridge University Press, 2007), 56.
[43] David Hare, *Bay at Nice*. Prompt 'Bible' Script, annotated 4.9.86, National Theatre Archive, RNT/SM/1/268, 1.

The Drama of Authenticity 107

Figure 2.1 *Bay at Nice* written and directed by David Hare. With Colin Stinton as the Assistant curator and Irene Worth as Valentina Nrovka. Cottesloe Theatre at The National Theatre, London, September 1986.

Source: Courtesy Conrad Blakemore / ArenaPAL.

of mud' that she even refuses to visit the museum's new extension, explaining that she 'would rather look at bare walls. At least they are cleanly painted' (*Bay* 304).

The visual conflict between the two pictorial grammars of French Neo-Classicism and Socialist Realism is overshadowed by the presence of Matisse's inspiring art,[44] which is ultimately associated with the freedom and joy that was lacking in Russia, where Valentina and other Russian modernists were not free to exhibit their art. Intriguingly, the fact that Matisse's alleged painting is propped up against a chair, hidden from the view of the spectators, teases their imagination; at the same time, by arousing the spectators' desire to see it, such a device invites them to be ready to sharpen their gaze. It is important to underline that the audience must rely on the words of the Assistant as he describes Matisse's painting to Valentina, not in terms of what it shows but what it leaves out:

> **Assistant** Well, it's like a sketch – I'm not speaking technically … […] I mean a kind of dry-run. For everything that follows. Except the foreground is bare. There is no woman. There is no violin. There is no chair. (*He shrugs.*) There is just a wall. A pair of curtains. Wallpaper. Open windows. The sea. (*There is a sudden silence. Then he shrugs again.*) It is either a copy. Or a beginning. (*Bay* 318–19)

In a way, Hare is suggesting that the audience of *The Bay at Nice* are more attentive viewers than the crowds of people who dutifully rush through museums yet hold little interest in trying to understand what is on display.

It is only at the end of the play that 'the background fades and the stage is filled with the image of the bay at Nice, a pair of open French windows, a balcony, the sea and the sky' (*Bay* 360).[45] As director of his own play, Hare then projected the image of the painting onto the back wall of the Cottesloe Theatre, thus finally giving the audience the thrill of recognition with the vision of what Matisse had painted and they had tried to recall or imagine during the play,[46] and at the same time inviting a consideration of the sorts of tools that might be useful in authenticating both a painting and the purpose and meaning of its exhibition. Hare also asks his audience to reflect on the role of an art museum and the fate of the painting if it is a real Matisse:

---

[44] Homden writes that Hare's choice of Matisse 'is the culmination of an admiration which hung a Matisse cut-out in William's bedroom in *Dreams of Leaving* and was expressed by Andrew and Rebecca in the abandoned first scene of *Pravda*'. (*The Plays*, 145).
[45] Henry Matisse, *Bay at Nice*, 1918, private Collection, oil on canvas, 90 × 71 cm.
[46] Hare, *Bay at Nice*. Prompt 'Bible' Script, 54.

Valentina   […] what will happen to it? They will put it on the walls of this hideous building. And the state will boast that they own it. And people will gawp at it and say 'What does it mean?' Or 'Well, I don't like it.' I am told that in the West now people only look at paintings when they are holding cubes of cheese on the end of the toothpicks. To me, that says everything of what art has become. (*Bay* 307)

No wonder Valentina denounces the danger of Matisse's painting losing its true spirit and becoming something 'the State will boast that they own' and museum visitors 'gawp at' without understanding its meaning (*Bay* 307). Hare does not miss the opportunity to point out how art has increasingly become a commodity, winking at his critic of contemporary American capitalism in *Wrecked Eggs* (the other play in double bill with *The Bay at Nice*) and bringing to the fore one of the most controversial issues of Thatcherite neoliberal ideology. Through Valentina, who recalls that 'in the West now people only look at paintings when they are holding cubes of cheese on the end of toothpicks', Hare alludes to the consequences of economic liberalism, which has turned the art world into a business and art's primary purpose into entertainment for the masses. It is perhaps even worth recalling the many ways in which Thatcherism affected both the style and the content of British theatre, which was so pervaded by the influence of the market that its favourite mantra became 'bums on seats'.[47]

The link between the practice of attribution and the logic of the market would be even more straightforward almost twenty years later, in Simon Gray's *The Old Masters*, which premiered at the Birmingham Repertory Theatre in 2004.[48] An art-historical play firmly grounded in historical research, *The Old Masters* is a middlebrow play that deftly exposes how morally murky the relationship between dealer and connoisseur can become. It looks back to a time when the distinction between original and copy became all the more urgent with the Old Master boom, which produced record prices and the emergence of a new type of collector, particularly the new American collectors, who were too busy or lacked sufficient interest to train their eye or sensibilities, and who therefore used to appoint the art

---

[47] Michael Billington, *State of the Nation. British Theatre since 1945* (London: Faber and Faber, 2007), 284.
[48] Simon Gray, *The Old Masters* (London: Faber and Faber, 2004). It was first presented at the Birmingham Repertory Theatre on 4 June 2004 by Greg Ripley-Duggan with Duveen Productions and Ted Tulchin in a Birmingham Repertory Theatre Production. It then moved to the Comedy Theatre (now Harold Pinter Theatre) from 1 July to 18 December 2004.

historian as 'a guiding authority for the collector' (and thus for the dealer as well).[49]

Set in the home of the world-famous American art historian Bernard Berenson (BB) at Villa I Tatti in 1937, when Benito Mussolini had already signed the military alliance with Germany, the play raises gripping moral and ethical questions about the validity and importance of artistic attribution, starting with another cause célèbre, the attribution of a celebrated painting, *L'adorazione dei pastori*.[50] Also known as the *Allendale Nativity*, it is famous for the long-standing dispute among experts as to whether it is a late Giorgione, a work by Giorgione's pupil, Titian, or a collaboration between the two artists (*Masters* 53–4).

The play focuses on the final dispute over the attribution of the painting and the subsequent break-up of 'the secret partnership'[51] between the expert connoisseur of Italian Renaissance art BB and the brilliant English art dealer Sir Joseph Duveen, 'a big shark in the turbulent waters of the art market, a creature who knew better than most how to ride the wave of American prosperity and to scare his rivals with a predatory show of force'.[52] Whereas *The Bay at Nice* pits two women in a battle of duty and desire, *The Old Masters* revolves around what Gray describes as 'an epic confrontation between the two morally crippled Titans',[53] who are described by BB's librarian and lover: Joe Duveen, 'a businessman, a salesman, an entrepreneur' and BB, 'a great man' who 'has taught people how to look at a painting and see into the soul of artists long dead', and who then, as he admits, was forced by circumstances of poverty to negotiate 'about money and reputation' (*Masters* 35). Indeed, the play rests on the 'clash of male egos' and the performance of two veterans, Edward Fox as the despotic expert and Peter Bowles as the wily dealer, who, under Harold Pinter's direction, alone 'justifies the play', as Billington wrote in his review.[54]

For all their differences, Duveen and BB were in complete agreement on one point. They were both 'profoundly suspicious and sometimes arrogantly dismissive of the scientific investigation of painting',[55] apparently fearing

---

[49] Germain Seligman, *Merchant of Art: 1880–1960. Eighty Years of Professional Collecting* (New York: Appleton-Century-Crofts, 1961), 124.
[50] Giorgione, *L'adorazione dei pastori* (*The Adoration of the Shepherds*), 1505–10, oil on panel, 90.8 x 110.5 cm, Samuel H. Kress Collection, National Gallery of Art, Washington.
[51] Colin Simpson, *The Artful Partners. The Secret Association of Bernard Berenson and Joseph Duveen* (London: J. Simpson, 1988), I.
[52] Brewer, *American Leonardo*, 101.
[53] Simon Gray, 'Author's Introduction', Simon Gray's website: http://simongray.org.uk/plays/the-old-masters/ (accessed 8 May 2023).
[54] Michael Billington, 'The Old Master. Comedy, London', *The Guardian*, 2 July 2004.
[55] Brewer, *American Leonardo*, 294.

its intrusion into the world of the connoisseurs. Reluctantly drawn into the dispute over the Hahns' *La Belle Ferronnière*, Duveen 'airily dismissed' the American Leonardo as a copy or a fake without seeing it,[56] and BB declared that it was 'a bad copy'. Although the American art historian 'frankly' admitted that he was 'not an expert on techniques or the chemical composition of pigments in paintings or the mechanical manner in which painters go about their work', he claimed that a lifetime of study of Italian paintings had nevertheless allowed him to acquire a 'knowledge that almost amounted to a sixth sense so that he was able to place a painting in its exact school or era'.[57] Gray's *The Old Masters* therefore shed light on one of the most obscure and controversial chapters in the history of art, exploring BB's contradictory positions on the science of attribution as, towards the end of his career, and after many a reckless attribution, he began to find his involvement in the art trade 'a source of anguished dissatisfaction'.[58] In a few lines, Gray's BB expresses the disillusionment and sense of failure that the real BB tried to exorcize in the confessional pages of *Sketch for a Self-Portrait*, where he blames himself for not always choosing 'the most spiritually profitable fields'. He admits that he should not have become 'that equivocal thing, an "expert"'[59] and openly condemns 'the pig trade' – a phrase used by the art historian and his wife Mary to describe the art trade, as Ernest Samuels writes in his biography of BB (and which was also the title of an earlier version of the play, *The Pig Trade*):[60]

> **BB** I have done nothing in my life, my life, except acquire, acquire my collections, acquire my reputation, acquire my I Tatti [...] There is a voice I hear, a piping voice, no, a shrill, jeering voice, that says well, well, it doesn't matter, nothing matters, you and Joe, Joe and you, you have earned nothing, you deserve nothing but each other –' (*Masters* 35)

Gray's BB thus reveals that he has sold his idealism off to the dealings of the art trade, of which Duveen is a master, and which involves 'buy[ing] low and sell[ing] high [...], conflicts of interests, dissimulation, lavish puffery'.[61] Chapter 4 offers a more detailed analysis of how *The Old Master* provides the audience with an informative insight into one of the most exciting periods

---

[56] Ibid., 12.
[57] Ernest Samuels, *Bernard Berenson. The Making of a Legend* (Cambridge, MA: Harvard University Press, 1987), 316–17.
[58] Ibid., 3.
[59] Bernard Berenson, *Sketch for a Self-Portrait* (Firenze: Pantheon, 1949), 38.
[60] Simon Gray, *The Pig Trade*, in *Four Plays* (London: Faber and Faber, 2004), 1–89.
[61] Samuels, *Bernard Berenson*, 3.

in art history, when the arrival of the wealthy American collectors, Frick and Huntingdon, Mellon and Kress, transformed the art market and changed the relationships between collectors, dealers, experts and museums. Suffice it, for now, to recall Duveen's witty and ferocious impersonation of dime store millionaire Samuel Henry Kress at the beginning of his career as a collector of European art and philanthropist, although the latter aspect is never mentioned in the play (*Masters* 48–50). Is Duveen different from the kind of crude dealer he pretends to despise when he tries to reconcile pricelessness with a price? Is BB? These are the questions Gray asks his audience as he attempts to re-create the identities of the two characters on stage with the same consistency that BB himself demanded in his attribution.

Confronted by Duveen, whom he accuses of being 'like a mere tradesman', talking of money, profit and loss (*Masters* 40), BB poses as the genius who has 'the eye, the mind, the memory' (*Master* 46) and remains true to his integrity despite his reputation, which is losing its value in the marketplace as both his partner and his wife remind him (*Masters* 59, 71). As if this were not enough, in depicting BB's struggle between erudition and commerce, the playwright does not forget to allude to BB's doubts about his earlier attribution of a Masaccio, the *Madonna of Humility*[62] and Mary's ghost-writing for him of the Four Gospels (as his four books were collectively known by several English-speaking art historians).[63]

Gray highlights the lies, double-dealing and corruption of the past that still resonate in the early 2000s, when conflicts of interest are still rife, with trustees of public galleries also running companies that through sponsorship take advantage of their positions. Take, for example, the bold sponsorships by Gilbert de Botton when he was a trustee of the Tate, or by Charles Saatchi when he was a trustee of the Whitechapel Art Gallery, as revealed by Chin-tao-Wu in her analysis of the sly ways in which free-market capitalism infiltrates art.[64]

The Old Masters concludes with BB alone at his desk, eyes closed, demonstrating one of the most essential skills of the connoisseur, the ability to recall the visual memory of a painting – in this case the *Allendale Nativity* – and finally conjure it up in words for the audience. As the sounds of war grow louder in the background and the waning of a world and the end of a culture

---

[62] Ibid., 375–6.
[63] BB's four books are *Venetian Painting in America* (1916), *The Study and Criticism of Italian Art* (1916), *Essays in the Study of Sienese Painting* (1918) and *Studies in Medieval Painting* (1930).
[64] Chin-tao Wu, *Privatising Culture. Corporate Art Intervention since the 1980s* (London: Verso, 2002), 116–21.

render any question of attribution irrelevant and idle, BB re-evaluates the painting and the reasons for its attribution by recalling the eyes and the hair of the two shepherds:

> **BB** Yes, because one can't see their faces! (*Laughs almost childishly.*) Isn't it ridiculous, that one never remembers that? And yet one should, because that's how it brings the eye – the whole eye – to Mary, Joseph and the baby – just as you'd do it on stage, a stage grouping, really, as elementary as that – crude almost, until the eye goes beyond, to the boys under the tree, beyond them to the church, then beyond to the mountains, the clouds – one has his hair cut *en brosse*, the other longer, almost ill-kempt, now, now, I've said it I shall remember it whenever needed – (*Little pause*) – It is needed now.
> *Sounds of war louder and louder.*
> Lights. Curtain. (*Masters* 77–8)

Here, perhaps, Gray draws on BB's *Rudiments of Connoisseurship*, in which the art historian follows the empiricism of his master, Giovanni Morelli, in considering minor details to be the most characteristic parts of a painting and the surest guide to attribution. Thus, he writes that the treatment of the hair 'is apt of being characteristic, because of its very nature' and assumes 'almost a calligraphic character';[65] this is why BB, in the play, attempts to remember the way Titian drew hair. Interestingly, he recalls the composition of the *Allendale Nativity* by comparing it to 'a stage grouping', thus making a connection between art and theatre. It is no surprise, then, that the Metropolitan Museum of Art, which, incidentally, had a long association with Sir Joseph Duveen,[66] hosted two staged readings of the play in the Met's auditorium, using the magic of PowerPoint both to evoke works of art from the period and introduce the cast of the production at the Long Wharf Theatre in New Haven (2011).[67]

---

[65] Bernard Berenson, *Rudiments of Connoisseurship* (New York: Schocken Books, 1962), 127, 126.

[66] As the Met's longtime chief spokesman Harold Holzer notes, the museum owns more than 120 European paintings that at some point passed through Duveen's galleries, and in 1968 acquired the Duveen Brothers' records (a vast amount of material including stock books, sales books, invoice books, shipping receipts, customer ledgers, loose photographs, 2,000 glass negatives and hundreds of correspondence files that include letters to, from and about clients, museums, scholars and other dealers), which were donated to the Research Library at the Getty Research Institute in 1996, though it has also since acquired a microfilm copy.

[67] Kate Taylor, 'A Drama of Attribution to Play Out at the Metropolitan Museum', *The New York Times*, 28 April 2011. https://archive.nytimes.com/artsbeat.blogs.nytimes.com/2011/04/28/a-drama-of-art-attribution-to-play-out-at-the-metropolitan-museum/ (accessed 27 September 2023).

Thus, in the face of the impending catastrophe of the Second World War and all the other conflicts that followed, BB challenges himself and his audience by questioning the meaning of art and ethics in a wartime situation:

> What does it matter a few lies or a few truths in the attribution of a Giorgione or a Titian, one's as good as the other when there's nobody left to look at them, just the duck [Mussolini] and Hitler and the new barbarians, who'll make bonfires of them along with all the books – Sophocles, Aeschylus, Plato, Titian, Giorgione, Leonardo. (*Masters* 73)

This crucial dilemma echoes, without resolution, from play to play, from Edgar's *Pentecost* to Hannah Khalil's recent *A Museum in Baghdad*, from decade to decade, continuing to haunt and torment artists, museum curators and playwrights.

Before Gray's *The Old Masters*, Alan Bennett had made up his mind about BB and the social sanctification of art. In 1964, he wrote a parody of an account of a visit to the American art historian BB entitled *Ta Ta I Tatti*. Later, in 1993, in his lecture *Going to the Pictures*, he described him not only as 'both intolerable and silly' but also 'a bit of a rogue' because 'for much of his life he was on a retainer from the art dealer Duveen, which meant that some of his attributions were more self-serving than scholarly'.[68] Little wonder, then, that BB receives similar treatment in Bennett's successful *A Question of Attribution*,[69] which premiered at the National Theatre on 1 December 1988 as part of a double bill entitled *Single Spies* with *An Englishman Abroad*. The most successful example of the unusual exploitation of the connoisseurship debate, *A Question of Attribution* recalls BB's mis-attributions rather than his expertise and how BB himself, however unwittingly, contributed to the market for forgeries. When he came across groups of Italian Renaissance drawings similar in style to Botticelli's, attributed to five different artists but with a family resemblance, he assumed the existence of an unknown artist and invented the 'Amico di Sandro – the friend of Botticelli', until, as 'the work of attribution progressed', he 'came to see that these drawings were actually the early work of the Florentine painter, Filippino Lippi. There was no Amico di Sandro. He had been invented to fit the evidence, but he did not exist' (*Question* 350).

---

[68] Alan Bennett, 'Going to the Pictures', in *Untold Stories* (London: Faber and Faber, 2006), 456.
[69] Alan Bennett, 'A Question of Attribution', in *Alan Bennett: Plays 2* (London: Faber and Faber, [1989] 1998), 301–51.

Oxford history graduate Alan Bennett conceives a play that is 'an inquiry in which the circumstances are imaginary, but the pictures are real'[70] and which interweaves a fascinating question of art attribution with equally intriguing investigations into the mysterious double life of Sir Anthony Blunt: professor of Art History at the University of London, acknowledged expert on French painter Nicolas Poussin, director of the Courtauld Institute of Art from 1947 to 1974 and Keeper of the Queen's Pictures from 1945 to 1972, he was also the 'Fourth Man' of the notorious Cambridge spies group. Exposed by MI5 and the British government in 1964, he was given immunity in return for the names of other spies from the period until 1979, when the Thatcher government publicly disclosed his status as a double agent acting for both the Secret Intelligence Service and the KGB. In the play, Bennett portrays Blunt before the scandal when, still undercover, he is gently interrogated by Detective Chubb in search of other spies, while Blunt himself investigates two Old Masters. In a much more complex way than in Hare's *The Bay at Nice* and Gray's *The Old Masters*, the 'question of attribution' announced by Bennett's title becomes the framework of the play, symmetrically investing both the refined art world of the Old Masters and the brutal world of Cold War espionage with an unpredictable and at times hilarious overlap of thematic layers and narrative situations. The uncertain nature of *The Triple Portrait*, a painting that conceals a third, a fourth and later a fifth man under its surface, only to be revealed by X-ray analysis, is an obvious metaphor for Blunt's multiple, hidden identities, and a fitting starting point for exploring the nature of authenticity and the process of authentication, both in art and life. Bennett skilfully intersects and overlaps the investigations of a connoisseur, Sir Anthony Blunt, on the one hand, and a detective, Chubb, on the other hand, the latter a fictional character invented by Bennett.

As well as discussing the practice of attribution, connoisseurship and forgery, Blunt instructs the audience on and off stage with academic lectures illustrated by slides projected on the screen, as the stage directions indicate. Thus, Bennett transforms the stage into a room in the Courtauld Institute where its 'sophisticated and metropolitan' director (*Question* 310) lectures on the Renaissance art world, sharing Bennett's humour and disenchantment. Alongside the lectures and the commitment to study and conservation, the various aspects of Blunt's professional life are staged, and the audience is even offered the spectacle of modern scientific techniques to ensure attribution. In more than one scene, Blunt is on stage with an unnamed Restorer, examining and analysing *Titian and a Venetian Senator* before and after cleaning, and

---

[70] Ibid., 301.

searching for the meaning of Titian's *Allegory of Prudence*, 'an emblematic painting, a puzzle picture'. He compares slides of the two paintings, which are projected onto a screen, and explains their relationship, appropriating the words of Erwin Panofsky and St John Gore (*Question* 309, 346–8).[71] He explains that art is rarely what it seems and that in a painting, 'there isn't a "hang of it"' (*Question* 325) and warns that paintings 'do not purport to be anything other than paintings', thus suggesting that it is rather the viewer who makes claim for them (*Question* 342–3). Consequently, he presents Titian's *Allegory of Prudence* as 'a puzzle picture', whose meaning is difficult to grasp and, following Panofsky, he invites Chubb (and the audience) to consider it not only as 'a visual paraphrase of the *Three Ages of Man*' but also as a modern allegory of prudence (*Question* 325–6).

He argues, therefore, that Chubb's misinterpretations and mistakes in interpreting the painting stem from the fact that he has adopted 'the techniques of facile identification favoured in [his] profession' as a detective, while ignoring that in art 'it isn't quite like that. Appearances deceive. Art is seldom quite what it seems' (*Question* 326). Undoubtedly, the X-ray, infrared and laser micro-analyses of Titian's paint and brushstrokes, invisible to the naked eye, add to the complexity of the concept of forgery, for all these techniques suggest that the façade lies, and reality is what lies behind it – a truth that applies not only to paintings but also to the character of Blunt.

Surprisingly, in the very first scene, Bennett's Blunt, defying any snobbery about connoisseurship, confesses to the Restorer that he has 'no eye' and declares that according to the hierarchy devised by art historian Kenneth Clark, he belongs to the group of people who, when looking at the Old Masters, 'see what it is when you tell them':

> **Blunt** I should warn you. I don't have an eye. K. Clark was saying the other day (I don't *think* the remark was directed at me) that people who look at Old Masters fall into three groups: those who see what it is without being told; those who see it when you tell them; and those who can't see it whatever you do. I just about make the second category. It means I can't date pictures. […] For an art historian it's rather humiliating. Like being a wine taster and having no sense of smell. (*Question* 310)

---

[71] In 'A Note on the Paintings' Bennett acknowledges the play 'owes a great deal' to two articles in which the attributions of two Old Masters paintings are discussed: 'Titian's *Allegory of Prudence*' by Erwin Panofsky (in *Meaning in the Visual Arts*, Peregrine, 1974) and *Five Portraits* by St John Gore (*Burlington Magazine*, 100, 1958)', 351–2. In Bennett, *Plays 2*, 303.

While serving as a means for the character to introduce himself unpretentiously to the audience, the reference to Baron Clark of Saltwood is also relevant for the connotations his name invites them to consider. A patron, collector and controversial director of the National Gallery in the years 1934–44, 'the most publicly visible Leonardo expert in Britain'[72] and therefore directly (even if reluctantly) involved in the dispute over Hahn's *La Belle Ferronnière*, as well as being the first to bring discussions of the twentieth-century art to a mass television audience, Clark was a great popularizer. According to the press release announcing the exhibition *Kenneth Clark: Looking for Civilization* at the Tate Britain (2014), his belief in the social importance of art and everyone's right to access to it 'anticipated much of today's culture of accessibility and democratisation of art in museums and galleries'.[73] Undoubtedly, Chubb would agree with his view that the primary function of galleries should not be scholarship or conservation but to feed the public's imagination. More importantly, one might think that Bennett himself was inspired by Clark's ideas when he decided to offer his audiences authentic Art-history lectures, which are generally restricted to a small elite of experts. Like Clark, Bennett believes that pictures and art museums 'belong as much to a boy or girl sleeping in a doorway in the Strand as they do to the benefactors whose names are emblazoned on the walls' and praises the National Gallery for being 'a free university of art'.[74] Moreover, in 1993, Bennett even took part in a television documentary about the Leeds city Art Gallery, *Portrait or Bust*, to 'advertise' his own 'ignorance in the hope that it would encourage people with similar feelings of inadequacy where art is concerned' to visit the gallery anyway.[75] In this sense, it is not surprising that during his interrogations in Blunt's room at the Courtauld Institute, Detective Chubb discovers an interest in iconology and a pleasure in strolling through art galleries and museums, such as the National Gallery or the British Museum. A parodic double for Blunt, Chubb even attempts to interpret and appreciate Old Master paintings, often discussing his clumsy and comical conclusions with the director of the Courtauld Institute:

> **Chubb**   Michelangelo? I don't think they are all that lifelike, frankly. The women aren't. They're just like men with tits, and the tits look as if they've been put on with an ice-cream scoop. Has nobody pointed that out? (*Question* 319)

---

[72] Brewer, *American Leonardo*, 240.
[73] Tate Press Release of the exhibition 'Kenneth Clark: Looking for Civilisation', *Tate*. https://www.tate.org.uk/press/press-releases/kenneth-clark-looking-civilisation (accessed 8 May 2023).
[74] Bennett, *Going to the Pictures*, 475.
[75] Alan Bennett, 'Portrait or Bust', in *Untold Stories*, 494–514.

Chubb has a naïve (or innocent?[76]) eye and a dilettantish but genuine passion for art, which prompts Blunt to remark wryly that he hopes 'the security of the nation is not being neglected in favour of your studies in iconography' (*Question* 325). Although it is only a joke, Blunt hits the nail on the head, for art really does seem to distract the detective, who even confesses that one morning he was about to forget one of his appointments when he wandered 'round the British Museum, sure to come across something of interest' (*Question* 314).

Blunt patiently guides Chubb (and the audience) through the intricacies and mysteries of the art world, often through witty exchanges full of very funny subtexts. Thus, as they watch black and white photographs of various alleged spies from the 1930s projected onto a screen alongside reproductions of Titian's *Allegory of Prudence*[77] and the *Triple Portrait*,[78] formerly attributed to Titian and part of HM the Queen's collection, the misunderstandings between the art historian/spy and the detective, who is ignorant of even the basics of art history, are inevitable and hilarious:

[…] *a new photograph comes up on the screen.*

Blunt   No. No. N … no.
Chubb   Sure?
Blunt   It's the neck. The *neck* could be Piero della Francesca.
Chubb   Who's he?
Blunt   Well, he was many things, but he wasn't a member of the Communist Party. (*Question* 312–13)

Thanks to Blunt, Chubb, who is himself an expert in investigation and interrogation and accustomed to distrusting appearances out of professional bias, discovers that iconology is a minefield and that gallery rooms are full of treacherous paintings to be approached with techniques not unlike those of criminal investigation and counter-espionage.

The debate on the mysteries of art and mis-attributions also sparks a number of witty and humorous conversations between Blunt and the Queen herself. In their sharp crosstalk, Bennett examines the problem of the

---

[76] Roger Shattuck, *The Innocent Eye. On Modern Literature and the Arts* (New York: Farrar Straus Giroux, 1984).
[77] Titian (and studio), *Allegoria della Prudenza* (*An Allegory of Prudence*), c. 1550–65, oil on canvas, 75.5 × 68.4 cm, The National Gallery, London.
[78] After Titian, *Titian and His Friends*, 1550–60, oil on canvas, 82.8 × 94.5 cm, Windsor Castle, Royal Collection Trust.

authenticity of works of art and explores the difference between forgeries and fakes. To HMQ, who sardonically protests at Blunt's role in proving that her 'pictures are fake' (*Question* 333) and who intends the use of the word 'fake' to mean the fraudulent imitation of something else, Blunt explains that the boundaries between truth and falsehood are often difficult to define. Just 'because something is not what it is said to be […] it doesn't mean it is a fake. It may just have been wrongly attributed'. 'A painting is a document' that 'has to be read in the context of art history' (*Question* 333), he argues, in line with the real-life Blunt,[79] who wrote that to appreciate an artist, 'it is essential to understand the intellectual climate in which he worked, and the ideas – religious, philosophical, or aesthetic – in which he believed and which influenced his working method as well as his paintings'.[80] He also argues that Old Masters are 'seldom forgeries':

> **Blunt** They are sometimes not what we think they are, but that's different. The question doesn't pose itself in the form, 'Is this a fake?' so much as 'Who painted this picture and why?' Is it a Titian, or a pupil or pupils of Titian? Is it someone who paints like Titian because he admires him and can't help painting in the same way? The public are rather tiresomely fascinated by forgery – more so, I'm afraid, than they are by the real thing. […] (*Question* 342)

Acknowledging that notions of truth and falsehood may change or contradict each other, Blunt contends that the study of forgeries themselves is critical because of what Jones calls 'the unrivalled potential of fakes as evidence of the sense of history possessed by their creators'.[81]

In response to his assertion that forgery is 'much more a feature of modern or relatively modern paintings than of Old Masters' (*Question* 343), HMQ reminds Blunt of the Vermeer forgeries by van Meegeren, one of the world's most skillful forgers. Publicly tried for high treason during the Second World War for selling Vermeer's *Christ with the Woman Taken in Adultery* to Hermann Göring, he saved himself by confessing that the work was his own, thus undermining the credibility of the experts. Elisabeth expresses her disbelief that van Meegeren could have fooled the art world for so long:

> **HMQ** […] Those were forgeries. Of Old Masters. […] Moreover, these Van Meegerens didn't seem to me to be the least bit like. Terrible daubs.

---

[79] Anthony Blunt, 'Standards-I', *The Spectator*, CLXI, II (16 September), 1938, 403–5.
[80] Anthony Blunt, *Nicholas Poussin* (London: Phaidon Press, 1967), ix.
[81] Jones, *Why Fakes?*, 12.

God knows, one is no expert on Vermeer, but if I could tell they were fakes why couldn't other people see it at the time? When was it, in the forties? (*Question* 343)

Echoing the Assistant curator's statement in *The Bay at Nice* that 'dating is what usually gives the forger away' (*Bay* 311), Blunt explains that it is time that reveals the age of a painting. Although a forger may reproduce the style and details of his subject in the most exact manner, as a painter he is nevertheless never of the original artist's time, and however slavishly he imitates, he does so in the fashion of his own time, so that with the passage of years it is this element which dates, which begins to seem old-fashioned and which finally unmasks him (*Question* 344). Blunt would therefore agree with David Lowenthal that 'revealing hidden assumptions about the past they claim to stem from, fakes advance our understanding no less than the truths that expose them'.[82] Indeed, as the small 2010 exhibition *Close Examination: Fakes, Mistakes and Discoveries* at the National Gallery would later show, paintings can look very different today from when they were created. Sometimes this is the result of natural processes, such as the ageing of materials; sometimes, human intervention has played a role, as in the case of 'the few *pentimenti*' in the *Annunciation*, of which the Palace footman Colin gives a technical description (*Question* 331). Interpreting 'the information gathered through scientific analysis in conjunction with art historical knowledge allows us to situate the painting within the context of its era, and to understand how it came to be the artwork we see in a gallery or museum today', as National Gallery curator Marjorie E. Wieseman writes in the catalogue for the National Gallery exhibition.[83]

Rather than forgeries, Blunt speaks rather of 'enigmas', or 'riddles', and claims that solving them is one of the tasks of art historians, although he reminds the Queen that one must never forget that 'a great painting will still elude us, as art will always elude exposition':

> **Blunt** […] The painting is a riddle, and this and similar riddles are quests one can pursue for years; their solution is one of the functions of art historian. But it is only one of his functions. […] Because, though the solution might add to our appreciation of this painting, paintings, we must never forget, are not there primarily to be solved.

---

[82] Lowenthal, *The Past Is a Foreign Country*, 190.
[83] Marjorie E. Wieseman, A *Closer Look. Deceptions and Discoveries* (London: National Gallery Company, 2010), 5.

A great painting will still elude us, as art will always elude exposition. (*Question* 348)

Appropriately, the play embraces hermeneutic uncertainty and leaves all the mysteries unsolved: those surrounding the two paintings – *The Triple Portrait* and the *Allegory of Prudence* – and Blunt's life, as well as the secret conspiracies of a still obscure chapter of British history. Significantly, at the end of the play, in front of new photographs of alleged spies, Blunt bursts out impatiently: 'Who are they all? I don't know if it matters. Behind them lurk other presences, other hands. A whole gallery of possibilities. The real Titian an Allegory of Prudence. The false one an Allegory of Supposition. It is never-ending' (*Question* 351).

While questioning the problematic relationship between connoisseurship and science, art scholarship and espionage, Bennett humorously uses Blunt's double (or triple) life as a paradigm of the impossibility of making a final decision about authenticity and identity. When, in one of her many double entendres, HMQ deliberately misinterprets Poussin, the French painter on whom Blunt is an expert, as the French word for 'chicken' (*Question* 335), she also reveals how often language fails to capture the complexity of real life, where people are not always who they think they are. HMQ plays cat-and-mouse with Blunt when she questions the honesty and legitimacy of the art establishment of connoisseurs, dealers and museums, who often opt for opportunistic judgments. Indeed, when HMQ suggests that 'the context of the painting matters' and that when confronted with a painting with 'the right background and pedigree' it must be difficult to think that 'it is not what it says it is', she is obviously also referring to Blunt's pedigree and immunity:

> **HMQ**   […] I suppose too the context of the painting matters. Its history and provenance (is that the word?) confer on it certain respectability. This can't be a forgery, it's in such and such a collection, its background and pedigree are impeccable – besides, it has been vetted by the experts. Isn't that how the argument goes? So if one comes across a painting with the right background and pedigree, Sir Anthony, then it must be hard, I imagine – even inconceivable – to think that it is not what it claims to be. And even supposing someone in such circumstances did have suspicions, they would be chary about voicing them. Easier to leave things as they are in every department. Stick to the official attribution rather than let the cat out of the bag and say, 'Here we have a fake.' (*Question* 344)

Through this crossfire of characters and the double network of references to the worlds of art and counter-espionage, Bennett invites the audience to think that even historians should try to understand Blunt's decision to become a spy in the light of the historical-political framework of the period. 'It seemed the right thing to do at the time' (*Question* 313), is Blunt's laconic explanation in the play: indeed, in analysing his character Bennett seems intent on adopting the same perspective suggested by art historian Marjorie Wieseman, who writes that 'our own attitudes and expectations also influence how we look at a painting, so we may respond to a work quite differently than its original audience long ago'.[84] Blunt's decision to spy for Russia in 1940, Bennett suggests, should therefore be reconsidered in the light of what the art historian would later describe as the great 'enthusiasm for any anti-fascist activity' following the rise of Hitler.[85] Blunt's story offers the playwright an opportunity to rethink the appeasement policy of the Tories, Baldwin and Chamberlain, and their belated response to the Nazi threat. Bennett's decision to actually play the role of Blunt himself clearly confirms his sympathy for him, as he writes in the introduction: 'Certainly in the spy fever that followed the unmasking of Professor Blunt I felt more sympathy with the hunted than the hunters.'[86] Indeed, the playwright never mentions that Blunt himself authenticated many of the London painter Eric Hebborn's forgeries, although it has never been clear whether he consciously collaborated with him, as Hebborn liked to imply, or whether he was actually deceived.[87] Confirming his sympathy, Bennett writes in his introduction that 'the trouble with treachery nowadays is that if one does want to betray one's country there is no one satisfactory to betray it to. If there were, more people would be doing it'.[88] He then refers to the Windscale nuclear accident of 1957 to argue that although governments regard treason 'the crime of the crimes', in his view concealing information can be as 'culpable' as betraying it:

---

[84] Ibid.
[85] Drawing Anthony Blunt's profile for the British Academy, Peter Kidson, Emeritus Professor and Honorary Fellow at the Courtauld Institute, suggested that historians in the future would 'be less censorious than his contemporary critics' and see his decision in 1940 to spy for Russia as 'his way of trying to keep the war against fascism going at a time when most right-wing opinion in the country was prepared to give up and get on with the Germans'. Peter Kidson, 'Blunt, Anthony Fredrick, 1907-1983', *The British Academy*, 38, 1983. https://www.thebritishacademy.ac.uk/publishing/memoirs/13/blunt-anthony-frederick-1907-1983/ (accessed 8 May 2023).
[86] Bennett, *Plays 2*, ix.
[87] Noah Charney, *The Art of Forgery. The Minds, Motives and Methods of Master Forgers* (London: Phaidon, 2015), 107.
[88] Bennett, *Plays 2*, x–xi.

> As I write, evidence is emerging of a nuclear accident at Windscale in 1957, the full extent of which was hidden from the public. Were the politicians and civil servants responsible for this less culpable than our Cambridge villains? Because for the spies it can at least be said that they were risking their own skins, whereas the politicians were risking someone else's. Of course, Blunt and Burgess and co. had the advantage of us in that they still had illusions. They had somewhere to turn.[89]

Moreover, distance from the past provides a fresh perspective that allows the playwright to reflect on the timeliness of government responses. If Baldwin and Chamberlain's response to the Nazi menace came late, the Thatcher government's decision to go to war in the Falklands was swift, apparently justified by the need to gain consensus and new credibility through a military expedition that was immediately promoted as a demonstration of newfound national solidarity. As he writes, the Falkland War helped him 'to understand how a fastidious stepping-aside from patriotism could be an element in characters as different as Blunt and Burgess'.[90] It is not the purpose of this volume to delve into the reasons for Blunt's betrayal, although it is perhaps important to mention that Blunt's decision was also influenced by aesthetic considerations. Indeed, a visit to the Hermitage Museum in Saint Petersburg during a trip to the Soviet Union in 1934 reinforced his conviction that Communism was a patron of the arts and that only a totalitarian state could promote the various artistic disciplines:

> The Renaissance was a great period, I agree; but at that time there were patrons whose money was used to develop the arts. They didn't worry about the growth of workers' productivity. As long as they supported art with money, art was alive. But when Patrons vanished, the quality of artistic production fell dramatically. Today art is more than ever dependent on money, yet the bourgeois state does nothing to develop it. Only a totalitarian state can assume the role of patron to encourage all the disciplines of art. [...] Where are the Sun Kings and the Medicis of today?[91]

It is a question that many other playwrights, not least Howard Barker, John Logan and Lee Hall, would ask in the decades that followed, as they sought

---

[89] Ibid., xi.
[90] Ibid., ix.
[91] Alan Bennett quoted in Richard Newbury, 'Anthony Blunt – Fourth Man and Royal "Fake"', *La Stampa*, 24 July 2009. https://www.lastampa.it/blogs/2009/07/24/news/anthony-blunt-fourth-man-and-royal-fake-1.37251793/ (accessed 8 May 2023).

to understand the reasons why art is so often intertwined with political and economic concerns.

Restoration or conservation?

David Edgar's intellectual thriller *Pentecost*, first produced by the Royal Shakespeare Company at The Other Place, Stratford-upon-Avon, on 12 October 1994,[92] stages another intriguing mystery story dealing with a question of attribution and involving a museum curator and a spy posing as (or being) a connoisseur. In his play of 'The Iron Curtain Trilogy', set in an unnamed post-communist country in South-East Europe,[93] Edgar uses museological issues to define the agenda of national identity, which entails an account of how a nation should or should not be 'told'.

The playwright drew inspiration from 'news reports, research and his own experience in Eastern Europe after the collapse of Communism', including a visit in 1990 to a church in Skopje, Macedonia, where the extraordinary frescoes decorating it raised doubts about the traditional Western assumption that the discovery of perspective originated in Europe and about Western Europe's superiority over other cultures. He explained:

> We were shown some extraordinary frescoes. They were painted around 1164, but they seemed remarkably naturalistic for painting of that period. It got me wondering what would have happened if a painter had got perspective 100 years before Giotto. I started reading about that and realised to my surprise just how dependent the Renaissance was on Arab geometry, for instance, and the extent of influence of Eastern art on Renaissance artists. [94]

In light of such considerations, the protagonist of *Pentecost*, Gabriella Pecs, curator of an unspecified national museum, begins to ask similar questions

---

[92] David Edgar, *Pentecost* (London: Nick Hern Books, 1995). After some cast changes it opened at the Young Vic in London, 31 May 1995. On both occasions it was directed by Michael Attenborough.

[93] Edgar, *Pentecost*, xx. On the national indeterminacy of the play's setting, see Janelle Reinelt and Gerald Hewitt, *The Political Theatre of David Edgar: Negotiation and Retrieval* (Cambridge: Cambridge University Press, 2011), 208; Janine Hauthal, ' "Provincializing" Post-Wall Europe: Transcultural Critique of Eurocentric Historicism in *Pentecost*, *Europe* and *The Break of Day*', *Journal of Contemporary Drama in English*, 3, 1 (2015): 28–46.

[94] David Edgar in Kramm Maggi, 'The Perspective Puzzle', *American Theatre*, 12, 9 (November 1995). *Gale Academic OneFile*, link.gale.com/apps/doc/A18009330/AONE?u=milano&sid=bookmark-AONE&xid=3f0fcc35. (accessed 31 August 2023).

when she discovers a fresco behind the surface of a large heroic revolutionary mural in an abandoned Romanesque church 'in a filthy little village, 20 kilometres off capital, and 17 off border' (*Pentecost* 4). Her curiosity is all the more understandable when one considers Edgar's stage notes, which state that the fresco, 'although stylistically Byzantine', is 'compositionally clearly very similar'[95] to Giotto's *The Mourning of Christ* in the Arena Chapel, Padua.[96] What if, Gabriella (and Edgar) wonder, the Italian masterpiece is just a copy of an original from an insignificant Eastern European country – a country whose national museums contain mostly folk art?

The vivid theatrical image of a newly discovered Giottesque fresco is thus at the centre of this ambitious state-of-Europe play, in which the correct attribution of the work of art is closely intertwined with the fate of a group of asylum seekers who break into the church where the fresco is located and take both the fresco and the art historians hostage in order to exchange them for permission to live somewhere in Europe. In the rubble heap of the Balkans, wracked by ultranationalism and financial instability and torn apart by violent ethnic conflicts that have destroyed many of the forms and functions of traditional sites of memory, the knot between heritage, national identity and politics unravels around the mysteries and fate of a fresco, challenging the audience with ethical dilemmas. Whose culture does a museum preserve? Who is the museum for? For the Orthodox or for the Catholic community? For tourists who rush into 'the biggest tourist trap since the Chinese terracotta army' (*Pentecost* 22), or for Asian, African and non-Western European refugees seeking asylum in the West? Why do heritage and art matter when people are dying?

In the first three scenes of the first act, Gabriella and Oliver Davenport, the British art historian she is working with on her attribution research, acknowledge the museum as a 'repository of memory, location of the collections that form the basis of cultural or national identity',[97] and make clear how 'visual representations are a key element in symbolizing and sustaining national communal bonds'.[98] Echoing Eilean Hooper-Greenhill, Gabriella acknowledges that meaning in a museum is constructed in relation to the collections that the museum holds and that the objects that make up a collection constitute a visual narrative:

---

[95] Edgar, *Pentecost*, xx.
[96] Giotto, *Il compianto su Cristo morto* (1303–6 about), 183 × 198 cm, Cappella degli Scrovegni, Padua.
[97] Crane (ed.), *Museums and Memory*, 4.
[98] Eilean Hooper-Greenhill, *Museums and the Interpretation of Visual Cultures* (London: Routledge, 2000), 25.

The beliefs, attitudes and values which underpin the processes of acquisition become embodied in the collections, as some objects are privileged, and others are left to one side. The public display of these collections makes a visual narrative that naturalises these underpinning assumptions and which gives them the character of inevitability and common sense.[99]

Gabriella seems fully aware that such visual narratives are 'not just reactive, depicting an existing state of being', but also 'purposefully creative' and capable of 'generat[ing] new social and political formations'.[100] She knows, therefore, that if her hypothesis were to be confirmed, her discovery would change the history of art, anticipating by almost a century the first use of the single-point perspective in Italy. And it would also change the narrative of the National Museum she works for. After years of humiliations and military occupation, 'despite all Turkish occupation, despite Mongol yoke' (*Pentecost* 42), the fresco would prove to the rest of Europe that her country had contributed more to Western culture than the proletariat quilts and painted carts that now fill the State Museum. It would also help restore the reputation of Eastern Europeans while confirming Eurocentric rhetoric nonetheless: 'Maybe then we may feel bit more universal, bit more grown up, maybe even bit more European' (*Pentecost* 42). Indeed, here Gabriella also introduces a reflection on the nature of a collection. Given that beliefs about what is and is not meaningful inform both collections and exhibitions, what might be the ideas and values behind a museum's decision to collect children's crayon drawings and old quilts and parts of painted carriages? What kind of identity and national pride might this collection express?

A good, left-leaning liberal, as he defines himself, Edgar believes that 'the definition of art should be widened, and should certainly include cultural artefacts which have not generally been regarded as high art'.[101] In considering the artification of quilts as one of the greatest collective and feminist cultural projects, he recalls 'The International Honor Quilt', a collection of 539 two-foot-long quilted triangles honouring women around the world, initiated by Judy Chicago in 1980, and 'The Names Aids Memorial Quilt', conceived by AIDS activist Cleve Jones in 1985. But he says he understands Gabriella's harsh attack on the museum collection she curates, which acknowledges 'the art of heroic revolutionary masses quite as good as Michelangelo' (*Pentecost*

---

[99] Ibid., 23.
[100] Ibid., 25.
[101] David Edgar in Duncan Wu, *Making Plays. Interviews with Contemporary British Dramatists and Their Directors* (London: Palgrave Macmillan, 2000), 131.

33),[102] and challenges his audience. Who gets to choose what is culturally significant? How does a conservator know what is significant enough to preserve? Once again, at the heart of a play, the question of attribution is only the first step in a complex process of conservation that raises many technical, ethical and philosophical challenges.

First of all, as Anthony Blunt thoroughly and persuasively argues in Bennett's *A Question of Attribution*, Edgar shows how difficult it is to interpret works of art and how this time the task may prove even more difficult given the limited authentication methods available. We might consider, for instance, Gabriella's use of her hairdresser sister's hydrogen peroxide as a solvent to clean the fresco (*Pentecost* 9). Moreover, the documents in which Gabriella finds references to the fresco are 'themselves fragmentary, subject to misquotation, mistranslation, printing errors' (*Pentecost* 35). A reference to the fresco appears in an account of a trial in 1425 by a certain Italian merchant, Signor Leonello Vegni, who was on trial and who, described as a spy as well as a connoisseur, was evidently used to mix up the true and the false, so 'it is hard to tell if when he writes he sees 'octagonal basilica with a fresco of our Holy Mother with dead Christ' is actually code for barrack with brigade of horse or ... just what it is' (*sic*) (*Pentecost* 6). The only other document confirming Vegni's words is a thirteenth-century national-patriotic poem written in Old Nagolitic, an obscure language with 'peculiar' rules (in which, e.g. 'words for "to" and "from" are actually "interchangeable"') (*Pentecost* 6).

Like *A Question of Attribution*, *Pentecost* also raises more complicated questions about the search for authenticity. It shows that works of art have a continuous history and that their current state 'records not only the moment of creation but also a whole subsequent sequence of events'.[103] Should the newly discovered fresco be conserved and stabilized, or should it be restored to its original splendour by removing the marks of subsequent centuries? Should the restoration destroy the mural of communist propaganda that covers it (Figure 2.2)?

Pentecost highlights these and other dilemmas about where this fresco should be kept. Should it be removed and placed in a museum, or should it remain in the church, which itself is a trigger of memory, changing its function over historical periods, as Gabriella reminds the audience in her ungrammatical English?

---

[102] Ibid., 131–2.
[103] Jones, *Why Fakes?*, 14.

Figure 2.2 *Pentecost* written by David Edgar and directed by Michael Attenborough. With Charles Kay as Oliver Davenport and Jan Ravens as Gabriella Pecs. The Other Place, Stratford-Upon-Avon, October 1994.

Source: Courtesy Henrietta Butler / ArenaPAL.

Gabriella One abandoned church. As well as warehouse, church is used by heroic peasantry for store potatoes. […] And before potatoes, Museum of Atheism and Progressive People's Culture. And before museum, prison. 'Transit Centre'. German Army. You can still the signatures of prisoners on wall. You note also wall is whitewash with clear mark of nail where Catholics hang pictures, how you say it, Via Dolorosa [Stations of the Cross] And underneath whitewash, pictures of our saints of orthodox religion.
[…]
When we are Hungary, it Catholic, when we are holy Slavic people, Orthodox. When we have our friendly Turkish visitor who drop by for few hundred years, for while is mosque. When Napoleon pass through, is house for horses. (*Pentecost* 5)

The debate over the most appropriate location for the fresco reopens an old wound, reminiscent of the Elgin Controversy and the current debate over the return of works of art and artefacts to their countries of origin by museums, as briefly mentioned in Hare's *The Bay at Nice*:

Assistant All art is loot. Who should own it? I shouldn't say this, but there isn't much justice in these things. If we examined the process whereby everything on these walls was acquired … we should have bare walls. (*Bay* 318)

This is a theme at the heart of Hannah Khalil's 2019 *A Museum in Baghdad*, the first play by a woman of Arab descent on the RSC's stage.[104] In this successful epic play about the opening of the Iraq Museum in Baghdad in 1926 and its reopening in 2006 after being looted during the US-led occupation of Iraq in 2003, Iraqi curator Mohammed Abdullah argues why artefacts found in Iraq must stay in Iraq and explains the importance of a museum to Baghdad, confirming the role of heritage in the construction of nationhood and somehow echoing Gabriella's words:

Mohammed Next you'll say she [a statue] should be back at the British Museum. But people must see her – *here*. We want this to be a tourist destination! Change the way people think about Iraq! (*Museum* 26)

---

[104] Hannah Khalil, *A Museum in Baghdad* (London: Methuen Drama, 2019). *A Museum in Baghdad* premiered on 11 October 2019, as a co-commission by the Royal Lyceum Theatre and the Royal Shakespeare Company at the Swan Theatre, Stratford-upon-Avon.

It is no coincidence that *Pentecost* draws attention to the inextricable tangle of semantics, history and politics and to the fact that 'the transfer of works of art from their original intended site to some museum' always implies the breaking of 'the link between creation and society, between art and mores, art and religion, art and life'.[105] The museum is no longer just a peaceful place for the muses, but also a place for collecting and preserving a memory that has often been stolen or extorted from another culture by force, cunning or money.[106]

On stage, Edgar sparks an academic battle between his allies Gabriella and Oliver, who are in favour of removing the fresco and exhibiting it in the National Museum, and Leo Katz, who fiercely opposes modern restoration methods, which he believes homogenize works of art and destroy the material evidence of their history. Their confrontation leads to an erudite discussion on the use of *strappo* or *stacco*, *coletta* or resin, reflectography or photogrammetry. In this part of the play, Edgar's stage notes go into great detail about the technique of removal:

> *On the platform, restorers in white dungarees are preparing the painting for removal from the wall. This involves painting a layer of glue on sections of the painting and then affixing 40 by 40cm pieces of loose cotton gauze – themselves steeped in glue – on the surface, stretched out gently by hand. This procedure starts from the bottom of the painting and moves upwards. […] The workstation area below has also developed. […] There are also microscopic machines now unpacked and in operation, and a big noticeboard on which a black-and-white, sectioned photograph of the painting is displayed, along with other lists and data, and reproductions of other Lamentations (including Giotto's at Padua). The computer is on and the screen is presently showing an outline of a section of the painting.* (Pentecost 26)

Such articulate precision confirms Edgar's interest in the subject, although he confesses that he has never been able to make up his mind as to which of Leo or Oliver was right about how to preserve the fresco (Figure 2.3).[107] Indeed,

---

[105] David Carrier, *Museum Skepticism. A History of the Display of Art in Public Galleries* (Durham: Duke University Press, 2006), 53.
[106] Caroline Patey, 'Il museo che non c'è. Note sulla dispersione del patrimonio in Gran Bretagna', *Altre Modernità/Other Modernities*, 5 (March 2011). https://riviste.unimi.it/index.php/AMonline/article/view/1025 (accessed 28 May 2023).
[107] Edgar cited in Wu, *Making Plays*, 129.

The Drama of Authenticity 131

Figure 2.3 *Pentecost* written by David Edgar and directed by Michael Attenborough. With Charles Kay as Oliver Davenport and Glen Hugill as Mikhail Csaba. The Other Place, Stratford-Upon-Avon, October 1994.

Source: Courtesy Henrietta Butler / ArenaPAL.

their dispute shows that the 'restoration establishment' has not reached a unilateral agreement on the conservation and display of artworks.

Pragmatically, Oliver Davenport, senior fellow at the Ruskin Institute, London, wants to make the fresco accessible and suggests that transferring it to the National Museum would be the best possible solution to satisfy everyone's needs: the rival Orthodox and Catholic churches vying for ownership, the international investors Deutschelectronic and Peruzzi and domestic tourism.

Leo Katz, a character inspired by James Beck, the Columbia University art historian and avowed critic of many high-profile restorations and re-attributions of works of art, takes an opposing view.[108] Significantly, Davenport introduces him by informing Gabriella of Katz's vehement attack on the cleaning of Michelangelo's sixteenth-century frescoes on the ceiling of the Sistine Chapel in Rome, quoting from Beck's own polemical volume *Art Restoration: The Culture, the Business and the Scandal* (1993).[109] Beck and Leo thus accuse restorers of ruining Michelangelo's masterpiece:

> **Oliver** […] You see, Gabriella, Professor Katz has made something of a career of bowling round the world attacking restoration beg their pardon conservation projects on the grounds that Michelangelo took 500 years of candle grease and overpainting into full account when he did the Sistine ceiling, and thus actually intended it should turn dark brown – […] Whereas, in fact, for all this guff about 'acknowledging the painting's history', what it comes down to for Professor Katz and ilk is that they want their art – and more crucially their artists – to be ancient, brooding and mysterious. So that we're rendered totally dependent on the insight of historians to explain their tortured genius to us. (*Pentecost* 32)

Echoing Beck's famous stance against one of the most controversial restorations of recent decades, Leo argues that the restorers were not trying to preserve or restore what was there but rather to re-create these ancient beauties by transforming them into something that pleases us today but that never existed. Leo/Beck argues against the 'unnecessary campaign of beautification' that has taken hold in museums and tends to turn paintings

---

[108] The reference is confirmed by Edgar himself in an interview with Gianni Cicali, 'A colloquio con David Edgar', 1 June 2003. https://drammaturgia.fupress.net/recensioni/recensione1.php?id=1487 (accessed 5 January 2021).

[109] James Beck and Michael Daley, *Art Restoration: The Culture, the Business and the Scandal* (London: John Murray, 1993), 56–9.

into works of art 'conforming to a bland museum look'.[110] It is a tendency with a long tradition, as BB confirms in Gray's *The Old Masters*, when, disgusted by a Bellini painting that Duveen has cleaned according to the American taste, he exclaims: 'Cleaned, cleaned, he has had it defiled ... defiled! [...] How ghastly this all is, how ghastly!' (*Masters* 23).

Leo also expresses his concern about the risks of the culture industry and warns Gabriella against the lure of that 'fucking Disneyland', which he seems to know very well. Not content with that, he even accuses Oliver of speculating on the fresco's removal and of complicity with the European sponsors who are financing it (also for predictably speculative purposes):

> **Leo** You really think, Peruzzi and Deutschelectronic, after all this, would transport you to the National Museum, assist you with the heavy lifting, and then slope off home?
> [...]
> Come on. It'd be – hey, we got the big bang here, you can't keep it to yourself, what say we take it on a little tour? Just think of all that currency. Or rather, while you guys are sorting out security, maybe more like an extended loan? Or even, now we come to think of it, wouldn't it be actually much happier, and much more accessible to doctors and professors of their ilk, in a nice new hi-tech California gallery with state-of-the-art air conditioning and three gold trowels from Architecture Quarterly? Hey, come on, Olly, wasn't that the deal? (*Pentecost* 45)

Aware of the risk of paintings becoming 'stars, of the Hollywood variety. With tours. And fans. And franchised merchandise. And – entourage' (*Pentecost* 45), Leo argues that a work of art is not an object to be owned or transported around the world as a celebrity to be exhibited and exploited. He then warns his colleagues that, once it enters the international showbiz circuit, the fresco will inevitably lose the right to remain in its 'original abode',[111] one of the inalienable rights listed in the 'Bill of Rights for a Work of Art' drawn up by Beck and Daley.[112] Finally, in line with Beck and Daley's belief that 'in principle, later transformations, adjustments and reformations added to the original' work of art 'should be left intact as marks of its history',[113] Leo argues that works of art 'do grow old' and 'their history is written on their faces, just

---

[110] Ibid., 191.
[111] Ibid., 177.
[112] Ibid., 176–91.
[113] Ibid., 181.

like it is on ours' (*Pentecost* 45). No wonder, then, that when he informs Anna Jedlikova, the magistrate who has to decide on the fate of the fresco, that there are names on the fresco from the time when the church was a torture chamber, and that these names would be scraped off as part of the procedures for removing the fresco, he touches a raw nerve and wins over the magistrate. Echoing Leo Katz's parallelism between painting and the people whose history is written on both, Jedlikova recalls one of the most reprehensible episodes in recent history, when Serb children dying of starvation in the Jasenovac concentration camp could not resist eating the cardboard tags with their names on them, thus erasing any trace of their identity and existence:

> **Jedlikova** […] in second World War, Serb children are transport to camp at Jasenovac, and they are so hungry that they eat cardboard tags around their neck. Which is their family, their age, their name. They eat their history. They die and nobody remember them.
> *Slight pause.*
> And now, already, here our past is being erased. And exiles with new names come back and restore old names of streets and squares and towns. But in fact, you cannot wipe it all, like a cosmetic. Because for 40 years it is not normal here. And so, we must remember. We must not eat our names. Otherwise, like Trotsky, we might end up with our jailor's. (*Pentecost* 38)

Through Jedlikova's warning to remember and her refusal to erase the traces of history from the fresco, Edgar shows that *any* historic work of art or building is always in a process of deliberate alteration, accidental change and natural decay. Whatever their convictions, Gabriella, Oliver, Leo, the conservators and the restorers are all inevitably part of the church's 'unrolling semiosis',[114] faced with the difficult choice of preserving the heroic revolutionary mural and the names of the prisoners on it or destroying it to expose the fresco underneath. Their discussion reveals the subjective and political nature of the conservation process. It demonstrates what the conservationist Erica Avrami argues about conservation as 'a creative process of valorising a given resource or element' to perpetuate 'a particular idea or narrative about a place or people', rather than as 'an impartial process of discerning some sort of intrinsic value'.[115] Decisions about the conservation

---

[114] Paul Eggert, *Securing the Past. Conservation in Art, Architecture and Literature* (Cambridge: Cambridge University Press, 2009), 239.
[115] Erica Avrami, 'Heritage, Values, and Sustainability', in Alison Richmond and Alison Bracker, *Conservation. Principles, Dilemmas and Uncomfortable Truths*

of a work of art reflect the complex ways in which it can be meaningful to different people at different times. Not surprisingly, all the characters attempt 'to appropriate this work of art for their own ideological, economic and political interests',[116] as Gabriella reveals: 'And I am thinking during all these days how everybody judge (sic) our painting. How for Catholic is spread of European culture, for national church expression of our holy Slavic soul. And for great Western intellectuals is either not so quite good photograph or megaphone of Good' (*Pentecost* 47).

With a coup de théâtre, the fresco takes on other meanings in the second part of the play, when a motley group of refugees from various 'troubled spots'[117] invade the church and hold Gabriella, Oliver and Leo hostage. In the first place, the fresco seems to be worth enough to be exchanged for passports and work permits. It also becomes a visual representation of intercultural 'hybridization',[118] as the multicultural group of asylum seekers, despite their different languages and cultures, are united in a common act of understanding (the Pentecost of the title). Towards the end of the play, before the US attack kills him and destroys the fresco, Oliver speculates on its transcultural origin, suggesting that, in addition to Christian narrative, both Arab geometry and optics and Byzantine iconography and fresco techniques are involved:

> **Oliver** […] medieval Europe was a chaos of diaspora. Every frontier teeming, every crossroads thronged. So it is frankly more than possible that a painter could have set off in the early years of the thirteenth century. From what perils we cannot imagine. And coming to this place, and being taken captive, and offering for his relieve to paint a picture, here, so akin to nature that its figures seem to live and breathe … […] An Arab colourist, who learns his fresco in the monasteries of Serbia and Macedonia. Who sees the great mosaics of the mighty churches of Constantinople. And who thinks, like any artist, I could do that too. And having thought some more that he could do it better. But his huge advantage over almost everybody else is not just that he has the classic geometry the Arabs kept alive for the best part of 800 years, nor yet again the optics they hypothesised around the first millennium, but the fact that nobody's explained to him that painters aren't supposed to use them.

(London: Routledge in association with the Victoria and Albert Museum London, 2009), 180.
[116] Edgar in Wu, *Making Plays*, 130.
[117] Edgar in Reinelt and Hewitt, *Political Theatre of David Edgar*, 239.
[118] Edgar in Wu, *Making Plays*, 146.

So, he has two eyes, and they tell him things have three dimensions, and he paints the world that way. With all that innocence, that freshness and that rage, we bring to things when we come up against them for the very first – first time. (*Pentecost* 98–9)

The fresco is therefore the product of the chaos of the medieval diaspora, which not only brought about this breakthrough in the art but also demonstrated the possibility of communication across languages and cultures. Edgar makes the fresco live on stage, a metaphor of how cultures actually interconnect, by having the actors perform in various languages that they – and the audience – are unlikely to understand, such as Polish, Arabic, Bulgarian and Turkish, thus extending 'the experience of incomprehension, disorientation and displacement referred to and embodied by the play's refugees'[119] to performers and audience alike. This medieval chaos, an unstable cultural space heavily influenced by migration, like the fictional world of *Pentecost*, shows a possible way of living in the subsequent chaos of this Balkan margin after the fall of the Berlin Wall, and hopefully also suggests at least the *possibility* of a happy ending, different from the rather dark ending of the play. The demolition of the wall with the fresco is a blunt act of violence, reminiscent of the events that have torn apart countries such as the former Yugoslavia since the dissolution of the Soviet Union, but it also recalls the joyous image of the fall of the Berlin Wall on 9 November 1989, when the German city was reunited.

Finally, the fresco raises another unresolved question about the value of art in relation to the value of human life. Leo, who is prepared 'to risk' the painting for his own survival, because he values the needs and rights of living human beings above those of a work of art, criticizes all those Western intellectuals who wrote 'polite letters' to the newspapers protesting against the destruction of architecture when Dubrovnik was burning under siege during the Bosnian war (*Pentecost* 75–7). On the one hand, Edgar alludes to the worldwide condemnation of the massive destruction of cultural heritage during the 1992–5 war in Bosnia, which eventually led to the recognition by international law of the destruction of cultural heritage as an aspect of genocide.[120] On the other hand, he invites the audience to reflect on the value that we place on human life versus our irreplaceable artefacts. The final image

---

[119] Hauthal, ' "Provincializing" Post-Wall Europe', 42.
[120] Helen Walasek, 'Cultural Heritage and Memory after Ethnic Cleansing in Post-Conflict Bosnia-Herzegovina', *International Review of the Red Cross*, 101, 910: Memory and War (April 2019): 275.

of the destruction of the fresco in *Pentecost*, reminiscent of other attacks on world-famous archaeological sites, looms large in the final scene of the play. It is an image that would reappear in the twenty-first century, especially after the destructive incursions carried out and publicized by ISIS in Syria and Iraq, and in Khalil's *A Museum in Baghdad*. The play, which revolves around the characters of two women, oscillates between two different temporalities that overlap and even interact: 1926, shortly after the birth of Iraq, and 2006, after the US invasion and occupation of Iraq. In 1926, the Baghdad Archaeological Museum (which became the Museum of Iraq) opened its doors for the first time, thanks in part to the mythologized Gertrude Bell, an English traveller, political administrator and archaeologist, who played a key role in the creation of Iraq as a modern nation after the dissolution of the Ottoman Empire in the wake of the First World War. In 2006, another woman, Ghalia Hussein, a fictional character inspired by the recently deceased Iraqi archaeologist Lamia Al-Gailani Werr, who was involved in the reconstruction of the museum in the twenty-first century, returns to Iraq after years abroad to oversee the restoration of the museum and is confronted by the spectrum of future violence that the play's audience know will arrive with the rise of the Islamic State. By bringing the colonial history of this museum to life, Khalil, who is herself of Palestinian-Irish heritage, asks why a country's treasures matter when people are dying and raises questions about the ways in which colonialism continues to influence both the destruction and the preservation of cultural artefacts housed within its walls. One of the characters, Nasiya, takes a stand against the museum's conservation policies and weighs the value of artefacts against human lives: 'This is all vanity, can't you see? People are starving while you worry about dead things – these things aren't alive, they're dust –' (*Museum* 79). Significantly, though, one of the Chorus lines at the end of the play – 'I was born in this city and I will die in this city' (*Museum* 80) – is an homage to Khaled Al-Assad, the archaeologist and curator of the ancient Semitic city of Palmyra in Syria, who was beheaded by ISIS for refusing to reveal the location of priceless artefacts.[121]

Despite being of a different generation and cultural background, Khalid shows a genuine interest in continuing Edgar's discussion of society's investment in cultural heritage and its role in assigning value to the artefacts and sites that make up that heritage.

Both Edgar and Khalid wrestle with and stage the ethical dilemmas faced by those who care for and preserve the cultural heritage, challenging their

---

[121] Annie Webster, '*A Museum in Baghdad*, and an Interview with its Author, Annah Khalil', *Arts Cabinet*, 2019. https://www.artscabinet.org/repository/a-museum-in-baghdad-and-an-interview-with-its-author-hannah-khalil (accessed 8 May 2023).

audiences in the process. Like *Pentecost*, *A Museum in Baghdad* has its own Pentecost, most palpably in the choric intonation of solemn phrases in both English and Arabic. Actors speaking in English and Arabic encourage the audience to hear and appreciate the sound of the Arabic language and to experience first-hand what it is like not to understand the words (*Museum* 2). In both cases, the theatre unlocks academic arguments and transforms them into emotional and topical stage action, although Khalil's play and Erica Whyman's production have been accused of 'a stodgy lack of theatricality'[122] and of presenting characters who never really come to life and are limited 'to mouth[ing] neo-colonialist points'.[123]

True stories about fakes: Towards a meta-modern experience?

The artistic director of Fire Exit, Scottish-based playwright David Leddy, approaches the concepts of forgery and authenticity from a different perspective. His play *Long Live the Little Knife*, developed with support from the Royal Shakespeare Company and the British Museum,[124] is a provocative and rambunctious reflection on 'artificiality and authenticity from a variety of different angles',[125] exploring the world of con artists, commercial fakes and art forgeries while engaging in a self-reflexive examination of the nature and possibilities of theatre and verbatim theatre in particular.

In his introduction to the play, Leddy claims to have found particularly interesting the thesis of Yale psychology professor Paul Bloom in *How Pleasure Works* that art forgeries pose 'a major challenge for our brains because they are both real and false simultaneously. They *are* beautiful and they were painted by a highly skilled artist but at the same time their *essence* is not what we believed it to be'.[126] They lack what Walter Benjamin

---

[122] Clare Brennan, '*A Museum in Baghdad* Review – The Tale of Two Women Trying to Preserve Iraq's Treasures', *The Guardian*, 3 November 2019. https://www.theguardian.com/stage/2019/nov/03/a-museum-in-baghdad-review-swan-stratford-rsc-gertrude-bell (accessed 20 August 2023).

[123] Robert Gore-Langton, 'Review of *A Museum in Baghdad*', *Daily Mail*, 2 November 2019.

[124] *Long Live the Little Knife* was first presented at Film City, Glasgow, from 7 to 9 February 2013. The version of the script published by Fire Exit in 2013 was first presented as part of the Edinburgh Festival Fringe from 1 to 25 August 2013 at the Traverse Theatre. It was funded by Creative Scotland and developed with support from the Royal Shakespeare Company and the British Museum.

[125] David Leddy, *Long Live the Little Knife* (Glasgow: Fire Exit, 2013), 8.

[126] Ibid., 7.

called the 'aura' of their uniqueness, which cannot be copied. Inspired by the idea that the value of an art object is 'rooted in our assumptions about the human performance underlying its creation' so that 'it's not just the object that we love, it's the story we believe to be hidden inside',[127] Leddy speculates on reality and fakery, mischievously playing on the audience's innate desire to believe in the essence of objects, as opposed to simply being swayed by their appearance. In particular the piece explores our contradictory attitudes towards fake art and fake designer goods. If we truly love a painting for its artistry, skill and beauty, why do we care so much about fakes?

Even before the show begins, Leddy involves the audience in a game of true/false, challenging their 'eye' and their ability to distinguish one from the other. From the outset, therefore, they are led to believe that the programme they receive at the entrance is 'a numbered, limited-edition artwork', the front of which is painted with 'an individual splatter design (Jackson Pollock style)' and signed by David Leddy, only to discover later that it is not Leddy's work, but a fake, as he writes in his stage notes.[128] In a further challenge to (or satirization of) their perspective, the audience are made to sit in an elaborate installation of paint-sprayed sheets of dust. As Leddy writes, it is as if Jackson Pollock had had a terrible explosion of paint in the middle of the room, except that it is not Pollock who has created the dust sheets in this case but the play's designer, Ali Maclaurin.

The production, too, intriguingly short-circuits the true and the false, consisting of different layers articulated by the overlapping of auto-fictional situations with the two actors, Sarah Jones and Andrew Smith (although the stage direction is clear about replacing these fictional names with the real names of the actors interpreting the roles), who take turns speaking (but often sharing the same narrative voice), and performing their roles as wife and husband, Liz and Jim. It is important to note that, while the play may not explicitly convey a political message, the names used, which are themselves drawn from the prequel *Thin Air*,[129] encapsulate the burning issues of

---

[127] Ibid. See also Paul Bloom, *How Pleasure Works. Why We Like What We Like* (New York: Random House, 2011), 1–4.

[128] Leddy, *Long Live the Little Knife*, 15.

[129] *Thin Air* is a seven-minute Shakespearean offshoot that was performed as part of a series of special late-night performances for visitors to the British Museum, itself as part of the major 2012 exhibition *Shakespeare: Staging the World*. This, in turn, was part of the World Shakespeare Festival designed for the Olympic Games. Significantly, the play was supposed to be 'a reaction to a specific exhibit, *Designs for the Union Flag of Great Britain*', the sheet of designs from around 1604 for the new British flag that shows various ways of combining the flag of St George for England with the flag of St Andrew for Scotland to symbolize their union through James VI and I. The designs document the problematic process of redefining and remapping the geographical and political borders between

individual and national identity, as Liz and Jim, who constantly switch between Cockney and Glaswegian accents, are a tongue-in-cheek reference to Elizabeth I of England and James VI of Scotland (whose marriage mockingly echoes James I's marriage metaphor for political union in his impassioned speech to his first parliament in 1604). They also reflect the uneasy political dynamics between England and Scotland in the past, the present and even in the future. Indeed, it is worth noting that when Leddy wrote *Thin Air* in 2012, discussions regarding a potential referendum on Scottish independence were already underway. The Scottish Independence Referendum Act, which addressed significant questions about nationality and the definition of 'Scottish' or 'English', was passed by the Scottish Parliament in June 2013 and received Royal Assent in August 2013, just a few days before the premiere of *Long Live the Little Knife*. Additionally, it is important to remember that, although David Leddy is English, the theatre company he founded and ran in Scotland for seventeen years, Fire Exit, would close at the end of June 2019 as a result of Creative Scotland's decision to axe the company's funding.[130] This perspective suggests that Leddy may approach the question of nationality and unity between Scotland and England from an unusual angle, as the uneasy border between true and false in the play seems to suggest.

Sarah Jones and Andrew Smith – whose roles at the Traverse were interpreted by Wendy Seager and Neil McCormack – are cast as actors and narrators and sometimes take on the roles of minor characters, requiring a range of different accents and tones. The action moves back and forth between their exchanges and their confrontation with the playwright, David Leddy (interpreted offstage by the stage manager), who introduces himself as the autobiographical/auto-fictional figure who 'wrote' the very play they are performing, a device much in keeping with the tradition of verbatim theatre.

The fast-paced seventy-five-minute narrative, which shatters any pretence of authenticity by exposing the artificiality of theatre and acknowledging the

---

England and Scotland as well as James I's dream of one nation, Great Britain, which was met with hostility on both sides of the border, only achieved a century later with the Act of Union, and prefaced years of uneasy relations between them. Taking a cue from one of the *Designs for the Union Flag of Great Britain*, which has been described as 'likening the two nations to man and wife'(Dora Thornton, 'Top Five: Exhibits from *Shakespeare: Staging the World* at the British Museum'. https://www.whatsonstage.com/west-end-theatre/news/top-five-exhibits-from-shakespeare-staging-the-wor_3428.html (accessed 15 May 2023), Leddy gives the names 'Liz' and 'Jim' to the two actors who alternate in their roles as husband and wife in both his plays *Thin Air* and *Long Live the Little Knife*. The play text of *Thin Air* is published in Leddy, *Long Live the Little Knife*, 105–24.

[130] Fire Exit theatre company was established in 2002 and closed in 2019. The website is an archive that is available online: http://fireexit.org/learn/ (accessed 8 May 2023).

presence of the audience, often unfolds at breakneck speed in fragmented and disjointed scenes which are at once comic and affecting. It tells how Liz and Jim, caught up in a turf war over fake vintage handbags, ambitiously decide to become 'the world's foremost, most accomplished' art forgers. Unable to paint, they cleverly become forgers to the nth degree:

Liz   We're fake forgers. We take other people's forgeries and pass them off as our own. We're such fakes, that even our forgeries are forgeries!
Jim   Fakes forger.
Liz   Double negative equals positive.
Jim   It's like forgery meets conceptual art!
Liz   Forgery meets conceptual art! (*Long* 62)

When their ingenious plan finally fails, they realize they have been manipulated and find themselves in the middle of a violent showdown between their mentor Madam, who runs a seedy prostitution business, and Oleg Bulgakov, a Russian oligarch and art collector who wants compensation for having bought their fake Pollock at fifteen times the market price. Indeed, after a series of unsuccessful ventures, Liz's miscarriage and Jim's castration, they come to the bitter conclusion that they 'are not the grifters' but 'the marks', 'not scammers but … Scamees!' (*Long* 76). In the end, however, they manage to pull off the biggest scam of their lives, forging both passports for Madam's girls, who are locked in her brothel as if in prison, and adoption papers for the Polish child they had believed to be Madam's daughter, when in fact she was one of the enslaved girls she had turned into sex workers for paedophiles.

The play mixes real and fake, sometimes hilariously and mockingly, sometimes movingly, and the question of what makes something real or fake runs through every aspect of the characters' lives, from Liz's 'fake labradoodle' – that is, a 'real' dog with 'no real pedigree' (*Long* 26) – to a fake PR agency (*Long* 50), and, presumably, a fake medium who pretends to connect them with their boss 'Wee Man' (*Long* 58). 'Champagne for my real friends, real pain for my sham friends', is the toast and motto of art dealer Mags De Angelo (*Long* 52), and Liz and Jim 'even mangle the brand name 'Prada' into 'Pravda', the legendary Russian newspaper whose name means 'truth'.[131] As Leddy writes, 'the word "real" appears ninety times in the script, roughly once every forty seconds',[132] while there is a plethora of words

---

[131] Leddy, *Long Live the Little Knife*, 8.
[132] Ibid.

belonging to the semantic field dealing with forgery and deception (fake, con, cheat, fraud, scam, counterfeit, bam, swindle). The massive use of slang is also a reminder of the arbitrary nature of language and shows how difficult it can be to get to the essence of reality through a language that constantly plays with Scottish, Cockney and Yiddish slang. Above all, there are the false identities and the false accents. As their identities and accents shift across time and gender, they force the audience to question what makes a man a 'real man', or a woman a 'real woman', what we mean by 'real love' and what makes a work of art worth its price.

Of the two, Liz is the most obsessed with authenticity, desperate for something real and enduring, and yet, paradoxically, she defines herself as 'a master of the modern scam' (*Long* 27), an expert in all three key elements, 'surveillance, espionage, wigs', even advising how to be 'a good con': 'a little wig, a little accent and a lot of disbelief' (*Long* 28). By her own admission, she has always been 'a big fan of the art forgers' (*Long* 32). She also has 'the eye!' or, rather, what she calls 'the Verrocchio!' (*Long* 49).[133] Leddy's pun on the name of the Italian Renaissance artist reveals a mocking approach to the question of the connoisseur's eye, one confirmed by his derisive description of Russian oligarch Oleg Bulgakov examining the fake Pollock Liza and Jim are trying to sell him (with the latter in the guise of an art dealer, 'Christopher'):

Liz	(Oleg)	What is your price?
Jim	(Christopher)	I write it on a piece of paper. Slide it across the table.
Liz	(Oleg)	I glance at the price. My huge eye, it squints.
Jim	(Christopher)	His huge eye squints.
Liz	(Oleg)	But my tiny eye, it trembles.
Jim	(Christopher)	His tiny eye, it trembles.
Liz	(Oleg)	You … have got … a deal. (*Long* 69)

Oleg Bulgakov, an art collector who is in some ways a parody of Charles Saatchi, is equipped with a 'huge' eye that squints and a 'tiny' eye that trembles both at the painting he is about to buy and at Jim's testicles, which he is about to castrate, after discovering the fraud (*Long* 75), perhaps even suggesting a link between the art trade and masculinity – a link already explored by Wertenbaker in *Three Birds Alighting on a Field*.

Ready to embark on their new careers as forgers, Liz and Jim recall those great forgers of art history who have managed to achieve the media fame they dream of emulating and become infatuated with their project

---

[133] 'Verrocchio' is also a reference to Leddy's 2007 sound art installation 'Verrocchio' in Glasgow's CCA, Centre for Contemporary Art (13 October–27 November).

of forging art. Perhaps inspired by the 2010 exhibition *The Metropolitan Police Service's Investigations of Fakes and Forgeries* at the Victoria and Albert Museum, they offer the audience a brief but fascinating guide to the world of art forgery,[134] from Han van Meegeren and John Myatt to Shaun Greenhalgh and his octogenarian parents, known as the 'Bolton family' (*Long* 32–5). Han van Meegeren, already mentioned by Her Majesty the Queen in Bennett's *A Question of Attribution* as an astonishing kind of forger, is number one on Liz and Jim's list, popular not only as a 'con artist' but also as 'a national hero':

> **Liz** Wait! I know who's number one. Han van Meegeren.
> **Jim** O.M.G.! Numero uno.
> **Liz** Picture this, reader. Holland. 1947. Van Meegeren's on trial for treason for selling off Dutch masters to Nazis. Potential death sentence.
> **Jim** Suddenly he tells the court (*Dutch accent*.) 'The picture I sold Hermann Göring is not by Vermeer. It's by van Meegeren. I painted it. It's a fake.'
> **Liz** Immediately, he's a national hero. He's not a collaborator, he's a con artist.
> **Jim** The authorities tell Herman Göring the Vermeer is a fake.
> **Liz** They say Göring looked as if 'for the first time he realised there was true evil in this world.' (*Long* 35)

Here, they recall Meegeren's story and the infamous anecdote that suggests a close connection between art, counterfeiting and the horrendous crimes of the Nazis, while also anticipating the sordid intrigues that underpin the play. The top five counterfeiters include the Boltons, described by Scotland Yard as 'the most diverse forgery team in the world ever', and John Myatt, a brilliant forger who, after being arrested and released, set himself up as a legal forger. Imitating the style of a staggering number of artists and fooling dealers in London and New York, such as Sotheby's and Christie's, Myatt began selling high-profile 'genuine fakes' signed with his name and even became the star of Sky Art's *Fame in the Frame* series[135] – something Liz would like to emulate in particular: 'I'd love my own telly show. Can you imagine? Reality TV about fakes!' What fascinates Liz and Jim even more

---

[134] Tom Hardwick, '"The Sophisticated Answer": A Recent Display of Forgeries Held at the Victoria and Albert Museum', *Burlington Magazine*, 152, 1287 (2010): 406–8.

[135] In the series he painted portraits of celebrities in the style of famous artists. Among them Ian Brown of the musical group The Stone Roses in the style of Cézanne, Stephen Fry in the style of Velazquez's pope and Jimmy Savile as Leonardo da Vinci's Vitruvian man (*Long* 34).

than the millions these forgers have made is the popularity they have gained since their arrest. Forgeries make headlines, and when a forger is caught, the scandal attracts more public interest than the impersonated artists themselves ever actually received. As Bennett's Blunt tells HMQ: 'The public are rather tiresomely fascinated by forgery – more so, I'm afraid, than they are by the real thing' (*Question* 342).

Liz and Jim are 'fake forgers' with a five-step plan: flood the market with fifty forgeries of a Pollock by fifty different artists and pass them off as their own; steal the original Jackson Pollock from the so-called University of Bumfuck using a method inspired by the sensational 1990 heist at the Isabella Stewart Gardner Museum in Boston; sell the fifty fake Pollocks, accompanied by fake certificates of authenticity to fifty 'real buyers', each of whom believes he is buying the stolen painting; deliberately get caught and 'take credit' not only for all fifty Pollock forgeries they commissioned but also for 'unsolved forgeries along the way'; and finally, return both the original painting and the money to the fifty buyers, thus avoiding prison but gaining fame as 'the world's foremost art forgers':

> **Liz** We will get our mugs all over the news.
> **Jim** Go viral.
> **Liz** Get famous.
> **Jim** Book deal.
> **Liz** Talk shows.
> **Jim** Reality T.V. (*Long* 35)

Leddy, like Bennett, seems to believe that the appeal of art forgery lies in the fact that the language of deception is universal and has social (and sometimes political) implications. Conceptual artist and art critic Jonathon Keats writes that art forgery breaks laws, damages markets and ruins reputations. As he explains, 'The aesthetic and intellectual barriers of high culture are levelled by a scandal', since 'recognizing the systemic weakness exploited by the swindler doesn't take the cultural knowledge required to appreciate the visual provocations in a Cubist painting'. Moreover, Keats argues, 'even those who aren't the victim (as collectors or curators or taxpaying citizens) are vicariously bamboozled, made to question how they'd have responded were the fraud directed at them'. He provocatively and paradoxically concludes that, in this sense, 'forgeries are more real than the real art they fake', stressing that legitimate art 'can only simulate the violations that forgeries perpetrate'.[136] It is a paradox that lies at the heart of the play, where

---

[136] Keats, *Forged*, 25.

the fake handbags Jim and Liz sell at the beginning of their story 'are not really real, though, not really':

> **Jim**   They are designer handbags, they're just not real.
> **Liz**   Well, they're not imaginary. They're not make-believe bags!
> **Jim**   They are not really real, though, not really.
> **Liz**   [...] What? Our contact steals the real materials from the real factory. Real leather, real zip, real label. Voila! Real designer handbag.
> **Jim**   That doesn't make it real.
> **Liz**   Geez peace, mammy-daddy! All the parts are authentic, it's just made somewhere else. Hand stitched at home, in fact, better quality. How is that not 'real'?
> **Jim**   It's just ... not! (*Long* 20–1)

Leddy pokes fun at the art world, and through Liz and Jim's scam, he not only shows how forgers need an elaborate system of creation, authentication, marketing and distribution, 'the whole framework of fraudulence',[137] but he also questions the veracity of contemporary art. The two protagonists know that 'provenance is the key to a successful forgery' and that they need to find both an efficient art dealer who is good at placing a forgery on the market and art collectors who are willing to buy the works of art.[138] As Bennett's HMQ claims, the art world's reliance on provenance (usually a history of ownership) is an assurance of a work's legitimacy. The art dealer who helps the two protagonists succeed is Margarita de Angelo (played by Jim with a thick New York City Italian accent). Starting from the premise that the art market is the only unregulated financial market in the world and the only place where you can 'artificially control prices and not go to prison', she draws up 'a ten-point plan':

> **Jim**   (*as Mags De Angelo – strong NY Italian accent*) Act one! Create a series of persona, the kind of schlemiels who actually collect art.
> [...] Act two! Choose an artist.
> [...] Act three! Buy Tamara's work and let people think you paid a fortune!
> [...] Act four! Re-sell Tamara's work to another alias at higher price.

---

[137] Ibid.
[138] Liz and Jim alternate in pretending to be 'a series of personas, the kind of schlemiels, who actually collect art': Chantelle Sturridge, making money from pornography websites, who needs a rapid investment she 'can hide from the taxman'; Mademoiselle Marie-Claude Roupette-Rouston, emphatically declaring she cares not for money but for beauty; and Christopher Morgan, 'uptight mummy's boy' (*Long* 49).

[…] Act five! Use a PR agent to tell journalists Tamara is a rising star!
[…] Six! Re-sell Tamara's work to another alias at an even higher price.
[…] Seven! Get drunk at people's parties. 'Accidentally' tell them how valuable it is.
[…] Eight! Lo! You have created a false demand. Nine! Flood the market my darlings!
[…] Act ten! You have made a small fortune!
Liz Then we disappear
Jim (*London accent*) Thin air. (*Long* 50–1)

Through Margarita de Angelo's cynicism, Leddy provides a hilarious, concise guide to both the anthropology and economics of the contemporary art market, describing the creation and rise of the 'branded' artist and 'art as the quintessential commodity, the ultimate example of the wonders of the capitalist system'.[139] Twenty years after Wertenbaker's first exploration of the art world in the aftermath of YBA in *Three Birds Alighting on a Field*, Leddy shows the extreme consequences of the liberal imperatives of a globalized economy in which 'the incomes of the main collectors have risen to unprecedented heights, and their influence broadened accordingly'.[140]

Significantly, in suggesting how to choose an unknown artist to launch, the art dealer Margarita humorously and disparagingly refers to the 'Charles Saatchi Methodology', firmly based on the global advertising tycoon's experience in advertising and marketing: 'Look for something with bam, with blam, with kerzam! Like a billboard. If it takes more than 2 seconds for you to understand, then it's a piece of shit!' (*Long* 49). Given Saatchi's status and reputation as a collector and art dealer, it is not surprising that Liz and Jim see the super-collector's acquisition policy as a model to emulate. Thus, in their search for the next young art star, they go to 'trawl the undergraduate shows' (*Long* 49), following the legendary Saatchi's habit of attending art school graduate shows to buy very cheap works by relatively unknown artists.[141] In the play, Saatchi's practice of art 'shopping' seems to be familiar even to the Russian oligarch Oleg Bulgakov, who buys 'the entire degree show' (*Long* 40) of an art student at the Glasgow School of Art, a notorious breeding ground for many young British artists, including Jenny Saville, whose work Saatchi actually bought at her graduation show.

---

[139] Rita Hatton and John A. Walker, *Supercollector. A Critique of Charles Saatchi* (London: Ellipsis, 2000), 156.
[140] Charlotte Gould and Sophie Mesplède (eds), *Marketing Art in the British Isles, 1700 to the Present. A Cultural History* (London: Routledge, 2012), 17.
[141] Gordon Burn, 'I Want It, I Want It all, and I Want It Now!', *The Guardian*, 7 December 1998, 2.

As a new artist to be launched, video artist Tamara Jones seems the 'perfect' choice, combining feminist irony with a Bill Viola-esque transcendentalism. Indeed, Mags describes her video of people falling through a waterfall in slow motion as 'plagiarised, sub-standard, Billy Viola bullshit!' (*Long* 49). Is the unknown video artist they may be promoting into the art world more fake than Bill Viola, the artist she is plagiarising? Is Viola's 'bullshit' real art? What is true and what is false? And even in the case of original artworks by Bill Viola, Leddy asks, should they be seen as the authentic expression of the artist or as a marketing and fashion product?

When is theatre true? In his introduction to the play, Leddy openly denounces theatre as an art form that 'constantly skates between artificiality and authenticity': 'You are looking at real people and real objects, but they are usually pretending to be something else.'[142] From this premise, the playwright plays with theatrical conventions, exposing the theatrical machinery before the audience's eye. Appropriately, the play begins with the stage manager, Chris, introducing the actors, Ms Sarah Jones and Mr Andrew Smith, who address the audience directly, pretending to be out of character. The audience's presence is thus acknowledged, and any illusions about a fourth wall are immediately shattered. After introducing themselves by their supposedly real names, Sarah and Andrew apologize for any lighting problems that might occur during the performance – a real, genuine failure of the technological equipment, reinforcing the idea that what is happening on stage might just be real (*Long* 42). The two actors, then, introduce their characters as a husband-and-wife team of counterfeiters who specialize in the trade of fake designer handbags: Jim, from Glasgow, and Liz, from London.

On stage, different narratives collide as the couple's storytelling is interwoven with role-playing moments in which they flash back to their supposed meeting with playwright Leddy, mixing autobiography and fiction in what Liz and Jim call 'faction', 'a wily combinations of fact and fiction' (*Long* 43). The playwright's part is read by the stage manager, who 'will pretend to be David Leddy', although she (gender may be changed if necessary) limits herself just 'to say the words' without acting (*Long* 17). Meanwhile, Liz and Jim tell the audience that their story of cheating inspired Leddy to edit the interviews he had conducted with them into a play in the style of 'verbatim theatre', revealing the paradox in the pretence of telling 'a true story about fakes, ha ha ha…' (*Long* 42).

As many commentators have pointed out, verbatim theatre has grown in popularity since the turn of the millennium because of a general distrust of

---

[142] Leddy, *Long Live the Little Knife*, 8.

politics, journalism and institutions, as well as the rise of reality television. According to David Lane, the theatre's reputation as a 'politicised and critical medium' for truth-telling has fuelled the public's desire for 'real' answers, providing a perceived clarity that other media could not.[143] Against this new wave of documentary and verbatim theatre, which appeals to contemporary audiences seeking the first-hand experience missing in everyday life, Leddy (the playwright who conceived *Long Live the Little Knife*, not the character in the play) questions the uneasy relationship between the fiction of theatre and the truth of reality. He confesses that he is sometimes 'uncomfortable' with audiences' often uncritical approach to the 'reality' presented (and thereby manipulated) by verbatim theatre, in which theatre-makers base their work on verbatim interviews with real people:

> We often treat it with complete transparency as if it is entirely 'true,' but just because somebody said something in an interview, it isn't necessarily true. Similarly, interviewers can lead subjects towards particular ideas, and writers can edit the text to focus on what they deem interesting or relevant. Suddenly 'truth' seems less transparent and more like it has been constructed by someone other than the interviewee.[144]

Firstly, as in the art world, where the provenance of a work of art is crucial to establishing its authenticity, the origin of the text spoken onstage (the source material) is equally crucial in verbatim theatre. Moreover, Leddy focuses on the risks of accepting the content of the interviews (the 'raw material' from which verbatim theatre is drawn) as authentic, and on the dramaturgical process of re-conceiving and re-articulating that material – a process which Minier describes as 'adaptive',[145] and which Jim and Liz describe as 'metanarrative' (*Long* 47). Indeed, not only could the author change Liz and Jim's appearance, their background and even their accents 'at the stroke of a pen', but he would probably also 'recycle old shit' from his old plays:

> **Liz** Jacques Derrida said all writing is autobiography! […] It means everything you write is a reflection of who you are. Even editing, it's still your idea of what's interesting, your 'autobiography.' (*Long* 47)

---

[143] David Lane, *Contemporary British Drama* (Edinburgh: Edinburgh University Press, 2010), 77–8.
[144] Leddy, *Long Live the Little Knife*, 9.
[145] Márta Minier, 'Adapting 'Real-Life' Material: Metatheatrical Configurations of Authorship and Ownership of Story in Contemporary British Verbatim Theatre', *Textus. English Studies in Italy*, 31, 2 (2018): 26.

Surprisingly, lowbrow Liz quotes Jacques Derrida and considers what she calls 'Verbatim Schmerbatim' in the light of what the French philosopher wrote about the theological text in which the author's own perspective on the real is guaranteed as authoritative. As Liz and Jim point out, in *Long Live the Little Knife*, as in any typical verbatim drama, the actual interview material goes through the 'intellectual and creative sieve of the author',[146] that is, the writer's own perspective on reality, as opposed to that of the interviewees or interviewer:

> **Stage Manager**   (*as David*) (*comically emotionless*)   I'm David Leddy. I'm a playwright. I feel so, so passionate about this idea. I would interview you then edit it into a play. A true story about fakes, ha ha ha …
> **Liz**   (*London accent*)   Interesting for you. I don't want my life gawped at by strangers.
> **Stage Manager**   (*as David*)   It's called verbatim theatre.
> **Liz**   (*London accent*)   He is taking the piss! You think I don't know that?
> **Jim**   (*Glasgow accent*)   Big yin, big yin … We tell lies for a living.
> **Liz**   (*Glasgow accent*)   What would be the point?
> **Stage Manager**   (*as David*)   Truth! Authenticity!
> **Jim**   (*London accent*) (*snorts*)   'Based on a true story'??!
> **Liz**   (*Glasgow accent*) Jus 'cause we say it in an interview, it does not mean it's true!
> **Jim**   (*Glasgow accent*) Yeah! Asks the polis!
> **Liz**   (*London accent*)   It could be a wily combination of fact and fiction.
> **Jim**   (*Glasgow accent*)   They call it 'faction'!
> **Liz**   (*London accent*)   And … you'll edit it. Any writer will tell you it's not the words, it's how you edit them.
> **Stage Manager**   (*as David*)   Only to cut out the … (*Turn page.*) … boring bits.
> **Jim**   (London accent)   It's not fair. It's our life, but you decide what to keep and what to cut.
> […]
> **Liz**   (*London accent*) You'll edit it to fit your artistic 'vision.'
> (*Long* 42–3, 47)

When Liz describes her painting teacher Anthony McAlpine by pointing out his beauty, Jim accuses her of exaggerating and 'rewriting history' (*Long* 41). Similarly, the Stage Manager/David Leddy meta-theatrically confirms

---

[146] Ibid., 24.

that storytelling always involves some degree of adaptation of reality, while claiming that his editing of Liz and Jim's story is limited to cutting out 'the boring bits', thereby acknowledging the problem of authorship. Significantly, in his introduction, Leddy also reflects self-reflexively on the problem of documentation and, more broadly, on the tension inherent in the form of verbatim theatre between factual accuracy and dramatic impact, aesthetic concerns and ethical commitments.

Indeed, despite the scepticism of the two characters and their arguments against verbatim theatre, which they perceive as 'untrue', the play ultimately tells a story that has a 'real' effect on the audience. In fact, while the audience is aware of the fakeness and simulation they are witnessing, as well as of their own performative selves, they are nonetheless still able to have an authentic experience. Far from the experience of the 'postmodern apathetic theatre' described by Birgit Schuhbeckon,[147] and perhaps precisely because of its sense of deception and its meta-dramatic frame, the play is entertaining, moving and has an ethical perspective. Beneath the farcical surface, *Long Live the Little Knife* is a scathing parody of the free-market economy that has commodified everything, from works of art to children's bodies, and thus performs a critical function in 'reveal[ing] and deal[ing] with society's hidden power-structures, instead of simply giving up in face of an overcomplicated world'.[148] Indeed, in keeping with a meta-modern 'structure of feeling'[149] that focuses on dialogue, collaboration, simultaneity and generative paradox, the performance is a rush of verbal, theatrical dexterity, pausing only for moments of surprising emotion and some uniquely terrifying revelations, swinging between wit and heart. While proclaiming itself a lie, it paints characters and a story that the audience really care about, achieving the perfect double bluff.

'Counterfeit … meets … conceptual!'

Liz and Jim's 'strapline for the reality show' they dream of, 'Counterfeit … meets … conceptual!' (*Long* 63) may well encapsulate the essence of Tim

---

[147] Birgit Schuhbeckon, 'Less Art, More Substance. New Tendencies in Contemporary Theatre', *Notes on Metamodernism*, 22 February 2012. http://www.metamodernism.com/2012/02/22/less-art-more-substance-new-tendencies-in-contemporary-theatre/ (accessed 8 May 2023).
[148] Ibid.
[149] Robin van den Akker, Alison Gibbons and Timotheus Vermeulen, 'Metamodernism: Period, Structure of Feeling, and Cultural Logic – A Case Study of Contemporary Autofiction' in David Rudrum, Ridvan Askin and Frida Beckman (eds), *New Directions in Philosophy and Literature* (Edinburgh: Edinburgh University Press, 2019), 41–54.

Crouch's *An Oak Tree*, a play in which deception or illusion has become the backbone of the performance. First performed at the Traverse Theatre in Edinburgh in 2005, the play takes its title from Michael Craig-Martin's conceptual work (1973) at Tate Modern, which consists of the display of a glass of water on a shelf and a printed text that appears to be a series of questions posed to the artist, along with his answers. Significantly, Crouch describes it as an important theatre text that questions the transformative power of art and audience engagement. As he explains:

> Craig-Martin's *An Oak Tree* makes me think about theatre's 'essential element.' When an actor plays Hamlet, for example, they are both the actor, *and* they are Hamlet. They are not themselves, but they are also not *not* themselves. A character in a play has no autonomous material form other than that of the actor who, fleetingly, through a process of nomination on their part and belief on ours, is deemed to be that character. A glass of water as a tree is only a little more ideologically out-there than Maxine Peake as a suicidal Danish prince. [...] A lot of time and effort is taken in theatre to narrow the gap between what the play says is something and what it actually is – to make the actor look like the character. But, in the spirit of Craig-Martin's glass of water, I want to explore how much of that is really necessary. How much can we discover in the de-materialised contract of belief that underpins all theatre and which allows two seemingly contradictory ideas to resolve effortlessly in one place. My *An Oak Tree* attempts a similar resolution to the artwork it's inspired by – not with glasses of water and trees, but with actors and characters, through story. Just like any play.[150]

Crouch uses words as 'the ultimate conceptual art form'[151] and, by playing with the unpredictability of live performance, re-shapes the relationship between text and performance in terms of transformation rather than transposition. By foregrounding this transformation which naturalist theatre seeks to conceal, and by challenging and reshuffling the relationships between text

---

[150] Tim Crouch, '*An Oak Tree:* Tim Crouch on the artwork that inspired his play', *National Theatre Website*, 22 June 2015. https://national-theatre.tumblr.com/post/122168645711/an-oak-tree-tim-crouch-on-the-artwork-that (accessed 20 August 2022).

[151] Tim Crouch argues: 'The word is the ultimate conceptual art form, inasmuch as the world is the symbol for an idea or thing, rather than the thing itself. When a word is used, we need to be aware of what it is unlocking in an audience's imagination.' Crouch in Stephen Bottoms, 'Authorizing the Audience: The Conceptual Drama of Tim Crouch', *Performance Research. A Journal of the Performing Arts*, 14, 1 (2009): 67.

and performance, Crouch invites his audiences to question both their own role and the ontological underpinnings of theatre itself.

It is difficult to describe this play, which consists of eight numbered scenes for two actors who play the 'Hypnotist' and the 'Father'. The father loses his daughter in a car accident and deals with his loss by claiming to have 'changed the substance' of a roadside tree where she died into that of his daughter (*Oak* 44–5). The man who drove the car is a stage hypnotist who has lost the power of suggestion since the accident. The play stages their first meeting after the accident, when the father volunteers for the hypnotist's act. While the Hypnotist is often played by Crouch himself, Father is played each night by a different actor, male or female, old or young, who knows nothing about the play before going on stage and is guided through the performance by the first actor (often Crouch) through spoken instructions and pages of script. To date, hundreds of actors have appeared in the play as the father (including Alanis Morissette, Laurie Anderson, Mark Ravenhill and Patrick Marber), each transforming it in their own way. Crouch admits:

> Every single father has been as different as every person is different as different as every interpretation of 'acting' is different. I suppose I could be fussy and say some second actors have spoken too quietly, too quickly, too slowly. I could say some have frozen, have misheard, misinterpreted. Maybe some have acted too much and some have not acted enough. At times, they've each done exactly what I thought I didn't want them to do. But, in so doing, they are each and every one a revelation. They have done the play in their own way. It will never be exactly how I want it – and thank God for that. It would be terrible if it were.[152]

Scripted exchanges between Crouch and the second performer alternate with the confrontation between the Hypnotist and the Father at the Hypnotist's show, as well as with the narration of the scene of the fatal car accident. Within this structure, the audience are involved in the action by being cast as the audience 'upstairs in a pub near Oxford Road', 'this time, next year', yet, at the same time, they are reminded that they are not coincidental with the audience they represent, and therefore addressed and welcomed as an audience in the theatre space in which the play is performed: 'In a short time I'll ask for volunteers, but I am not asking you. I'm asking some people in a pub a year from now. So don't get up' (*Oak* 18–19). They are both in the

---

[152] Tim Crouch, 'Who's the Daddy?', *The Guardian*, 3 August 2005. https://www.theguardian.com/stage/2005/aug/03/theatre (accessed 8 May 2023).

present tense of 'now' and in the future tense of the hypnotic world 'a year from now' (*Oak* 19).

The play exposes the transformations (or frauds?) that theatre tries to hide, like a piano stool standing for a tree, or an actor trying to play a role that they have never seen or known before in any way. Besides, how can the audience judge how free the actor in the role of the Father is to act, since they can never be quite sure what is in the script and what is not? And how can the audience trust the Hypnotist when he promises to tell the truth?

> **Hypnotist** I will never lie to you. You will see no false things tonight. Nothing phoney. No plants, no actors. The people you will see on stage tonight, ladies and gentlemen, apart from me, will be genuine volunteers. You will be stars of the stars of this evening's –
> […]
> I'm just the hypnotist; you are the stars of the show.
> Come up and give me a piece of your mind.
> Your mind.
> Your mind. (*Oak* 19–21)

Is the Hypnotist a fraud and his hypnosis a sham? Constantly shifting between being himself and being an actor, revealing the act of acting and involving the audience in a performance in which it is never sure where the acting begins and ends, is Crouch a deceiver? Audiences' habitual ways of engaging with theatre and performance are short-circuited, while wondering if there can ever be a performer on stage who is not acting at all. Confronted in different and even contradictory ways, the audience is invited to become aware of its own role in the process of producing meaning, and at the same time is led to emotionally experience the illusions/delusions of theatre, despite the absurdity of such a response. Indeed, if it is likely that few viewers of Craig-Martin's piece actually 'see' the glass of water as an oak tree, spectators of Crouch's play actually see the piano stool as a tree. The play is not only a response to Craig-Martin's conceptual work, it goes beyond it, for despite the non-illusionist set and acting, the actors become characters, and Crouch's 'hypnotic' world unfolds in the audience's imagination, so that the confrontation between a grieving father and mother over the death of their daughter is genuinely moving. Is this theatre's revenge on the visual arts? Although in different terms, Crouch's audience, like Leddy's, also participates in that 'reconstruction exercise' at the heart of meta-modern theatre, which is more complex than a simple suspension of disbelief: precisely because they are aware of the fiction of the situation and of their own performative selves, the spectators are free to have an authentic experience.

3

Staging the art gallery

Black boxes and white cubes: From Beckett to Crouch

How do playwrights imagine – and directors (re)create and stage – art galleries and artworks?

Taking account of the complexities and paradoxes of the hermeneutics of theatre, both dramatic and post-dramatic, this chapter traces a trajectory from plays that suggest a mimetic reconstruction of the spaces of art galleries and/or artist's studios on stage, in competition with the spectacle of art, to those that shatter all the familiar dramaturgical landmarks in favour of a radical reconfiguration of the conventions of visual representation, leading to a range of other, non-mimetic representations of such art spaces.

Mimicking the art gallery onstage is the most elementary form of the encounter between theatrical and art gallery interests. The stage serves as a setting for galleries or collections that playwrights, like art curators, imagine and sometimes describe or sketch in their stage directions. In many cases, they seemingly aim to achieve an 'ideal' staging of such art spaces that is implied in the play text and that directors and designers (re)create through the physical presence of canvases, drawings and sculptures. The catalogue of works of art and masterpieces that have been displayed on stage is very rich and ranges from paintings borrowed directly from living artists, such as William Tillyer's aforementioned abstract landscape for Wertenbaker's *Three Birds Alighting on a Field*, to commissioned reproductions of masterpieces, such as Rothko's *Seagram Murals* by Richard Nutborne for Michael Grandage's production of John Logan's *Red* at the Donmar Warehouse. Whatever their function within the plot, all these works of art capture the audience's attention and sharpen their gaze, paradoxically even (and especially) in those cases where what is seen onstage is only the back of the canvas or empty frames. William Hogarth's portrait of Sarah in Nick Dear's *The Art of Success*, described in Chapter 1, or Galactia's epic Battle of Lepanto in Howard Barker's *Scenes from an Execution,* which will be investigated in the following pages, trigger action and speculation and become powerful visual challenges precisely because they are never revealed, emerging only through what is implied by the characters' actions and conversations.

On the other hand, the stage has increasingly become a laboratory where the playwright can experiment with the interaction between exhibiting, performing and storytelling, and actively engage both director and audience in a different way. Indeed, the void of Samuel Beckett's stage as an empty black box, yet one mutely invaded by a complex system of artistic references, seems to have paved the way for generations of playwrights. Drawing, as Beckett did, on the grammars of the visual arts, they have challenged both the conventions of naturalistic theatre and the traditional authorial function of the playwright in guiding the audience through a predetermined and closed dramatic experience. Increasingly, they have made the stage a significant forum for discussion about the relation between displaying and performing, while experimenting with a range of new dramatic forms.

Having abandoned any attempt at naturalism, playwrights – or, rather, theatre-makers – have tended instead towards the production of 'post-dramatic' plays, in which the reduction of explicit stage directions is a theatrical (textual) challenge that contributes to the openness of the plays and requires creative intervention, both in terms of staging and meaning-making. At the intersection of theatre, visual arts and performing arts grammars, they have adopted the sorts of conceptual framing strategies that have been perhaps more often associated with performance artists, placing the emphasis on the creative process of making rather than on the text, as discussed in Duška Radosavljević's *Theatre Making* (2013). My key case studies in this chapter are Martin Crimp's *Attempts on Her Life*, Mark Ravenhill's *pool (no water)* and Tim Crouch's *ENGLAND*. While redefining the role of the text in theatre, these three plays invite directors, designers and actors as well as audiences to participate directly in the process of 'theatre-making' of both art galleries and artworks, thus subverting logocentric discourses of power and confirming the need to rethink the long-lived opposition between narrative and drama/performance.

This stage is a gallery

What is more static, and less dramatic, than a picture hanging on the wall? And yet, paintings can often stoke the imagination of characters and audience, both off and on stage.

Timberlake Wertenbaker told the anecdote of having seen a film as a child in which someone entered a painting and began to live in that landscape, and of having been 'pursued by this possibility ever since'.[1] In similar terms, in Lenkiewicz's *Shoreditch Madonna*, Martha affirms: 'I like visiting the Virgin

---

[1] Timberlake Wertenbaker quoted in Bush, *Theatre of Timberlake Wertenbaker*, 259–60.

and St Anne at the National Gallery. I like to sit and watch them until they start to move' (*Shoreditch* 187). The power of the visual evoked by Martha was, on the contrary, demolished by the 'almost criminally lazy' designer Paul Burgess, who, according to Charles Spencer, instead failed 'to put any works of art on stage'.[2]

However, the dream of a painting coming to life before the viewer's eyes seems to have been realized in many other plays and productions, which sometimes compete with the visual potential of the paintings by offering ravishing productions. Such is the case with Cornish company Kneehigh's lavish 2016 production of Daniel Jamieson's play *The Flying Lovers of Vitebsk*, in which Marc Chagall's multiple canvases dedicated to his wife Bella and himself are repeatedly staged through the seamless interplay of the two extraordinarily multi-talented performers, Marc Antolin and Audrey Brisson.[3] Director Emma Rice, who wowed audiences and critics with an exhilarating combination of dialogue, music, dance, circus skills and set design, says she wanted to immerse herself in Chagall's sensuous and seductive work:

> The colours are intoxicating and his magical, detailed and surprising subjects seem to dart around your heart, mind and soul. The worlds he creates capture another life and a time that I wish I could visit. His paintings allow to do this. They welcome us into this lost and precious world. Green cows and flying Rabbis, intimate kisses and airborne brides; he fills the canvas with dreams, and we all want to share them. His mind was brimming with wonder and it would take the hardest heart not to long to jump into Chagall's world, to fly up and look down through his unique eyes.[4]

Among many others, Chagall's painting *The Birthday* (1915) is brought to life on the stage when, in a fluid moment of physical theatre, actor Marc Antolin, playing Chagall, strokes a thick paintbrush along the curve of his wife Bella Chagall/Audrey Brisson's spine, bending her back until her lips meet his in

---

[2] Charles Spencer, 'Shoreditch Madonna', *Daily Telegraph*, 15 July 2005, reprinted in *Theatre Record 2–15 July 2005*, 947.

[3] Daniel Jamieson, *The Flying Lovers of Vitebsk* (London: Oberon Books, 2017). The original version of *The Flying Lovers of Vitebsk* was performed as *Birthday* by Theatre Alibi in 1992. The Kneehigh production in association with Bristol Old Vic was first performed at Bristol Old Vic on 27 May 2016 and first performed in Kneehigh's Asylum on 14 July 2016.

[4] Emma Rice, 'Q&A between Paul Crewes & Emma Rice. Taking the journey: An Interview with Director Emma Rice', *TheWallis.org/Lovers*, 2018. https://www.thewallis.org/ckeditor/userfiles/files/wallis1718_PerfProg_Feb_WebInterviews%20FLOV.pdf (accessed 8 May 2023).

Figure 3.1 *Sunday in the Park with George.* Music and lyrics by Stephen Sondheim. Book by James Lapine. With Maria Friedman as Dot and Philip Quast as George. Director Steven Pimlott. Designer Tom Cairns. Orchestrations Michael Starobin. Music Director Jeremy Sams. Choreographer Aletta Collins. Lyttelton at the National Theatre, London, March 1990.

Source: Courtesy Richard Mildenhall / ArenaPAL.

an upside-down kiss, even though it is Bella, and not Marc, who leans back on stage to capture the mood of the production (which is not about Chagall's art but rather about the love that sustained him).

It is also worth remembering here George Seurat's *Un dimanche après-midi à l'Île de la Grande Jatte*, which came to life in Sam Buntrock's revival of Stephen Sondheim and James Lapine's multi-award-winning 1984 musical *Sunday in the Park with George*, at the Menier Chocolate Factory in 2005 and then in the West End, at the Wyndham's in 2006 (Figure 3.1). The show, which famously juxtaposes Seurat's pictorial composition with the technical traumas of a modern conceptualist, magically paints a picture through songs, words, music and moving graphics. Drawn in and out of the painting, computer-generated figures animate the back wall of the stage, appearing on a blank, bare canvas and then coming to life singing and speaking, thanks to a sophisticated projection design that 'combines technical wizardry with an emotional charge'.[5]

---

[5] Michael Billington, 'Sunday in the Park with George', *The Guardian*, 25 May 2006, reprinted in *Theatre Record 21 May–3 June 2006*, 617.

The set, designed by David Farley, is a whitewashed room that could be a studio or gallery, but also functions as a canvas, allowing the painting to grow and change as George works on it.

The animation, by Timothy Bird, gives the audience the feeling that they are peering into the artist's mind and watching the creative process unfold. From the very beginning the piece is visually stunning, as reported by Sarah Hemming, who boldly attempts a parallelism between Seurat's pointillist art and the production's computer technologies:

> And just as Seurat's innovative technique allows us to see two colours but mix them in the eye, the production enables us to see 'real' people and his representations simultaneously, to appreciate the gap between their messy, emotional lives and his orderly, calm recreations of them. This makes the moment when they finally assume the positions frozen forever on canvas strangely moving.[6]

In the way that the set designers and directors have managed, here, to convey the aura of famous masterpieces, the stage might be said to rival (or even surpass) the creative and collaborative potential of the art gallery, offering audiences the exciting privilege of witnessing the artistic process of creation and being shown how to view works of art as they are passionately discussed by the artists themselves.

The staging of a famous painting as a tableau vivant offers a moment that allows the audience to experience the pleasure of recognition. But recognition can be both gratifying and risky, as David Pownall wrote of the tableau vivant that opened Alan Strachan's 1977 production at Greenwich Theatre of his *An Audience Called Edouard* (1978), a dramatization of Edouard Manet's painting *Le déjeuner sur l'herbe*. As he explains, he was disappointed by Strachan's decision to raise the curtain on a tableau vivant of Manet's painting, because he felt that this striking visual moment at the very beginning of the performance prevented the audience in the auditorium from direct engagement with the action on stage:

> Manet is painting *Déjeuner sur l'Herbe* on an island in the Seine. Karl Marx arrives, clambering out of the river (the backstage was a giant tank of water), having been pursued across Paris by the police. Manet is not a character. The audience is Manet, and it is painting the picture. The five

---

[6] Sarah Hemming, 'Sunday in the Park with George', *The Guardian*, 25 May 2006, reprinted in *Theatre Record 21 May-3 June 2006*, 620.

characters, two upper-class layabouts and two female models, and Marx, do not interact with the Manet audience, they talk behind his back.

[...] In the case of *An Audience Called Edouard*, there was a major mistake in how the audience was brought onto the island. The opening of the play was the famous picture, familiar to most people with an interest in art, a moment of recognition for the audience that always drew applause. However, there was a price to be paid for it.

This visual moment in all its splendour was in the wrong place, its substance tossed away. The picture should have come together at the end, its power to please held back, allowing audience anticipation to run through the length of the play.

I had to agree not to attend rehearsals because there could be no alteration of the script. [...] Not being able to foresee the wasteful effect of realising the picture right at the beginning was proof of a blind spot in my imagination. I should have seen the mistake as I wrote. Stagecraft is a special gift that comes and goes.[7]

The need for authenticity, especially in biographical plays, has sometimes led directors and stage designers to adopt the model of the diorama, which is often used in museums to reproduce the studios of deceased artists as permanent installations to be gazed at with voyeuristic wonder. Canvases on easels or on walls help to re-create the atmosphere of a gallery or an artist's studio and to encourage audiences to endow the performance with authenticity, even when the biographical material is rearranged and manipulated in the interests of stagecraft and theatricality rather than biographical truth.

The set designed by theatre designer Tim Hatley for Pam Gems' biographical play *Stanley*, about the great English artist Stanley Spencer, first performed by the Royal National Theatre at the Cottesloe on 1 February 1996, is particularly significant in this respect. *Stanley*, which revolves around the eponymous artist's two marriages and his ambition to build a cathedral to display his works, fails to provide a historically accurate account of Spencer's life and art, according to Kenneth Pople, Spencer's chief biographer, who strongly opposed Gems' dramatization.[8] Nevertheless, the play was a huge commercial success, thanks in no small part to the set by Hatley, who won

---

[7] David Pownall, *Writing Master Class* (London: Oberon Books, 2013). Digital version accessed online at British Library, unnumbered.

[8] In a letter to the production's stage manager, Angela Fairclough, Pople accused Gems of rearranging and distorting the material 'into entertainment without enlightenment' for the sake of box-office appeal. Kenneth Pople, 'Letter to Angela Fairclough'. 14 December 1995. Production File for *Stanley*, RNT/SM/1/397, National Theatre Archive, NT Studio, London.

a Lawrence Olivier Award for his design, which was intended to immerse the audience in Spenser's artistic vision of religious iconography and carnal sensuality. One of the most prolific designers in British theatre, who has worked internationally and crossed the boundaries between drama, dance and opera, Hatley belonged to a new generation of set designers. Alongside the generation of playwrights of the 1990s, they made subtle changes to the visual appearance of plays, and in the process made a powerful contribution to the new British theatre, whose strength lies precisely in the combined creativity of writer, actor, director and set designer. Hatley's design transformed the Cottesloe with pews, murals, ladders and scaffoldings on three sides, producing a Spencerian chapel of the Cookham and Glasgow Resurrection scenes, the walls full of torsos and limbs and of Biblical scenes that appear to characterize Spencer's tormented imagination. With the Cottesloe seemingly transformed into a kind of secular cathedral, Hatley was acting as Spencer himself in attempting to fulfil the artist's desire to paint a chapel. No wonder Hatley sells his sketches and paintings as works of art.[9] According to William Feaver, the real Spencer liked charades and would have loved the notion of the Cottesloe transformed into a scene-painter's vision of the Church House, with *The Resurrection, Cookham* under scaffolding, strips of Clydeside shipbuilding down the sides, Bach on the organ and plenty of space in which to talk and talk.[10] Nor is it surprising that London's Rona Gallery has made 'a cameo of the art of the set designer' by dedicating an exhibition to Pamela Howard, theatre designer and professor of scenography at Central St Martin's College of Art and Design.

Such an illusion of authenticity has also been discussed by Ursula Canton, who interviewed students after a performance of Nicholas Wright's *Vincent in Brixton* (2002), a play which deals with Vincent van Gogh's time in London, and which is based entirely on 'bits and pieces of evidence' that served as a basis for the playwright's 'speculat[ion] about what might have happened',[11] as the programme note reveals. Although the play is largely fictional, Canton found that, thanks to Richard Eyre's vivid reconstruction at the Cottesloe in 2002, many students genuinely believed that they had learned something factual about the painter.[12]

---

[9] Linda Relph-Knight, 'Stunning Scenic Routes', *Design Week*, 21 February 1997.
[10] William Feaver, 'Stanley', *Observer*, 4 February 1996, reprinted in *Theatre Record 29 January – 11 February 1996*, 128.
[11] Nicholas Wright, 'The Secrets at the Layers ...' in *Vincent in Brixton* (London: Nick Hern Books), vii–ix, viii.
[12] Ursula Canton, 'We May Not Know Reality, but It Still Matters – A Functional Analysis of "Factual Elements" in the Theatre', *Contemporary Theatre Review*, 18, 3 (2008): 322.

And yet, directors' attempts to re-create an art gallery on stage are not always successful or universally acclaimed. Michael Billington suggested that the real place for Edward Hopper's painting *Summer in the City* should remain the gallery wall and not the stage of Toby Farrow's 2001 play of the same title at the BAC.[13] Similarly, reviewing Lenkiewicz's *The Painter*, a bio-drama about William Turner, Charles Spencer complains that Ben Stones' set, strewn with sketches and canvases, 'doesn't feature much in the way' of Turner's art, even though the intimate Arcola auditorium, created in the converted space of the abandoned Reeves paint factory where Turner and Constable bought their colour blocks, seemed the perfect location for a play portraying the young Turner in the years when he was starting to build his reputation. With a wink at Philip Larkin's dictum that art about art isn't really art at all, the reviewer concludes that unlike Turner's paintings, Lenkiewicz's play 'largely fails to blaze with light and illumination'.[14] In his opinion, the audience was not led to share the author's admiration for the master of British watercolour landscape painting, which is, on the contrary, shown in the play by a collector and enthusiast, Hereford: 'I'm an admirer. A fan. It's fascinating for me. To see you in your own environment. You're the first in your department, Mr Turner, you really are' (*Painter* 53). The play may have not had the aura, but it left the audience curious to learn more about the artist's life and work. While Billington was critical of the production, he acknowledged as a 'positive by-product' that it made you 'want to rush to the Tate to look at Turner's paintings with their impression of what Hazlitt called "tinted steam"'.[15]

In an attempt to re-create the atmosphere of an art gallery or studio, playwrights often use slide projections. Such slideshows are particularly suitable for illustrating paintings that are the subject of a lecture or discussion, giving the audience the chance to see them clearly. As noted in Chapter 2, in Alan Bennett's *A Question of Attribution*, slides of *The Triple Portrait* before and after cleaning as well as Titian's *Allegory of Prudence* accompany both Sir Anthony Blunt's discussion with the restorer about their correct attribution (*Question* 309, 320, 323) and Sir Blunt's lecture on attribution (*Question* 346–8). In addition, the projection on a single screen of reproductions of Titian paintings, alternating with black-and-white photographs of various alleged spies from the 1930s, visually reinforces the link between the refined world of the Old Masters and the ruthless world of Cold War espionage, while also giving rise to inevitable and hilarious misunderstandings.

---

[13] Michael Billington, 'Edward Hopper Takes to the Stage', *The Guardian*, 5 January 2001, 6.
[14] Charles Spencer, 'The Painter', *Daily Telegraph*, 17 January 2011, reprinted in *Theatre Record 1–28 January 2011*, 29.
[15] Michael Billington, 'The Painter – Review', *The Guardian*, 16 January 2011, 7.

Since art can be appreciated on a variety of levels depending on the cultural (and often social) background, awareness and sensitivity of the spectator, it can become the occasion for comical and hilarious conversations full of misunderstandings and misinterpretations, as well as a reflection on the audience's ability to fully grasp the meaning of works so deeply rooted in art history. The highly entertaining tone of the exchanges about art between art historian Sir Anthony Blunt and the detective Chubb, who does not even know the basics of art history, reappears in Lee Hall's *The Pitmen Painters*. Professor Robert Lyon's first lecture in his 'Art appreciation' course, illustrated with slide projections of works by some of the Old Masters, sparks off a lively and hilarious exchange of ideas with his students:

> **Lyon**   [...] And ...
> *He changes the slide to show the ceiling of the Sistine Chapel.*
> Perhaps the crowning achievement of the entire period, of course, is Michelangelo's Sistine Chapel. You have heard of the Sistine Chapel?
> **Jimmy**   Is that the one in Blaydon?
> **Lyon**   Where? No. Blaydon?! No, this is Rome. You do recognise these images, don't you? *The Last Judgement*? *The Creation of Adam*.
> **George**   We haven't really seen much art, actually. That's why we hired you, like.
> **Harry**   To be quite honest with you – we were more keen on Introductory Economics, but we couldn't find a tutor.
> **Lyon**   May I ask you, have you ever been to a gallery?
> **George**   We've never been anywhere. We're pitmen. (*Pitmen* 11)

Professor Lyon's lectures highlight the cultural gulf between the university lecturer and the men of Ashington – not to mention the mutual difficulty in understanding each other, the latter speaking the Northumbrian dialect in sharp contrast to Lyon's Standard English. On the other hand, such scenes seem to reaffirm the educational function of public art galleries and theatres, asking who the target audience of art and theatre is and, more importantly, to what kind of audience such performances might be addressed in the first place.

An art gallery for all

In *The Pitmen Painters* at the Cottesloe Theatre in 2008, Lee Hall and director Max Roberts take the audience on the 'great Art Pilgrimage' that connoisseur, collector, and patron Helen Sutherland organized for the group of pitmen painters both in real life and on stage. Hall and Roberts literally transform the stage into the art galleries that the Group visited or in which they began to exhibit their work. Sharing Robert Lyon's belief in the educational function of art museums, director and designer entertain and educate the audience about the masterpieces on display. They also envisage a new and inclusive art gallery to display the works of the pitmen painters alongside the great masterpieces of art history, in line with the political and somewhat utopian ideal of a new, accessible and friendly space for workers' participation.

The projection of only a few images, as indicated by Hall in the stage directions, allows director Roberts and set and costume designer Gary McCann to conjure up art galleries on stage: Rock Hall Mansion, the Royal Academy, the Tate Gallery and the two galleries where the pitmen painters had their first exhibitions in 1938 and 1941, Bensham Grove Settlement (Gateshead-on-Tyne) and Laing Art Gallery in Newcastle.[16] McCann, who has been involved in productions of opera, musicals, and theatre with some of the world's most significant companies all over the globe, deployed a broadly minimalist design in his re-creation of such galleries as well as the 'Hut', the studio where the pitmen have their class. In fact, the stage is almost bare except for a few canvases leaning against the three walls and wooden chairs arranged in different ways: in rows when the pitmen listen to the teacher, lined up facing the audience or with their backs to the audience when they comment on their paintings or horseshoe-shaped for the committee meeting. According to Roberts, 'as the play goes through, the paintings are revealed so by the end of the play there is a little gallery'.[17]

Indeed, Hall himself suggests in his stage directions how to evoke the atmosphere of an art gallery on stage, while rejecting any attempt at mimetic naturalism. For the scene at the Royal Academy, 'Lyon walks into the scene as if moving around the exhibition' (*Pitmen* 67), while, for the Group's first exhibition at Bensham there should be 'the usual loud noise, but this time it is the sharp baying of an audience at a gallery' (*Painter* 82). When discussing and arguing about the merits of their paintings, the actors gather around the paintings on the easel. In Hall's view, the discussion around a painting, even if static, is itself very dramatic:

> Where the drama is, is in the drama of ideas, and people arguing between each other. The act of analysing individual paintings was actually a very interesting

---

[16] The Exhibition at the Laing Art Gallery of 1941 is the only one mentioned in the play, even if the gallery had hosted a previous one in March 1938. See William Feaver, *Pitmen Painters. The Ashington Group 1934–1984* (Newcastle upon Tyne: Northumbria Press in association with Ashington Group Trustees, 2010), 67.

[17] Max Roberts at the National Theatre with Lee Hall and William Feaver on *The Pitmen Painters*, 4 June 2008, National Theatre Archive, Platform Video Recording RNT/AE/1/2/132.

Figure 3.2 *The Pitmen Painters* written by Lee Hall and directed by Max Roberts. With David Whitaker as Jimmy Floyd, Christopher Connel as Oliver Kilbourn, Michael Hodgson as Harry Wilson, Phillippa Wilson as Helen Sutherland, Brian Lonsdale as Young Lad, and Ian Kelly as Robert Lyon. Cottesloe Theatre at The Royal National Theatre, London, May 2008.

Source: Courtesy Elliott Franks / ArenaPAL.

and dramatic form. […] Actually, it was about what drama is fundamentally about, which is about people struggling to articulate something.[18]

At other times, the actors look towards the audience pretending to contemplate invisible canvases, while the works of art are often projected in magnified detail behind them. The audience is thus led to look simultaneously at both the works of art flowing across the screens as the characters talk about them and at the characters contemplating them. The playwright involves them in the discussion of the painting by showing them the individual details under scrutiny. At the same time, he creates a distance that allows them to take a critical stance towards the action and the appreciation of the paintings.

Rock Hall, near Alnwick, in Northumberland, leased by wealthy collector Helen Sutherland between 1929 and 1939, is the first art gallery visited by the Group of pitmen painters and re-created by Hall and McCann (Figure 3.2).

---

[18] Lee Hall quoted in Robert Simonson, 'Watching Paint Dry: How Playwrights Turn Art-Making Into High Drama', *Playbill*, 6 October 2010. https://playbill.com/article/watching-paint-dry-how-playwrights-turn-art-making-into-high-drama-com-172202 (accessed 27 September 2023).

This visit provides the playwright with the opportunity to reiterate the social and cultural distance between the self-taught painters and the sophisticated Helen Sutherland, who, nevertheless, became an early patron of their Group. While Sutherland condescendingly refers to Rock Hall mansion as 'a kind of spiritual sanctuary' (*Pitmen* 59), whose collection includes an 'exquisite' Henry Moore's sketch of *A Woman Reclining*, 1933, and a Ben Nicholson painting, all white, 'a circle with a square cut out', the pitmen are more astonished and intimidated by the wealth and 'the many settees' she has than by her art collection. George tells his mates not to sit on the sofa or 'they'll think yer common' (*Pitmen* 52). Harry, the staunchest socialist of the Group, does not miss the opportunity to remind everyone that 'every single thing in this room's been paid for by some poor stevedore breaking his back in some P&O engine sixteen hours a day' (*Pitmen* 52). As for the works of art displayed, they fail to understand what they mean and to appreciate their experimental value. Harry dismisses an Alfred Wallis as 'a load of rubbish', George thinks the head of Moore's sketch 'is a bit small', and Young Lad naïvely and comically concludes, 'Ne wonder she [Helen Sutherland] thinks Jimmy [Jimmy Floyd, one of the pitmen painters] is a genius, if this is what she normally buys' (*Pitmen* 53).

When they are in the Royal Academy for what is apparently the largest exhibition of Chinese art ever to be shown outside China, their experience is condensed into a debate over a long and fairly simple watercolour of 'a bird on a branch, a tree by a stream', which appears split across the three screens. Again, it is a moment of a confrontation, although, in this case, it is also the occasion for Oliver and George to show their freedom in judging art and their understanding of what makes art, art. Indeed, arguing against their tutor Lyon, who finds the Chinese works 'formulaic', Harry values them in the light of a long tradition and even quotes 'Roger Fry and that whole Omega lot – tradition of craftsman' (*Pitmen* 66–9), demonstrating his growing knowledge and artistic sensibility.

When the Group moves into the Tate, a slide show begins, with a photograph of the gallery projected on the central screen, along with 'slides of the guys on the steps, and inside examples of the art mentioned' (*Pitmen* 69): besides the famous picture of the Group published in William Feaver's book, which inspired the play, there are paintings by Cézanne, Utrillo, Blake, Turner and van Gogh, who, as noted in Chapter 1, is their favourite. The van Gogh Room is full of masterpieces, more than the Tate actually has. It is a gallery conjured up through images of paintings that the pitmen painters saw in books, which are projected on the three screens together with huge close-ups of their details, illustrating the pitmen's discussion of the Dutch artist's work. As a slideshow of the aforementioned works begins, including

Self-Portrait, Starry Night, Sunflowers, The Bedroom and the early drawing of the miners (*Pitmen* 73–5), van Gogh's art is praised as collective, spiritual, 'breathing life' and belonging to all.

Significantly, Hall not only transforms the stage into the galleries that the pitmen painters visit, but also turns it into the 'Hut', the laboratory/studio in which they attend Professor Lyon's course and learn to appreciate art. It is here that they discuss the genesis, meaning and composition of masterpieces as well as their own work, instructing the audience, involving them in their personal appreciation of the paintings and entertaining them with the comic situations and observations that arise from the differing opinions on the works. The Hut is shown as a site both of production and critical debate, and for personal and social improvement.

In the Live Theatre and National Theatre co-production, director and designer followed Hall's stage directions and opted for a projection of the pitmen painters' works on screens between Brechtian-style captions, which 'cut across the naturalism of the scene' (*Pitmen* 37) and helped to reinforce the political meanings of the play. By alternating slides of the pitmen's paintings with series of slides providing social and historical context (dates, places, historical events) and statistical data about the pitmen's working conditions (average hours worked, average take-home pay, etc.), as well as archival material, including photographs of the men on whom the characters are based, Roberts and McCann attempted to set the scene before each act, informing the audience about the history of the Group and thereby to encourage the audience to take a particular political stance. The audience was asked to consider the living conditions of the pitmen painters, as well as the right of the working classes to knowledge, culture and education. The audience, vicariously taking part in the 'Art Appreciation' class, could join in the discussion of Oliver's linocut on the theme of 'Work' and ponder Harry's definition of the work as 'a glorification of the exploitation of the common man' (*Pitmen* 21) because they could see the work. As the stage notes indicate, Oliver's image of a miner burrowing into the coalface is projected on the central screen, while the second and third screens show each of the details that are mentioned, the head, the shoulder, the boots, the roof, the light (*Pitmen* 23) (Figure 3.3).

When it is his turn to present his work, Harry politicizes his portrait of a miner chained to the attributes of his job, arguing that he intended to depict metaphorical chains, 'chains of oppression tied to the wheel of industry' and a clock representing 'the tyranny of the wage-slave system' (*Pitmen* 23, 24). He rejects Young Lad's interpretation of the pipe as a Freudian symbol, claiming that his work 'is about politics and that's that' (*Pitmen* 25).

Through these confrontational dialogues, Hall conveys the idea that Pitmen Painters were both a collective enterprise and a loose affiliation of

Figure 3.3 *The Pitmen Painters* written by Lee Hall and directed by Max Roberts. With David Whitaker as Jimmy Floyd, Deka Walmsley as George Brown, Michael Hodgson as Harry Wilson, Ian Kelly as Robert Lyon, Christopher Connel as Oliver Kilbourn, and Brian Lonsdale as Young Lad. Cottesloe Theatre at The Royal National Theatre, London, May 2008.

Source: Courtesy Elliott Franks / ArenaPAL.

different individuals trying to find their way. He therefore presents them as articulate, politicized and confident, as they were in fact (as evidenced, e.g. by the thirteen articles they wrote between 1936 and 1938 for the *Ashington Collieries Magazine*, which became the group's platform). Accordingly, when given a theme, they appropriate and develop it in different ways. Invited to draw inspiration from 'the Deluge', for example, Harry conceives *The East Wind*. This painting stemmed from Harry's desire for 'something more from round here' (*Pitmen* 32) and became one of the Group's exemplary pictures, despite George's judgement that it is 'technically' not a deluge at all. Indeed, this image of a street corner with 'some folk who are heading into the wind and others who are waiting round the corner' (*Pitmen* 33) is the first of the Group's factual accounts of 'the impact of a wind straight off the North Sea',[19] something everyone in Ashington felt and knew. Jimmy's account of how his deluge became the image of a dog, *The Bedlington Terrier*,[20] is an amusing

---

[19] Feaver, *Pitmen Painters*, 27.
[20] All the pictures the characters produce in the play were originally painted by their namesakes, with the exception of William Scott's *Bedlington Terrier* of 1937, which is attributed to Jimmy Floyd.

theatrical moment (*Pitmen* 28–31), while, on a more serious level, Oliver has the opportunity to reflect openly on his own personal empowerment as he paints his *Deluge*, a work depicting houses swept away by the violence of a storm, which Feaver describes as 'ordinariness drowned in emotion'.[21] Oliver's *Deluge* is much appreciated by his classmates, while Jimmy's abstract contribution to the 1939 War Ministry's commission for a painting on 'Preparation for Battle', *The Blob*, is heavily criticized as 'bourgeois formalism'. Dismissed as a work 'mimicking a style which is actually somebody's else's', it sparks a debate about the relationship between social classes and art subjects, fuelled by Oliver's idea that 'there can't be one lot of things that posh people can draw and another lot of things for us' (*Pitmen* 97).

More images of the Group's paintings are shown on the three screens as the stage is transformed into Bensham, Gateshead, the space that hosted the Group's first exhibition. A series of images of their work are projected behind Lyon, who addresses the audience and introduces the Ashington Group as the first and only group of working people who have made art. The audience observe them as he claims that the exhibition is 'the evidence that […] in every mine, every street, workplace, is the potential for works of art to blossom and grow and amaze us with their riches' (*Pitmen* 83–4). Hall leaves the selection of the paintings to be projected to the director Max Roberts and designer Gary McCann, who ultimately presented a virtual/digital Ashington Group exhibition featuring painting of everyday life in the pit or at work, very different from the YBA's conceptual works that were much talked about in the 1990s. Among them were Jimmy Floyd's *The Miner* (c. 1939), *Bait Time* (1946), *Pigeon Crees* (c. 1938); George Blessed's *Whippets* (c. 1939); Oliver Kilbourn's *Mother and Child* (c. 1939), *The Dogs* (1936), *Evening Paper* (1936), *Football* (c. 1937), *My Life as a Pitman* (*The Deputy's Kist*) (1976); Andy Foreman's *The Bar: Playing Dominoes* (c. 1936); Harry Wilson's *Ashington Collier, Northumberland, 1936*; and Andy Rankin's *Pit Accident* (1938). There are scenes of toil, pit accidents and struggle, but also of shops, pubs, seaside and countryside, domestic scenes, children playing and people socializing. Audiences are entertained and educated by such a rich collection of works they may never have seen or heard of.

It is important to point out, with art historian and critic Susannah Thompson, that playwright Lee Hall himself can be seen as an 'intermediary', along with figures such as Robert Lyon, Helen Sutherland, William Feaver and their contacts in the art world. Thompson rightly suggests the playwright's account of the Ashington's Group was 'sensitive to the men's own need to

---

[21] Feaver, *Pitmen Painters*, 22.

reclaim their history' and provided a platform, however fictional, for the men to respond to their patrons and to correct some of the latter's assumptions. Not surprisingly, much of the dialogue between Oliver Kilbourn and Harry Wilson is based on Feaver's book. As a visual record of the mining community in the mid-20th century, argues Thompson, these works are a 'testament to the determination of the miners to represent themselves rather than being represented'[22] and can be seen as a successful example of the participation in the artistic production that Hall encourages and promotes. Indeed, by exhibiting the works of the almost unknown Ashington Group alongside masterpieces by famous painters, Hall seeks to realize his utopic project of a near future in which the working classes would have access to education and could create works of art worthy of display in art galleries and museums. At the height of the Groups' success and near the end of the play, Hall's utopia is expressed by George Brown and Harry Wilson, speaking in the language of the southeast Northumberland coalfields:

> **George** Nebody's ganna be satisfied with just coming off their shift and vegetating – they're all ganna want what we want. For centuries and centuries they kept aal the good stuff for themselves. But they're not gonna leave yer Shakespeare or Goethe just for the upper classes now – it's ganna belang to us.
> **Harry** This is just the start. This place'll be an academy. In years to come it'll be teeming with artists in here: bakers, pitmen, housewives. […] Everybody actually living a proper creative life. (*Pitmen* 122).

Notoriously, the Group's (and Hall's) utopian agenda of museums and culture for all fell apart, and the play ends on a disconsolate note as the final words on the screen register: 'No university of Ashington was founded. Woodhorn Colliery was closed in 1981. In 1995, the call for the "Common ownership of the means of production and exchange" was excised from the Labour Party constitution' (*Pitmen* 124). The hopes of the 1945 election were dashed. New Labour's rhetoric of regeneration in the 1990s and 2000s proved unable to undo the devastating effects of Tory policies in the 1980s. The piece ends with a reminder of how New Labour undermined the socialist and collectivist ethos that defined the left in the 1970s and 1980s by controversially rewriting Clause IV, a fundamental principle of the Labour Party constitution, which had established public ownership as the party's main goal. In spite of all this,

---

[22] Susannah Thompson, ' "But ye de de art, divvint ye?" Authenticity, Identity and the Historicization of the Pitmen Painters', *Visual Studies*, 28, 3 (2013): 213.

the Ashington Group's amateur paintings have survived and continue to engage with contemporary politics and history, thanks in no small part to the success of Hall's play.

To exhibit or not to exhibit?

While Hall's *The Pitmen Painters* turns the stage into an art gallery full of works, Howard Barker's visually extravagant *Scenes from an Execution* explores the complex mise en scène of a single, yet controversial and extraordinary painting, the exhibition of which poses problems both at the level of the play-text, for the character of the Doge of Venice who commissions it and has to decide whether or not to display it publicly (as seen in Chapter 1), and at the level of the performance, for the director who has to decide whether or not to show it.

The huge painting at the centre of the piece is a depiction of the battle of Lepanto (1572), commissioned by the Doge to honour the Venetian Republic and painted by a fictitious artist, Galactia, 'divorced, promiscuous and combative' (*Scenes* 272). With a violence reminiscent of Artemisia Gentileschi's work and inspired by Andrea Vicentino's monumental representation of the battle in his fresco in the Sala dello Scrutinio at the Doge's Palace,[23] Galactia's stomach-churningly realistic depiction of the battle as a 'great waterfall of flesh' (*Scenes* 287) contradicts the hagiographic intentions of the Doge, who is humiliated and enraged by a painting that shows the atrocities of war and the suffering of the victims on both sides, the Holy League and the Ottomans. Through the conflict between the Doge and Galactia, who is first sent to prison and then treated as a celebrity when her work is finally and triumphantly exhibited in the Doge's Palace thanks to the mediation of the art critic Rivera, Barker questions the subversive potential of art exhibitions, reflects on the chains that inevitably bind artists to their patrons and interrogates artists' responsibilities to their art and themselves.

Originally conceived as a radio drama and first broadcast on BBC Radio 3 on 14 October 1984, *Scenes from an Execution* is an ambitious attempt to extend the expressive range of radio drama and to visualize virtually the whole of a Renaissance costume drama, including Galactia's epic painting. In fact, as always on radio, it is the words that conjure up the spectacle of the events and make the painting visible. Barker himself explained that in writing the play he had attempted 'to actually use the act of painting as a

---

[23] Andrea Vicentino, *La Battaglia di Lepanto* (1595–1605), oil on canvas, 520 × 1390 cm, Sala dello Scrutinio, Doge's Palace, Venice.

radio technique – the practice of visual representation as it occurs in an artist's mind'.[24]

Since it exists entirely as the listener's projection, evoked by the dialogues and a talking Sketchbook that seems to parody the *ut pictura poësis* topos, the image of Galactia's battle of Lepanto is apparently free to acquire an immediacy that no conventional painting can match. In the process, the narrative invites listeners to enter what Heiner Zimmermann has called Barker's *musée imaginaire* and share 'the memories of paintings' that had a part in the making of the play.[25] In fact, Barker, a painter himself who emphasizes the close relationship between his oil paintings and his theatre in his own preface to the catalogue of an exhibition of his paintings at the Musée des Beaux Arts in Caen in 2008–9,[26] engages his audiences with a museum of pictures. While explicit references to specific paintings in the plays are rare, he refers to the paintings that inspired his plays in programme notes and commentaries. Departing from the long iconographic tradition, from Tintoretto to Veronese, of celebrating victory and the sanctity of the Crusade, Galactia's depiction of the battle shows the fury of the fighters and the bodies of the wounded, in the style of the Vicentino painting:

> **Sketchbook** Painting the Dying. The dead and the dying occupy one third of the entire canvas, which is no less than six hundred and six square feet, an area not strictly in accordance with the sketch submitted to the authorities. They lie sprawled, heaped, and doubled against gunwales and draped over oars, with expressions of intolerable pain, and by a method of foreshortening, their limbs, attached and unattached, project uncomfortably towards the viewer … (*Scenes* 276)

The character of Prodo, 'the Man with the Crossbow Bolt in His Head' (a nickname written in capital letters like the titles of works of art) confirms the inspiration, as he looks like a copy of the man in the foreground of the fresco with the crossbow bolt embedded in his bald skull. But alongside

---

[24] Barker in Tony Dunn, 'Interview with Howard Barker'. *Gambit. International Theatre Review*, 11 (1984): 34.
[25] Heiner Zimmermann, 'Memories of Paintings in Howard Barker's Theatre', in David Ian Rabey and Sarah Goldingay (eds), *Howard Barker's Art of Theatre. Essays on His Plays, Poetry and Production Work* (Manchester: Manchester University Press, 2013), 193.
[26] On Barker's painting see Michel Morel, 'Howard Barker's Paintings, Poems and Plays: 'In the Deed' Itself', or the Triple Excavation of the Inchangeable', in Rabey and Goldingay (eds), *Howard Barker's Art of Theatre*, 183–91.

this Renaissance source, the description of the painting by Galactia and the Sketchbook seem to allude to much more contemporary inspirations. One cannot help but think of Francis Bacon's obsession with slaughterhouses, meat and carcasses when the Sketchbook lingers on the description of mutilated bodies (*Scenes* 276) or when Galactia, defining the battle as a 'butchery', focuses on depicting 'meat sliced':

> **Galactia**   I am painting the battle, Prodo. [...] One thousand square feet of canvas. Great empty ground to fill. With noise. Your noise. The noise of men minced. Got to find a new red for all that blood. A red that smells. (*Scenes* 257)
>
> **Galactia**   And when I show meat sliced, it is meat sliced, it is not a pretext for elegance. Meat sliced. How do you slice meat? (*Scenes* 271)

Although Galactia's Battle of Lepanto can never be as eloquent as when it is invisible, stage productions have tried to make it visible. In the theatre, the painting becomes a visual problem for the director, who has to (re)present it through the use of theatrical effects that, by definition, inhibit the exercise of the individual spectator's imagination.

David Fielding's stage set for the minimalist 1990 production at the Almeida Theatre, directed by Ian McDiarmid and starring Glenda Jackson, was almost bare: a claustrophobic black box with three black-tiled walls covered with chalk sketches of anatomical details (skulls, skeletons of legs and hands, bony pelvis), human figures, and black-and-white drawings that in some way reflect the play's main themes and characters, such as the sketch of the man whose body is pierced with arrows (an allusion to both Antonello da Messina's painting *Saint Sebastian* and the character of Prodo in the play) (Figure 3.4).

In this space, which seems more an anatomical theatre than an art gallery, Galactia's painting was only shown once, when it is revealed to Carpeta, and was represented by a large white cloth which was stretched over the heads of the actors, and which itself was suffused with light. However, Elissa Guralnick asks provocatively, 'Who in that audience attended to the cloth in an effort to fill it with phantasmal shapes and figures, when standing beneath it, competing for attention, were Galactia and Carpeta? Very likely, no one.'[27]

The Wrestling School's abstract 1999 revival of the play at the Barbican Pit (21 September–9 October), directed by Barker himself and starring Kathryn

---

[27] Elissa S. Guralnick, *Sight Unseen. Beckett, Pinter, Stoppard, and Other Contemporary Dramatists on Radio* (Athens: Ohio University Press, 1996), 27.

Figure 3.4 *Scenes from an Execution* written by Howard Brenton and directed by Ian McDiarmid. With Glenda Jackson as Galactia, Johnathan Hyde as the Doge of Venice, Kevin McNally as Carpeta, Ralph Nossek as the Cardinal Ostensibile, Jeremy Child as Suffici, and Julian Forsyth as Pastaccio. Almeida Theatre, London, January 1990.

Source: Courtesy Ivan Kyncl / ArenaPAL.

Hunter as Galactia (Figure 3.5), challenged audiences with an elusive image designed at once to capture their imagination and to encapsulate the play's many tensions and contradictions.

As is typical of his 'catastrophic' theatre, Barker conjures up disturbing but compelling imagery that has the unsettling resonance of a dream, creating surprising and haunting incongruities. A contraption by designer Tomas Leipzig confronted the audience as they entered the auditorium: a mechanical pulley raised a large dripping white sail out of a deep iron well, creating the (miked and amplified) sound of a rhythmic plunge into the water, and thus helping to establish 'the keynote of human ingenuity and the unstable terrain of Venice, and its distinctive element of dissolution'.[28]

It was a very powerful stage image, almost an art installation, which aroused many questions. Was the dripping canvas repeatedly hauled from

---

[28] David Ian Rabey, *Howard Barker: Ecstasy and Death. An Expository Study of His Drama, Theory and Production Work, 1988–2008* (Berlin: Springer Nature, 2009), 109.

Staging the Art Gallery 175

Figure 3.5 *Scenes from an Execution* written by and directed by Howard Barker. With Kathryn Hunter as Galactia. Barbican Pit, London, September 1999.

Source: Courtesy Geraint Lewis / ArenaPAL.

the well a sail from one of the galleys at Lepanto? Was it a painting? When Galactia is released from prison and crouches foetally centre stage, this canvas suddenly emerged soaked in blood. Was it Galactia's painting? Or was it the representation of her capitulation, as Paul Taylor seemed to suggest, since, once unhooked, it turned out to be a dress that Galactia put on? Indeed, as he wrote,

> Kathryn Hunter wrestled her way into it in a manner that thrillingly shows a desperate overcoming of revulsion. Then she rises and, by an arch of the back and a tilt of the head, transforms herself from dissident detainee into a cocktail-sipping socialite at the private viewing of her paintings. The image of Galactia in a cross between a stylish frock and a butcher's apron brings home with a hideous clarity the cost of compromise and the state's domestication of violence'.[29]

Barker's abstract and highly evocative set was designed to emphasize both the timelessness of the play and its modern relevance, as its scathing analysis of the ways in which power seeks to manipulate and domesticate subversive art remained sadly relevant. The scene was immediately made contemporary by the disturbing scene of the three soldiers in wheelchairs, their heads hanging and bandaged, recalling more recent wars, from the Falklands to the Gulf War or the Bosnian War. Moreover, as many critics have pointed out, the tendency of Lucy Weller's costume designs simultaneously to evoke both sixteenth-century Venice and twentieth-century haute couture contributed to the creation of this complex overlapping of heterogeneous time periods. This acidly funny play that spares no one (artists, critics or patrons) spoke both to and of the England at the end of the millennium. As Carole Woodis contended, 'With its female artist forced to become her own pickled exhibit to keep up with the Damien Hirsts of end-of-millennium conceptualism, issues of integrity and female creativity have hardly gone away. Rather, they've multiplied'.[30]

In Sweet Pea Productions' small-scale revival at The Hackney Empire Acorn, London, in 2007, director William Oldroyd threaded a sense of urgency that made the play's relevance to the contemporary world even more explicit. Sam Marlowe described Robert Goodale's Urgentino as being 'as eager to befriend the culturally chic as Tony Blair inviting Oasis to No

---

[29] Paul Taylor, 'Scenes from an Execution', *Independent*, 27 September 1999, reprinted in *Theatre Record 10–23 September 1999*, 1232.
[30] Carole Woddis, 'Scenes from an Execution', *Herald*, 1 October 1999, reprinted in *Theatre Record 10–23 September 1999*, 1234.

10',[31] while Lyn Gardner suggested that if Tony Blair had seen this play, he might have thought twice before taking the country to war in Iraq.[32] Gardner described Goodale's Urgentino, meanwhile, as 'urbane, cultured and expedient' and as 'more director of the Tate than the Byzantine Doge'.[33] Designer Signe Beckmann's hyper-modern all-white set resembled a white cube, where Galactia's oil painting was a blank wall that functioned, almost entirely, as an invitation for the viewers' more or less private or collective projections.

In the successful 2012 revival directed by Tom Cairns at the Lyttleton Theatre, the first Barker play at the National Theatre, Hildegard Bechtler's stark, looming set resembled 'a monolithic empty gallery',[34] whose austere verticals and avoidance of realism recalled the best of Barker's own productions for the Wrestling School. Indeed, Lyttleton's equipment met Bechtler and Cairn's ambitions, lifting and moving large walls that looked like paintings themselves, transforming the stage into an art gallery, as suggested by Fiona Shaw, who interpreted Galactia: they looked like 'sort of Mondrian paintings. You have an archbishop or a cardinal sitting next to a tall wall, and suddenly you're in a Francis Bacon, or you were in something more classical, something Renaissance'.[35]

The looming sets evoked the epic nature of Galactia's canvas without actually showing it, although some tableaus sometimes seemed to suggest parts of it. After all, the idea of an art gallery was further reinforced by transforming the Sketchbook into a contemporary curator in modern clothes rather than a storyteller or the voice of Galactia's creative energy, as it had been in the original radio play. Gerrard McArthur, as the Sketchbook, appeared in a floating white cube (Figure 3.6), while below Galactia sketched her painting or arranged the actors on stage in tableaux bathed in a blue light that made them look artificial and different from the real action on stage, eventually presenting them as possible groups of figures in her painting.

At times, the Sketchbook paced the stage delivering his lines as if he were describing the work of art (or details of it) in a gallery. Indeed, the production

---

[31] Sam Marlowe, 'Scenes from an Execution', *The Times*, 16 January 2007, reprinted in *Theatre Record* 1–28 *January 2007*, 31–6.
[32] Lyn Gardner, 'Scenes from an Execution', *The Guardian*, 17 January 2007, reprinted in *Theatre Record* 1–28 *January 2007*, 32–6.
[33] Caroline McGinn, 'Scenes from an Execution', *Time Out London*, 17 January 2007, reprinted in *Theatre Record* 1–28 *January 2007*, 36.
[34] Andrzej Lukowskj, 'Scenes from an Execution', *Time Out London*, 9 October 2012, reprinted in *Theatre Record* 23 *September – 6 October 2012*, 1051.
[35] Fiona Shaw in conversation with Hanna Berrigan, 'Acting Barker', in James Reynolds and Andy W. Smith. *Howard Barker's Theatre: Wrestling with Catastrophe* (London: Bloomsbury Methuen Drama, 2015), 175–88.

Figure 3.6 *Scenes from an Execution* written by Howard Barker and directed by Tom Cairns. With Fiona Shaw as Galactia, Gerrard McArthur as the Sketchbook, and Phoebe Nicholls as Rivera. Lyttelton Theatre at the National Theatre, London, October 2012.

Source: Courtesy Marilyn Kingwill / ArenaPAL.

resonated with the 2010s. Fiona Shaw/Galactia was a modern Artemisia Gentileschi, whose disturbing painting *Judith Beheading Holofernes*, among other things, inspired Barker's play *Judith* (1990).[36] But she also prowled the stage in a smock revealing her body like 'a Renaissance Tracy Emin'.[37] Thus, Galactia's ultimate success is made all the more resonant and topical by the reference to Emin and her uneven career. Notoriously, Emin began as a maverick and controversial outsider and then became an establishment-branded artist, betraying her roots and original subversive intentions (according to some critics), and content, like other YBAs, 'to play the well-remunerated role of court dwarf'.[38] With a similarly ascendant parabola, Galactia, whose imprisonment leads the audience to believe that she is about to be killed, is instead released and her painting is exhibited – indeed, she is even invited to the Doge's party. In a short-circuiting of art and theatre, the creative and biographical entanglement between Galactia and Emin suggests some sort of sisterhood in art and life, and even an overlap with Barker himself. In fact, Dan Rebellato sarcastically reads both the play itself as 'an allegory' of the very project of reviving *Scenes from an Execution* at the National Theatre and Galactia's capitulation as Barker's when he decides to have his play produced in a venue that had previously repeatedly excluded him:

> Barker has made such a thing of his opposition to the National that it inevitably is going to seem that being embraced by the National might serve as a kind of neutering of his own oppositional stance, as much as the Doge's ultimate patronage robs Galactia of her radicalism. [...] For some reason, the production now has her in an elegant black dress. Throughout the play, she's been in rough linen clothes, in earthen colours. Now she looks dressed up to the nines. And why not? It's not every day you have a major painting unveiled by the state. But this anticipates her capitulation to state power at the end of the play. In the other productions I have seen (and the original radio production) she shows up at the hanging in a state of horror, refusing to believe that her painting can have been so neutered. It is witnessing the power of the state that brings her to her knees. The last words of the play are her decision to buckle to power. Here though, she turns up in a killer dress, a laugh on her lips. Her demeanour appeared to say, how silly I was, why

---

[36] Ibid., 180.
[37] Michael Billington, 'Scenes from an Execution', *The Guardian*, 6 October 2012, reprinted in *Theatre Record* 23 September – 6 October 2012, 1051.
[38] Julian Stallabrass, *High Art Lite. The Rise and Fall of Young British Art* (London: Verso, 2006), 308.

can't we just get along? Of course, she accepts the Doge's invitation to dinner; she's already dressed for it. And this, in turn, seems to become a kind of apology for Howard Barker. Of course, he allows the National to perform his work on their stage. Why wouldn't he? How silly we all were; why can't we just get along?[39]

It is also important to remember that Barker is known to have repeatedly sent manuscripts of plays to the National Theatre, with the rejections often seen as evidence that he, much like Galactia rejoicing in her imprisonment, remained true to his aesthetic and theatrical vision. As such, the fact that his work was subsequently produced by the National Theatre, with very little input from the Wrestling School, further complicates the relationship between Barker's aesthetic and his explicit aim of resisting dominant and popular theatrical modes, conventions and commitments. It is no coincidence, then, that in response to his undoubted neglect by the British theatre establishment (including the Arts Council, which withdrew funding for Wrestling School in 2007), Barker chose to stage at the National Theatre precisely *Scenes from an Execution*, a play in which, in Brechtian style, his questioning of the ethics of art and the artist complicates an apparently simple defence of artistic integrity. Indeed, he shows the commissioning Doge not as some vulgar philistine but as a patron with a genuine passion for art. Galactia herself is not only brilliant and talented but also 'unsympathetic', 'selfish', 'arrogant and vain', as her lover Carpeta defines her. He also cleverly uses the art critic Rivera to demonstrate how even the most transgressive art can be co-opted by the state. Above all, Galactia's 'yes' at the end of the play is ambiguous, as it can be interpreted as final acquiescence or defiance. In Barker's own words: 'What is the style that will carry us through the times in which we live?'[40]

The artist's studio

As art historian David A. Scott explains, 'The voyeuristic experience of gazing at a replica of an artist's studio invokes awe at the faithful reproduction of the milieu of the artist in his or her intimate surroundings',[41] even when none of

---

[39] Dan Rebellato, 'Scenes from an Execution'. http://www.danrebellato.co.uk/spilled ink/2013/3/11/scenes-from-an-execution, 2012 (accessed 8 May 2023).
[40] Howard Barker, lecture at The Wresting School Summer School, University of Exeter, 20–2 August 2009, in David Ian Rabey, 'Introduction: The Ultimate Matter of Style', in Rabey and Goldingay (eds), *Howard Barker's Art of Theatre* (Manchester: Manchester University Press, 2013), 2.
[41] David A. Scott, *Art Authenticity, Restoration, Forgery* (Los Angeles: Cotsen Institute of Archaeology Press, 2016), 410.

these may be authentic in terms of spatial location or artefactual content, as the French conceptual artist Daniel Buren noted in his important essay *The Function of the Studio* (1979).[42] Suffice it to mention the success as a tourist attraction of the reconstruction of Eduardo Paolozzi's supposedly original studio on display at the Edinburgh National Gallery of Scotland, moved from its original locale in Chelsea, London. Similarly, Francis Bacon's studio was moved from 7 Reece Mews in South Kensington and carefully reconstructed for its permanent housing in Dublin's Hugh Lane Gallery, where it is exhibited as 'a shrine to his Saturnine genius'.[43] Bacon's reconstructed studio, 'preserved as it is in its Plexiglas shell', resembles 'an empty stage set, or an old-style natural history museum display. As such, it lacks only its taxidermized protagonist',[44] argues art historian and curator David J. Getsy, who strongly criticizes this touristic exploitation that has missed 'the chance to make a useful critical contribution to the understanding of Bacon – or of modern art'.[45] However, the recent exhibition at the Whitechapel, *The Artist's Studio*,[46] has confirmed the artist's studio as a physical space, a genre and a theme that has been re-imagined and explored by artists themselves, documented by photographers and filmmakers and preserved in situ or reconstructed within art museums and galleries.

Not surprisingly, this site of artistic creation has also held a certain amount of visual fascination for playwrights, providing both a setting and a subject for their plays. Playwrights have thus capitalized on the tendency within the art world to fetishize not only the work of art but also the place where artists have traditionally conceived it – a kind of cultish tendency that, as has been demonstrated again and again, retains its hold on the collective imagination. Whether conceived as workshops, social networks or states of mind, artists' studios have captivated audiences through their associations with freedom from convention, unbridled creativity, bohemian lifestyles and the struggle for success. They offer the opportunity to think about the spatial relationship of the studio both to the artwork and to the visitor. The artist's studio is also an arena where artists of different generations, genders and

---

[42] Daniel Buren, 'The Function of the Studio', *October*, 10 (Autumn 1979): 56–7.
[43] Robert Storr, 'A Room of One's Own, a Mind of One's Own', in Mary Jane Jacob and Michelle Grabner (eds), *The Studio Reader: On the Space of Artists* (Chicago: University of Chicago Press, 2010), 62.
[44] David J. Getsy, 'The Reconstruction of the Francis Bacon Studio in Dublin', in Jacob and Grabner (eds), *The Studio Reader*, 103.
[45] Ibid., 103.
[46] Dawn Ades, Iwona Blazwick, Inês Costa, Richard Dyer, Hammad Nasar, and Candy Stobbs, *The Artist's Studio. A Century of the Artist's Studio. 1920-2022* (London: Whitechapel Gallery, 2022).

perspectives might argue or fall in love, or else discuss aesthetic and politics. On stage the studio fascinates, challenges and evolves, questioning the very basis of why art is made as well as our own relationship to it.

Particularly in the recent resurgence of documentary or biography plays, the need to present the life and work of artists as 'authentic' has led directors and set designers to appropriate the model of dioramic representation that has notoriously been exploited in museums to re-create deceased artist's studios to be displayed as permanent installations for voyeuristic consumption. Playwrights write long stage directions where they describe the studio in detail and instruct actors on how to act like 'genuine artists', while theatre directors and set designers, while acting in the manner of museum curators, actually end up presenting replicas of artist's studios that can seem more authentic and meaningful than those hosted in situ or museums, if only because inhabited by living actors. Part of these plays' success, apart from the performers' interpretation, is surely due to the illusion of absolute reality that the set conveys to the audience; indeed, it induces them to share the atmosphere of the artist's studio and plunge into their life, even though they also implicitly understand the performed version of events, as well as the locations which they see, are a fictitious construct. And yet – due precisely to this somewhat confusing mixture of fact and fiction – one might also venture to ask how many audience members, by the end of the play, might genuinely believe they have learned something factual about the painter in question.

The stage frames the studio, which in turn frames the artist and their work by displaying 'finished works, works in progress, abandoned works, sketches – a collection of visible evidence, viewed simultaneously, that allows an understanding of process'.[47] It is precisely this aspect of the work, which according to Daniel Buren is 'extinguished by the museum's desire to "install",[48] that is presented on the stage, where the two spaces of studio and gallery overlap, thus providing visually arresting entertainment that is undoubtedly voyeuristic and somewhat exploitative, but also potentially instructive. What is more, the theatre rivals art galleries and museums in the way that, by capitalizing on the mythology of the artist, stage designers have more than once been able not only to convey the so-called aura of the studio but also to stage 'authentic' experiences of artists in the 'practiced place',[49] offering the audience the thrilling privilege of being allowed to witness the artistic process of creation and thus to be brought into contemplative contact with the supposed genius of the artist.

---

[47] Buren, *Function of the Studio*, 56.
[48] Ibid.
[49] Grabner, *Studio Reader*, 5.

John Logan's *Red*, a play about the convoluted history of Mark Rothko's Seagram murals, 'one of the enduring myths of the twentieth-century art, with the solitary figure of the misunderstood artist defending the gravitas of his project at its centre',[50] is one of the most significant examples of plays that demonstrate the dramatic potential of the artist's studio on stage.

Logan invites the audience to enter the mysterious locus of Rothko's creative act and share in the process of 'the ecstatic insemination with an idea, the birth of the work, the difficulties of the process, the exhausted *auteur*', to quote Brian O'Doherty.[51] Director Michael Grandage and set designer Christopher Oram attempted to re-create an exact replica of Rothko's studio at the Donmar Playhouse in 2009.[52] Although Logan claimed that it is 'really not about art at all, it's not about painting', but 'about teachers and students, mentors and protégés, fathers and sons',[53] the site-specificity of the Seagram Murals, 'an interrelated system'[54] of murals conceived for a specific space, which was one of Rothko's main concerns, inevitably became one of Logan's main concerns (Figure 3.7).

According to Borchardt-Hume, the curator of the 2008–9 Rothko exhibition at the Tate, Rothko realized in the late 1940s and early 1950s that the impact of his paintings depended mainly on their interaction with the surrounding space[55] – a conclusion he reached before Buren would insist that only in the studio is the work 'closest to its reality' and 'thus totally foreign to the world into which it is welcomed (museum, gallery, collection)'.[56] This is why, in exhibiting his work, Rothko sought 'to recapture the experience of his own encounter with [it]' and 'to create a position of empathy between the viewer and himself by emulating the conditions of his studio, which for him always remained the true spiritual home of his work'.[57] Rothko became increasingly concerned with controlling every aspect of the display of his works in museums and galleries in order 'to create a *place*',[58] as evidenced by

---

[50] Achim Borchardt-Hume, 'Shadows of Light: Mark Rothko's Late Series', in *Rothko: The Late Series* (London: Tate Publishing, 2008), 15.

[51] Brian O'Doherty, *Studio and Cube. On the relationship between where art is made and where art is displayed* (New York: Princeton Architectural Press, 2007), 29.

[52] For a detailed analysis see M. Cavecchi, 'Il museo in scena. I Seagram Murals di Rothko sul palco di John Logan', *Acme – Annali della Facoltà di Studi Umanistici dell'Università degli Studi di Milano*, LXXI (2018), 191–207.

[53] Logan in Neena Arndt, 'A Conversation with Playwright John Logan', *Theatre Goodman On Stage*, 27, 1 (September–December, 2011): 7. https://www.goodmantheatre.org/Documents/OnStage/1112/RedNSA_OnStage.pdf (accessed 8 May 2023).

[54] Riccardo Venturi, *Mark Rothko. Lo spazio e la sua disciplina* (Milano: Electa, 2007), 11–5.

[55] Borchardt-Hume (ed.), *Rothko*, 15–28.

[56] Buren, *Function of the Studio*, 54.

[57] Borchardt-Hume (ed.), *Rothko*, 17.

[58] Ibid., 16.

Figure 3.7 *Red* written by John Logan and directed by Michael Grandage. With Eddie Redmayne as Ken. Donmar Warehouse, London, 2009.

Source: Courtesy Johan Persson / ArenaPAL.

the list of 'suggestions' he sent to the Whitechapel for his 1961 exhibition[59] and as is fully explained by his double on stage:

> **Rothko** (*he gestures to his paintings*) The more you look at them the more they move … They float in space, they breathe … Movement, communication, gesture, flux, interaction; letting them work … They are not dead because they're not static. They move through space if you let them, this movement takes time, so they are temporal. They require *time*. […] That is why it's so important to me to create a *place*. A place the viewer can contemplate the painting over time and let them move. (*Red* 19–20)

Given this premise, it is obvious why the staged representation of the true spiritual home of Rothko's work, the studio, becomes crucial in Logan's imagined set design. Indeed, he devotes a long and detailed stage note to

---

[59] Whitechapel Art Gallery, *Mark Rothko. A Retrospective Exhibition: Paintings 1945–1960* (London: Fosh & Cross, 1961).

suggesting how Rothko's Bowery studio might be re-created onstage. It was the studio – at the time located in a former basketball court on the first floor of a large building on the corner of Bowery and Prince Street, in New York's Lower East Side – that Rothko famously chose because it replicated the space of the Four Seasons restaurant where the murals were to be hung:

> Rothko's studio is an old gymnasium. The hardwood floor is splattered and stained with hues of dark red paint. There is a cluttered counter or tables filled with buckets of paints, tins of turpentine, tubes of glue, crates of eggs, bottles of Scotch, packets of pigment, coffee cans filled with brushes, a portable burner or stovetop, and a phone. There is also a phonograph with messy stacks of records. [...] Most importantly, representations of some Rothko's magnificent *Seagram Mural* paintings are stacked and displayed around the room. Rothko had a pulley system that could rise, lower and display several of the paintings simultaneously. The paintings could be repositioned throughout the play, with a different arrangement for each scene.
> There is also an imaginary painting 'hanging' right in front of the audience, which Rothko studies throughout the play.
> Alternately, the entire setting could be abstract. (*Red* 7)

A successful cinema scriptwriter and a son of that American 'hyperreality' that demands 'the real thing' even at cost of fabricating 'the absolute fake', Logan, while leaving the director the option of an empty and abstract set, describes in detail how to reconstruct Rothko's studio in a 'credible' way (to cite the word Umberto Eco uses in his work *Faith in Fakes. Travels in Hyperreality* when he speaks of the Getty Museum's effort to reconstruct and present the Greek and Roman past).[60] Grandage and Oram accepted Logan's challenge of transforming the Donmar Warehouse stage into Rothko's studio by fabricating an absolute but plausible fake. Thus, the opening image of Alfred Molina interpreting Rothko, who sits in an Adirondack chair with his back to the audience looking at one of his murals at the beginning of the play, was inspired by Hans Namuth's famous 1964 photograph of the artist in a garage he used as a studio in East Hampton – not in the Bowery studio, where he created the murals at the centre of the play.[61] In both the photograph and stage design, the emphasis is on the studio as a place of contemplation, where the act of looking reveals Rothko's 'unwavering belief in art's potential

---

[60] Umberto Eco, *Faith in Fakes. Travels in Hyperreality* (London: Minerva, 1997), 34.
[61] Hans Namuth's photograph is published in Borchardt-Hume (ed.), *Rothko*, 22–3.

to convey transcendental truths, a belief that by the 1960s ran a growing risk of appearing merely rhetorical, especially to a younger generation of artists'.[62]

To make it look as authentic as possible on the Donmar stage, the studio is also a unique space of production:

> [...] when two men prime a canvas on stage, you're seeing a real thing happen; the paint is really splattering over the actors. I wanted to do a work play, a play about all the things artists do. They're not sitting around talking about painting – they're painting. They're stretching canvases, washing brushes, eating, doing all the minutiae of what they do.[63]

In fact, at the Donmar, Rothko's studio was even equipped with the large pulley system that the artist used in his Bowery studio to see the pictures vertically as they would be hung, so that throughout the play several different canvases were brought out and hoisted up on the pulleys. It is important to note that Logan requires some of the Seagram murals to be displayed in the studio, forcing the director and set designer to make decisions about the arrangement of the works on stage. The stage is transformed into an artist's studio, but also into a gallery, where questions about the relationship between the place where art is made and that where it is exhibited, and the dynamics between the work of art, the artist and the viewer, intersect with crucial meta-theatrical reflections.

During the performance, canvases were stretched over wooden frames and paint was heated on a small stove; according to assistant director Paul Hart, they even tried 'to make the theatre smell like a painter's studio, spraying turps and oil smells around the room' and 'boili[ing] up new paint mixtures [...] on an almost daily basis'.[64] Thus, while in Lenkiewicz's *The Painter* the smell of the paint has a dramatic function as Turner's pregnant widowed friend Sarah is annoyed by the smell of the turpentine, which makes her feel sick, and asks the British painter not to come near her for a while (obviously an excuse to keep him at a distance, as she feels he is emotionally distant from her) (*Painter* 12), the smell of turpentine and oil in *Red* is part of an attempt to re-create Rothko's studio in such a way the viewer/spectator can perceive it as truly authentic, whatever authentic might mean. Eddie Redmayne, who played Ken, the young man who arrives for an interview with the already famous Rothko, confesses that one of the great challenges of the production

---

[62] Borchardt-Hume (ed.), *Rothko*, 25.
[63] Logan in Arndt, *A Conversation with Playwright John Logan*, 8.
[64] Paul Hart in Domonic Francis, 'Study Guide for *Red* by John Logan', 10. https://donmar.s3.amazonaws.com/behindthescenes/older/Red.pdf (accessed 8 May 2023).

Figure 3.8 *Red* written by John Logan and directed by Michael Grandage. With Alfred Molina as Mark Rothko and Eddie Redmayne as Ken. Donmar Warehouse, London, 2009.

Source: Courtesy Johan Persson / ArenaPAL.

was to try not only to re-create the world of the studio but also 'to inhabit that world': 'So things like physically priming the canvases, making the paint, moving the easels and stretching the canvases, all those things are wonderful but challenging, because you have to get them so sorted that hopefully they become second nature to you and you don't look like a fraud'[65] (Figure 3.8).

Stage actions and movements are therefore of pivotal importance for this 'work play' to succeed. Movement, an intrinsic element of Rothko's paintings, which are characterized by a constant 'tension between the blocks of colour', thus 'exist[ing] in a state of flux – movement' (*Red* 19), reverberates from them to Logan's stage and reaches a powerful climax when artist and assistant, backs to the audience, jointly prime an eight feet square canvas, covering its white rectangular expanse with reddish-brown paint 'in a silent dance-like unison',[66] to the rhythm of Beethoven's *Ninth Symphony* and in a state almost of erotic and creative ecstasy:

[65] Ibid., 18.
[66] Paul Seven Lewis, '*Red* Starring Alfred Molina – Review', *One Minute Theatre Reviews*, 21 May 2018. https://www.youtube.com/watch?v=D4TGny6GvHo (accessed 8 May 2023).

> *Rothko waits for the music.*
>
> *With theatrical panache, Rothko waits for the exact moment the music thunders most dramatically and then –*
>
> *He begins to paint –*
>
> *He moves very quickly –*
>
> *Using strong, broad strokes he sweeps across the top of the canvas as quickly as possible – big, horizontal gestures – moving fast to make sure the base layer is even and smooth –*
>
> *Ken does the same for the bottom half of the painting –*
>
> *Some of Rothko's paint drips and splashes down on Ken –*
>
> *It is like choreography, they move in sync, they move toward each other and then cross, Rothko lurching back awkwardly as he continues to paint so Ken can dive in under him gracefully as he continues to paint –*
>
> *The thin, watery paint splatters and splashes as they dip their brushes and assault the canvas –*
>
> *It is hard, fast, thrilling work –*
>
> *The music swells –*
>
> *And then they are done.*
>
> *The white canvas is now an even, flat plain of dark plum.* (Red 37)

It is a coup de théâtre, one of the rare moments of sympathy and even communion between two characters of different generations who argue about art and life. Synchronizing their movements, Rothko and Ken work in a musical and choreographic crescendo of emotional intensity in front of spectators who are allowed to witness a moment of pure, frenetic artistic creation, even if it is completely fake.

It is perhaps worth noting here that the performance sets in motion a collective engagement with Rothko's art of which Rothko himself might not have approved, since he detested 'the whole machine for the popularization of art – universities, advertising, museums, and the Fifty-seventh Street salesmen'.[67] It is a list to which he might have added theatres as well, as confirmed by his words to John Fisher: 'When a crowd of people looks at a painting, I think of blasphemy. I believe that a painting can only communicate directly to a rare individual who happens to be in tune with it and the artist.'[68] In the light of such words, it is no surprise that he broke his contract with the Four Season restaurant and that, not long before his death, he arranged for his murals to be hung in a purpose-built Chapel for

---

[67] Mark Rothko, according to John Fisher in 'Portrait of the Artist as an Angry Man', *Harper's Magazine*, 1 July 1970, 16–23.

[68] Ibid.

the newly founded University of St Thomas in Houston, Texas.[69] To Rothko his paintings looked better in this high, shadowy space, which, seemed 'a preface to transcendence'.[70]

Leaving aside any assumptions about Rothko's possible reaction to such a display of his work in *Red*, the play undoubtedly encourages one to question the relationship between the artwork and the viewer and even between the original and the copy. It is quite remarkable how the play invites the audience to understand and appreciate Rothko's inimitable art by presenting on stage copies of the murals created for the occasion by scenic artist Richard Nutborne. These copies are only fakes, and yet, for many spectators they are their only link with the abstract painter's art, while for others they may be far more meaningful than the originals, as they are able to 'wrap' and 'embrace' viewers/spectators more than the originals displayed in a cold room at the Tate Modern. As Elyse Sommer writes in her review, Rothko's re-created paintings in such a context are 'powerful; not just props, but vivid characters'.[71] Indeed, the audience were not only allowed to witness the artistic process of creation but also had the extraordinary privilege of looking at these paintings while they are passionately discussed by their own creator in an emotional and vehement, sometimes violent, exchange between two men of different generations and status, each of whom openly learns from the other not only about art, their lives and the world they live in, but also, above all, a kind of mutual respect and appreciation based upon their shared humanity.

By contrast with Logan's work, a non-mimetic recreation of the artist's studio is offered by multimedia performance company Breach Theatre in their production of *It's True, It's True, It's True*, one of the hits of the 2018 Edinburgh Fringe Festival,[72] which cleverly stages the transcript of the 1612 rape trial of Artemisia Gentileschi's rapist Agostino Tassi on the back of a devising process with the cast. Exploring issues of sexual harassment, gender inequality, the abuse of power and the inadequacy of the legal system in dealing with rape cases, this all-female, multi-roling, politically engaged play

---

[69] Borchardt-Hume (ed.), *Rothko*, 21.
[70] O'Doherty, *Studio and Cube*, 22.
[71] Sommer Elyse, 'The Donmar Warehouse Production of *Red* at Broadway's Golden Theater', *CurtainUp*, 4 April 2011. http://curtainupcom.siteprotect.net/redrothko.html (accessed 8 May 2023).
[72] Commissioned by New Diorama Theatre, the show ran at the Edinburgh Fringe in 2018. Its reprise at the Barbican (31 March–9 April 2020) was cancelled due to the Covid-19 emergency. A film version, shot on location in a former chapel, was specially staged for TV and directed by Billy Barrett and Rhodri Huw. The film was produced by Artemisia Films and Breach and was commissioned by The Space for the BBC as part of the 'Shock of the Nude' season in 2021.

seeks to exorcize 'the ghost of the male-dominated studio',[73] and to give voice and agency to Artemisia Gentileschi, the artist and the woman:

> It was this voice – already bold, visionary and uncompromising at only seventeen years old – that inspired us throughout the making of this show, in a room filled with rage, tears, laughter and love of a similarly impassioned creative team. Just as the artists of Gentileschi's time imagined and painted biblical figures in the clothes and buildings of their own society, so we heard Artemisia speak to us directly in the 21st century. We hope that in reading, watching or performing this text, you'll hear her loud and clear.[74]

Artemisia Gentileschi is made to speak to us directly in the twenty-first century through a superimposition of past and present. The soundtrack mixes baroque, punk and contemporary, and the costumes 'clash together the historical and the contemporary, with sharp jackets and outsized cuffs and collars contrasting with velvet cloaks, fake beards, and ornate dress'.[75]

Luke W. Robson's set design is particularly revealing, being conceived as a staging area that is at the same time 'a kind of real, historical legal space' and 'an imaginative space'.[76] The courtroom and Artemisia's studio overlap on a stage that has become a kind of laboratory where the unresolved interplay between fiction and history is examined and pursued at various levels (legal, theatrical, and artistic), as the triple repetition in the title perhaps over-emphasizes.[77] Truth is sought in the courtroom where Artemisia is on trial, and with her 'the countless women who have come forward with accounts of rape before and after her',[78] but the representation of the trial, with the handful of characters called as witnesses, is also tightly interwoven with the exploration of both the nature of tribunal theatre and of art history's attempt at historical accuracy. The play disrupts simultaneously the specific performance and mise-en-scene techniques of tribunal theatre and challenges the traditional notion of the studio as a masculine, largely private

---

[73] Dawn Ades, 'Photography and the Artist's Studio', in Ades, Blazwick, Costa, Dyer, Nasar, and Stobbs, *The Artist's Studio*, 15.
[74] Breach, 'Notes on the Text. Staging', *It's True, It's True, It's True* (London: Oberon Modern Plays, 2018) unnumbered.
[75] Ibid.
[76] Ibid.
[77] The words '*It's True, It's True, It's True*', spoken by the 17-year-old Artemisia Gentileschi, come down to us in a 1612 trial transcript which is held in the State Archives in Rome and was displayed at the National Gallery in the first major exhibition of Artemisia's work in the United Kingdom (3 October 2020–24 January 2021).
[78] Breach, *Notes on the Text*.

space where the lone male genius works, and where the female model is the object of his gaze (and sometimes abuse).

The non-mimetic recreation onstage of the artist's studio is strictly related to the company's investigation into the accuracy of verbatim theatre. *It's True, It's True, It's True* is a fiercely political play that questions the authorial adaptation of 'real-life' material, implying narrative unreliability, and disrupts the use of scenography and methods of staging usually attuned to tribunal plays, whose primary aim is 'to create the illusion of authenticity'.[79] It is all about 'perspective', a key word that refers to the technique Agostino Tassi was asked to teach Artemisia (*True* 21): in one sense, this refers to the representation of objects in three-dimensional space on the two-dimensional surface of a painting, but it can also call attention here to the way visual arts and theatre view and represent reality. It is also, of course, the specifically female perspective from which Artemisia paints male stories. As Artemisia, interpreted by actress Ellice Stevens, tells the court, 'It's not just about the story, is it? It's about how you choose to paint it, what you make it say' (*True* 14).

It's not just about the story, is it? It's about how you choose to *stage* it. Challenging verbatim theatre's claim to truth, the play – which is based on a four-hundred year old court transcript 'hand-written by [a] notary whilst the testimonies were given, […] later patched together, transcribed and translated several times' before reaching the rehearsal room – is designed in such a way that it is difficult 'to pinpoint' where 'documented history ends' and 'imagination begins'.[80] Notably, actress Ellice Stevens and director Billy Barrett feel it necessary 'to clarify some of the liberties' they have taken in editing the recorded court proceedings ('largely due to the limits of an hour-long three hander').[81] They also openly state that they altered the documentary material to suit their own political agenda. By acknowledging that the very process of transposition of the transcript onto the stage involves a certain degree of manipulation, Barrett exposes the (meta)fictional nature of his *jeu théâtral* and challenges the audience to observe and rethink how theatre works. As director Barrett explains in his conversation with the art historian Letizia Treves, who was curating the (then) forthcoming Artemisia exhibition at the National Gallery, their performance was designed to draw

---

[79] Derek Paget, '"Verbatim Theatre": Oral History and Documentary Techniques', *New Theatre Quarterly*, 3, 12 (1987): 317–36; Duška Radosavljević, *Theatre-Making. Interplay between Text and Performance in the 21st Century* (London: Palgrave MacMillan, 2013), 128.
[80] Breach, *Notes on the Text*.
[81] Ibid.

the audience into the inner workings of a theatrical experience, 'where suddenly an actor can go and grab a cloak and throw it on and a beard and be the elder in *Susanna and the Elders*'.[82] Barrett and Robson blur borders and design the stage as both a courtroom and an artist's studio with props that refer simultaneously to different realms: 'Step ladders that fold into chairs and tables standing in for legal benches and witness boxes, and a paint trolley wheeling out for Susanna's garden and Holofernes' bed', as they write in the staging notes in the published play-text.[83]

Ellice Stevens, Sophie Steer (in the Edinburgh production and Harriet Webb in the London one) and Kathryn Bond – the three performers of the terrific all-female cast – snappily switch characters by changing costumes in front of the audience and rotating the part of the judge; meanwhile, verbatim reports mix with agit-prop, slapstick in the tradition of the British film comedy and tableaux inspired by visual arts. Like the real-life Artemisia, who often put her own features in her pictures and turned herself into muse, martyr, Amazon warrior or avenging Queen, the actress Ellice Stevens, who plays the roles of Artemisia, Susanna and Judith, is a woman both of the seventeenth and twenty-first century, struggling to be believed, fighting against a patriarchal system that sets a man's world above woman's and that 'internalizes misogyny to such an extent that women become the judge and jury of each other'.[84]

No wonder, then, that in this shifting, ambiguous stage space (half courtroom, half artist's studio) Artemisia at one point asks the judge for permission to show one of her paintings as a piece of evidence to demonstrate that she is a victim of Tasso's stalking, thus transforming the courtroom/stage/studio into an art gallery. It is one of the witnesses, Tuzia, who, surprised by this request, draws attention to this transformation: 'What is this now, a gallery?' (*True* 10). At this point, as in the various cases already discussed in the previous paragraphs, Artemisia's painting of *Susanna and the Elders*[85] is brought to life, as 'Artemisia pulls down a large painted backdrop of the sky, replicating Gentileschi's painting, and undresses to her underwear to become Susanna, draped in a sheet. The other two become Narrators, and dress in the cloaks and beards of The Elders as they speak' (*True* 11). In this

---

[82] The National Gallery, '*It's True, It's True, It's True*: Becoming Artemisia Gentileschi', *YouTube*, 17 October 2018. https://www.youtube.com/watch?v=lMpAInIof_M (accessed 8 May 2023).

[83] Breach, *Notes on the Text*.

[84] Maddy Costa and Andy Field, *Performance in an Age of Precarity* (London: Bloomsbury, 2021).

[85] Artemisia Gentileschi, *Susanna e i vecchioni* (1610), olio su tela, 170 × 119 cm, Collezione Graf von Schönborn, Pommersfelden.

art gallery, Ellis Stevens/Artemisia, 'more Pussy Riot than Kenneth Clark', as Laura Freeman wrote,[86] passionately presents her canvas, which represents a very different narrative of the biblical story from that previously presented by male painters. Improvising an art history lecture, she even compares her own version with that of Alessandro Allori[87] and re-enacts Susanna as she appears in the two paintings. Whereas in Artemisia's painting, Susanna is seen as 'not welcoming' the male gaze of the Elders, Allori's Susanna appears as 'encouraging'. In her re-staging of Allori's Susanna, Stevens becomes more like a woman in a shampoo commercial or Barbara Windsor in *Carry on Camping*. As the stage directions suggest, 'She offers her naked body to the Elders' gaze (and the audience's gaze as well) in an over-the-top seductive way, culminating in a comic gag of the Elders chasing her around the theatre, 'Benny Hill-style, at one point running through the audience' (*True* 15). By dressing up, or rather undressing, to become the subject of her painting and play the role of Susanna, Stevens directly challenges the viewers, who are invited to participate rather than be mere voyeurs as she and the Elders 'take up and hold the positions from Gentileschi's painting, in which the Elders reach out for Susanna, and she turns away from them' (*True* 14). Interestingly, in this case, the process of creation taking place in this studio/stage/courtroom/art gallery is not shown as celebrating the mythology of the artist engaged in 'the mysterious business of creation',[88] but rather as passionately lecturing the judge and spectators by explaining the artist's choices in order to prove her truthfulness and thus present herself as a victim. Indeed, Stevens challenges the court and the audience with her erotic provocation, exposing her naked body to the tribunal of their gaze.

One of the achievements of the production is that the audience becomes an active listener, invited to look at the past to examine issues of rape, consent and the injustices of the current legal system. The play succeeds in making this abrupt leap to modern-day sensibilities by stealthily declaring Artemisia and the women she painted feminists through a kind of noisy 'riot grrrl' party. Indeed, Breach Company is interested in raising awareness and eliciting an emotional response to the issue of rape, with a rock grand finale that is somehow reminiscent of agit-prop techniques. Close to the end of the play, Stevens/Artemisia brings to life another of her paintings, the 1620–1 version of *Judith Beheading Holofernes* at the Uffizi Gallery, Florence. In this case, she

---

[86] Laura Freeman, 'Painting: The Extraordinary Life and Art of Artemisia Gentileschi', *The Spectator*, 11 April 2020.
[87] Alessandro Allori, *Susanna e i vecchioni* (1561), oil on canvas, 202 × 117cm, Musée Magnin, Digione.
[88] O'Doherty, *Studio and Cube*, 38.

acts not as the protagonist but as Judith's trusted servant, Abra, while Judith enters the stage as 'a rock star, a guardian angel, the embodiment of rage' (*True* 48), driving Abra/Stevens/Artemisia to take revenge on Holofernes/Tassi. Significantly, according to the stage directions, it is Artemisia (and not Judith, as in the painting) who 'screams, a howl of rage' and beheads Holfernes (*True* 49). Not only does she proclaim her innocence, but she also acknowledges the autobiographical inspiration behind her art, thus taking a position in the historical art debate on the side of those art critics who read her work in the light of her autobiography – 'I put all those things in my art – because I'm painting my experience' (*True* 51).

In the final scene, as Judith victoriously holds the decapitated head of Holofernes in her hand and sings Patty Smith's *Gloria*, joined by the other two actresses, Artemisia speaks her epilogue over the music, informing the audience that Agostino Tasso has been found guilty of her rape and banned from Rome (only to be called back shortly afterwards to work for a papal commission), and of her achievements: both artistic, as the first woman artist to be admitted to the Academy of Arts in Florence and as a woman and a mother who taught her daughter how to paint. Her anger is palpable, but so is her fierce determination to get even: to live, to paint and to overcome the slanders of men who hardly deserve her contempt. The women aptly choose to perform a part of Smith's song that works to absolve themselves of the crime they have just committed – 'Jesus died for somebody's sins but not mine' – and also to describe Artemisia's pride and challenge to patriarchal rule: 'People say "beware!" / But I don't care / The words are just / Rules and regulations to me, me / I-I walk in a room, you know I look so proud / I'm movin' in this here atmosphere, well, anything's allowed.' In the end, Artemisia acknowledges that she has put her 'anger' and 'sadness' as well as her 'happiness' into her art, affirming her own agency and independence from the judgment of men: 'And men would tell me I couldn't do that, that there wasn't an audience for it. And to them, I would say: "as long as I live / I will have control over my being. My lordship, I'll show you what a woman can do"'.

In a musical crescendo, Stevens/Artemisia/Judith leads the other actresses into the cathartic finale, as the refrain, in which Smith's words are altered, is 'sung, screamed, and roared by all three cast members' (*True* 52), as if addressing a stadium full of girls united in a sisterhood of enthusiasm and solidarity with a cry against patriarchal rule or male abuses of power and a sense of entitlement over women's bodies that echoes the #MeToo rallying cry:

> We're at the stadium, and two thousand girls are calling their names out to me. Marie, Ruth, telling the truth. We can all hear them, we can all see.

Gloria
Gloria
Gloria
Gloria (*True* 52)

The artist's studio/courtroom has become the stage of a rock concert, where the performance releases and in turn receives amazing flows of energy that fuse the performers and the audience together in this act of rebellion and resistance against patriarchal power, dancing, shouting, singing along with the actresses. This climactic moment could not be further away from Logan's *Red*, where, on the contrary, the audience is cast in the role of voyeur, interested, educated, amazed, but never really an active part of the action. Almost inevitably, on Logan's stage, as well as in most of the studios reconstructed in art museums, the mythology of the artist as a being immersed in the mysterious activity of creation in his studio has transformed the creative act into a bourgeois fetish by which the visitor/spectator acknowledges the power of the work of art but at the same time trivializes its subversive potential.

'Making' the art gallery on stage

While mainstream theatre production in Britain remains largely dramatic and playwright-oriented, three post-dramatic plays – Martin Crimp's *Attempts on Her Life* (1997), Mark Ravenhill's *pool (no water)* (2006) and Tim Crouch's *ENGLAND* (2007) – show how different kinds of dramaturgy are redefining the role of the text in the theatre. Open to multiple readings and inviting practitioners, as well as audiences to intervene directly, the three playwrights have conceived plays (and performances) that subvert both traditional theatrical conventions and logocentric discourses of power, while winking at, or conversing with, what happens in the world of the art gallery. Rather than showing art galleries and artworks, the three authors present the process of the 'making' of the art galleries on stage, prompting the audience (and in the case of Crimp, directors, designers, actors, light technicians, musicians, too) to imaginatively visualize the works of art that are not onstage and yet are more or less explicitly evoked in the texts. They simultaneously draw attention to the audience's own participatory sense-making, thus outlining a new post-Beckett theatre of absence.

All three plays mark a transition from playwriting to theatre-making and straddle the line between traditional theatre conventions and the anarchic openness of performance, relying on the imaginative power of the word and the use of performance techniques to question the increasing influence of performance art on the theatre. Although exploiting different dynamics, in the three plays the production of meaning is effectively dislocated, materialized somewhere in the liminal space between the written text and the physical performance on stage.

Crimp's *Attempts on Her Life* is a post-dramatic play consisting of 'Seventeen Scenarios for the Theatre', in which the performative dimension is suspended as both speakers and setting are indeterminate and the text does not feature any stage directions except for the dashes to indicate figural speech and change of speaker. The play therefore requires the director and actors to become co-writers of a performance text that attempts to define the unknowable and polymorphous character of Anne (or Annushka, Anny, Annie and Anya, but mostly referred to simply as 'she') who never appears on stage and whose voice is never heard. Instead, her physical presence is replaced by images, descriptions and traces that transform her into a work of art or even a mirrored gallery through which the play satirizes the many contradictory images of women in post-modern age. In Scenario 11, 'Untitled (100 words)', Crimp presents an (absent) 'sensational' art installation that is the result of creative decision-making open to almost everyone involved in the production, from the director to set and light designers, not to mention the actors. In this play, in which the critique of media representation also implies a probing analysis of theatre as a representational art form, the art installation also prompts a meta-theatrical reflection on the new form of theatre Crimp is experimenting with. It is the kind of theatre that one of the speakers in the scenario describes as eschewing 'the outmoded conventions of dialogue and so-called characters lumbering towards the embarrassing dénouements of the *theatre*' (*Attempts* 50–1, emphasis in original) in favour of a different mode of representation, which Crimp himself explores in the play. Like the scenario itself, Anne's installation raises provocative questions about the role the spaces of the theatre and the gallery played in the postmodern, mediatized society of the 1990s, even before Tony Blair made them the pinnacles of his Cool Britannia.

Nearly a decade later, on the stage of *pool (no water)*, a pseudo-confessional play about art, friendship, jealousy and aesthetic opportunism, the author of the 1990s zeitgeist drama, *Shopping And F***ing*, Mark Ravenhill, and Scott Graham and Steven Hoggett, the directorial and choreographic team behind physical theatre company Frantic Assembly, use their rehearsal process to devise a gallery of choreographed artworks. They turn the stage into a multifunctional pool/hospital/art gallery that hosts high-impact art installations and performances, which are themselves the result of acts of physical creativity and crafting inspired by the visual suggestiveness and themes of Nan Goldin's photographic work. Through a performance that owes as much to theatre as it does to live art practice, and that combines text, music, movement and acting, *pool (no water)* generates meanings, connections and images that depend essentially on the receptivity of the audience, while staging and questioning the spectacularization of pain in art. In the educational *Comprehensive Guide* of the play, Scott Graham explains the importance of rehearsal as a process that focuses on the live encounter between performer and audience, because 'the play is not about the events. It is primarily about the character and the audience'.[89]

Conceived as 'a play for galleries', Crouch's *ENGLAND* uses the art gallery as a laboratory for experimenting with interaction between modes of storytelling, performance and exhibition in order to attempt 'to minimise the division between the stage and the audience'.[90] On the one hand, borrowing from the visual arts, where the viewer is expected to work hard to find meaning, Crouch relinquishes complete control of the work's content and allows the audience's imagination to meander, designing a performance in which structure is balanced by lack of form, unpredictability and randomness. Like *An Oak Tree*, in *ENGLAND* 'theatre is something that is created "live", and it is created through decision-making and choice-taking' while audiences are involved in 'a whole series of different processes, of choices and decisions'.[91] On the other hand, while attempting to minimize the distance between himself as a performer and the audience, he physically and metaphorically leads the audience through the rooms of real and imaginary galleries.

Crouch challenges the contemporary visual artists on their own ground by placing dirty, pulsating life at the centre of an ideal, awe-inspiring, sanitized white cube. In contrast to the white cube gallery's signification of *emptiness*, Crouch's narration offers a profusion and complexity of references and makes his spectators experience a *fullness*, by effectively placing them in the middle of an interaction between his predetermined text and the actual (and therefore un-determined) performance experience.

While making the audience aware of the theatrical situation and the artificial mechanisms of constructing the imaginary worlds they conjure

---

[89] Scott Graham, '*pool (no water)*' by Mark Ravenhill. Pool. For students (aged +16), teachers & art educationalists, 3. https://www.yumpu.com/en/document/view/27937257/pool-no-water-resource-pack-frantic-assembly (accessed 8 May 2023).
[90] Tim Crouch in conversation with Seda Ilter, in Seda Ilter, '"A Process of Transformation": Tim Crouch on *My Arm*', *Contemporary Theatre Review*, 2, 4 (2011): 399.
[91] Ibid., 400.

up through words and images, both Crouch and Ravenhill induce their audiences to play along and to 'gain authentic experience' in these fake situations. In fact, Crouch and Ravenhill captivate their audiences with a series of moving and engaging narratives, allowing for authentic individual experiences and the creation of individual meanings. They seem therefore to share the meta-modern sensibility, which, as Daniel Schulze writes, 'allows for authentic experience that is not a parody or nostalgia but is genuinely real while everyone knows that it is a fake'.[92]

Displaying the absence: Martin Crimp's *Attempts on Her Life*

As mentioned in Chapter 1, in Scenario 11, 'Untitled (100 words)', Crimp sketches a controversial installation of the suicidal artist Anne through a dialogical/polylogical exchange between speakers, although it remains unclear who and how many they are, of what gender and age, and in what environment their exchanges take place. It is from their words that the installation, which displays various objects associated with suicide attempts, emerges as an ostensibly autobiographical work:

> - What we see here are various objects associated with the artist's attempts to kill herself over the past few months. For example: medicine bottles, records of hospital admissions, polaroids of the several HIV positive men with whom she has had intentionally unprotected intercourses, pieces of broken glass …
> - Suicidal notes.
>
> - … yes, and the walls of the gallery have of course been lined with her many suicidal notes. In addition to the polaroids there are rather unpleasant, I have to say, video recordings of the attempts themselves. Well, I don't know about other people, but after a few minutes of this I rather began to wish she'd succeeded the first-time round. (*Attempts* 45)

What seems particularly intriguing about this play, is that while visual art is thematically present, it is also conspicuously absent from a stage where nothing happens but language, in the wake of Beckett's theatre of absence and his concern with not-seeing. As would be expected in a play where every 'attempt' stakes a claim for Anne/Annushka/Anny/Annie/Anya's presence

---

[92] Daniel Schulze, *Authenticity in Contemporary Theatre and Performance. Make It Real* (London: Methuen, 2017), 58.

and at the same time emphasizes her 'absence' ('She says she is not a real character, not a real character like you get in book or on TV, but a lack of character, an absence she calls it, doesn't she, of character' (*Attempts* 25)), spectators are never offered the image of the installation. Rather, they are invited to imagine Anne's work through the verbal clues given by the speakers, usually anonymous egomaniacal art critics who react in various ways, discussing its meaning and value.

In Crimp's scenario, then, the stage is a gallery displaying an installation that exists only in the mind of the viewers/spectators. It is a place where the visual has been replaced by the auditory, and where the performative power of the dramatic discourse invites the viewer/spectator to imagine the art installation and think critically about the fictive artist's psychological characteristics in light of female stereotypes created and exploited by media.

Either 'a landmark work' or an 'undigested exhibition' (*Attempts* 46), the installation of the suicidal artist Anne is revealed through the contrasting personal reactions of anonymous art critics. Arguments about the blurring of life and art are rehearsed: if viewers accept the work as a record of real suicide attempts, they are 'mere voyeurs in Bedlam'; if 'Anne' is just pretending, then the work has no artistic integrity:

> - Her own victim? If she really is – as it appears – trying to kill herself, then surely our presence here makes us mere voyeurs in Bedlam. If on the other hand she's only play-acting, then the whole work becomes a mere cynical performance and is doubling disgusting. (*Attempts* 50)

The installation catalyses deeply held cultural beliefs that associate the representation of women with mental illness and even death. This is a connection reinforced by Crimp's appropriation of Carl G. Jung's list of one hundred unrelated words, which the psychoanalyst developed and used to test a subject's mental health.[93] Echoing the style of those contemporary art critics who dismiss abstract and conceptual art – '*Why* can't people learn to draw? *Why* can't people learn to paint? Students should be taught *skills*, not ideas' (*Attempts* 47; emphasis in original) – one of the anonymous critics asks whether Anne should receive psychiatric treatment. This position sums up the attitude of many actual critics, who consider the works of art and the plays they cannot understand to be the products of a sick mind, somehow echoing the hateful prohibition of so-called degenerate art banned by the

---

[93] Solange Ayache, 'Theatre and Psychoanalysis: Or Jung on Martin Crimp's Stage: "100 Words"', *Sillages Critiques*, 10, 2009. https://journals.openedition.org/sillagescritiques/1838 (accessed 8 May 2023).

Nazis (*Attempts* 48). 'Where does the 'life' – literally in this case – end, and the 'work' begin?' (*Attempts* 46). There is no doubt that the question raised by Anne's installation intercepts an analogous debate in both the contemporary art world and theatre, where similar questions are being asked about the relationship between representation, lived experience and the construction of the self. Crimp is alluding perhaps more than anything here to the reaction to the controversial play *Blasted*, for which Sarah Kane became the target of personal attacks. Jack Tinker's notorious review of *Blasted*[94] and Charles Spencer's infamous review of Kane's *Phaedra's Love* at the Gate Theatre in 1995 – 'It's not a theatre critic that's required here, it's a psychiatrist' – resonate in the scenario as one of the speakers affirms: 'What we see here is the work of a girl who quite clearly should've been admitted not to an art school but to a psychiatric unit [...] a mental hospital. Somewhere where she could / receive treatment' (*Attempts* 47–8).

According to Crimp's fictional art critics, the artist's (absent) body itself becomes an object and a work of art:

> - [...] She is offering us no less than the spectacle of her own existence, the radical *pornography* – if I may use that overused word – of her own broken and abused – almost *Christ*-like – body.
>   [...]
> - An object, yes. But not the object of *others*, the object of *herself*. *That's* the scenario / she offers.
>
> - But surely we've seen all that. Haven't we seen all that in the so-called 'radicalism' of the sixties stroke seventies?
> (*Attempts* 50–1, emphasis in original)

It is precisely the various art critics' references to crucifixion iconography (Francis Bacon's included, perhaps),[95] degenerate art and body art that somehow direct the audience to imagine Anne's work. In fact, by placing Anne's installation in the tradition of body performance art, which began to explode in the early 1960s, one art critic suggests that Anne should be considered a member of a large community of women artists who have

---

[94] 'Some will undoubtedly say the money might have been better spent on a course of remedial therapy' (Jack Tinker, 'The Disgusting Feast of Filth', *Daily Mail*, 19 January 1995, reprinted in *Theatre Record 1–28 January 1995*, 42).

[95] Crimp's early radio play *Six figures at the Base of a Crucifixion*, broadcast on BBC Radio 3 on 2 December 1986, is reminiscent of Francis Bacon's *Crucifixion* series of paintings. In a personal interview with Vicky Angelaki, Crimp referred to Bacon as a painter sharing his same effort engaging in the imaginative depiction of the contemporary (*The Plays of Martin Crimp. Making Theatre Strange* (London: Palgrave Macmillan, 2012), 69, n. 90).

produced explicit forms of performance in which bodies critically engage with ways of seeing – performances, moreover, which have 'inscribed women as given to be seen but not as given to see' in order to expose their 'link with representational structures of desire in commodity capitalism'.[96] Anne seems to have entered a fruitful dialogue with many artists, including perhaps the pioneering Carolee Schneemann, who was among the first women artists to introduce her body and her sexuality as a part of her work and its materiality; Marina Abramovic, who acted as 'the object' in her daring *Rhythm 0* (1974), inviting visitors to freely interact with her body; Hannah Wilke, whose photographic *Intra-Venus Series* (1992) documents the realities of her physical and psychological transformation caused by cancer treatment; and, last but not least, Tracey Emin, 'Mad Tracey from Margate', whose uncompromisingly autobiographical and confessional work scrutinizes her relationship with her own body and explores the possibilities of self-representation and self-expression.

Rejecting claims of 'narcissism', 'undigested exhibitionism' or cynical pretence on the part of the artist, one critic eulogizes Anne's deliberate objectification of her body and qualifies her gesture as a subversive form of 'radical pornography', perhaps alluding, and not without irony, to the performances of sex worker/performance artist Anne Sprinkle. Indeed, she used pornographic imagery in art spaces to subvert the traditional male gaze that has so often perpetuated the oppression of women. As already mentioned, the speakers leave open the question of whether 'she' is a victim or is simply acting. It is a doubt that reappears later in Scenario 16, 'Pornó', where 'the principal speaker is a very young woman', as the stage directions indicate (the only instance in which a performer is described). She defines pornography as 'actually a way of taking control' because 'rather than *consuming* the images' (emphasis in original) she 'is producing them'. At the same time, her faltering control over her performance and her increasing reliance on prompts from off stage to continue the speech may be an expression of mounting dissent: 'She seems to have forgotten what to say: but this should imply a distress which is never allowed to surface' (*Attempts* 67).

Like all those avant-garde works that have aroused controversy and continue to arouse unease, Anne's installation is deemed inappropriate and repulsive by the less progressive art critics of the group, in large part because its negotiation of the body contradicts the long-established codes of female representation in Western art history and visual culture. No doubt these art critics would be more appreciative of Constance Charpentier's

---

[96] Rebecca Schneider, *The Explicit Body in Performance* (London: Routledge, 1997), 3.

more aesthetically pleasing painting *Young Woman Drawing* (1801), hanging on the walls of the house described in Scenario 2, 'Tragedy of Love and Ideology' (*Attempts* 11). On the contrary, the more progressive art critic (a woman, in Katie Mitchell's production) interprets Anne's artistic act of becoming '*her own victim*' as 'the only way to avoid becoming a victim of the patriarchal structures of late twentieth-century capitalism' (*Attempts* 49; emphasis in original), echoing all those body artists who seek to expose how the logic of commodity capitalism shapes both the way the body is seen and the way desire is structured. This is mirrored in the response of the actual critics. When she directed the play as a special performance for Max Stafford-Clark at the Dixon Drama Studio, York, on 27 May 2002, theatre scholar Mary Luckhurst claimed that Anne is clearly 'an interrogative device' used 'to expose misogyny and exploitation of women, both institutionally and internationally, with corporate mentalities in the first world countries implicated before anyone else'.[97] Similarly, Vicky Angelaki explains that 'she' is absent precisely because the art industry has taken over her function: she is an abstraction whose voice is given by others to her or to the product that she will become, leading to yet another act of consumption, this time by critics and audiences.[98]

It is no coincidence, then, that in both Tim Albery's first production at the Royal Court and Katie Mitchell's ten-year-anniversary revival at the Lyttleton, the stage became a television studio, somehow confirming that, after the massive media response to the *Sensation* exhibition at the Royal Academy, talking about art has often seemed to have become more important than art itself. In both productions, the scenario has been conceived as a live television art show, allowing the audience to draw parallels between the dialogue on stage and that which they regularly encounter on television panel discussions, and emphasizing the humour of the scenario.[99] It should be remembered here that Crimp prioritizes spectacle over plot, thus transferring the responsibility for meaning-making from the playwright to the theatre company producing the play, as suggested in his note to the play's first edition: 'Each scenario in words – the dialogue – unfold[s] against a distinctive world – a design – which best exposes its irony'.

At the National Theatre, Mitchell and designer Vicki Mortimer's high-tech production made extensive use of live video, projection and music

---

[97] Mary Luckhurst, 'Political Point-Scoring: Martin Crimp's *Attempts on Her Life*', *Contemporary Theatre Review*, 13, 1 (2003): 55.
[98] Angelaki, *Plays of Martin Crimp*, 62.
[99] Katie Mitchell revived *Attempts on her Life* at the Lyttleton Auditorium of the National Theatre (8 March–10 May 2007). She also directed an Italian production of *Attempts*

to give overt scenic form to Crimp's intermedial discourse. The actors' performances were filmed and relayed in real time as a live feed on screens placed in different areas of the stage. Working on a play as free as *Attempts on Her Life*, 'can be very exciting', but 'it can also be very frightening' and Mitchell was aware that the company, especially the actors, 'needed a very clear framework to work around to alleviate that fear, and also to give the production a sense of coherence'. She worked with them and together they devised a set of circumstances based around a live television show, imagining Tracey Emin as one of the panellists, by which the action of the play could be framed.[100] For the performers and possibly the audience the choice of Emin added significance to both the scenario and the installation, as she is an artist who first became known for the frank sexuality of her confessional works and for appearing drunk and disorderly on the Channel 4 television programme *Is Painting Dead?* after attending the Turner Prize dinner in 1997. In this two-way conversation between theatre and visual arts, one might also wonder whether the spectators at Mitchell's revival of *Attempts on Her Life* also thought of Emin's iconic *My Bed* (1998), which, in the best tradition of young British art, became an overnight sensation when it was installed at the Tate Gallery as part of the 1999 Turner Prize shortlist. Mitchell's audience would have probably remembered that both Anne's suicidal installation and Emin's bed are emotional and psychological narratives written through an assemblage of objects, which seek boldly to challenge a range of aesthetic and social norms. They would have noted that Anne's and Emin's installations have been a source of both comment and controversy, often interpreted as straightforward and unproblematically autobiographical rather than as constructed artworks to be critiqued for the emotional and material forms of disruption they enact.

Not only does the conspicuous figure of Tracey Emin hover over the show, but Mitchell also chooses to represent Anne's abstraction and polyvalence on stage through an assemblage of different images: women dressed in red who move around the stage during the different scenarios,

---

on her Life (Tracce di Anne) at the Piccolo Teatro in Milan in March 1999. Nicholas de Jongh wrote about the 'cultural jargon spouted in Radio 3's *Night Waves* style' echoed by Albery in the Scenario 11 (Nicholas de Jongh, '*Attempts on Her Life*', *Evening Standard*, 13 March 1997. In *Theatre Record 12–25 March 1997*, 311), while Michael Billington saw the scenario of Katie Mitchell as 'a specific *Newsnight Review* parody', in which noted panellist Tom Paulin and radical feminist Germaine Greer 'sound-alikes argue over the meaning of Anne as art-object'. (Michael Billington, 'Review of *Attempts on Her Life*', *The Guardian*, 15 March 2007, 309).

[100] National Theatre Education. '*Attempts on her Life* by Martin Crimp. Background Pack'. http://d1wf8hd6ovssje.cloudfront.net/documents/Attempts_bkpk.pdf, 3 (accessed 1 June 2023).

perhaps suggesting that they are the different Anne's in the show, as well as video projections of faces and details of women's bodies that could be hers. Thus, the actors playing the art critics in Scenario 11 sit in a studio-like setting in one corner of the stage and comment on Anne's installation, while triptychs of photographs or videos are projected overhead on three huge screens above the stage, somehow defusing the verbal power of the scene. Forms of verbal imagery compete in the audience's mind with on-screen images and videos, which attempt to visualize some of the elements composing the art installation: close-ups of women's faces and mouths, images of a woman lying in a hospital bed on an intravenous drip, videos showing the preparatory treatment before a mastectomy, an attempted suicide by overdose and a woman dressed in red walking towards the audience at the beginning of the scenario and away from the audience, with their backs to them, at the end of the scenario, a wall of flames unfolding on the three screens, its pattern of glowing waves reminiscent of Bill Viola's video/sound installation *Fire Woman* (2005). Anne's installation is thus transformed into a media-simulation, forcing the audience's gaze, simultaneously drawn by different media, to wander between heterogeneous sign systems and discourses. The high-tech performance articulates both a reflection and a critique of the mediatized experience of postmodern reality, as the chaotic abundance of visual impressions makes it impossible for the overloaded spectator either to focus on the performance or to feel sympathy for the performers, and leaves them instead simply to 'crave some human warmth from the stage'.[101]

Transplanting the white cube: Tim Crouch's *ENGLAND*

ENGLAND has a privileged relationship with the gallery space, not least because it happens in a gallery, which, according to the playwright, must remain a gallery:

> I want the gallery to remain a gallery and not to be transformed into a theatre. […] you come to a gallery, and in the process of being in a gallery, we start to take you somewhere else, not through material transformation, not through sets, not through anything like that, but through language, through text.[102]

Despite his profound interest in the visual arts, Crouch declares himself as 'passionate about words' and 'the universes they can create in the audience's

---

[101] Alice Jones, 'Attempts on Her Life', *Independent*, 15 March 2007, reprinted in *Theatre Record 12–15 March 2007*, 309.
[102] Crouch in Ilter, *Process of Transformation*, 402.

heads'.[103] As the stage hypnotist in *An Oak Tree* who leads his actors and spectators to believe that a tree is a girl, Crouch invites the audience to use the imagination to see with the 'mind's eye'[104] the gallery he conjures through the skilful interaction between modes of storytelling, performance and exhibition. Visitors/spectators, therefore, find themselves at the centre of a complex intertextual experience designed to encourage them to exercise their agency and thus to position themselves physically within the performance (being free to move around the gallery and aware of themselves and others as bodies in the room), while also taking a perspective on the aesthetic and ethical issues the play is about.

As mentioned previously, in *ENGLAND*, the theatrical performance and the gallery situation coincide with the two performer/guides leading the audience for a gallery tour, engaging them in multiple layers of viewing as they explain the history of the art space they are in (in the case of the première, the Edinburgh Fruitmarket Gallery), introduce the artist of that particular performance (for the première it was Alex Hartley) and invite the audience to 'look' at the works on the walls (Figure 3.9).

Intriguingly, Crouch not only stages the performance of his storytelling in the middle of an art exhibition, thus including the exhibition itself within his performance, but he also evokes other virtual and invisible art galleries by inventing and evoking a world of artistic references that invisibly stir the audience's imagination.

Look! Look! Look! Once the invitation has been accepted, the visitor/spectator quickly realizes, on the one hand, just how many traces of the visual arts are scattered throughout the piece, and on the other, that the sheer seriality of their referencing suggests the accumulation typical of art galleries and museums – to the extent that one might even attempt to organize them in the various rooms of a gallery.

First and foremost, the two actor/guides invite the audience to visit the couple's private collection at their London home, a place 'like heaven' that looks very much like an art gallery. It is perhaps not by chance that they live in Southwark, the highly aestheticized borough, home of Tate Modern. It is a duplex, with white walls which spectators are brought to compare to those of the white cube gallery described by Brian O'Doherty, whose work, *Inside the White Cube. The Ideology of the Gallery Space* (1999) is a major influence on

---

[103] Crouch in Caridad Svich 'Tim Crouch's Theatrical Transformations: A Conversation with Caridad Svich', *HotReview.org*, 2006. http://www.timcrouchtheatre.co.uk/shows-2/england/booking-info (access 8 May 2023).
[104] Stephen Bottoms, 'Materialising the Audience: Tim Crouch's Sight Specifics in *ENGLAND* and *The Author*', *Contemporary Theatre Review*, 21, 4 (2011), 447.

Figure 3.9 *ENGLAND* written by Tim Crouch, and directed by Karl James and a smith. With Tim Crouch and Hannah Ringham. The Fruitmarket Gallery at The Traverse Theatre at The Edinburgh Festival, August 2007.

Source: Courtesy Geraint Lewis / ArenaPAL.

this play. The duplex is also 'a converted jam factory' (*E* 17), a building whose redevelopment ironically recalls that of the former Bankside Power Station turned into Britain's exclusive gallery of international modern art.

As already noted in Chapter 1, some of the painters belonging to the lead character's personal collection are painters of the YBA generation who contributed to *Sensation*, such as Marc Quinn, Gary Hume and Tacita Dean:

> This is where we live, my boyfriend and me. […] We live in London. […] We have a duplex.
>
> We have white walls.
>
> It's like heaven here!
>
> Here.
>
> Here.
>
> We don't have much here, but what we have is pretty amazing.
>
> We have a Marcus Taylor on the wall. He's a favourite of ours. His colours are amazing.
>
> My boyfriend believes that art shouldn't just be in galleries. / It belongs in people's everyday lives.
>
> /Art is for all!
>
> He's not a collector. He just gets what he likes.
>
> We have a Gregory Crewdson and a small Gary Hume.
>
> We have a Marc Quinn and Tacita Dean.
>
> In the other room, seriously, we have a small Willem de Kooning. / Seriously.
>
> / Seriously. It's not a joke. (*E* 17–18)

The mention of YBAs is no mere coincidence. Indeed, it is largely through allusions to YBA that signs of illness and death creep into the two guides' tale, penetrating the lives and words of the two characters far beyond their description of the symptoms of the protagonist's heart disease. Once the story of the protagonist's deteriorating health emerges, one might be led (as I was) to re-evaluate this set of YBA works in relation to their profound exploration of what Norman Rosenthal aptly describes as 'metaphors of sensations'[105] and their persistent focus on the vulnerability of the human body. A subtle yet sturdy thread weaves together the narrative of illness, predominantly unfolding within hospital corridors and private clinics, with the works of the artists it evokes. As a spectator myself, I might mention, for example, Marc Quinn's meditation on identity and mortality, *Self* (1991), a sculpture of his head made from his own frozen blood; Tacita Dean's interest in the obsolescence of her chosen materials and elements in the process of disappearing, becoming a series of memento mori of the here and now; or Gary Hume's famous *Doors* series, among which are those resembling hospital swing doors, whose highly lacquered and reflective surfaces place the viewer both inside and outside the space they circumscribe, perhaps to convey the idea of the transition from health to illness and death.

The couple also owns a Gregory Crewdson. His photographic series, *Twilight*, displayed at the White Cube in 2002, where threat and danger creep into ordinary suburban life, perhaps also catches a glimpse of the lives of the two protagonists. The couple's 'favourite', however, is a Marcus Taylor. 'His colours are amazing' (*E* 17–18) they say, and this clue might lead spectators (as it led me) to think of his colour field canvases, inspired by Rothko, whose edges are completely painted, creating the artworks' own frame, and of his constant search for beautiful experiences created by intimate interactions between the canvas and the viewer – an interaction Crouch himself is very keen on exploring.

But the finest piece of the couple's collection is a small study by abstract expressionist Willem de Kooning, 'one of the most famous American painters in the world' (*E* 19). 'The painting is unfinished from a series of two studies for a canvas he did in 1952' (*E* 19) and is worth a million pounds. In this case, the emphasis is on the value of the piece, which is more than twice the amount paid at auction in 1995 (*E* 19). Not surprisingly, by focusing on the commodification of art and the exploitation of others in art's name, albeit in passing, Crouch invites his spectators to question the legacy of contemporary art itself, torn between creativity and the market in a world where the gallery space plays a crucial role in the process of endorsement and where, in fact, the gallery is *the* space of legitimation. Furthermore, the reference to De Kooning highlights the link between art, death and market, according to which 'it's always good to buy art just before the artist dies, because after they die it goes up in value' (*E* 19). In addition, this reference unveils the unstable and contradictory nature of contemporary art, at the same time 'deadly' and 'healing'. On the one hand, the two actor/guides are less concerned with De Kooning's art than with his Alzheimer's disease and the possible connection

---

[105] Brooks Adams, Lisa Jardine, Martin Maloney, Norman Rosenthal, and Richard Stone, *Sensation: Young British Artists from the Saatchi Collection* (London: Thames & Hudson, 1997), 11.

between his illness and the lead in the paint he used, even though there is no actual evidence for this fatal link: 'Art is deadly!' (*E* 19). On the other hand, they invite the audience to imagine sitting in a cardiology waiting room and to recognize 'the importance of art in recuperation and contemplation' (*E* 30), considering how 'artworks can bring many therapeutic benefits to patients, visitors and staff within a hospital environment' (*E* 36).

At this point, other collections and gallery rooms emerge from the narrative. Guy's Hospital has an art trail that connects the works of art in the hospital with information about the artists and the therapeutic benefits of art in health. Likewise, on the walls of the clinic in the Royal County of Berkshire hang 'a genuine Bridget Riley, a Damien Hirst spin painting, and a photograph by Sam Taylor-Wood' (*E* 25). On the walls of the doctor's surgery, meanwhile, hang prints by Raoul Dufy, David Hockney and Seurat. Even if there is no explicit reference to specific art pieces, except Hirst's spinning paintings, one might suppose that this collection is inspired by an interest in colour therapy as well as in the interaction between forms and colours. From Bridget Riley's elementary shapes – lines, circles, curves and squares – triggering optical vibrations and illusions that draw the viewer in, to French Fauvist painter Raoul Dufy's colourful, decorative style; from George Seurat's painted stippling creating harmony and balanced emotions to the godfather of British art David Hockney's vivid world of lush, verdant nature. The artworks Crouch hints at are part of a collection intended to help patients: 'The patients like to look at the paintings. It helps them to feel better about their illnesses' (*E* 25), and to 'feel better about going to die. It can make you live longer!' (*E* 30).

A dedicated room within this gallery deserves to be reserved for Damien Hirst. The narrator/guides make specific reference to his spin paintings (*E* 43), famous for their vibrant colours and eloquent titles that begin with the word 'Beautiful'. It is precisely this adjective that catalyses the connection between Hirst's works and the play, in which 'beautiful' serves as a recurring descriptor for the lives of the two protagonists, their collection of art, the gallery space, Southwark Cathedral and even the atrium of London's Guy's Hospital. It may also be worth mentioning the exhibition *Damien Hirst: No Sense of Absolute Corruption* at the Gagosian Gallery in New York in 1996. There, the spin paintings were made to rotate mechanically on the wall, implying that movement was essential because the moment they stopped, they began to rot and stink, suggesting too that Hirst's colourful and beautiful spin paintings somehow conceal the same sense of decay that sweeps away the beautiful but fragile lives of the two protagonists in *ENGLAND*. However, the allusion to Hirst extends beyond the realm of spin painting, potentially operating in a more nuanced yet profound way. The theatre-maker's descriptions of hospitals as aestheticized and sanitized spaces, devoid of any visible traces of blood or flesh, are reminiscent of Hirst's captivating collection of medicine cabinets, in which the exhibition of pills, bottles, surgical instruments, skeletons and anatomical models intertwines the sombre motifs of bodily frailty with the unsettling allure of medical advancements and technology. By juxtaposing or overlapping the images of 'aseptic' hospitals and 'anaesthetized' galleries, the theatre-maker raises profound questions about the role of the theatre as a space that actively engages with and examines real-life experiences. Unlike the sterile white cube gallery, the theatre is a domain that welcomes the outside world, allowing it to seep in and be thoroughly explored. Referring explicitly to O'Doherty, Crouch writes:

> Some galleries should have antiseptic hand wash dispensers outside their entrances. Their aesthetics are so clean and other-worldly that they appear to disdain the mortal and infected mayhem of everyday life - and this before we've even looked at the art. I feel the same about churches … and of course, hospitals […] Theatre, I think, is less capable of such clean immortal lines. Its raw material is less controlled, more prone to disease. I never feel I need to wash my hands before I see a play.[106]

It is significant, then, that despite the narrative's consistent focus on the aesthetic attributes that define the white cube gallery, hospitals and even churches – such as pristine white walls, clean lines and an almost sacred silence – the invisible art galleries evoked by Crouch are made to share with the theatre its inherently mortal essence, highlighting theatre's ability to transcend mere aesthetics and tap into the raw, mortal core of our existence. Furthermore, Crouch's consistent allusions to artists and works extending beyond those exhibited in the gallery create an aesthetics of accumulation that fundamentally challenges the minimalism of the white cube.

ENGLAND is a play for galleries that fully engages the audience's imagination, inviting them to decipher signs and clues that simultaneously allude to different visual realms and galleries. These include the physical gallery in which the performance takes place, the galleries evoked by Ringham and Crouch's narration and ultimately the myriad other galleries that each member of the audience conjures up in their own unique way. Known for his careful consideration of the audience's role in his performances, Crouch seems to be targeting a discerning elite. This audience not only comprehends the narrative's allusions to contemporary artists and appreciates the artworks on display in the gallery where the performance takes place but also shows a genuine curiosity

---

[106] Tim Crouch, Programme for the 2009 news from nowhere production of ENGLAND at London's Whitechapel Gallery (8 May–16 June 2009).

about the world of contemporary art, recognizing the theatre-maker's dialogue with Brian O'Doherty and perhaps even having read his influential essays. Nevertheless, while it is undeniable that audiences at cultural venues such as the Royal Court or the Whitechapel often have 'high cultural capital', this play can be understood and appreciated on different levels by different audiences. These audiences, however, share the common freedom to move around the gallery and to grasp the dark undertones that unfold in the second act when a precious work of art is exchanged for a human life in a distant Eastern country.

Significantly, in the programme for the 2009 production at the Whitechapel Gallery in London, Crouch aptly references Marcel Duchamp's concept of 'art coefficient', which explores the delicate balance between the artist's 'unexpressed but intended and the unintentionally expressed'. Moreover, he acknowledges that 'inside both theatre and visual art exists the chaotic element of the audience and the unpredictability of its reception'.[107] Indeed, the references to works of art or artists made by the two guides may or may not trigger recollection of specific works or associations within the audience's minds. Nevertheless, the spectators can activate their newfound agency, fuelled by their active involvement in the performance, as described in Chapter 1. This agency allows them to forge unique connections, interpretations and associations, depending on their own fields of interest and personal and cultural experiences, which cannot be fully controlled by the playwright, and which contribute to a personal and transformative experience within the context of the play. For each individual spectator, a quick reference to an artist or a work of art becomes the centre of a very complex and receptive dynamic that is part of a unique intellectual adventure.

A choreographed collection: Mark Ravenhill and Frantic Assembly's *pool (no water)*

On the stage of Mark Ravenhill's *pool (no water)* at the Drum Theatre Plymouth (2006),[108] a peculiar, intangible art gallery is conjured up in a performance that owes something to both theatre and live art practice.

A pseudo-confessional play, *pool (no water)* is the result of a collaborative and group-based creative process involving playwright Ravenhill, who describes himself as a text-oriented playwright, and Frantic Assembly. An ensemble formed in Sheffield in 1984 and today widely recognized as one of Europe's leading experimental companies, Frantic Assembly is an

---

[107] Tim Crouch in the Playbill for the 2009 production at London's Whitechapel Gallery.
[108] A Frantic Assembly, Drum Theatre Plymouth and the Lyric Hammersmith Production, *pool (no water)* was first performed at the Drum Theatre Plymouth on 22 September 2006.

experimental theatre group engaged in a search for new artistic forms. It presents itself as a company with a 'unique style' that combines 'movement, design, music, and text',[109] highly physical performance vocabulary and innovative staging of both devised and theatre-based work. Indeed, *pool (no water)* is arguably a multimedia and transmedia production, prompted, as Ravenhill himself explains, by American photographer Nan Goldin's work. 'Her intimate portraits of bohemian, drug-addled, multisexual friends, of the ill and the bruised' inspired the story of friendship and illness, which Ravenhill summarizes as follows: 'A group of friends, who have become very close at art college, feel huge jealousy as one of them becomes a massively successful artist. They go to stay with her and, when she is badly injured in an accident, realise they can use her as material for their next work of art.'[110]

Ravenhill conceives an open narrative text with no stage directions, lines of the script not allocated to any of the unnamed characters and a cast of four speakers, A, B, C and D (although, as Ravenhill himself writes, 'other productions don't have to follow this'[111]), who are performed by Keir Charles, Cait Davis, Leah Muller and Mark Rice-Oxley. They form the collective voice of unnamed speakers who act as artists known as 'the Group'. Engaged in various social and charitable projects and disparagingly dismissing themselves as 'hypocritically do-gooding, new Labour-era bohemians who design murals for heroin babies and the like',[112] they admit to being bitterly jealous of one of them, an unnamed 'she', whose art has become so successful that she can afford the ultimate status symbol of her own swimming pool.

The storytelling serves as a collective autobiographical reflection on the past as the speakers tell their own story in retrospect, addressing the audience rather than themselves as if they were being interviewed for a documentary about their artist friend, 'she',[113] while they are in constant movement, walking, running, jumping, climbing and dancing. Through this bursting physicality as well as repetition and variations that emphasize the temporal distance between their telling and experiencing selves, they unfold the story of their friend's terrible accident and coma after falling into an empty pool, and their subsequent decision to turn her twisted and bruised body into both a sex toy (this means 'a man unzipping himself into her mouth', and another man taking the patient's finger, wetting it with his tongue and placing it

---

[109] Frantic Assembly website https://www.franticassembly.co.uk/about (accessed 8 May 2023).
[110] Mark Ravenhill, 'In at the Deep End', *The Guardian*, 20 September 2006.
[111] Mark Ravenhill, *pool (no water)*, in, *Plays: 2* (London: Bloomsbury, 2008), 294.
[112] Donald Hutera, 'pool (no water)', *The Times*, 28 September 2006, reprinted in *Theatre Record 22 October – 4 November 2006*, 1297.
[113] Graham, *pool*, 11.

somewhere up his backside,[114] as an annoyed Quentin Letts described in his review) and a work of art.

While 'she' lies in coma in a hospital bed, Ravenhill's artists, numb to feeling and even convinced that, somehow, she deserves this accident, begin to document their friend's recovery and to rearrange the scene. They decide to capitalize on her hospitalization, gleefully using her maimed body as photographic material for the lucrative artwork they intend to make of her misfortune, and so follow in the footsteps of other immoral, parasitical, opportunist artists, like Simon in Crouch's *My Arm* or Evelyn in Neil Labute's play *The Shape of Things*, which premièred at the Almeida in 2001.[115] In *pool (no water)*, the speakers/artists seem to be particularly cruel, as the pain of their comatose lifelong friend does not arouse an ounce of sympathy but rather invites them to re-frame it in the guise of a heartless artistic representation. They 'start to arrange, start to order, start to catalogue' (*pool* 302), thus transforming the injured body into an art object by bringing its exhibition value to the fore:

> We can't remember now. It doesn't matter. Oh of course it matters to curators it matters to historians. But to us it doesn't matter at all. But one of us first thought of taking a camera.
> [...]
> And you see now – look – what it's done to her. Now the blood's been cleaned away. The body bruised and swollen into shape no other humans yet achieved. Her limbs in plastic. Her neck in plastic. Her mask. The drips and the tubes. And the machines that inhalate and beeeep. A moving ... a timeless picture of the ...
> [...]
> It appeals. It tempts. There is beauty here. We know, we've spent our life hunting it out and there is beauty here.
>
> And we stand and we look and at last we're moved by the intense beauty of that image.
> [...]
> And the light was good and the potential for composition was all there and to honest it was easy easy easy easy to come up with those images that so later seemed striking.
> [...]

---

[114] Quentin Letts, 'pool (no water)', *Daily Mail*, 2 November 2006, reprinted in *Theatre Record 22 October – 4 November 2006*, 1298.

[115] Evelyn secretly exploits her would-be lover by turning him into her 'installation thingie' without his consent. Neil Labute, *The Shape of Things* (London: Faber and Faber, 2001), 128.

And the temptation to arrange – just to move the bed … so … so the composition was … get her head in the light, so. The temptation was great, and we were weak. So we wheel her into the light and actually move the limbs and head – checking of course not to disrupt the tubes and drips and … science and art can work together happily.

It took a few moments to snap. An image a record a frame.

(*pool* 306–7)

The moment the seduction of the aestheticization invades the care ward and the group begins to share with the audience both their view of the friend as a thing of beauty and their own art project, the hospital bed becomes an art installation. The stage, whose bed right at the centre suggests a hospital room, is thus transformed into an art gallery that presents high-impact art experiences/performances. It is no wonder, therefore, that Miriam Buether's dazzling, white-tiled 'surreal space that combines the bottom of a swimming pool with a hospital room'[116] was an aseptic white space, 'rendered more chilly and clinical' by Natasha Chivers' lighting (fluorescent whites, limes and mauves),[117] that impressed the actors with its 'strong clean lines' (Figure 3.10), perhaps conceived as a new variant of the antiseptic white cube gallery that Crouch compares to hospitals and clinics in *ENGLAND*.

The body of the 'she' in the hospital bed is therefore the first work of art to be exhibited in this pool/hospital/art gallery. Given Frantic Assembly's artistic practice, the 'she' can be seen, here, as an installation, or a choreographed piece of body art performance, which emerges through collaborative creation and decision-making that are themselves formed on the basis of a collective process of 'research and development'.[118]

The primary visual inspiration for this image and for the Group's artistic project is the American counter-cultural artist and activist Nan Goldin's pioneering work, intense and painful as a punch in the stomach: *Falling into an Empty Pool* (2000),[119] a series of photos recording her and her friend's stay in hospitals, which perhaps suggested the main action/accident in the play, and also her successful *The Ballad of Sexual Dependency*, a 'record-keeping of her day-to-day-life'.[120] It is a deeply personal narrative, based

---

[116] Graham, *pool*, 14.
[117] Susannah Clapp, 'pool (no water)', *Daily Mail*, 2 November 2006, reprinted in *Theatre Record* 22 October – 4 November 2006, 1299.
[118] Graham, *pool*, 4.
[119] Nan Goldin, 'Falling into an Empty Pool, India, 2000', in John Jenkinson (ed.), *Nan Golding, The Devil's Playground* (London: Phaidon, 2003), 214–35.
[120] Nan Goldin, *The Ballad of Sexual Dependency* (London: Secker & Warburg, 1989), 9. The *Ballad*, which was first published in 1986, also exists as a live multimedia presentation and video tape. Including over 700 images and a soundtrack, *The Ballad*, which is

Staging the Art Gallery 215

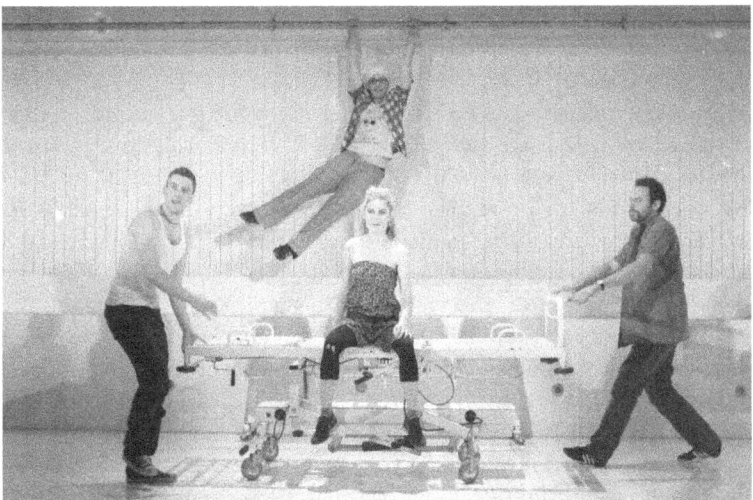

Figure 3.10 *pool (no water)* written by Mark Ravenhill. A production by Frantic Assembly, with Keir Charles [green shirt], Leah Muller [printed dress], Cait Davis [checked shirt, glasses], and Mark Rice [yellow vest]. Lyric Theatre Hammersmith, London, November 2006.

Source: Courtesy Geraint Lewis / ArenaPAL.

on the experiences of the artist herself and of her 're-created family' of nonconformist, multisexual, drug-addicted, AIDS-affected friends. Yet, it is important to emphasize that for Goldin, photographing is a moment of emotional connection with the subjects of her photographs, who are aware and content to be part of her work. In her programmatic introduction to *The Ballad of Sexual Dependency*, she writes:

> I photograph directly from my life. These pictures come out of relationships, not observation. [...] The instant of photographing, instead of creating distance, is a moment of clarity and emotional connection for me. There is a popular notion that the photographer is by nature a voyeur, the last one invited to the party. But I'm not crashing;

constantly reedited and updated, began its public life on the club circuit in New York City and has since been included in the Whitney Museum of American Art Biennial in 1985 and in the Berlin Film Festival in 1986. The text is available online: https://americansuburbx.com/wp-content/uploads/2012/09/nan-goldin-ballad-of-sexual-dependency.pdf (accessed 8 May 2023).

this is my party. This is my family, my history. [...] My family of friends is still based on interdependency, continuity, love, and tenderness.[121]

While Goldin claims the 'authenticity' of her work – 'a record of what things really looked like and felt like'[122] – Ravenhill's collective of artists are precisely those voyeurs who 'crash', who invade their friend's intimacy without permission or respect, and with the twin aims of achieving artistic success and making money ('We are already thinking interviews – exhibitions – catalogue – sale' (*pool* 307)). They also know that what they are doing is 'wrong', even 'disgusting', because, as they admit, they are not doing it 'for her'. Their photographic record is not authentic, because they arrange her body in such a way as to meet the requirements of an exhibition (*pool* 313). Having done 'very good work with the underprivileged', they believe it is time for them 'to be privileged' (*pool* 315).

Goldin's chronicle of the suffering caused by AIDS seems to have been the inspiration not only for the stage image of 'her' in bed but also for 'her' first truly successful work. As it emerges from the Groups' words, 'she' used their friend Ray's 'blood and bandages and catheters and condoms' after his death from AIDS to create pieces that were 'sold to every major collector in the world' (*pool* 295). Did 'she' exploit the aestheticization of suffering according to the relentless logic of consumption, like the Group after her accident? Or did 'she' rather use it for much more personal and ethical purposes like Nan Goldin? Indeed, Goldin was sincerely interested in documenting the effects of the burgeoning HIV/AIDS crisis of the 1980s and also in recording her life, despite her awareness that 'photography doesn't preserve memory as effectively' as she thought it would: 'I always thought if I photographed anyone or anything enough, I would never lose the person, I would never lose the memory, I would never lose the place. But the pictures show me how much I've lost'.[123]

And what about the installation that the 'she' artist conceives, after recovering and exerting her ownership of the images her friends have taken of her broken body? As 'she' re-orients the project into a self-representational mode of performance photography, other visual inspirations come to mind, not least Goldin's many self-portraits. Indeed, her famous *Nan One Month after Being Battered* (1984), which shows Goldin with a swollen, bloodshot eye and bruised face and which was conceived as a testament to the destructive power of an abusive relationship, resonates in significant ways

[121] Ibid.
[122] Ibid.
[123] Ibid.

with the abusive relationship presented by the play. What are the true artistic and ethical motives behind the injured artist's project? Is it an attempt to assert some form of control over her life, enabling her to remember, as it is for Nan Goldin? Or is it ego-driven opportunism, as some references to her 'business acumen and her opportunism' suggest? As the co-artistic director of Frantic Assembly, Scott Graham explains, 'The artist's success brings power and her power brings success. Once the world's eyes are on her she knows how to market and sell herself perfectly. This is the expertise that the Group will never have.'[124]

But these Goldin-like pieces are not the only works in the pool/hospital/art gallery. Another work conjured up in Ravenhill/Buether's gallery derives from David Hockney's iconic paintings of Los Angeles' swimming pools of the 1960s and 1970s. It is no coincidence that the pool that emerges from the characters' description clearly recalls Hockney's sun-drenched swimming pools in a Californian artificial paradise: 'The poooooool. / And we go. / It takes so many hours to fly to this strange new world and there are palm trees and heat haze in the dusk of the airport' (*pool* 299). Like Hockney's swimming pools, Ravenhill's seems to open up an idyllic world of leisure and sexual openness, a far cry from the greyness and pain of Britain which the group of friends have left behind.[125]

Empty of human presence, although the splash under the diving board implies the presence of a diver, *The Little Splash* (1966), *The Splash* (1966) and *The Bigger Splash* (1967), perhaps among the most famous paintings of the British artist, intriguingly intertwine and overlap with the play's visual imagery of the waterless swimming pool in which, similarly, the 'she'/diver is absent. In fact, 'she' is thrice absent: physically absent as she is never on stage; absent as a human being, incapable of connecting with other people; and artistically absent, as her 'being absent' is 'that quality in her work that sells' (*pool* 295).

In both the play (and performance) and the paintings, the act of jumping into the pool is only to be imagined by the audience and gallery visitors. In the play, however, there is an attempt to visualize it:

> I'll always remember that moment, always. Just something … all of us standing there naked in the dark. Sometimes now when the painkillers aren't working I try to visualize that moment […]

---

[124] Graham, *pool*, 28.
[125] David Hockney is referred to among the sources of inspiration in Scott Graham, *pool*, 31. In particular there is a reference to his painting *The Cruel Elephant*, where an unknowing elephant is standing on the words 'ants ants ants': 'This is like their relationship. The characters are the ants crushed under this crass behemoth'.

Come on she squeals come on the pool!

And then she's running and whooping through the darkness as she launches herself as you can just see her up in the sky, up against the sky, the arc of her body through the night up and up and up and up.

She seems so high. She's flying. She's an angel. A drunken laughing goddess angel.

And then she arcs down and we're clapping and we're cheering. (*pool* 301)

While in the play, it certainly is a 'she' who jumps into the pool, the paintings leave the viewer wondering who has just dived in. While in the paintings there is no one in sight and the scene is almost entirely still (apart from the splash), in the play, a group of drunk and noisy friends is having good time. However, the first perception of the Group watching their friend launching herself into the pool is not too different from that of the viewer who looks at Hockney's silent canvas:

And then.

Some of us thought we heard the splash. You do. When you think there's going to be a splash then you hear a splash. You do the work. But we didn't hear the splash. There was no splash. (*pool* 301)

'You do the work'. The Group's initial reaction is to experience the same perception and the same emotions aroused by the paintings, which invite the viewer to 'hear' what is silent and is only visually conveyed, except that in the play, the spectator's 'work' is followed not by the sound of a splash but of a crack:

There was

The crack

The cracking of her body.

The harsh cracking of her body against the concrete.

(*pool* 301)

But there are a number of other ways in which we might reflect upon the intertwining of Ravenhill and Hockney's works. First, the representation of jumping and diving is an aesthetic challenge for both the artist and the playwright. Hockney is said to be fascinated by the challenge of depicting a substance in motion that is essentially transparent to the eye and of freezing in a still image something which is never still. Rejecting the possibility of recreating the spray with an instantaneous gesture in liquid on canvas, he took about two weeks to complete the painting, which provides an interesting contrast to the artist's subject matter. Hockney explained:

> When you photograph a splash, you're freezing a moment and it becomes something else. I realise that a splash could never be seen this way in real life, it happens too quickly. And I was amused by this, so I painted it in a very, very slow way.[126]

According to Graham, Frantic Assembly faced a similar challenge. The company felt that the metaphorical, ironic, symbolic accident of jumping into an empty swimming pool had to be represented through the 'simplicity of the words', because that moment had to be 'the perfect communion of storytelling and the audience's imagination'. They felt there was no point in reciting or dancing it, because they could rely on the audience to understand what it meant to jump and land in an unexpectedly empty swimming pool:

> The contrast between the joy of the leap into the air and the pain of the crash onto the tiles is so extreme yet so vivid. Who cannot imagine that feeling of abandon followed by the confusion of the slightly extended length of the fly, the unexpected angles and views, before the unspeakable cruelty of landing?[127]

It is all about soliciting empathy from the audience because the characters need to be understood.

Finally, both *pool (no water)* and *The Splashes* deal with jealousy. Hockney himself offers jealousy as a key for interpreting his painting *A Bigger Splash*:

> What do you think of when you look at *A Bigger Splash*? Is there a word that sums up how the painting makes you feel? It's OK if that word is 'jealous' as *A Bigger Splash* is an immediately seductive image. It makes us think of holidays and escapism – or perhaps the sort of life most of us can only dream about.[128]

---

[126] David Hockney quoted in Catherine Kinley, *David Hockney: Seven Paintings* (London: Tate Gallery, 1992), 5.
[127] Graham, *pool*, 27.
[128] Tate, 'Understanding David Hockney's *A Bigger Splash*'. https://www.tate.org.uk/art/artworks/hockney-a-bigger-splash-t03254/understanding-david-hockneys-bigger-splash (accessed 8 May 2023).

Jealousy, specifically the jealousy of four minor artists for their successful friend, is also the driving idea behind *pool (no water)*, which unashamedly explores this very human and yet dark emotion. The swimming pool to which the friends are invited is both a status symbol and a visualization of their envy. The substance-abusing foursome are so jealous that they even project blame onto 'she' for the death of another of their friends, Sally, who died from cancer:

'It was you who killed Sally.'

God.

'Because none of us was meant to be wealthy, none of us was meant to be recognised, none of us was meant to fly. We're the Group. And there's balance. And you took away the balance. One of us goes up, then one of us goes down. It's a natural law. Don't you understand the most basic natural law? Well of course you do – understood it and ignored it – on purpose – and killed Sally. Chose to kill Sally. Cunt. Cunt. Cunt.

(pool 298)

With Icarus' arrogance, she 'flew' (not 'leapt') too high and therefore deserved to crash. No wonder her friends perceive her dive as the flight of an angel launching itself up into the sky, 'up and up and up and up' (*pool* 301):

[…] there is justice in this. Something is shaping our ends.

For Sally, for Ray, for us, this had to be.

You see you flew – yes – you reached out your wings and you flew above us. And that's okay. You tried and congratulations. For trying. But you thought that could last? Flying above the ground, looking down on our lives in the city below? You really thought that could last? Of course that couldn't last. And now you've crashed right down. And that hurts doesn't it? I understand. That hurts.

(pool 303)

Graham suggests that the very act of jumping into the swimming pool and finding it empty could be 'a pessimistic metaphor for the lives of the artist and that of the four characters'. Significantly, 'she' is denigrated not for leaping but for 'flying', as if it were wrong to even try:

Here the characters place themselves in a catastrophic heap at the bottom of the pool, watching the artist fly over and eventually join them. This is how they see life, not just in the depiction of the [she] artist's attempts at superiority but in their role as broken failures, twisted on the tiles of the emptied pool. This attitude is bitter and worn. It has leapt and found the pool empty.[129]

The admission of jealousy remains one of the greatest and still relevant taboos,[130] as demonstrated by Frantic Assembly's 2008 successful production of *Othello*. Jealousy is also the feeling the company wants the audience to experience:

> It cannot just be the story that you meet here. The audience must be made to confront the idea of artistic jealousy. We felt the audience had to be implored to at least put themselves in the shoes of the characters. And this imploring is direct from the characters themselves. Why else do they speak? This is not the theatre of events unfolding. This is confessional and specifically the confession of despicable events that will ultimately demand sympathy, horror and revulsion [...] But there is no tension or engagement if these acts are purely despicable. The audience has to be led to believe or appreciate the need for these acts, or at least what inspired them. The characters have to go somewhere towards the point where what they are presenting to you is a possible version of you in the same situation.[131]

Ravenhill focuses on an emotion, jealousy, that was already embedded but hidden in Hockney's painting, allowing both the Frantic Assembly performers to express it freely and the audience to re-imagine Hockney's artificial paradise, and thus to reconsider the beauty of his swimming-pool, set in clean-lined and geometrical spaces, surrounded by minimalist architecture, immaculate green lawns, vibrant blue skies and blue water, as a backdrop for a story of envy, cynicism and bloodshed. After the accident, one of the friends attempts to visualize the image of 'her' body and, at the same time, to engage the audience:

> Her body – her body is broken in our head. A picture but not – it's not a feeling you know? And you would have thought above all else an artist would – (*pool* 305)

But it is the choreography, more than the words, that makes the audience aware of the characters' inner feelings. At one point in the play, after eight

---

[129] Graham, *pool*, 21.
[130] Ibid., 26.
[131] Ibid., 15.

weeks of visiting the comatose woman, the four friends hear the news that she is conscious: 'Two months and Sleeping Beauty is … Oh.' (*pool* 309). As co-artistic director of Frantic Assembly Steven Hoggett explains, the realization that 'she' has finally recovered triggers an 'explosion' of the performers' true feelings, which oscillate violently between behaving in a way they know is right and behaving in a way they cannot help but express, despite their best efforts to keep it secret. In the rehearsing process, Graham and Hoggett asked the performers to improvise around two ideas: one of 'goodness', inspired by religious illustrations, which led them to 'play with the idea of kisses and cherubs', morphing the static images of religious iconography into a choreography that takes inspiration from famous images that usually show outstretched arms and faces turned slightly upwards, bathed in the diffused light that emanates from the sunbeams behind their heads – examples of which are littered throughout the history of art. The second idea was based 'around the words "shit" and "fuck"', which, Hoggett explains, not without irony, are not so well represented in art history or iconography and therefore pose a greater challenge when trying to create physical material that represents them. However, he concludes, 'the results were fascinating. Most material seemed to centre itself either on the hands (particularly the fingers) or the gut (clutching, omitting, retching)'.[132] Based on these two ideas, they choreographed to Imogen Heap's *Just for Now*. The interplay between the delicate melody of the harp and the unhinged, almost panicky rhythmic, track steered the movement of a sequence that oscillated between the two states, asking the performers to take 'the physicality out of a sense of naturalism and gesture and move towards the extreme'.[133] Through non-verbal communication, which required a shift in choreographic style from naturalism towards the extreme, the audience was made aware of this emotional explosion. More than that, they were invited to 'dive' into the turbulent waters of conflicting emotions to reach the shore they felt was the safest.

The intention of Frantic Assembly's performers is to involve the audience in an event and never to allow them to dismiss what they see as safe because it is 'only' a play. They literally force the audience to visualize the world they describe through words and physical movement, but also to share the conflicting feelings of the characters on stage, creating their own synergy with the play. It is precisely through this synergetic experience that the audience can visualize the art gallery and also 'sympathize' with its hidden, carefully choreographed masterpiece.

---

[132] Steven Hoggett, 'Your Friend Is Conscious' in ibid.
[133] Ibid.

4

The price of everything

Art is money-sexy

What is art? And what determines its value? One of the characters in Timberlake Wertenbaker's *Three Birds Alighting on a Field* (1991) challenges the audience with questions about the true nature of art and what makes it valuable:

> **Jeremy** I read yesterday about an Italian clerk who had saved great Italian paintings from the Nazis. He knew exactly which ones to save, well, it wasn't difficult, he saved the Raphaels, the Leonardos … If we had an invasion here, what would I save? Would I save this painting? Would I save it because it is worth half a million, or was, yesterday, or would I save it because I was convinced humanity would be the poorer without it? Would humanity be the poorer without it? (*3 Birds* 20)

Jeremy's cynical speculation resurrects the familiar, unanswerable question of longevity, while hiding the suspicion (if not fear) that contemporary art is no more than a hoax. The eternal question of the value of art, which has become even more contentious with the rise of the modern art market, with works of art valued in both aesthetic and commercial terms, recurs in several contemporary plays in which art dealers, collectors, artists and art critics are prompted to explore the relationship between the art world and neoliberal capitalism in a range of different ways. As the previous chapters have already shown, this concern has appeared in a growing number of plays since the shift from the welfare state to the art market and the increasing hybridization of state support and corporate patronage. Indeed, playwrights have turned their attention to such phenomena as the commercialization, marketing and consumption of art, denouncing the danger of the pernicious influence of philistinism and commodification on the art world. Significantly, while questioning the art world, they also explore the world of theatre and the entertainment industry. While the Conservatives spent the whole of the 1980s installing a new economic and cultural hegemony in Britain, by the end of the 1990s, this mixed economy of funding – part state subsidy, part business sponsorship and part box office – was in crisis.

The whole system of theatre funding had become so commercialized that even subsidized theatre companies had succumbed to the 'pressure to be successful businesses': 'Theatres rebranded themselves, acquired logos, learnt to use niche marketing, made sponsorship deals, redesigned their foyers and expanded their bar activities. Audiences became customers and shows became products. The box office was king.'[1]

In *The Art of Success* (1987), Nick Dear shows that many of the commercial strategies in the British art world had in fact already been experimented with during the preceding centuries, thanks in large part to 'a specifically national history in which the role of commerce has both attached stigma to local creativity by hindering some practices and encouraged the development of marketing innovations'.[2] He thus presents the *enfant terrible* of British art, William Hogarth, as a businessman and brings to the fore pressing issues common to both the eighteenth and twentieth centuries, such as the commodification of art or the nature of ambition and 'the degree of compromise one will accept'.[3] First of all, Dear's Hogarth is an artist deeply steeped in the spirit of 'negotiation', ready to accept secret commissions from Prime Minister Robert Walpole.[4] Incessantly and obsessively, the ongoing artistic discussion revolves around power, money and the changing nature of both market and audience. This is not only because Dear's Hogarth, like his alter ego, is in need of cash and happens to have the flair and inclinations of a businessman but also because the value of art is undergoing a substantial revolution. The eruption of 'modern' finance in the cultural scene of the eighteenth century, along with its attendant crises, bankruptcy, investment, profit and loss, had a momentous effect upon the world of collecting, which was no longer the exclusive domain of taste and gentility but increasingly a matter related to wealth, as Robert Walpole reminds his interlocutors on stage. The prime minister is a greedy art collector, very much aware of the new financial potentialities attached to works of art:

---

[1] Aleks Sierz, *Modern British Playwrighting. The 1990s* (London: Methuen Drama, 2012), 34.
[2] Charlotte Gould and Sophie Mesplède, 'Introduction. From Hogarth to Hirst: Three Hundred Years of Buying and Selling British Art', in *Marketing Art in the British Isles, 1700 to the Present. A Cultural History* (New York: Routledge, 2012), 7.
[3] Nick Dear, *The Art of Success*, in *Plays One* (London: Faber and Faber, 2000), vii.
[4] This is not an episode corroborated by historians, but one which nonetheless testifies to the artist's somewhat pacified relations with the controversial politician: 'The fact that the Act [Licensing Act] went through so smoothly is a demonstration, if it were needed, that Hogarth was not regarded by Walpole as a threat.' David Bindman, *Hogarth and His Times. Serious Comedy* (Berkeley: University of California Press, 1988), 77.

> My houses are stuffed full of art, you know. It's such a damned good investment. I got a Titian last year for two pounds ten. It's already worth double that. I love art, I love it more than any other property, they're so neat and compact, those rectangles of wealth. (*Art* 67)

In reshaping the figure of Hogarth, the playwright would appear to embrace art historian Frederick Antal's interpretation of the eighteenth century artist as 'the most business-like of artists in a milieu pervaded by a business spirit'.[5] As he shows Hogarth's transactions with 'low lives' and, in particular, the lives of women, Dear clearly points that the art market rubs shoulders with the ways of prostitution, as the artist's lover Louisa suggests without equivocation when told he is a famous painter: 'Well isn't that a nice thing to be? A profession as old as my own' (*Art* 21).

The budding marketability of art fuelled the question of its visibility and accessibility to the public; in the absence of public spaces to show one's works, there were no easy solutions to these new problems. And Hogarth was truly ingenious at devising intelligent strategies to create interactions with the public that were profitable both financially and artistically:

> **William**   I'm doing a print of Sarah Sprackling. […] Plan to have an edition on sale straight after the poor woman's turned off. Get in while she's still fresh in the public imagination – all those crowds who will bay at the hanging – last portrait of the deceased – got to be an earner. (*Art* 43)

He was also aware that, in a time when patronage by royalty and aristocracy 'had begun to recede but was not entirely displaced', diversification was necessary; as Antal explains, Hogarth was 'discovering completely new classes of consumers' and exploring the potentialities of 'a public extending in scope far beyond the middle classes'.[6] Not content with capitalizing on Malcolm's/Sprackling's scandalous fame, the artist considers the opportunity of catering to different types of public. Perhaps the first English artist to produce a painting of a criminal, as distinct from an engraving, Hogarth produced a sketch of Sarah Malcolm (National Gallery of Scotland, Edinburgh) for the aristocratic connoisseur Horace Walpole. At the same time, 'after wide advertisement, he published a simplified version of this as an engraving, knee-length against a dark background. *The Gentleman's Magazine* published

---

[5] Fredrick Antal, *Hogarth and His Place in European Art* (London: Routledge & Kegan Paul, 1962), 13.
[6] Antal, *Hogarth and His Place in European Art*, 57.

a woodcut after this composition, but a summarized version, showing the head and shoulders only'.[7] Hogarth used to diversify his artistic production and, according to Paulson, apparently 'still distinguished at this time between the serious modern moral subjects, to be painted, subscribed, and sold at his house, and an ephemeral catch-penny print'.[8]

In *Painting for Money* (1996), David Solkin showed that 'none better than William Hogarth knew how to hybridize genres with a view to catering to the needs of a new pool of buyers informed by values of their own'.[9] Eager to circumvent aristocratic patronage, 'with unique business acumen',[10] like his historical counterpart, Dear's Hogarth creates his own market and substitutes the middleman with subscription. In his typically colourful language, the stage version of Hogarth flaunts his commercial agenda:

> **William**   What I am gonna do is, I'm gonna do a set of prints that'll be dirt cheap to buy, right, I mean fuck, I don't care if you wrap your fish in them, but what I'm thinking of is this: they'll infiltrate. My modern moral subjects. They'll sneak into people's homes – ordinary people – and creep up on to the walls and they'll hang over the bedsteads and they'll niggle. They will take on the old prejudices and they'll worry them by the throat […] they won't sicken, but they'll nag. (*Art* 59)

Nick Dear's irreverent and fantastical William Hogarth, untrammelled by the limitations of history and verisimilitude, displays the drama of art as it unfolds since its very beginning, certainly, but yet more importantly, as it explodes in the 1980s. Entrepreneurialism combined with a casual disregard for rules and conventions of the art market makes Hogarth Damien Hirst's contemporary. It is worth noting that Hirst, whose career has thrived from the start due to sponsorship, effectively blends the provocative nature of cutting-edge art with sponsorship from the very bourgeois world that the avant-garde once aimed to question and defy.[11]

The historic Hogarth has become a lens through which Dear explores and assesses the tragicomedy of contemporary art, all of a sudden made spectacular

---

[7] Ibid., 56.
[8] Ronald Paulson, *Hogarth. High Art and Low. 1732–1750*, vol. 2 (New Brunswisk, NJ: Rutgers University Press, 1992), 10.
[9] Charlotte Gould and Sophie Mesplède, 'From Hogarth to Hirst: three Hundred Years of Buying and Selling', in *Marketing Art in the British Isles, 1700 to the Present: A Cultural History* (London: Routledge, 2012), 20.
[10] Gould and Mesplède, *From Hogarth to Hirst*, 20.
[11] Julian Stallabrass, *Art Incorporated. The Story of Contemporary Art* (Oxford: Oxford University Press, 2004), 129–33.

by globalization, a financial economy, the appeal of scandal, towering prices, hedge funds and other rogue proceedings which interact with aesthetics, craftsmanship and talent. No wonder, then, that Timberlake Wertenbaker's dissection of Thatcherite Britain, *Three Birds Alighting on a Field*, revives the long-running debate on national taste, raises questions about art as a rewarding financial investment and ponders the issue of what constitutes legitimation in the contemporary art world. 'Art is sexy, art is money, art is money-sexy, art is money-sexy-social-climbing-fantastic', reads the pink-lit billboard of an unlikely artist Laura Hellish, quoting the former director of the Metropolitan Museum of Art, Thomas Hoving (a piece which is auctioned off in the first scene of the play). This is a scene designed to remind the audience not only that the elite use their corporate positions to advance their personal interest and social status through their involvement in arts sponsorship but also that London is the art capital of the world with its two leading auction houses, Christie's (founded in 1766) and Sotheby's (1744), which still compete for international supremacy. Art patronage, fierce competition between artists, auctions, branded galleries and processes of endorsement to determine which works are to be considered worthy of a potential place in art history lead the playwright to explore the difference between the intrinsic and the exchange value of a work of art, and also to question the relationship of the theatre to both the market and those public bodies financially and medially involved in its management, as seen in Chapter 1.

Through the mirror of the art world, Wertenbaker reveals the Faustian pact between art and business that threatens the very creative independence that investment should make possible, both in the visual arts and theatre:

> **David**   [...] I've just agreed to the Tate – at least the art world understands business, can't say that about theatres I deal with. [...] Well done with the million, Yoyo, hope they don't waste it on something too modern. You can always state a preference for tunes, you know. Don't let them intimidate you with all this artistic independence nonsense. You paid the money, you call the tune. (*3 Birds* 10–11)

David's words encapsulate Wertenbaker's realization that everything would change with the arrival of capitalist sponsorship and anticipate her resignation from the Royal Court's board, which she challenged by inviting it to investigate the nature and consequences of private sponsorship rather than simply the means of obtaining it.[12] Concerned about the business-oriented

---

[12] Sophie Bush, *The Theatre of Timberlake Wertenbaker* (London: Bloomsbury, 2013), 254–5.

nature of corporate sponsorship,[13] which has become a crucial component of every major theatre company in Britain, Wertenbaker urges the audience to reflect on the too-tight knot between art (both fine art and theatre) and economics and to imagine possible ways out of the market logic. She even points to a possible direction, by resigning from the Royal Court board in protest against private sponsorship and proposing, at the end of *Three Birds Alighting on a Field*, a friendly, warm and women-run art gallery that challenges the capitalist and macho way of perceiving, exhibiting and experiencing art.

By the turn of the millennium, the entrenchment of corporate finance in the theatre world was an inescapable reality, and, in 1998, the Royal Court was renamed after the Jerwood Foundation, a charitable arts organization which funded the renovation of its building in Sloane Square on the condition that the theatre add the name 'Jerwood' to both of its auditoriums.[14]

Not surprisingly, the commercial value of art is still a contentious topic in many plays of the new millennium, starting with Simon Gray's *The Old Master* (2004), which shows how the value of a work of art is distorted when money and reputation are at stake. The play revolves around the famous dispute over the attribution of an Old Master painting between the connoisseur and American art historian Bernard Berenson, who at that point in his career was accused of prostituting his connoisseurship and compromising his reputation, and Joseph Duveen, whose firm Duveen Brothers, based in London, Paris and New York, was seen as the most important art and antiques dealers from the late nineteenth to the mid-twentieth century. Gray sets the action at that moment when the international reputation of the British art market was on the rise; Duveen arrived on such a set selling Old Master paintings at high prices to those American 'robber barons' who had been alternately condemned and admired for their unrestrained and sometimes illegal pursuit of wealth. The latter eventually became some of the

---

[13] In 1989, when the accounting firm Deloitte offered financial advisory services to the Royal Court, the proposal, echoing the contemporary business rhetoric that encouraged arts organizations' entrepreneurialism, stated that the firm would provide the Royal Court with 'support and advice in a proactive and business-orientated manner', and help the theatre 'in the areas of financial control, management information, accounting systems, computerisation, and marketing initiatives'; it also suggested key objectives for the theatre which included '"running your company in a more commercial manner" and "raising your chances of producing box office successes"'. George W. Eccles, 'Letter to Stephen Morris'. 3 March 1989. General Finance Papers, THM/273/2/4/1, English Stage Company/Royal Court Theatre Archive, V&A Theatre and Performance Archive, Blythe House, London. Quoted in Alex Ferrone, *Stage Business and the Neoliberal Theatre of London* (Basingstoke: Palgrave Macmillan, 2021), 8–9.

[14] Sierz, *Modern British Playwrighting*, 33.

most influential American collectors of Old Master art, bringing to the art market the same ruthlessness that had helped them amass their enormous fortune: Henry Clay Frick, Henry Huntingdon, Andrew Mellon and Samuel Kress, to name just a few.

In the play, Duveen explains how the arrival of a new generation of collectors changed the relationship between the dealers and their clients. In the past, dealers sometimes nurtured their clients, the Fricks, the Mellons or the Huntingtons, who were 'eager to be taught both about taste and attribution, and to develop their own discerning eye',[15] while many of the new collectors were 'too busy or without a sufficiently deep interest to train the eye or the sensibility', as art dealer Germain Seligman noted in his memoir of the family business, *Merchants of Art 1880–1960: Eighty Years of Professional Collecting* (1962). Duveen admits that the philistine collectors represented by Samuel Kress are completely deaf to the nuances of art. They are used to dealing in huge sums of money and accordingly expect quick results and large profits: 'Frick and Mellon had something, whatever you call it, that a man like Kress hasn't even a whiff of. Not a whiff of whatever-you-call-it in Kress' (*Masters* 47). In a crescendo of incredulity, horror and fascination, Duveen recounts how Simon Kress, 'the new man. The new American' (*Masters* 47), founder of a chain store and one of the most important collectors of Italian Renaissance and European artwork, haggled equally over the price of 'sacred and luminous masterpieces' and cheap shawls sold on the street of Algiers, because to him they were both ultimately commodities:

> **Duveen** Yes, there he is, sitting in a café in Algeria – […] Kress, Kress, Samuel Kress […]. And along comes one of those street traders, selling shawls […] so Kress calls him over, has a look at one of these shawls, quite a good shawl, not a bad shawl, a street trader's shawl but of a quality […] so our man Kress, he can't let the opportunity slip by, even in a café in Algiers on his holiday – with a trader who trades he has to trade a little, what else is there for him to do – so he begins, how much are they? Ah, and in dollars how much, ah, and if he buys two shawls now how much in discount, and the discount for three how much, how much, say, if he buys half the stock he sees before him, would he get a couple from the half he leaves behind thrown in free, ah, and how many shawls does this trader have apart from what's on his hand-barrow, ah, well, then put the stock on top of this stock how much discount … So on

---

[15] John Brewer, *The American Leonardo. A Tale of Obsession, Art and Money* (Oxford: Oxford University Press, 2009), 32.

he goes and on, until at the end, he makes his purchase [...] the deal of a lifetime, because when he's sold every single one of them, which he will do, he'll have made a clear profit of three hundred and forty-eight dollars [...] Six months ago I let him into my private gallery, into the very heart of it, where I keep one of my most sacred shrines. My Amico di Sandro. [...] And he looked at this – this truly – of a grace, a charm, a religious tenderness, of a holiness and a lustrousness – as I said to him. Whispered to him. Holiness. Lustrousness. (*whispering intently*). Luminousness. And he squinted at it for eight, nine, ten seconds, and he said, 'How much?' So. So I doubled the sum that came into my head and added fifty thousand. He said, that room back there, the one we came through, there were six paintings, who were they by? Well, I said, there were two Titians, a Gainsborough, a Tintoretto, a Botticelli and an Uccello. And how much are those, he asked? Well, I said, and I began to give him the price of each. Ah, he said, but if I bought the lot. I named a price, a price, a sum, a sum so huge – ah, he said, now if I bought this sacred and luminous masterpiece here, and three of those other masterpieces in there, what kind of discount would you give me, ah, and if I took all six and the sacred and luminous, what would you throw in free, and what discount on all six, and so – and so – I was the street trader in Algiers, BB, I began to bargain, yes, before I knew it, I was bargaining with Mr Five and Dime over Amico di Sandro and a fistful of price-reduced masterpieces. (*The Old Master* 48–50)

Apart from his overt crassness and lack of taste, how does Kress' attitude to art differ from that of Duveen or Berenson, whose attributions were often influenced by the value the art market placed on artists?

The commodification of art, potentially corrupt relationships between art experts and art dealers, conflicts of interest and questionable mechanisms for determining the commercial value of a work of art: while describing the art world of the 1930s and 1940s, Gray winks at the flourishing of the art trade at the dawn of the new millennium, which has placed a rapidly changing London in the centre of the world art market, with its attendant gossip, mystery and even crime both serious and petty.

But the most exhaustive lecture on the mysteries and deregulation of the art market comes from Jim, one of the characters in David Leddy's *Long Live the Little Knife*, a play that explores the world of con artists, commercial fakes and art forgeries. In the scene in question, Jim is pretending to be Italian art dealer Margareta De Angelo, alias Mags. Jim/Mags not only confirms that it has become the norm to buy through dealers, now posing as experts and curators, rather than directly from the artist, but also exposes 'the sometimes shady mechanics of the art market', considered as 'an example of free market economics' (*Long* 48):

Jim   (*Mags*) (*clears throat, suddenly serious*)   The art market is the world's only unregulated financial market. It's the only place you can artificially control prices and not go to prison. (*Long* 48)

In this unregulated world of secretive deals, speculation, tax breaks, insider trading, hedging and market manipulation, Jim/Mags acts freely, comforted by the fact that 'if you do this with stocks and shares you go to prison for insider dealing' while 'in the art world it's complete legal' (*Long* 51). Jim/Mags' way of pumping up the market and speculating on the work of Tamara Jones – the young woman they present as a supposedly promising artist with a successful career ahead of her – is a plan in ten acts, involving all the major players in the art market, the auctioneers, the press, and a significant number of dealers, which is graphically visualized in the backdrop (Figure 4.1).

Jim/Mags' reckless audacity is obviously a parody of Charles Saatchi's prodigious entrepreneurial flair for market speculation and tactical dealings. One of the new super-collectors who consider art as speculative investment and follow the liberal imperatives of a globalized economy, he 'buys art for investment purposes and uses the whole apparatus of gallery, loans, exhibitions and catalogues to increase the status and value of his holdings'.[16] Described by many as a modern-day Medici, Charles Saatchi has been credited with 'single-handedly changing the course of contemporary art in Britain through his role of presiding genius behind the generation of Young British Artists',[17] wielding enormous power in the contemporary art market, and often making or breaking artists' reputations.

In any case, as Julian Stallabrass writes, Saatchi's 'business practices, with which his collecting is entangled, are highly secretive', and while he 'often buys with considerable publicity (except when he is defending the prices of artists in his collection), he usually sells in great secrecy'.[18] He has shown repeatedly that he has 'the eye', but he 'still needs confidants and inside-trackers and guides, what some people in London refer to as his "sniffer dogs", if he wants

---

[16] Rita Hatton and John A Walker, *Supercollector. A Critique of Charles Saatchi* (London: Ellipsis, 2000), 159.
[17] Chin-tao Wu, 'The Collector as Phoenix: Can Charles Saatchi Rise from the Ashes?', in Gould and Mesplède, *From Hogarth to Hirst*, 165.
[18] Julian Stallabrass, *Highartlite. The Rise and Fall of Young British Art* (London: Verso, 2006), 206.

Figure 4.1 *Long Live the Little Knife* written and directed by David Leddy. With Wendy Seager and Neil McCormack. Fire Exit production. Traverse Theatre, Edinburgh, August 2013.

Source: Courtesy Tommy Ga-Ken Wan.

to be first, and he has always wanted that.'[19] No wonder Jim/Mags and his accomplice Liz look to Saatchi for inspiration:

    Jim   (*Mags*)   I love it! Act two! Choose an artist.
    Liz   We trawl the undergraduate shows.
    Jim   (*Mags*)   It's a city of the blind. Look for something with bam, with blam, with kerzam! Like a billboard. If it takes more than 2

---

[19] Gordon Burn, 'I Want It, I Want It All, and I Want It Now!', *The Guardian*, 7 December 1998, 2.

seconds for you to understand, then it's a piece of shit! ... I call this 'The Charles Saatchi Methodology.' (*Long* 49)

In this brisk exchange, Leddy ridicules Saatchi's well-known practice of arriving at art-school degree shows to buy works from unknown artists at a very early stage in their career in bulk and at low prices, sometimes purchasing whole shows. Like him, Liz and Jim/Mags go 'shopping',[20] trying to buy art where it is cheap and sell it where it is expensive, and thus potentially reaping huge profits when an artist achieves blue-chip status on the market. Through Liz and Jim/Mags, Leddy also mocks Saatchi's attraction to high-impact, shock-value art due to his years as an advertising executive and his lack of attention span, as Rita Hatton and John A. Walker argue in their hostile critique,[21] while also obliquely recalling that his advertising agency, Saatchi & Saatchi, ran Margaret Thatcher's election campaigns.

Through verbal pyrotechnics and a brilliant closing *coup de théâtre*, *Long Live the Little Knife* exposes the close connection between the art world and the market, revealing the art gallery as a potentially ideal place for accommodating those who wish to buy high-priced paintings in anonymity. Entertaining and moving, it asks the audience to think about 'the final blood-price of a world where nothing is real but cash',[22] while also exposing the dark side of art galleries as a privileged site of cultural production linked to criminal activities such as forgery, prostitution and paedophilia. This is also the case with Scottish playwright David Harrower's award-winning solo epic play *Ciara* (2013), likewise presented at the 2013 Edinburgh Fringe Festival, and perhaps, like Leddy's play, intended as a broader reflection on Scotland's changing cultural identity on the eve of the referendum on political independence from Britain.[23]

Indeed, the play's eponymous protagonist, Ciara, is not only the owner of the fictional art gallery 'Belisama' but also describes the art world as 'a pit of snakes' full of 'charlatans, cut-throats', 'businesspeople, entrepreneurs, property developers, footballers', who live 'in big hooses' with 'big big

---

[20] 'Going shopping' is the expression used by sculptor Richard Wentworth to describe Saatchi's unusual way of buying art. Quoted in Burn, 'I want it'.

[21] Hatton and Walker, *Supercollector*, 115.

[22] Joyce Macmillan, 'Review of Long Live the Little Knife', *Scotsman*, 9 February 2013, reprinted in *Theatre Record 29 January–11 February 2013*, 121.

[23] Indeed, the play is the culmination of a process which had already led Harrower to write that to redefine themselves, the Scots needed to better understand themselves, exchange ideas, confront their enduring myths, expose injustices and explore their past, and that the vitality of contemporary Scottish theatre was an expression and a determinant of national cultural and political identities. (David Harrower and David Greig, 'Why a new Scotland must have a properly funded theatre', *Scotsman*, 25 November 1997, 15).

walls to fill' (*Ciara* 19, 21). For these people, Ciara suggests, art is simply a commodity to be owned and exhibited; at the same time, she also reveals the connections between her gallery and the legacy of her gangster father. For its Traverse Theatre debut, Anthony Lamble's set showed just 'a bleak, premonitory brick warehouse, with a single mattress and a sinister metal chain suspended from the ceiling',[24] a derelict industrial warehouse on the brink of a process of gentrification that provides a perfect backdrop for both Glasgow's changing face and Ciara's quest for control over her story and her life. Indeed, although she is a gangster's daughter and wife, she is, as the Traverse's new artistic director Orla O'Loughlin notes, 'not ultimately being victimized by her experience, but surviving in a man's world and actually proving herself every bit the equal if not the better of the criminal fraternity'.[25]

Following in the footsteps of Julia and Biddy in *Three Birds Alighting on a Field*, this play is once again centred upon a strong female figure who wishes to gain control over both her own history and her own life – and who, despite the burning of her art gallery 'Belisama', is eventually entrusted with the task of running an art space. This new space, which is part of 'Glasgow's exciting riverside development', is one in which artists will work 'with the local community even though community around Tradeston is a somewhat hopeful term' (*Ciara* 60–1).

Is female entrepreneurship in the arts the only way to ethical, community-based, truly meaningful art?

All the beauty and the bloodshed

British playwrights have often explored not only the many faces of art, its strengths but also its compromises, though perhaps without the outcry that has characterized similar denunciations by other artists, not least the American activist Nan Goldin. Her art, her human rights activism and her crusade against the Sacklers, a billionaire family who knowingly created an epidemic and then funnelled money to museums in exchange for tax write-offs and naming rights to galleries, are articulated in Laura Poitras' epic docufilm *All the Beauty and the Bloodshed* (2022), which interweaves Goldin's deeply personal and urgently political past and present.

---

[24] Talya Kingston, 'Ciara by David Harrower', *Theatre Journal*, vol. 66, 2 May 2014, 264.
[25] Orla O'Loughlin quoted in Kingston, *Ciara*.

Taking their cue from Nan Goldin's work, Mark Ravenhill and Frantic Assembly prompt an exploration of the ambiguous factors that underpin the spectularization of suffering in art. In *pool (no water)*, they show that while art can be at the service of the community, helping to raise awareness and draw attention to taboo or controversial issues, it can also, conversely, use controversial topics as a mere 'springboard' to success. A present in which the Group of artist friends behave like a bunch of 'bad people' (*pool* 298, 300) is set against a past 'when it all seemed to mean so much, when everything was so full of meaning' and the Group used to do 'very good work with the underprivileged', caring for them so passionately:

> God, do you remember when we are all together when it all seemed to mean so much when everything was so full of meaning yes it was all drenched in meaning and we all cared we all cared so so passionately? Do you remember do you remember do you remember do you remember do you remember the days? Ah yes happy happy happy happy happy happy happy days. (*pool* 300)

What happened then? What changed them? What drives them to capitalize on their friend's hospitalization, maliciously using her maimed body as photographic material for their lucrative art project and even physical abuse? Is the envy of their successful artist friend 'she' really the reason for such a change? And what about this figure, 'she' who has gained fame through her bold artistic use of the story of her friend Ray, as 'she used Ray's blood and bandages and catheter and condoms. Pieces that sold to every major collector in the world' (*pool* 295–6)? How should the audience view her work? As an important step in representing the impact of AIDS through art, or as a predatory appropriation of a friend's pain for the sake of success? What about her intentions when, after her recovery, 'she' regains agency and claims ownership of the images her friends have produced of her body, thereby redirecting her methodology from voyeurism to self-objectification and confessional art?

Ravenhill has a rather pessimistic view of the motives of art. In the cynical and even brutal world of the play, art is just 'Selling. Packaging. Promoting. Launching' (*pool*, 317), and art and humanity seem almost incompatible: 'I am so happy that art has gone away and now we can be people. That is wonderful' (*pool* 309). Giving up art and enjoying family and ordinary life seems the only way to find peace and meaning. No Californian swimming pool with pool boys and personal trainers who could have been porn stars, but a paddling pool in the garden. No sets and photo projects, but children spontaneously photographing their mother (*pool* 323).

But while Ravenhill wonders what art is actually for, once again winking at the controversy surrounding the meaning of YBA,[26] Quentin Letts reminds him that he himself is part of the art system he condemns, since, unlike Wertenbaker, he does not seem to ask too many questions about where the money comes from that finances the theatre in which he presents his work:

> The Lyric Hammersmith, since you ask, receives money from the likes of Deutsche Bank, the smart London solicitors Harbottle & Lewis, the Heritage Lottery Fund and the Government's Sure Start programme. The programme for this show includes an advert for Latymer Prep School. Mr Ravenhill may aver that he has depicted the decadence of today's art crowd. Maybe he is satirising them. But he is also one of them. This production is not entirely without merit. […] But it is basically little more than a masturbatory fantasy, paid for in the first instance by corporate-sponsor suckers and, later, by a coarsened, diminished society.[27]

Despite Ravenhill's apparent disinterest in such an issue, it is clear that the need for ethical clarity has increased. Artists and intellectuals have begun to demand clear ethical positions from the institutions they work for on issues of environmental sustainability, inequality, citizenship, the legacy of colonialism, questions of democracy and human rights. They have begun to question the blurred boundaries between the public and the corporate, which have led to a disturbing level of corporate interference both in the art world and in theatre. They have begun to challenge the well-established tradition of seeking the halo of philanthropy by supporting the arts. We might think here, for example, of the recent 'BP or not BP?' campaign against art patron BP, the oil and gas company accused of ecocide, and the British actor and director Mark Rylance, who recently resigned from the Royal Shakespeare Company,

---

[26] Tim Walker writes that, hearing the four friends talk among themselves about 'her', 'the audience quickly gets the impression of a woman such as Tracey Emin – fashionable, unlovable, lucky and of debatable talent'. (Tim Walker, 'pool (no water)', *Sunday Telegraph*, 12 November 2006, reprinted in *Theatre Record* 22 October – 4 November 2006, 1300). Scott Graham's list of the sources of inspiration for the play include the work of another of the artists featured in the Royal Academy's *Sensation* exhibition, Ron Mueck, along with a scathing review of his life-size, hyper-realistic sculptures of naked bodies, by Jonathan Jones, who polemically asks what art is. (Scott Graham, *pool (no water) by Mark Ravenhill. A Comprehensive Guide. For students (aged +16), teachers & art educationalists*, 31. https://www.yumpu.com/en/document/view/27937257/pool-no-water-resource-pack-frantic-assembly (accessed 15 May 2023).

[27] Quentin Letts, 'pool (no water)', *Daily Mail*, 2 November 2006, reprinted in *Theatre Record* 22 October – 4 November 2006, 1298.

refusing to be a shill for BP (a company that 'wilfully destroys the lives of others alive and unborn').[28]

Letts' review of Ravenhill's *pool* reveals that while some playwrights denounce the predatory values promoted by global capitalism, their plays are themselves often products of the very market economy they critique; meanwhile, as Alex Ferrone argues in his book *Stage business and the neoliberal theatre of London*, such plays' production histories and formal innovations also tend to reproduce the strategies and practices of neoliberal labour markets.[29] In making this argument, Ferrone offers a reading of both Albery's and Mitchell's productions of *Attempts on Her Life*, which visually highlight the performers constantly at work on stage (perhaps reminding the audience of the creative work that goes on in the run-up to opening night). Ferrone sees here the basis of an analogy between the shift in focus in post-dramatic plays from the creative labour of meaning-making (traditionally the domain of the playwright) to the significance of directors, designers (etc.) and the wider 'outsourcing of labour that has become a fixture of the worldwide neoliberal economy'; it does not seem unlikely, Ferrone concludes, that contemporary theatre 'may have absorbed the strategies of neoliberal consensus politics, whether unwittingly or under duress'.[30]

Tim Crouch's *ENGLAND* (2007) is perhaps one of the best examples of a play that, although conditioned and constrained by its position within the market economy, seems to resist, if not disrupt, the ethos of capitalism through its form, content, themes, and, most importantly, collaborative 'labour' practices that place the audience in the unique position of 'experientially' taking a stand against the connection between capital and art that, while seemingly innocuous, reveals sordid links between the art world and the illegal trafficking of human organs. Significantly, this act of resistance takes place in an art gallery, which has come to represent the very heart of neoliberal practices, policies and ideologies. Indeed, even though it is often presented as being every bit as immaculate, timeless and apolitical as the white cube gallery would like to be, the art gallery finds itself in a complex relationship with capitalism and inequality, not least because the purchasing and accrual of artworks is a major part of what it does while its own value as an institution is largely determined by the works of art it has to offer.

---

[28] Mark Rylance quoted in Matthew Taylor, 'Mark Rylance Resigns from RSC over BP Sponsorship', *The Guardian*, 21 June 2019. https://www.theguardian.com/stage/2019/jun/21/mark-rylance-resigns-from-royal-shakespeare-company-rsc-over-bp-sponsorship (accessed 27 September 2023).
[29] Ferrone, *Stage Business*, 2.
[30] Ibid.

In Crouch's play the connection of art and capitalism is clear from the beginning, as Crouch and Ringham introduce the gallery hosting the performance (in the case of the premiere, the Fruitmarket Gallery) while openly thanking the Scottish Arts Council (although at other times it is the gallery's founders who are openly thanked) for making possible the refurbishment of the building, the current exhibition and the performance of *ENGLAND*: 'Thank you Scottish Arts Council. If it weren't for you we wouldn't be here. / You saved our lives' (*E* 14). After this introduction, in which they associate capital, albeit in passing, with the provision and circulation of works of art outside of fiction, the two actors refer to corporate philanthropy. Indeed, they reveal that the protagonist's father-in-law donates part of his company's profits to the Presbyterian Church and that he once sponsored a sculpture park to support a cancer ward, encouraging the audience to appreciate his philanthropic commitment. They do not mention, of course, the common practice of corporations and wealthy businessmen-cum-collectors using art as a commodity for advertising and branding purposes and to promote their interests.[31] Nor do they mention that these figures tend to be bankers and hedge fund managers, fossil fuel oligarchs and opioid profiteers, from Frick and Kress, the robber barons of yesteryear, to the Sackler family, currently under fire for their central role in the opioid addiction crisis, as denounced by Nan Golding and others, all laundering their reputations through lavish tax-deductible donations:

> My boyfriend's father is Presbyterian. His company donates ten per cent of its profit to the church.
>
> He sponsored a sculpture park for a cancer ward in Atlanta in Georgia.
>
> My boyfriend's father did well in America.
>
> He puts back what he gets out! (*E* 22)

The discourse of both actors about the beneficial social effects of capitalism and so-called social responsibility, as well as their gratitude towards the owners of capital and their investments in worthwhile artistic or philanthropic projects, is used from the outset to hide the fact that capital gain is the real goal of corporations. Art is a commodity, as they repeatedly make clear.

First of all, the protagonist's boyfriend is a wealthy Dutch American art-dealer, who 'understands the market' (*E* 20) and tells people what to buy, 'what's up and what's down' (*E* 15). He 'believes in art' and believes that art is a

---

[31] Chin-tao Wu, *Privatising Culture: Corporate Art Intervention since the 1980s* (London: Verso, 2002), 129–31.

commodity that has an exchange value: 'Good art is art that sells!' (*E* 29). Not surprisingly, what he and his girlfriend/boyfriend seem to appreciate most about their De Kooning painting is its monetary value: 'It's worth more than this duplex!' Significantly, thanks to an idiomatic expression – 'My boyfriend paid an arm and a leg for it' (*E* 19) – the protagonist hints, albeit indirectly and without realizing it, the possibility of human organs becoming an exchange currency, thus foreshadowing the purchase of a heart in the second act. Indeed, the two performers, Crouch and Hannah Ringham, aestheticize the human body, inviting the audience to marvel at a heart with atrial fibrillation through the same imperatives ('Look!') they use as artistic guides:

> Look at the muscles in the heart. Look at them thickening.
>
> Look at how the pumping chamber gets smaller and
> keeps the heart muscle from relaxing properly between
> contractions. Look how the chambers of the heart stiffen as
> the muscle thickens.
>
> It's happening to me here.
>
> This is the picture.
>
> Look!
>
> Look! (*E* 37–8)

In a context where art is perceived as a commodity and the audience is constantly invited to see the world in aesthetic terms, the protagonist's diseased heart is seen as a work of art, just as an arm or blood are conceptual art objects in Crouch's *My Arm* or in Mark Quinn's *Self*. As decay and death slowly begin to contaminate the 'beautiful' life of the privileged protagonists, it becomes clear that the human body can be equated with a commodity to be looked at, sold, bought and consumed. Hassam's heart is thus effectively treated as a work of art, selected and priced, to be 'relocated' for the pleasure of a privileged few.

Presenting capitalism as a multicultural, cultivated and sometimes philanthropic system, uncritically celebrating privilege, reifying and valorising every element of life, the performers of *ENGLAND* embody the universal language of global capitalism. The two performers address the audience, who is free to move around the gallery space, as a united, art-loving community, willing wholeheartedly to embrace the language and perspective presented in the play and perhaps even to feel gratified by a cultural background that allows them to keep up with the various references to artists and places. This shared understanding creates a strong sense of unity and consensus that persists until the second act.

In Act Two, in a narrative shift, the audience is led into a separate room within the art gallery, representing a distinct temporal, spatial and epistemological realm in the story. Here, the protagonist, who has had a heart transplant, visits the widow of the heart donor, a computer programmer called Hassam, to express her gratitude by gifting the woman an expensive work of art. At this juncture, the audience is invited to take their seats and assume a more traditional stance. However, they remain actively engaged as participants, embodying the character of the wife, as the stage directions suggest: 'A different room in the gallery. Seats for the audience. The wife is us, the audience. When the audience enter the space, it is her entering the space. The Interpreter interprets her words and translates what is said to her' (*E* 44). The two performers take turns as the 'Interpreter' and the protagonist from Act One, here identified as 'English', who emerges as a representative of a Western capitalist and neocolonialist ideology that has no qualms about destroying and erasing lives for its own benefit. The Interpreter acts as an intermediary between 'English' and the grieving Widow, providing the audience with a unique opportunity to see the world from a profoundly different perspective that challenges their attitude to the story being told. The exchange between English and Widow brings to light a clash between a privileged, prejudice-laden Western society and a vulnerable Global South nation, depicted as a helpless victim of Western greed. In this context, the theme of placing one art form in a space designed for another – a theatre performance in a gallery – resonates not only with the transplantation of one heart into another body but also with that of one culture into another.[32]

Through this exchange facilitated by the Interpreter, it becomes evident that, from the widow's perspective, the transplant was the tragic outcome of her husband's murder. What is more, she unwittingly played a role in this unfortunate sequence of events. Pressured by immense emotional distress and precarious economic conditions, she found herself compelled to sign the consent for the transplant. To compound matters, the woman reveals that her husband's body was never returned to her and she received only a meagre sum of money. In this sense, the character of the widow symbolizes the marginalized and voiceless individuals who endure various forms of social, economic, physical and epistemic violence within the context of neocolonialism and global capitalism. This includes the Turkish man whose kidney was illicitly procured by another art dealer, Biddy, at a hefty price from

---

[32] Tim Crouch quoted in Carmela Maria Laudando, 'The Risky in-betweenness of Performing Audiences', *Alicante Journal of English Studies*, 26 (2013): 52.

the organ black market, in Wertenbaker's *Three Birds Alighting on a Field* (*3 Birds* 70). *ENGLAND* exposes the neocolonialist practices of globalized capitalism, such as the outsourcing of cheap labour and raw materials (human organs included) to developing countries for the benefit of a privileged British few and at the expense of the voiceless inhabitants of an unnamed Islamic nation. However, it is possible to say, with Ferrone, that while the formal characteristics of such so-called post-dramatic plays 'analogize the diffusion of labour under global capitalism', in *ENGLAND*, 'the delegation of creative and emotional labour' is intended 'as a shift towards collaboration that might actually represent a kind of resistance to neoliberalism, rather than simply a blind absorption of its strategies'.[33]

The Interpreter plays an important role. An English person from Manchester, who speaks four languages and lives in this unnamed country, the interpreter seems to understand the situation, sympathizing with the widow while trying to protect her from the English's culturally insensitive remarks by not translating or mistranslating everything that reveals her prejudices and callous indifference. The Interpreter's unfaithful but respectful translation and distance from the privileged English contributes to and facilitates a process of dis-identification of the audience with the privileged position of English into which they have been seduced in Act One. In fact, no real exchange seems to occur between English and Widow. When the Interpreter reports that Widow wants to listen to English protagonist's breast and to embrace her, this embrace never comes, as the audience/Widow remains in her seat and the performance ends with a series of questions that show English's inability or unwillingness to understand:

English: What is she saying?

> What?
>
> What is she saying?
>
> What did she say?
>
> What did she say? (*E* 62)

At this point, the important role of the audience becomes clear. According to Cristina Delgado-Garcia, this is where the potential for 'progressive politics' lies, as the second act reveals the audience's complicity in an unethical process of domination. Positioned between the privileged few and the unrepresented

---

[33] Ferrone, *Stage Business*, 168.

other, Hassam's widow, the audience is invited to find its own position within the economies of power presented in the play.[34] As Delgado-Garcia argues, 'the spectators' impossible identification with the subaltern' disrupts their previously ascribed identity of belonging to a global, culturally-aware and free Western subject alongside the performers and protagonists. Indeed, in the second act, *ENGLAND* not only encourages the spectators' rejection of their privileged subject position but also 'actively promotes the spectators' repudiation of their initial identity by revealing the effects that the economic transactions of the privileged have on others'. In this way, *ENGLAND* places the audience in a position 'where no identification is possible' (neither with the collective subject represented by the English nor with the subaltern), thus prompting them to reconfigure their own sense of singular and collective subjectivity.[35]

Significantly, the art gallery is also characterized in a nuanced if not fully paradoxical manner, as *ENGLAND* exposes the contradictions inherent in the place where art is shown and acquires monetary value. On the one hand, the gallery seems to epitomize the notion of cultural capital as an 'instrument of domination' in the terms developed by the French sociologist Pierre Bourdieu.[36] The collective subject embodied by the protagonist, enmeshed in a convivial, uncritical and privileged inhabiting of the world, confirms art as a form of hegemonic ideology, in which its transmission from one generation to the next (i.e., from the boyfriend's father to his son, who is to be taught 'what is to be done' (E 34)) serves to maintain and reproduce the dominant position of a ruling class. In this sense, the art gallery enacts a 'symbolic violence'.[37] On the other hand, the art gallery is an arena that exposes conflicts and contradictions and requires the visitors/spectators to undergo politically charged operations that seem to be in line with those encouraged by the new museology's view of the visitor as an autonomous maker of meaning. One might be tempted to conclude that in *ENGLAND*, Crouch, while challenging the modernist white cube aesthetics, somehow embraces the model of the post-museum proposed by museum theorist Eilean Hooper-Greenhill as 'a process of experience' in which the exhibition of the works of art is one among other forms of communication, and in

---

[34] Cristina Delgado-García, 'Political Gestures in a Post-Political Scenario: Tim Crouch's *ENGLAND*', in *Rethinking Character in Contemporary British Theatre: Aesthetics, Politics, Subjectivity* (Berlin: Walter de Gruyter, 2015), 180.

[35] Ibid., 194.

[36] Pierre Bourdieu, *Distinction: A Social Critique of the Judgement of Taste* (London: Routledge & Kegan Paul, 1984), 228.

[37] Pierre Bourdieu and Alain Darbel, quoted in Seph Rodney, *The Personalisation of the Museum Visit. Art Museums, Discourse, and Visitors* (London: Routledge, 2019), 28.

which a set of shared dynamic processes allow for the inclusion of many voices and perspectives.[38] Indeed, in the fiction, the audience is characterized both as the privileged English protagonist and the donor's widow but also as a collection of individuals subjected to an experience of 'disidentification'.[39] Above all, Crouch's gallery/stage, like the post-museum, is a site from which to redress social inequalities. Despite its problematic entanglements with neoliberal finance, Crouch's theatre articulates important social critiques and evokes deep emotions in its audiences, the impact of which should not be underestimated.

In his critical overview of the growing dominance of marketplace thinking in museum affairs, the independent scholar-practitioner Robert R. Janes concludes that 'a museum's mission can assume both the imperatives of the marketplace and the challenges of social responsibility. The essential ingredients are the board and staff leadership required to enable these disparate aims to coexist within the mission'.[40]

Both the stage and the art gallery are insidiously permeated by neoliberal economics and politics that tend towards the marketization of cultural life; but they can also remain sites of profound emotional experience and passionate social and/or political engagement. Ultimately, as some of the plays discussed in this volume show, they can offer glimpses of utopian and resilient hope in the midst of darker realities.

---

[38] Eilean Hooper-Greenhill, *Museums and the Interpretation of Visual Culture* (London: Routledge, 2000), 152.
[39] Delgado-García, *Political Gestures*, 189.
[40] Robert R. Janes, 'Museums, Corporatism and the Civil Society', in Bettina Messias Carbonell (ed.), *Museum Studies. An Anthology of Contexts*, 2nd edn (Malden, MA: Wiley-Blackwell, 2012), 558.

Bibliography

Ackerley, Chris J., and Stanley E. Gontarski. *The Faber Companion to Samuel Beckett*. London: Faber and Faber, 2004.

Adams, Brooks, Lisa Jardine, Martin Maloney, Norman Rosenthal and Richard Shone (eds). *Sensation. Young British Artists from the Saatchi Collection*. London: Thames & Hudson with the Royal Academy of Arts, 1997.

Ades, Dawn, Iwona Blazwick, Inês Costa, Richard Dyer, Hammad Nasar and Candy Stobbs. *The Artist's Studio. A Century of the Artist's Studio. 1920–2022*. London: Whitechapel Gallery, 2022.

Aidin, Rose. 'The YBAs: The London-based Young British Artists', *Smarthistory*, 7 September 2018. https://smarthistory.org/YBA-3/ (accessed 8 May 2023).

Angelaki, Vicky, *The Plays of Martin Crimp. Making Theatre Strange*. London: Palgrave Macmillan, 2012.

Antal, Fredrick. *Hogarth and His Place in European Art*. London: Routledge & Kegan Paul, 1962.

Arndt, Neena. 'A Conversation with Playwright John Logan', *Theatre Goodman On Stage*, 27, 1 (September–December 2011): 1–21. https://www.goodman theatre.org/Documents/OnStage/1112/RedNSA_OnStage.pdf (accessed 8 May 2023).

Aston, Elaine. *Feminist Views on the English Stage. Women Playwrights, 1990–2000*. Cambridge: Cambridge University Press, 2009.

Atik, Anne. *How It Was. A Memoir of Samuel Beckett*. London: Faber and Faber, 2001.

Avrami, Erica. 'Heritage, Values, and Sustainability'. In Alison Richmond and Alison Bracker. *Conservation. Principles, Dilemmas and Uncomfortable Truths*, 177–82. London: Routledge with the Victoria and Albert Museum, 2009.

Ayache, Solange. 'Theatre and Psychoanalysis: Or Jung on Martin Crimp's Stage: "100 Words"', *Sillages Critiques*, 10, 2009. https://journals.openedition.org/sillagescritiques/1838 (accessed 8 May 2023).

Barker, Howard. *Scenes from an Execution*. In Howard Barker, *Collected Plays*, vol. 1, 251–305. London: John Calder, 1990.

Barker, Howard. 'Judith. A Parting from the Body'. In Howard Barker, *Collected Plays*, vol. 3, 241–66. London: John Calder, 1990.

Beck, James, and Michael Daley. *Art Restoration: The Culture, the Business and the Scandal*. London: John Murray, 1993.

Beckett, Samuel. 'That Time'. In *Samuel Beckett. The Complete Dramatic Works*, 385–95. London: Faber and Faber, 1986.

Beckett, Samuel. *The Letters of Samuel Beckett. 1929-1940.* Edited by Martha Dow Fehsenfeld and Lois More Overbeck. Cambridge: Cambridge University Press, 2009.

Bennett, Alan. 'A Question of Attribution'. In Alan Bennett, *Alan Bennett: Plays 2*, 301-51. London: Faber and Faber, 1998.

Bennett, Alan. 'Going to the Pictures'. In Alan Bennett, *Untold Stories*, 453-76. London: Faber and Faber, [2005] 2006.

Bennett, Alan. 'Portrait or Bust'. In Alan Bennett, *Untold Stories*, 494-514. London: Faber and Faber, [2005] 2006.

Bennett, Susan. *Theatre & Museums.* Basingstoke: Palgrave Macmillan, 2013.

Berenson, Bernard. *Rudiments of Connoisseurship.* New York: Schocken Books, 1962.

Berenson, Bernard. *Sketch for a Self-Portrait.* Firenze: Pantheon, 1949.

Berenza, Jessica. 'Freeze: 20 Years on', *The Guardian*, 1 June 2008. https://www.theguardian.com/artanddesign/2008/jun/01/art (accessed 8 May 2023).

Berghaus, Gunter. 'Happening in Europe: Trends, Events, and Leading Figures'. In *Happenings and other Acts*, edited by Mariellen R. Sandford, 368-71. London: Routledge, 1995.

Bicknell, Sandra, and Graham Farmelo, *Museum Visitor Studies in the 90s.* London: Science Museum, 1993.

Bignamini, Ilaria. *William Hogarth: Nationalism, Mass Media and the Artist.* Vancouver: Vancouver Art Gallery, 1980.

Billington, Michael. *State of the Nation. British Theatre since 1945.* London: Faber and Faber, 2007.

Billington, Michael. '*Attempts on Her Life*', *The Guardian*, 15 March 2007, 309.

Billington, Michael. 'Edward Hopper Takes to the Stage', *The Guardian*, 5 January 2001, 6.

Billington, Michael. 'Men judge the plays, put on the plays and run the theatres', *The Guardian*, 25 November 1999, 10.

Billington, Michael. 'Scenes from an Execution', *The Guardian*, 6 October 2012. In *Theatre Record* 23 *September – 6 October 2012*, 1051.

Billington, Michael. 'Sunday in the Park with George', *The Guardian*, 25 May 2006. In *Theatre Record 21 May–3 June 2006*, 617.

Billington, Michael. 'The Moralist's Lewd Progress', *The Guardian*, 11 July 1986, 18.

Billington, Michael. 'The Old Master. Comedy, London', *The Guardian*, 2 July 2004.

Billington, Michael. 'The Painter – Review', *The Guardian*, 16 January 2011, 7.

Billington, Michael. 'Three Birds Alighting on a Field', *The Guardian*, 11 September 1991. In *Theatre Record 10–23 September 1991*, 1119.

Bindman, David. *Hogarth and His Times: Serious Comedy.* London: British Museum Press, 1997.

Bishop, Claire (ed.). *Participation. Documents of Contemporary Art.* London: Whitechapel Gallery with MIT Press, 2006.

Blair, Tony. 'Blair's speech on the arts in full', *The Guardian*, 6 March 2007. https://www.theguardian.com/politics/2007/mar/06/politicsandthearts.uk1 (accessed 20 August 2023).

Blazwick Iwona, and Frances Morris. 'Showing the Twentieth Century'. In *Tate Modern the Handbook*, edited by Iwona Blazwick and Simon Wilson, 28–39. London: Tate Publishing, 2000.

Bloom, Paul. *How Pleasure Works. Why We Like What We Like*. New York: Random House, 2011.

Blunt, Anthony. *Nicholas Poussin*. London: Phaidon Press, 1967.

Blunt, Anthony. 'Standards-I', *The Spectator*, CLXI, II, 16 September 1938, 403–5.

Boon, Richard. *The Cambridge Companion to David Hare*. Cambridge: Cambridge University Press, 2007.

Borchardt-Hume, Achim (ed.). *Rothko: The Late Series*. London: Tate Publishing, 2008.

Bosanquet, Theo. 'Philip Ridley On … Revisiting *The Pitchfork Disney*', *WhatsOnStage*, 30 January 2012. https://www.whatsonstage.com/west-end-theatre/news/philip-ridley-on-revisiting-the-pitchfork-disney_5566.html (accessed 7 May 2023).

Bose, Mihir, and Cathy Gunn. *Fraud: The Growth Industry of the Eighties*. New York: HarperCollins, 1989.

Bottoms, Stephen. 'Authorizing the Audience: The Conceptual Drama of Tim Crouch', *Performance Research. A Journal of the Performing Arts*, 14, 1 (2009): 65–76.

Bottoms, Stephen. 'Materialising the Audience: Tim Crouch's Sight Specifics in *ENGLAND* and *The Author*', *Contemporary Theatre Review*, 21, 4 (2011): 445–63.

Bourdieu, Pierre. *Distinction: A Social Critique of the Judgement of Taste*. London: Routledge and Kegan Paul, 1984.

Brater, Enoch. *Beyond Minimalism. Beckett's Late Style in the Theater*. New York: Oxford University Press, 1987.

Breach. *It's True, It's True, It's True*. London: Oberon Books, 2008.

Brennan, Clare. '*A Museum in Baghdad* review – the Tale of Two Women Trying to Preserve Iraq's Treasures', *The Guardian*, 3 November 2019. https://www.theguardian.com/stage/2019/nov/03/a-museum-in-baghdad-review-swan-stratford-rsc-gertrude-bell (accessed 20 August 2023).

Brewer, John. *The American Leonardo. A Tale of Obsession, Art and Money*. Oxford: Oxford University Press, 2009.

Bridgemont, Andrew. *Red on Black*. https://www.youtube.com/watch?v=q6FahHUHvww (accessed 1 May 2023).

Brook, Carolina, and Valter Curzi (eds). *Hogarth Reynolds Turner: British Painting and the Rise of Modernity*. Milan: Skira. 2014.

Bruce, Chris. 'Spectacle and Democracy: Experience Music Project as a Post-Museum'. In *New Museum Theory and Practice. An Introduction*, edited by Janet Marstine, 129–51. Oxford: Blackwell, 2006.
Buck, Louisa. *Matters. The Dynamics of the Contemporary Art Market*. London: British Council, 2004.
Buren, Daniel. 'The Function of the Studio', *October*, 10 (Autumn 1979): 51–8.
Burn, Gordon. 'I Want It, I Want It All, and I Want It Now!', *The Guardian*, 7 December 1998, 2.
Bush, Sophie. *The Theatre of Timberlake Wertenbaker*. London: Bloomsbury, 2013.
Canton, Ursula. *Biographical Theatre. Re-Presenting Real People?* Basingstoke: Palgrave Macmillan, 2011.
Canton, Ursula. 'We May Not Know Reality, but It Still Matters – A Functional Analysis of "Factual Elements" in the Theatre', *Contemporary Theatre Review*, 18, 3 (2008): 318–27.
Carbonell, Bettina Messias (ed.). *Museum Studies. An Anthology of Contexts*. Malden, MA: Wiley-Blackwell, 2012.
Carlson, Marvin. *The Haunted Stage: The Theatre as Memory Machine*. Ann Arbor: University of Michigan Press, 2001.
Carrier, David. *Museum Skepticism. A History of the Display of Art in Public Galleries*. Durham: Duke University Press, 2006.
Cavecchi, Mariacristina. 'From Playwriting to Curatorship. An Investigation into the Status of Beckett's Stage Objects'. In *The Exhibit in the Text. The Museological Practices of Literature*, edited by Caroline Patey and Laura Scuriatti, 161–82. London: Peter Lang, 2009.
Cavecchi, Mariacristina. 'Hogarth's Progress in Nick Dear's *The Art of Success*'. In *Enduring Presence. William Hogarth's British and European Afterlives*. Book 1: *Aesthetic, Visual and Performative Culture*s, edited by Caroline Patey, Cynthis E. Roman and George Letissier, 183–204. Oxford: Peter Lang, 2021.
Cavecchi, Mariacristina. 'Il museo in scena. I Seagram Murals di Rothko sul palco di John Logan', *Acme – Annali della Facoltà di Studi Umanistici dell'Università degli Studi di Milano*, LXXI (2018): 191–207.
Cavecchi, Mariacristina. 'Quando il teatro va al museo. Una storia di oggi', *Altre Modernità*, 5 (2011): 26–44. https://riviste.unimi.it/index.php/AMonline/article/view/1027 (accessed 8 May 2023).
Cavecchi, Mariacristina. 'Samuel Beckett, Visual Artist'. In *The Tragic Comedy of Samuel Beckett. 'Beckett in Rome'*, edited by Daniela Guardamagna and Rossana M. Sebellin, 122–42. Rome: Laterza-Tor Vergata University Press, 2009.
Cavecchi, Mariacristina. 'The New Art Galleries on the Contemporary British Stage'. In *The Museal Turn*, edited by Sabine Coelsch-Foisner and Douglas Brown, 299–313. Heidelberg: Winter, 2011.
Charney, Noah. *The Art of Forgery. The Minds, Motives and Methods of Master Forgers*. London: Phaidon, 2015.

Cicali, Gianni. 'A colloquio con David Edgar', www.drammaturgia.it, 1 June 2003. https://drammaturgia.fupress.net/recensioni/recensione1.php?id=1487 (accessed 5 January 2021).

Clapp, Susannah. 'pool (no water)', *Daily Mail*, 2 November 2006. In *Theatre Record* 22 *October–4 November 2006*, 1299.

Clark, Kenneth. 'The Ideal Museum', *ARTnews*, 52, 9 (January 1954): 28–31. Re-published as 'The Ideal Museum: Art Historian Kenneth Clark on the Formation of Western Institutions, in 1954', *ARTnews*, 19 March 2021. https://www.artnews.com/art-news/retrospective/kenneth-clark-the-ideal-museum-1234587297/ (accessed 8 May 2023).

Collings, Matthew. *Blimey! From Bohemia to Britpop: The London Artworld from Francis Bacon to Damien Hirst*. London: 21 Publishing, 1997.

Cook, Mark. 'Shoreditch Madonna', *What's on*, 20 July 2005. In *Theatre Record 2–15 July 2005*, 949.

Costa, Maddy, and Andy Field, *Performance in an Age of Precarity*. London: Bloomsbury, 2021.

Coveney, Michael. '*The Art of Success*/The Other Place', *Financial Times*, 10 July 1986, 25.

Crane, Susan A. (ed.). *Museum and Memory*. Stanford: Stanford University Press, 2000.

Crimp, Martin. *Attempts on her Life*. London: Faber and Faber, 1997.

Croft-Murray, Edward. 'An Exhibition of Forgeries and Deceptive Copies: Held in the Department of Prints and Drawings from 9 February 1961', *The British Museum Quarterly*, 24, 1/2 (August 1961): 29–30.

Croke, Fionnula (ed.). *Samuel Beckett: A Passion for Paintings*. Dublin: National Gallery of Ireland, 2006.

Crouch, Tim. *An Oak Tree*. London: Oberon Books, 2005.

Crouch, Tim. *ENGLAND. A play for galleries*. London: Oberon, 2007.

Crouch, Tim. *My Arm*. London: Faber and Faber, 2003.

Crouch, Tim. '*An Oak Tree*: Tim Crouch on the Artwork That Inspired His Play', *National Theatre Website*, 22 June 2015. https://national-theatre.tumblr.com/post/122168645711/an-oak-tree-tim-crouch-on-the-artwork-that (accessed 20 August 2022).

Crouch, Tim. 'Appendix 3: Tim Crouch – Interview'. In Duška Radosavljević, *Theatre-Making. Interplay between Text and Performance in the 21st Century*, 216–24. New York: Palgrave Macmillan, 2013.

Crouch, Tim. 'In Conversation with Seda Ilter'. In Seda Ilter, ' "A Process of Transformation": Tim Crouch on *My Arm*'. *Contemporary Theatre Review*, 2, 4 (2011): 394–404.

Crouch, Tim. 'Who's the Daddy?', *The Guardian*, 3 August 2005. https://www.theguardian.com/stage/2005/aug/03/theatre (accessed 8 May 2023).

D'Monté, Rebecca, and Graham Saunders (eds). *Cool Britannia? British Political Drama in the 1990s*. Basingstoke: Palgrave Macmillan, 2008.

de Jongh, Nicholas. 'Attempts on Her Life', *Evening Standard*, 13 March 1997. In *Theatre Record 12–25 March 1997*, 311.
Dear, Nick. 'The Art of Success'. In *Dear. Plays One*, 1–98. London: Faber and Faber, 2000.
Dear, Nick. *The Hogarth Plays*. London: Faber and Faber, 2018.
Delgado-García, Cristina. 'Political gestures in a post-political scenario: Tim Crouch's *ENGLAND*'. In Delgado-García, *Rethinking Character in Contemporary British Theatre: Aesthetics, Politics, Subjectivity*, 148–99. Berlin: Walter de Gruyter, 2015.
Dillon, Brian. 'Ugly Feelings'. In Ann Gallagher. *Damien Hirst*, 21–37. London: Tate Publishing, 2012.
Dodd, Ian. 'Three Birds Alighting on a Field', *Tribune*, 20 September 1991. In *Theatre Record 10–23 September 1991*, 1116.
Domonic Francis, 'Study Guide for *Red* by John Logan', 1–30. https://donmar.s3.amazonaws.com/behindthescenes/older/Red.pdf (accessed 8 May 2023).
Duncan, Carol. *Civilizing Rituals: Inside Public Art Museums*. London: Routledge, 1995.
Dunn, Tony. 'Interview with Howard Barker'. *Gambit. International Theatre Review*, 11, 48 (1984): 33–44.
Eccles, George W. 'Letter to Stephen Morris'. 3 March 1989. General Finance Papers, THM/273/2/4/1, English Stage Company/Royal Court Theatre Archive, V&A Theatre and Performance Archive, Blythe House, London.
Eco, Umberto. *Faith in Fakes. Travels in Hyperreality*. London: Minerva, 1997.
Edgar, David. *Pentecost*. London: Nick Hern Books, 1995.
Eggert, Paul. *Securing the Past. Conservation in Art, Architecture and Literature*. Cambridge: Cambridge University Press, 2009.
Einberg, Elizabeth. *William Hogarth. A Complete Catalogue of the Paintings*. New Haven: Yale University Press, 2016.
Elyse, Sommer. 'The Donmar Warehouse Production of *Red* at Broadway's Golden Theater', *CurtainUp*, 4 April 2011. http://curtainupcom.siteprotect.net/redrothko.html (accessed 8 May 2023).
Etchells, Tim. *Certain Fragments*. London: Routledge, 1999.
Evans, Lloyd. 'Attempts on Her Life', *The Spectator*, 24 March 2007. In *Theatre Record 12–15 March 2007*, 312.
Evans, Lloyd. 'Shoreditch Madonna', *The Spectator*, 23 July 2005. In *Theatre Record 2–15 July 2005*, 949.
Eyre, Hermione. 'Philip Ridley: The Savage Prophet', *Independent*, 18 September 2011. https://www.independent.co.uk/arts-entertainment/films/features/philip-ridley-the-savage-prophet-395320.html (accessed 8 May 2023).
Falk, John H., and Lynn D. Dierking, *The Museum Experience Revisited*. London: Routledge, 2013.
Feaver, William. *Pitmen Painters. The Ashington Group 1934–1984*. Newcastle upon Tyne: Northumbria Press with Ashington Group Trustees, 2010.

Feaver, William. 'Stanley', *Observer*, 4 February 1996. In *Theatre Record 29 January–11 February 1996*, 128.
Ferrone, Alex. *Stage Business and the Neoliberal Theatre of London*. Basingstoke: Palgrave Macmillan, 2021.
Findlen, Paula. 'The Modern Muses. Renaissance Collecting and the Cult of Remembrance'. In *Museum and Memory*, edited by Susan A. Crane, 161–78. Stanford: Stanford University Press, 2000.
Fisher, John. 'Portrait of the Artist as an Angry Man', *Harper's Magazine*, 1 July 1970: 16–23.
Fisher-Lichte, Erica. *The Transformative Power of Performance: A New Aesthetics*. London: Routledge, 2008.
Flam, Jack D. *Matisse on Art*. Oxford: Phaidon, [1973] 1978.
Freeman, Laura. 'Painting: The Extraordinary Life and Art of Artemisia Gentileschi', *The Spectator*, 11 April 2020, 44–5.
Gallagher, Ann. *Damien Hirst*. London: Tate Publishing, 2012.
Gardner, Lyn. 'Scenes from an Execution', *The Guardian*, 17 January 2007. In *Theatre Record 1–28 January 2007*, 36.
Getsy, David J. 'The Reconstruction of the Francis Bacon Studio in Dublin'. In *The Studio Reader: On the Space of Artists*, edited by Mary Jane Jacob and Grabner, 99–103. Chicago: University of Chicago Press, 2010.
Goldin, Nan. *The Ballad of Sexual Dependency*. London: Secker & Warburg, 1989.
Goldin, Nan. 'Falling into an Empty Pool, India, 2000'. In *Nan Golding, The Devil's Playground*, edited by John Jenkinson, 214–35. London: Phaidon, 2003.
Gore, St John. *Five Portraits*. Burlington Magazine, 100 (1958), 351–2.
Gore-Langton, Robert. 'Review of *A Museum in Baghdad*', *Daily Mail*, 2 November 2019.
Gould, Charlotte, and Sophie Mesplède (eds). *Marketing Art in the British Isles, 1700 to the Present. A Cultural History*. London: Routledge, 2012.
Graham, Scott. *pool (no water) by Mark Ravenhill. A Comprehensive Guide*. https://www.franticassembly.co.uk/resources/pool-no-water-resource-pack (accessed 4 June 2023).
Gray, Simon. *The Old Masters*. London: Faber and Faber, 2004.
Gray, Simon. *The Pig Trade*. In Simon Gray, *Four Plays*. London: Faber and Faber, 2004, 1–89.
Gross, John. 'You be Ted & I'll be Sylvia', *Sunday Telegraph*, 19 September 1999. In *Theatre Record 10–23 September 1999*, 1194.
Guralnick, Elissa S. *Sight Unseen. Beckett, Pinter, Stoppard, and other Contemporary Dramatists on Radio*. Athens: Ohio University Press, 1996.
Gussow, Mel. *Conversation with Stoppard*, London: Nick Hern Books, 1995.
Hall, Lee. *The Pitmen Painters*. Faber and Faber: London, 2008.
Halliburton, Rachel. 'The Art of Success', *Evening Standard*, 17 June 2002. In *Theatre Record 4–17 June 2002*, 808.

Hamilton, Rachel Segal. 'This Week's Art Funding News', *The Guardian*, 13 May 2011. https://www.theguardian.com/culture/culture-cuts-blog/2011/may/13/arts-funding-news+(8 (accessed 8 May 2023).

Hardwick, Tom. ' "The Sophisticated Answer": A Recent Display of Forgeries Held at the Victoria and Albert Museum', *Burlington Magazine*, 152, 1287 (2010): 406–8.

Hare, David. *The Bay at Nice*. Prompt 'Bible' Script, annotated 4.9.86, National Theatre Archive, RNT/SM/1/268.

Hare, David. 'The Bay at Nice'. In *David Hare. Plays: 2*, 301–60. London: Faber and Faber, [1986] 1997.

Harrower David, and David Greig, 'Why a New Scotland Must Have a Properly Funded Theatre', *Scotsman*, 25 November 1997, 15.

Hatton, Rita, and John A. Walker. *Supercollector. A Critique of Charles Saatchi*. London: Ellipsis, 2000.

Hauck, Gerhard. *Reductionism in Drama and the Theatre. The Case of Samuel Beckett*. Potomac, MD: Scripta Humanistica, 1992.

Hauthal, Janine. ' "Provincializing" Post-Wall Europe: Transcultural Critique of Eurocentric Historicism in *Pentecost*, *Europe* and *The Break of Day*', *Journal of Contemporary Drama in English*, 3, 1 (2015): 28–46.

Hemming, Sarah. 'Sunday in the Park with George', *The Guardian*, 25 May 2006. In *Theatre Record 21 May–3 June 2006*, 620.

Hemming, Sarah. 'Variation on a cloning classic', *Financial Times*, 3 February 2022, 18.

Hewison, Robert. *Cultural Capital. The Rise and Fall of Creative Britain*. London: Verso, 2014.

Hewison, Robert. *The Heritage Industry. Britain in a Climate of Decline*. London: Methuen, 1987.

Hewison, Robert. 'A Rake and a Rebel in a Morality Play That Mirrors Our Time', *Sunday Times*, 19 November 1989, 9.

Hewison, Robert. 'Rebirth of a Nation', *The Times*, 19 May 1993.

Higgins, Charlotte. 'How Nicholas Serota's Tate Changed Britain'. *The Guardian*, 22 June 2017. https://www.theguardian.com/artanddesign/2017/jun/22/how-nicholas-serota-tate-changed-britain (accessed 7 May 2023).

Higginson, Craig. 'The Art of Success', *Time Out London*, 29 May 1996. In *Theatre Record 6–19 May 1996*, 615.

Holdsworth, Nadine. *Joan Littlewood's Theatre*. Cambridge: Cambridge University Press, 2011.

Homden, Carol. *The Plays of David Hare*. Cambridge: Cambridge University Press, 1995.

Hooper-Greenhill, Eilean. *Museum and the Interpretation of Visual Culture*. London: Routledge, 2000.

Huston, Diehl. ' "Does not the Stone Rebuke Me?": The Paulina Rebuke and Paulina's Lawful Magic in *The Winter's Tale*'. In *Shakespeare and the*

Cultures of Performance, edited by Paul Yachnin and Patricia Badir. London, Routledge, 2013, 69–82.

Hutera, Donald. 'pool (no water)', *The Times*, 28 September 2006. In *Theatre Record 22 October–4 November 2006*, 1297.

Huyssen, Andreas. *Twilight Memories: Marking Time in a Culture of Amnesia*. London: Routledge, 1995.

Ilter, Seda. ' "A Process of Transformation": Tim Crouch on *My Arm*', *Contemporary Theatre Review*, 21, 4 (2011): 394–404.

Innes, Christopher. *Modern British Drama. The Twentieth Century*. Cambridge: Cambridge University Press, 2002.

Jacob, Mary Jane, and Michelle Grabner (eds). *The Studio Reader: On the Space of Artists*. Chicago: University of Chicago Press, 2010.

Jamieson, Daniel. *The Flying Lovers of Vitebsk*. London: Oberon Books, 2017.

Janes, Robert R. 'Museums, Corporatism and the Civil Society'. In *Museum Studies. An Anthology of Contexts*, edited by Bettina Messias Carbonell, 549–61. Malden, MA: Wiley-Blackwell, 2012.

Jenkinson, John (ed.). *Nan Golding, The Devil's Playground*. London: Phaidon, 2003.

Joachimides, Christos M., Norman Rosenthal and Nicholas Serota (eds). *A New Spirit in Painting*. London: Royal Academy of Arts, 1981.

Jones, Alice. 'Attempts on Her Life', *Independent*, 15 March 2007. In *Theatre Record 12–15 March 2007*, 309.

Jones, Jonathan. 'Reflected Glory. G2's Human Logo Project at Tate Modern', *The Guardian*, 30 October 2003. https://www.theguardian.com/culture/2003/oct/30/1 (accessed 8 May 2023).

Jones, Mark (ed.). *Fake? The Art of Deception*. London: British Museum Publications, 1990.

Kalb, Jonathan. *Beckett in Performance*. Cambridge: Cambridge University Press, 1989.

Kane, Sarah. 'Interview with Nils Tabert, "Gespräch mit Sarah Kane" '. In *Playspotting: Die Londoner Theaterszene der 90er*, edited by Nils Tabert, 8–21. Rowohlt: Reinbeck, 1998.

Kane, Sarah. 'Sarah Kane: Why Can't Theatre Be as Gripping as Footie?', *The Guardian*, [From the Guardian Archive, 1998] 12 January 2015. https://www.theguardian.com/stage/2015/jan/12/sarah-kane-theatre-football-blasted (accessed 8 May 2023).

Keats, Jonathon. *Forged. Why Fakes Are the Great Art of Our Age*. Oxford: Oxford University Press, 2012.

Kennedy, Dennis. *Looking at Shakespeare. A Visual History of Twentieth-Century Performance*. Cambridge: Cambridge University Press, 1993.

Khalil, Hannah. *A Museum in Baghdad*. London: Methuen Drama, 2019.

Kidson, Peter. 'Blunt, Anthony Fredrick, 1907–1983', *The British Academy*, 38, 1983. https://www.thebritishacademy.ac.uk/publishing/memoirs/13/blunt-anthony-frederick-1907-1983/ (accessed 8 May 2023).

Kingston, Talya. 'Ciara by David Harrower', *Theatre Journal*, 66, 2 (May 2014): 264–6.
Kinley, Catherine. *David Hockney: Seven Paintings*. London: Tate Gallery, 1992.
Kirschenblatt-Gimblett, Barbara. *Destination Culture: Tourism, Museums and Heritage*. Berkeley: University of California Press, 1998.
Labute, Neil. *The Shape of Things*. London: Faber and Faber, 2000.
Lane, David. *Contemporary British Drama*. Edinburgh: Edinburgh University Press, 2010.
Laudando, Carmela Maria. 'The Risky in-betweenness of Performing Audiences', *Alicante Journal of English Studies*, 26 (2013): 45–58.
Leddy, David. *Long Live the Little Knife*. Fire Exit: Glasgow, 2013.
Leddy, David. 'Thin Air'. In David Leddy, *Long Live the Little Knife*, 105–24. Fire Exit: Glasgow, 2013.
Lenkiewicz, Rebecca. *Shoreditch Madonna*. In Rebecca Lenkiewicz, *Plays One*, 115–201. London: Faber and Faber, 2013.
Lenkiewicz, Rebecca, *The Painter*. London: Faber and Faber, 2011.
Letts, Quentin. 'pool (no water)', *Daily Mail*, 2 November 2006. In *Theatre Record 22 October–4 November 2006*, 1298.
Lewis, Paul Seven. '*Red* Starring Alfred Molina – Review', *One Minute Theatre Reviews*, 21 May 2018. https://www.youtube.com/watch?v=D4TGny6GvHo (accessed 8 May 2023).
Lloyd, David. *Beckett's Thing. Painting and Theatre*. Edinburgh: Edinburgh University Press, [2016] 2018.
Lowenthal, David. *The Past Is a Foreign Country*. Cambridge: Cambridge University Press, 1985.
Luckhurst, Mary. 'Political Point-Scoring: Martin Crimp's *Attempts on Her Life*', *Contemporary Theatre Review*, 13, 1 (2003): 47–60.
Luckhurst, Mary, and Jane Moody (eds). *Theatre and Celebrity in Britain, 1660-2000*. Basingstoke: Palgrave Macmillan, 2005.
Lukowskj, Andrzej. 'Scenes from an Execution', *Time Out London*, 9 October 2012. In *Theatre Record 23 September–6 October 2012*, 1051.
MacDonald, James. 'Review of *Blasted*'. *The Observer*, 22 January 1995. In *Theatre Record 1–28 January 1995*, 43.
Macmillan, Joyce. 'Review of *Long Live the Little Knife*', *Scotsman*, 9 February 2013. In *Theatre Record 29 January–11 February 2013*, 121.
Maggi, Kramm. 'The Perspective Puzzle', *American Theatre*, 12, 9 (November 1995). *Gale Academic OneFile*, link.gale.com/apps/doc/A18009330/AONE?u=milano&sid=bookmark-AONE&xid=3f0fcc35 (accessed 31 August 2023).
Malvern, Sue. 'The Spaces of British Art: Patronage, Institutions, Audiences'. In *The History of British Art*, edited by Chris Stephens, 198–221. London: Tate Publishing, 2008.
Marlowe, Sam. 'Scenes from an Execution', *The Times*, 16 January 2007. In *Theatre Record 1–28 January 2007*, 36.

Marstine, Janet (ed.). *New Museum Theory and Practice. An Introduction*. Oxford: Blackwell, 2006.

Mathews, Patricia. 'Returning the Gaze: Diverse Representations of the Nude in the Art of Suzanne Valadon', *The Art Bulletin*, 73, 3 (1991): 415–30.

McAvera, Brian. *Picasso's Women*. London: Oberon, 1999.

McCarten, Anthony. *The Collaboration*. London: Methuen Drama, 2022.

McClellan, A. (ed.). *Art and its Publics: Museum Studies at the Millennium*. Malden, MA: Blackwell, 2003.

McGinn, Caroline. 'Scenes from an Execution', *Time Out London*, 17 January 2007. In *Theatre Record 1–28 January 2007*, 36.

McShine, Kynaston. *The Museum as Muse: Artists Reflect*. New York: Museum of Modern Art, 1999.

Miller, M. H. 'Nicholas Serota: 'The Concept of the Museum Is in Constant Evolution', *ARTnews*, 1 July 2016. http://www.artnews.com/2016/01/07/nicholas-serota-the-concept-of-the-museum-is-in-constant-evolution/ (accessed 8 May 2023).

Minier, Márta. 'Adapting "Real-Life" Material: Metatheatrical Configurations of Authorship and Ownership of Story in Contemporary British Verbatim Theatre', *Textus. English Studies in Italy*, 31, 2 (2018): 23–40.

Morel, Michel. 'Howard Barker's Paintings, Poems and Plays: "In the Deed" Itself, or the Triple Excavation of the Inchangeable'. In *Howard Barker's Art of Theatre. Essays on His Plays, Poetry and Production Work*, edited by David Ian Rabey and Sarah Goldingay, 183–91. Manchester: Manchester University Press, 2013.

Morphet, Richard. *The Hard-Won Image. Traditional Method and Subject in Recent British Art*. London: Tate Gallery Publications, 1984.

National Gallery, '*It's True, It's True, It's True*: Becoming Artemisia Gentileschi', *YouTube*, 17 October 2018. https://www.youtube.com/watch?v=lMpAInIof_M (accessed 8 May 2023).

National Theatre Education. '*Attempts on Her Life* by Martin Crimp. Background Pack'. http://d1wf8hd6ovssje.cloudfront.net/documents/Attempts_bkpk.pdf, 3 (accessed 1 June 2023).

Newbury, Richard. 'Anthony Blunt – Fourth Man and Royal "Fake"', *La Stampa*, 24 July 2009. https://www.lastampa.it/blogs/2009/07/24/news/anthony-blunt-fourth-man-and-royal-fake-1.37251793/ (accessed 8 May 2023).

Nittve, Lars. 'How Tate Modern Transformed London – and Beyond', *Apollo. The International Art Magazine*, 31 May 2016. https://www.apollo-magazine.com/how-tate-modern-transformed-london-and-beyond/ (accessed 8 May 2023).

O'Connell, Michael. *The Idolatrous Eye. Iconoclasm and Theater in Early-Modern England*. Oxford: Oxford University Press, 2000.

O'Connell, Michael. 'The Idolatrous Eye: Iconoclasm, Anti-Theatricalism, and the Image of the Elizabethan Theater'. *ELH*, 52 (Summer 1985): 279–310.

O'Doherty, Brian. *Inside the White Cube. The Ideology of the Gallery Space*. London: University of California Press, [1976] 1999.

O'Doherty, Brian. *Studio and Cube. On the Relationship Between Where Art Is Made and Where Art Is Displayed*. New York: Princeton Architectural Press, 2007.

O'Donoghue, Nathalie. 'Edinburgh 2018: BWW Q&A – Picasso's Women', *Broadway World*, 2 July 2018. https://www.broadwayworld.com/westend/article/EDINBURGH-2018-BWW-QA--Picassos-Women-20180702 (accessed 8 May 2023).

Paget, Derek. '"Verbatim Theatre": Oral History and Documentary Techniques', *New Theatre Quarterly*, 3, 12 (1987): 317–36.

Panofsky, Erwin. *Meaning in the Visual Arts*. Harmondsworth: Peregrine, 1974.

Patey, Caroline. 'Il museo che non c'è. Note sulla dispersione del patrimonio in Gran Bretagna', *Altre Modernità/Other Modernities*, 5 (March 2011). https://riviste.unimi.it/index.php/AMonline/article/view/1025 (accessed 28 May 2023).

Paulson, Ronald. *Hogarth. High Art and Low. 1732–1750*, vol. 2. New Brunswick, NJ: Rutgers University Press, 1992.

Pople, Kenneth. 'Letter to Angela Fairclough'. 14 December 1995. Production File for *Stanley*, RNT/SM/1/397, National Theatre Archive, NT Studio, London.

Pownall, David. *An Audience Called Edouard*. London: Nick Hern Books, 2020.

Pownall, David. *Writing Master Class*. London: Oberon Books, 2013.

Preziosi, Donald, and Claire Farago (eds). *Grasping the World: The Idea of the Museum*. Aldershot, VT: Ashgate, 2004.

Prior, Nick. 'Having One's Tate and Eating It: Transformations of the Museum in a Hypermodern Era'. In *Art and Its Publics: Museum Studies at the Millennium*, edited by Andrew McClellan, 51–74. Malden, MA: Blackwell, 2003.

Rabey, David Ian. *Howard Barker: Ecstasy and Death. An Expository Study of His Drama, Theory and Production Work, 1988–2008*. Berlin: Springer Nature, 2009.

Rabey, David Ian, and Sarah Goldingay (eds). *Howard Barker's Art of Theatre. Essays on His Plays, Poetry and Production Work*. Manchester: Manchester University Press, 2013.

Radosavljević, Duška. *Theatre-Making. Interplay between Text and Performance in the 21st Century*. New York: Palgrave Macmillan, 2013.

Ratcliffe, Michael. 'Review of *The Art of Success*', *The Observer*, 13 September 1986. In *Theatre Record 2–15 July 1986*, 754.

Ravenhill, Mark. *pool (no water)*. In Mark Ravenhill, *Plays: 2*, 293–323. London: Bloomsbury Methuen Drama, 2008.

Ravenhill, Mark. 'In at the Deep End', *The Guardian*, 20 September 2006.

Rebellato, Dan. '"Because It Feels Fucking Amazing": Recent British Drama and Bodily Mutilation'. In *Cool Britannia? British Political Drama in the*

1990s, edited by D'Monté, Rebecca and Graham Saunders, 192–207. Basingstoke: Palgrave Macmillan, 2008.

Reinelt, Janelle, and Gerald Hewitt. *The Political Theatre of David Edgar: Negotiation and Retrieval*. Cambridge: Cambridge University Press, 2011.

Relph-Knight, Linda. 'Stunning Scenic Routes', *Design Week*, 21 February 1997.

Reynolds, James, and Andy W. Smith. *Howard Barker's Theatre: Wrestling with Catastrophe*. London: Bloomsbury Methuen Drama, 2015.

Rice, Emma. 'Q&A between Paul Crewes & Emma Rice. Taking the Journey: An Interview with Director Emma Rice', *TheWallis.org/Lovers*, 2018. https://www.thewallis.org/ckeditor/userfiles/files/wallis1718_PerfProg_Feb_WebInterviews%20FLOV.pdf (accessed 8 May 2023).

Rich, Frank. '*Art of Success* Makes Hogarth the Warhol of the 18th Century', *New York Times*, 21 December 1989. https://www.nytimes.com/1989/12/21/theater/review-theater-art-of-success-makes-hogarth-the-warhol-of-the-18th-century.html (accessed 20 August 2019).

Ridley, Philip. *The Pitchfork Disney*. London: Methuen Drama, (1991) 2015.

Ridley, Philip. *The Poltergeist*. London: Methuen Drama, 2020.

Ridley, Philip in conversation with Aleks Sierz, ' "Putting a New Lens on the World": The Art of Theatrical Alchemy', *New Theatre Quarterly*, 25, 2 (May 2009): 109–17.

Ridley, Philip interviewed by Theo Bosanquet, 'Philip Ridley On … Revisiting *The Pitchfork Disney*', *WhatsOnStage*, 30 January 2012. https://www.whatsonstage.com/west-end-theatre/news/philip-ridley-on-revisiting-the-pitchfork-disney_5566.html (accessed 8 May 2023).

Ridley, Philip. 'Philip Ridley Q&A', *Exeunt Magazine*, 23 April 2012. https://exeuntmagazine.com/features/exeunt-philip-ridley-qa/3/ (accessed 8 May 2023).

Roberts Richard J. (ed.). 'Study Guide for *Red* by John Logan', *Indiana Repertory Theatre*, 2014. https://d1fl2pbib0u1tq.cloudfront.net/pdf/Study%20Guides/20142015/IRT%20Study%20Guide%20for%20Red.pdf (accessed 8 May 20023).

Rodney, Seph. *The Personalization of the Museum Visit: Art Museums, Discourse, and Visitors*. London: Routledge, 2019.

Samuel, Raphael (ed.). *Patriotism: The Making and Unmaking of British National Identity*. London: Routledge, 1987.

Samuels, Ernest. *Bernard Berenson. The Making of a Legend*. Cambridge, MA: Harvard University Press, 1987.

Saunders, Graham. *'Love Me or Kill Me': Sarah Kane and the Theatre of Extremes*. Manchester: Manchester University Press, 2002.

Schneider, Rebecca. *The Explicit Body in Performance*. London: Routledge, 1997.

Schuhbeckon, Birgit. 'Less Art, More Substance. New Tendencies in Contemporary Theatre', *Notes on Metamodernism*, 22 February 2012. http://

www.metamodernism.com/2012/02/22/less-art-more-substance-new-tendencies-in-contemporary-theatre/ (accessed 8 May 2023).

Schulze, Daniel. *Authenticity in Contemporary Theatre and Performance. Make It Real*. London: Methuen, 2017.

Scott, David A. *Art Authenticity, Restoration, Forgery*. Los Angeles: Cotsen Institute of Archaeology Press, 2016.

Seligman, Germain. *Merchant of Art: 1880–1960. Eighty Years of Professional Collecting*. New York: Appleton-Century-Crofts, 1961.

Serota, Nicholas. *Experience or Interpretation: The Dilemma of Museums of Modern Art*. London: Thames and Hudson, [1996] 2000.

Serota, Nicholas. 'The 21st-Century Tate Is a Commonwealth of Ideas', *The Art Newspaper*, 1 July 2016. https://mefsite.wordpress.com/2016/07/01/the-art-newspaper-the-21st-century-tate-is-a-commonwealth-of-ideas/ (accessed 7 May 2023).

Shattuck, Roger. *The Innocent Eye. On Modern Literature and the Arts*. New York: Farrar Straus Giroux, 1984.

Shaw, Fiona in conversation with Hanna Berrigan, 'Acting Barker'. In *Howard Barker's Theatre: Wrestling with Catastrophe*, edited by James Reynolds and Andy W. Smith, 175–88. London: Bloomsbury Methuen Drama, 2015.

Sierz, Aleks. *In-Yer-Face Theatre. British Drama Today*. London: Faber and Faber, 2001.

Sierz, Aleks. *Modern British Playwrighting. The 1990s*. London: Methuen Drama, 2012.

Sierz, Aleks. 'Attempts on Our Lives (2): 1997–2007'. In 'Programme for Martin Crimp's *Attempts on Her Life* at the Lyttelton Theatre', directed by Katie Mitchell, National Theatre, 2007. Production File for *Attempts on Her Life*, RNT/PP/1/2/272, National Theatre Archive, NT Studio, London.

Simonson, Robert. 'Watching Paint Dry: How Playwrights Turn Art-Making Into High Drama', *Playbill*, 6 October 2010. https://playbill.com/article/watching-paint-dry-how-playwrights-turn-art-making-into-high-drama-com-172202 (accessed 27 September 2023).

Simpson, Colin. *The Artful Partners. The Secret Association of Bernard Berenson and Joseph Duveen*. London: J. Simpson, 1988.

Soncini, Sara. 'Hogarth in Drag. Acts of Transvestism in *The Grace of Mary Traverse* and *Mother Clap's Molly House*'. In *Enduring Presence. William Hogarth's British and European Afterlives*. Book 1: *Aesthetic, Visual and Performative Cultures*, edited by Caroline Patey, Cynthis E. Roman and George Letissier, 163–82. Oxford: Peter Lang, 2021.

Spencer, Charles. 'Shoreditch Madonna', *Daily Telegraph*, 15 July 2005. In *Theatre Record 2–15 July 2005*, 947.

Spencer, Charles. 'The Painter', *Daily Telegraph*, 17 January 2011. In *Theatre Record 1–28 January 2011*, 29.

Spencer, Charles. 'Three Birds Alighting on a Field', *Daily Telegraph*, 12 September 1991. In *Theatre Record 10–23 September 1991*, 1119.

Stafford-Clark, Max. 'Artistic Director's Statement', programme for *Three Birds Alighting on a Field* at the Royal Court, 1991, TWA, BLMC, Add 79386.

Stallabrass, Julian. *Art Incorporated. The Story of Contemporary Art*. Oxford: Oxford University Press, 2004.

Stallabrass, Julian. *High Art Lite. The Rise and Fall of Young British Art*. London: Verso (1999), revised and expanded edition, 2006.

Stangos, Nikos (ed.). *David Hockney by David Hockey: My Early Years*. London: Thames and Hudson, 1976.

Stein, Sarah. 'Sarah Stein's Notes, 1908'. In Jack D. Flam, *Matisse on Art*, 41–6. Oxford: Phaidon, [1973] 1978.

Steiner, Wendy. 'Art; In London, A Catalogue of Fakes', *New York Times*, 29 April 1990, 37. https://www.nytimes.com/1990/04/29/arts/art-in-london-a-catalogue-of-fakes.html (accessed 8 May 2023).

Stephens, Chris (ed.). *The History of British Art*. London: Tate Publishing, 2008.

Stephens, Simon. 'David Hare Talks to Simon Stephens'. *Royal Court Theatre Playwright's Podcast*, season 1, episode 5, 6 January 2017. https://royalcourttheatre.com/podcast/episode-5- david-hare-talks-to-simon-stephens (accessed 7 May 2023).

Stoppard, Tom. *After Magritte*. London: Faber and Faber, 1971.

Stoppard, Tom. *Artist Descending a Staircase*. In Tom Stoppard, *The Plays for Radio. 1964–1991*, 109–56. London: Faber and Faber, 1971.

Storr, Robert. 'A Room of One's Own, a Mind of One's Own'. In *The Studio Reader: On the Space of Artists*, edited by Mary Jane Jacob and Michelle Grabner, 49–62. Chicago: University of Chicago Press, 2010.

Svich, Caridad. 'Tim Crouch's Theatrical Transformations: A Conversation with Caridad Svich', *HotReview.org*, 27 October 2006. http://www.timcrouchtheatre.co.uk/shows-2/england/booking-info (access 8 May 2023).

Tate Gallery. 'In the Gallery. Rothko on Stage', *Tate*. https://www.tate.org.uk/art/artists/mark-rothko-1875/rothko-on-stage (accessed 8 May 2023).

Tate Gallery. 'Understanding David Hockney's *A Bigger Splash*', *Tate*. https://www.tate.org.uk/art/artworks/hockney-a-bigger-splash-t03254/understanding-david-hockneys-bigger-splash (accessed 8 May 2023).

Tate Gallery Press Release. 'Kenneth Clark: Looking for Civilisation', *Tate*, 6 January, 2014. https://www.tate.org.uk/press/press-releases/kenneth-clark-looking-civilisation (accessed 8 May 2023).

Taylor, Kate. 'A Drama of Attribution to Play Out at the Metropolitan Museum', *The New York Times*, 28 April 2011. https://archive.nytimes.com/artsbeat.blogs.nytimes.com/2011/04/28/a-drama-of-art-attribution-to-play-out-at-the-metropolitan-museum/ (accessed 27 September 2023).

Taylor, Matthew. 'Mark Rylance Resigns from RSC Over BP Sponsorship', *The Guardian*, 21 June 2019. https://www.theguardian.com/stage/2019/jun/21/mark-rylance-resigns-from-royal-shakespeare-company-rsc-over-bp-sponsorship (accessed 27 September 2023).

Taylor, Paul. 'Scenes from an Execution', *Independent*, 27 September 1999. In *Theatre Record 10–23 September 1999*, 1232.
Thompson, Donald. *The $12 Million Stuffed Shark: The Curious Economics of Contemporary Art*. Basingstoke: Palgrave Macmillan, 2008.
Thompson, Susannah. ' "But ye de de art, divvint ye?" Authenticity, identity and the historicization of the Pitmen Painters', *Visual Studies*, 28, 3 (2013): 207–17.
Thornton, Dora. 'Top Five: Exhibits from *Shakespeare: Staging the World* at the British Museum', 18 July 2012. https://www.whatsonstage.com/west-end-theatre/news/top-five-exhibits-from-shakespeare-staging-the-wor_3428.html (accessed 15 May 2023).
Tinker, Jack. 'The Disgusting Feast of Filth', *Daily Mail*, 19 January 1995. In *Theatre Record 1–28 January 1995*, 42.
Tubridy, Derval. 'Samuel Beckett and Performance Art', *Journal of Beckett Studies*, 23, 1 (2014): 34–53.
Tulsa, John. *Art Matters: Reflecting on Culture*. London: Methuen, 1999.
Turner, Cathy, and Synne Behrndt, *Dramaturgy and Performance*. Basingstoke: Palgrave Macmillan, 2008.
Turner, Luke. 'Metamodernism: A Brief Introduction', *Notes on Metamodernism*, 12 January 2015. https://www.metamodernism.com/2015/01/12/metamodernism-a-brief-introduction/ (accessed 8 May 2023).
van den Akker, Robin, Alison Gibbons, and Timotheus Vermeulen. 'Metamodernism: Period, Structure of Feeling, and Cultural Logic – A Case Study of Contemporary Autofiction'. In David Rudrum, Ridvan Askin and Frida Beckman (eds). *New Directions in Philosophy and Literature*, 41–54. Edinburgh: Edinburgh University Press, 2019.
Venturi, Riccardo. *Mark Rothko. Lo spazio e la sua disciplina*. Milano: Electa 2007.
Vermeulen, Timotheus, and Robin van den Akker, 'Notes on metamodernism', *Journal of Aesthetics & Culture*, 2 (2010): 1–14.
Walasek, Helen. 'Cultural Heritage and Memory after Ethnic Cleansing in Post-Conflict Bosnia-Herzegovina', *International Review of the Red Cross*, 101, 910 (April 2019): 273–94.
Walker, Tim. 'pool (no water)', *Sunday Telegraph*, 12 November 2006. In *Theatre Record 22 October–4 November 2006*, 1300.
Walsh, Kevin. *The Representation of the Past: Museums and Heritage in Post-Modern World*. New York: Routledge, 1992.
Wardle, Irving. 'The Gap between Life and Dreams', *The Times*, 10 July 1986, 19.
Webster, Annie. '*A Museum in Baghdad*, and an Interview with its Author, Annah Khalil', *Arts Cabinet*, 2019. https://www.artscabinet.org/migration/a-museum-in-baghdad-and-an-interview-with-its-author-hannah-khalil (accessed 8 May 2023).
Wertenbaker, Timberlake. Draft/copy of letter to Lindsay Posner, 14 January 1991, TWA, BLMC, Add 79217. 3003C.

Wertenbaker, Timberlake. *The Line*. London: Faber and Faber, 2009.
Wertenbaker, Timberlake. *Three Birds Alighting on a Field*. London: Faber and Faber, 1992.
Whitechapel Art Gallery. *Mark Rothko. A Retrospective Exhibition: Paintings 1945–1960*. London: Whitechapel Art Gallery, 1961.
Wieseman, Marjorie E. A *Closer Look. Deceptions and Discoveries*. London: National Gallery Company, 2010.
Wilson, Snoo. *Reclining Nude with Black Stockings*. http://www.snoowilson.co.uk/Reclining%20Nude.pdf (accessed 15 January 2023).
Woddis, Carole. 'Scenes from an Execution', *Herald*, 1 October 1999. In *Theatre Record 10–23 September 1999*, 1234.
Woddis, Carole. 'You Be Ted & I'll Be Sylvia', *Jewish Chronicle*, 17 September 1999. In *Theatre Record 10–23 September 1999*, 1194.
Wolfe, George C. *The Colored Museum*. New York: Grove Press, 1985.
Wright, Nicholas. *Vincent in Brixton*. London: Nick Hern Books, 2002.
Wu, Chin-tao. *Privatising Culture: Corporate Art Intervention since the 1980s*. London: Verso, 2002.
Wu, Duncan. *Making Plays. Interviews with Contemporary British Dramatists and their Directors*. London: Palgrave Macmillan, 2000.
Zimmermann, Heiner. 'Memories of Paintings in Howard Barker's Theatre'. In *Howard Barker's Art of Theatre. Essays on His Plays, Poetry and Production Work*, edited by David Ian Rabey and Sarah Goldingay, 69–85. Manchester: Manchester University Press, 2013.

Index

Abramovic, Marina 201
Aidin, Rose 75
Al-Assad, Khaled 137
Al-Gailani Werr, Lamia 137
Albery, Tim 202, 203 n.99, 237
Allen, James 47
Allori, Alessandro 193
Anderson, Laurie 152
Andrews, Michael 46
Angelaki, Vicky 200 n.95, 202
Annigoni, Pietro 102
Antal, Frederick 225
Antolin, Marc 157
Antonello da Messina 173
art galleries and museums
   Andy Warhol Museum, Pittsburgh 69 n.109, 84
   Barbican Arts Centre, London 58
   Battersea Arts Centre, London 69 n. 109
   Bensham Grove Settlement, Gateshead-on-Tyne 164
   Bernard Jacobson Gallery, London 83
   British Museum, London 93–4, 93 n.3, 117–18, 129, 138, 138 n.124, 139 n.129, 140 n.129
   Centre for Contemporary Art, Glasgow 142 n.133
   Courtauld Institute of Art, London 115, 117, 122 n.85
   Donnaregina Museum (Complesso Monumentale Donnaregina) Naples 85
   Experience Music Project (MoPoP), Seattle, Washington 80
   Fondazione Arnaldo Pomodoro, Milan 84
   Fruitmarket Gallery, Edinburgh 68, 81, 83, 84, 85, 86, 87, 205, 206, 238
   Gallery Different, London 87
   Gagosian Gallery, New York 209
   Getty Museum, Los Angeles 185
   Hayward Gallery, London 50, 69 n.109
   Henry Art Gallery, Seattle 85
   Hermitage Museum, Saint Petersburg 18, 105, 106–7, 123
   Institute of Contemporary Arts, London 69 n.109
   Iraq Museum, Baghdad 129
   Isabella Stewart Gardner Museum, Boston 144
   Knoedler Gallery, London 99
   Laing Art Gallery, Newcastle Upon Tyne 164, 164 n.16
   Marian Goodman Gallery, New York 28
   Metropolitan Museum of Art, New York 52, 113, 113 n.66, 227
   Musée des Beaux Arts, Caen 172
   Museum of Modern Art, New York 1, 25 n.31
   National Gallery of Art, Washington 110 n.50
   National Gallery of Ireland, Dublin 21, 22
   National Gallery of Scotland, Edinburgh 181, 225
   National Gallery, London 1, 18, 21, 34, 40, 88, 89, 93, 93 n.4, 117, 118 n.77, 120, 157, 190 n.77, 191, 192 n.82
   National Portrait Gallery, London 20, 22, 31
   Rona Gallery, London 161

Royal Academy of Arts, London 3, 12, 46, 59, 60, 62, 63, 101, 164, 166, 202, 236 n.26
Saatchi Gallery, London 2, 49
Scottish National Gallery of Modern Art, Edinburgh 63
Serpentine Gallery, London 50, 70
Tate Gallery, London 1, 3, 18, 23, 25, 27, 27 n.33, 28, 32, 35, 46, 49, 50, 68, 76, 76, 99, 112, 117, 117 n.73, 162, 164, 166, 203, 227
Tate Modern, London 3, 4, 12, 18, 19, 25, 58, 60, 75–82, 87, 89, 90, 91, 151, 177, 183, 189, 205, 219 n.128
The Gallery Soho, London 89
Tokyo Metropolitan Art Space, Tokyo 69 n.109
Uffizi Gallery, Florence 193
Victoria and Albert Museum, London 82, 99, 143
Washington State University Museum of Art, Washington 80
White Cube, London (*see also* O'Doherty) 2, 67
Whitechapel Art Gallery, London 77, 78 n.117, 82, 84, 112, 181, 184, 210 n.106, 211, 211 n.107
Whitney Museum of American Art, New York 215
Yale Center for British Art, New Haven 85
Artaud, Antonin 19
Ashington Group 35, 164–71
Atik, Anne 21, 22
Attenborough, Tom 89, 124, 124 n.92, 128, 131
Auerbach, Frank 46, 48, 101
Avrami, Erica 134

Bacon, Francis 23 n.23, 32, 46, 101, 102, 173, 177, 181, 200, 200 n.95
Baldwin, Stanley 122, 123

Barker, Howard 5, 29, 123, 172, 172 n.173, 177, 180 n.40
Judith. A Parting from the Body 179
Scenes from an Execution 29–31, 102, 155, 171–80
Barrett, Billy 89, 189 n.72, 191, 192
Baselitz, Georg 85
Baudrillard, Jean 95
Bechtler, Hildegard 177
Beck, James 132–3
Beckett, Samuel 5, 8, 12, 14, 15, 20–4, 31, 155, 156, 195, 198
That Time 20, 21–2, 31
Beckmann, Signe 177
Beethoven, Ludwig, van 187
Bell, Gertrude 137
Benjamin, Walter 41, 99, 138
Bennett, Alan 10, 13, 18, 31, 94, 95, 115, 147, 162
A Question of Attribution 2, 13, 18, 94, 95, 100, 102, 104, 114–24, 127, 143, 162, 163
Going to Pictures 33
Portrait or Bust 117
Berenson, Bernard (BB) 5, 94, 110–15, 112 n.66, 228, 230
Berman, Ed 25
Billington, Michael 54, 55 n.78, 110, 162, 203 n.99
Bird, Timothy 159
Blair, Tony 58, 176, 177, 196
Blake, William 166
Blessed, George 169
Bloom, Paul 138
Blunt, Sir Anthony 13, 94, 115–23, 122 n.85, 127, 144, 162–3
Boltanski, Christian 40
Bond, Edward 65
Bond, Kathryn 192
Borchardt-Hume, Achim 183
Bottoms, Stephen 84, 85 n.127
Bourdieu, Pierre 242
Bourgeois, Louise 79, 82
Bowles, Peter 110

Breach Theatre 88, 189
  It's True, It's True, It's True 88–9, 189–95
Bridgemont, Andrew
  Red on Black 32–3, 32 n.42
Brisson, Audrey 157
Broughton, Pip 44
Brown, George (*see also* Ashington Group) 168, 170
Brown, Ian 143
Bruce, Chris 80
Buck, Louisa 48
Buether, Miriam 214, 217
Buntrock, Sam 158
Buonarroti, Michelangelo 117, 126, 132, 163
Buren, Daniel 181, 182, 183
Burgess, Guy 123
Burgess, Paul 157

Cabaret Voltaire, Zurich 43
Cairns, Tom 158, 177, 178
Canton, Ursula 161
Cardiff, Janet 83
Cerciello, Carlo 84
Cézanne, Paul 143 n.135, 166
Chagall, Marc 5, 157–8
Chamberlain, Neville 122, 123
Chapman, Dinos and Jake 60
Charles, Keir 212, 215
Charpentier, Constance 201
Chicago, Judy 126
Chivers, Natasha 214
Church, Jonathan
  You Be Ted and I'll Be Sylvia 67
Churchill, Caryl 48
  A Number 40–1, 42
Cicali, Gianni 132
Clark, Sir Kenneth 34, 94, 116–17, 193
Collings, Matthew 47
Collins, Aletta 158
Collishaw, Mat 71
Connel, Christopher 165, 168

Constable, John 9, 50, 60, 85, 162
Craig-Martin, Michael 151, 153
Crewdson, Gregory 207, 208
Crimp, Martin 15, 23
  Attempts on Her Life 15, 24, 64–5, 156, 195, 196, 198–204, 237
Crouch, Tim 5, 6, 8, 9, 10, 12, 15, 74, 74 n.115, 80, 84 n.125, 85 n.127, 98, 155, 197 n.90, 243
  An Oak Tree 6, 8, 14, 95, 96, 151–3, 197, 205
  ENGLAND 8, 9, 12, 15, 34, 68, 76–81, 83–6, 156, 195, 197, 204–11, 214, 237–43
  My Arm 6, 8, 69–74, 213, 239

da Vinci, Leonardo 13, 104, 111, 114, 117, 143 n.135, 223
Davis, Cait 212, 215
De Botton, Gilbert 112
De Kooning, Willem 207, 208, 239
Dean, Tacita 68, 83, 85–6, 207, 208
Dear, Nick
  The Art of Success 12, 13, 15, 43–7, 43 n.56, 56, 94, 96–104, 224–7
Degas, Edgar 5, 9, 55, 56, 57
Delgado-Garcia, Cristina 241–2
Derrida, Jacques 148, 149
Devlin, Es 40–41
Dierking, D. Lynn 27 n.34, 27–8
Dillane, Stephen 86
Duchamp, Marcel 25, 87, 211
Dufy, Raoul 209
Duncan, Carol 17
Duveen, Joseph 5, 13, 94, 110–14, 133, 228–30

Eco, Umberto 185
Edgar, David 2, 10, 95
  Pentecost 2, 13, 18, 94, 95, 114, 124–38
Eliasson, Olafur 79–80
Elisabeth I 140

Elizabeth II (HMQ) 102, 119–21, 144, 145
Emin, Tracey 3, 47, 48, 59, 60, 62, 62 n.93, 63, 65, 65 n.101, 66–7, 68, 71, 82, 179, 201, 203, 236 n.26
Ergen, Mehmet 9
Essiedu, Paapa 40
Etchells, Tim 95
exhibitions
  A New Spirit in Paintings (Royal Academy, London, 1981) *46*
  A School of London: Six Figurative Painters (touring exhibition, 1987) *46*
  An Exhibition of Forgeries and Deceptive Copies (British Museum, London, 1961) *93 n.3, 94*
  Artemisia (National Gallery, London, 2020–2021) *88*
  Beyond Caravaggio (National Gallery, London, 2016–2017) *89*
  Close Examination: Fakes, Mistakes and Discoveries (National Gallery, London, 2010) *93*, *120*
  Counterfeits, Imitations and Copies of Works of Art (Burlington Fine Arts Club, London, 1924) *93*, *94*
  Damien Hirst: No Sense of Absolute Corruption (Gagosian Gallery, New York, 1996) *209*
  David Hockney: Moving Focus Print from Tyler Graphics Ltd (Tate Gallery, London, 1986) *99*
  David Hockney: Still Lives and Landscapes (Knoedler Gallery, London, 1986) *99*
  Dora Maar (Tate Modern, London, 2020) *87*
  Duchamp, Man Ray, Picabia (Tate Modern, London, 2009) *25*
  Fake? The Art of Deception (British Museum, London, 1989) *93–4*
  Freeze (Docks Offices, London, 1988) *3, 12, 43, 59*
  Howard Barker: Peintures (Musee des Beaux Arts, Caen, 2008–9) *172*
  Kenneth Clark: Looking for Civilization (Tate Britain, London, 2014) *117*
  Landscape in Britain 1850–1950 (Hayward Gallery, London, 1983) *50*
  Mark Rothko. A Retrospective Exhibition: Paintings 1945–1960 (Whitechapel Art Gallery, London, 1961) *184, 184 n.59*
  Mark Rothko 1903–1970 (Tate Gallery, London, 1987) *49*
  Muse, Model or Mistress? (Gallery Different, London, 2018) *87*
  Museum Photographs (Marian Goodman Gallery, New York, 1990) *28*
  New York Art Now (Saatchi Gallery, London, 1987–8) *49*
  Picasso 1932 – Love, Fame, Tragedy (Tate Modern, London, 2018) *87*
  René Magritte (Tate Gallery, London, 1969) *25*
  Rothko: The Late Series (Tate Modern, London, 2008–2009) *89*
  Salon des Refusés (Paris, 1863) *43*
  Sensation (Royal Academy, London, 1997) *3, 12, 59–62, 64, 64 n.96, 68, 71, 85, 103, 202, 207, 236 n.26*
  Shakespeare: Staging the World (British Museum, London, 2012) *139 n.129, 140 n.129*
  Some Went Mad, Some Ran Away (Serpentine Gallery, London, 1994) *70*
  The Artist Studio. A Century of the Artist's Studio. 1920–2022 (Whitechapel Art Gallery, London, 2022) *181*

The Hard-Won Image. Traditional Method and Subject in Recent British Art (Tate Gallery, London, 1984) *46–7*
The Metropolitan Police Service's Investigations of Fakes and Forgeries (Victorian and Albert Museum, London, 2010) *143*
The Museum as Muse: Artists Reflect (Museum of Modern Art, New York, 1999) *1*
Woman with a Red Hat (Fruitmarket Gallery, Edinburgh, 2018) *85*
Eyre, Richard 161

Fairclough, Angela 160 n.8
Falk, H. John 10, 27–8, 27 n.32
Farley, David 159
Farrow, Toby 162
Feaver, William 34, 35 n.47, 161, 164 n.17, 166, 169, 170
Ferrone, Alex 237, 241
Fielding, David 173
Fielding, Henry 44
Fisher, John 188
Flying Elephant Productions 86
Floyd, Jimmy (*see also* Ashington Group) 165, 166, 168, 168 n.20, 169
Fludd, Robert 18
Forced Entertainment 95
Foreman, Andy 169
Fox, Edward 110
Frantic Assembly 9, 196, 211, 212, 214, 215, 217, 219, 221, 222, 235
Freeman, Laura 193
Freud, Lucien 7, 46, 101
Freud, Sigmund 44, 67, 167
Frick, Henry Clay 112, 229, 238
Friedman, Maria 158

Fry, Roger 166
Fry, Stephen 143 n.135, 166
Fun Palace 19

Gardner, Lyn 177
Gems, Pam 160, 160 n.8
 Stanley 5, 160–1
Gentileschi, Artemisia 5, 30, 88–9, 171, 179, 189–94, 192 n.85
Genzken, Isa 84
Getsy, J. David 181
Gilmour, Alexander 9 n.18
Gilot, Françoise 86
Giorgione 23, 23 n.23, 110, 110 n.50, 114
Giotto di Bondone 40, 124, 125, 125 n.96, 130
Goldin, Nan 197, 212, 214–16, 214 n.119–120, 217, 234, 235, 238
Goodale, Robert 176, 177
Göring, Hermann 119, 143
Gouel, Eva 86
Graham, Scott 196, 197, 217, 219, 220, 222, 236 n.21
Grandage, Michael 90, 155, 183, 184, 185, 187
Gray, Simon
 The Old Masters 5, 13, 94, 100, 104, 109–14, 109 n.48, 115, 133, 162, 163
Greenhalgh, Shaun 94, 143
Greer, Germaine 203 n.99
Greig, David 233 n.23
Gromada, John 97
Guralnick, Elissa 173

Hall, Lee 12, 66, 123
 The Pitmen Painters 5, 14, 18, 34, 35, 66, 163–71
Hall, Sir Peter 18, 18 n.7
Halliburton, Rachel 47
Hambling, Maggie 48
Han, Andrée and Harry 13, 104
Hare, David 7–8, 95

The Bay at Nice 13, 94, 104–9, 110, 115, 120, 129
Harrower, David 233, 233 n.23
  Ciara 233–4
Hart, Paul 186
Hartley, Alex 84, 85, 205
Harvey, Marcus 59, 64, 103
Hatley, Tim 160–1
Hatoum, Mona 60, 63
Hatton, Rita 233
Hauck, Gerhard 24
Hayden, Henri 21
Hazlitt, William 162
Heap, Imogen 222
Hebborn, Eric 122
Hemming, Sarah 159
Hewison, Robert 41, 58
Hindley, Myra 59, 64, 103
Hirst, Damien 3, 43, 47, 48, 53, 60, 64, 64 n.96, 66, 67, 70, 71, 72, 72 n.112, 176, 209–10, 226
Hitler, Adolf 114, 122
Hockney, David 60, 99, 99 n.25, 100, 209, 217, 217 n.125, 218, 219, 221
Hodgson, Michael 165, 168
Hogarth, William 5, 13, 15, 43–7, 43 n.54, 94, 96–103, 155, 224, 224 n.4, 225, 226
Hoggett, Steven 196, 222
Höller, Carsten 79
Holzer, Harold 113 n.66
Hooper-Greenhill, Eilean 80, 125, 242–3
Hopper, Edward 162
Hoving, Thomas 52, 227
Howard, Pamela 161
Hume, Gary 207, 208
Hunter, Kathryn 174, 175, 176
Huntingdon, Henry 112, 229
Huw, Rhodri 189 n.72

Innes, Christopher 64 n.96

Jackson, Glenda 29, 173, 174

Jacob, Sally 48, 54
Jacobson, Bernard 48, 83
James, Karl 68, 73, 206
James I of England and Ireland (VI of Scotland) 139 n.129, 140, 140 n.129
Jamieson, Daniel
  The Flying Lovers of Vitebsk 157–8
Joachimides, M. Christos 46
Jones, Cleve 126
Jones, Jonathan 79, 236 n.26
Jones, Mark 119
Joplin, Jay 2
Jung, G. Carl 199

Kalb, Jonathan 23
Kane, Sarah 59, 63–5, 64 n.96, 200
Kapoor, Anish 79
Kelly, Ian 165, 168
Khalil, Hannah 6, 137–8
  A Museum in Baghdad 2, 6, 114, 129, 129 n.104, 137, 138
Khokhlova, Olga 86
Khrushchev, Nikita 104 n.39
Kidson, Peter 122 n.85
Kilbourn, Oliver (*see also* Ashington Group) 165, 168, 169, 170
King, Gillian 47
Kirschenblatt-Gimblett, Barbara 17
Kitaj, Ronald Brooks 46
Kossoff, Leon 46, 48
Kress Henry, Samuel 112, 229–30, 238
Kwei-Armah, Kwame 6

Labute, Neil
  The Shape of Things 89, 213, 213 n.115
Lamble, Anthony 234
Lapine, James 158
Larkin, Philip 162
Leddy, David 10, 12, 95, 138, 149, 153
  Long Live the Little Knife 14, 67, 95–6, 100, 138–50, 138 n.124, 140 n.129, 230–3

Thin Air 139–40, 139 n.129, 140 n.129
Lees, Irene 87
Lenkiewicz, Rebecca
   Shoreditch Madonna 40, 67, 156–7
   The Painter 9, 162, 186
Lespinasse, Gaby 86
Letts, Quentin 213, 236–7
Lippi, Filippino 114
Littlewood, Joan 19
Lyric Hammersmith Production
   211 n.108
Logan, John 123, 195
   Red 11, 14, 89–91, 155, 183–9, 195
Lonsdale, Brian 165, 168
Lowenthal, David 120
Lucas, Sarah 60, 71
Luckhurst, Mary 202
Lyon, Robert (*see also* Ashington
   Group) 35, 163–4, 165, 166, 167,
   168, 169

Maar, Dora 86, 87
MacDonald, Hettie 73
MacDonald, James 65
Maclaurin, Ali 139
Madonna (Louise Veronica
   Ciccone) 68
Magritte, René 25, 25 n.31, 27–8, 76
Malcolm, Sarah 101, 103, 225
Manet, Edouard 159–60
Mapplethorpe, Robert 98, 99
Marber, Patrick
   Closer 18, 36–40
Marx, Karl 159–60
Mathews, Patricia 57
Matisse, Henri 105, 108–9
McArthur, Gerrard 177, 178
McAvera, Brian 5, 86, 87
   Picasso's Women 86–7
McCann, Gary 164, 165, 167, 169
McCarten, Anthony
   The Collaboration 6–7
McCormack, Neil 140, 232
McDiarmid, Ian 29, 173, 174

McGreevy, Thomas 21, 22
McGuire, Stryker 58
McShine, Kynaston 1
Mellon, Andrew 112, 229
Michel-Basquiat, Jean 6, 51
Miller, Graeme 83
Mitchell, Katie 65, 202–3, 237
Molina, Alfred 185, 187
Monet, Edouard 5
Moore, Henry 166
Moorthy, Rani 7
   Whose Sari Now 7
Morelli, Giovanni 113
Morissette, Alanis 152
Morris, Frances 90
Mortimer, Vicki 38, 202
Mueck, Ron 71, 236 n.26
Muller, Leah 212, 215
museums (*see* art galleries)
Mussolini, Benito 110, 114
Myatt, John 143

Namuth, Hans 185
Nazli, Leyla 9
Nicholson, Amelia 47
Nicholson, Ben 166
Noble, Adrian 97
Nutborne, Richard 155, 189

O'Doherty, Brian (*see also* White
   Cube) 77, 78, 183, 205, 210, 211
O'Loughlin, Orla 234
Ofili, Chris 47, 59
Old Masters 21, 45, 49, 56, 115, 116,
   116 n. 71, 119, 162, 163
Oldroyd, William 176
Olivier, Fernand 86
Oram, Christopher 91, 183, 185

Paines Plough 44
Panofsky, Erwin 116, 116 n.71
Paolozzi, Eduardo 181
Paulin, Tom 203 n.99
Peppiatt, Michael 46

Perugino, Pietro 21, 22
Picasso, Pablo 5, 48, 86, 87, 102
Pimlott, Steven 158
Pinnock, Winsome 6, 55 n.78
Pinter, Harold 110
Poitras, Laura 234
Pollock, Jackson 67, 139, 141, 142, 144
Pomodoro, Arnaldo 84
Pope, Alexander 45
Pople, Kenneth 160, 160 n.8
Posner, Lindsay 54, 55 n.77
Poussin, Nicolas 115, 121
Pownall, David
  An Audience Called Edouard 159–60
Preziosi, Donald 17
Price, Cedric 19
Puvis de Chavannes, Pierre 55

Quast, Philip 158
Quinn, Mark 3, 68, 71, 72, 207, 208

Radosavljević, Duška 9, 15, 84
  n.125, 156
Rankin, Andy 169
Raphael 223
Rasa Productions, Manchester 7
Ravenhill, Mark 15, 23, 43 n.54, 59,
  152, 196, 198, 236
  pool (no water) 6, 9, 15, 24, 156,
  195, 211–22, 235–7
Read, Katie 32 n.42
Rebellato, Dan 63 n.96, 179
Redgrave, Collette 86–7, 87 n.129
Redmayne, Eddie 184, 186–7
Rembrandt, Harmenszoon van Rijn
  23 n.23
Renoir, Pierre-Auguste 55
Reynolds, Joshua 45, 46
Reza, Yasmina 52
Rhapsody of Words Productions 89
Rice-Oxley, Mark 212
Rich, Frank 98, 99
Ridley, Philip 5, 10, 10 n.20, 12, 60, 61,
  62, 62 n.91, 63, 63 n.94

Poltergeist 10, 66–7, 82
The Pitchfork Disney 10, 59, 61–2
Riley, Bridget 209
Ringham, Hannah 68, 76, 206, 210,
  238, 239
Riopelle, Jean-Paul 21
Ripley-Duggan, Greg 109
Roberts, Max 163, 164, 164 n.17, 165,
  167, 168, 169
Robson, Luke W. 190, 192
Rock Hall, Northumberland 164–6
Roque, Jacqueline 86
Rosenthal, Norman 46, 60, 68,
  207–8
Rothko, Mark 32, 33, 49, 89–91, 155,
  183–9, 208
Royal Shakespeare Company (RSC) 6,
  43, 58, 124, 129, 129 n.104, 138,
  138 n.124, 236, 237 n.28
Rylance, Mark 236–7

Saatchi, Charles 50, 59, 60, 64 n.96,
  68, 75, 82, 112, 142, 146, 231–3
Sams, Jeremy 158
Savile, Jimmy 143 n.135
Saville, Jenny 146
Schiele, Egon 9 n.18
Schneemann, Carolee 201
Schulze, Daniel 93, 198
Scott, David A. 180
Scott, William 168 n.20
Scuhbeckon, Birgit 150
Seager, Wendy 140, 232
Seligman, Germain 229
Serota, Sir Nicholas 3, 4, 12, 32, 46, 68,
  76, 78, 81, 90
Serra, Richard 32
Seurat, George 158–9, 209
Shaw, Fiona 177, 177 n.35, 178, 179
Sierz, Alek 62, 63 n.94
smith, a 68, 206
Smith, Patty 194
Smith, Simon 67
Solkin, David 226

Sommer, Elyse 189
Sondheim, Stephen
    Sunday in the Park with
    George 158–9
Spencer, Charles 157, 162, 200
Spencer, Stanley 5, 160, 161, 200
Sprinkle, Anne 201
Stafford-Clark, Max 48, 49, 54, 83, 202
Stallabrass, Julian 72, 72 n.112, 231
Starobin, Michael 158
Steer, Sophie 192
Stein, Sarah 105
Stevens, Ellice 191, 192, 193, 194
Stinton, Colin 107
Stones, Ben 162
Stoppard, Tom 5, 12
    After Magritte 25–8, 76
    Artist Descending a Staircase 25
Strachan, Alan 159
Stravinsky, Igor 100
Struth, Thomas 28
Stubbs, George 85
Sutherland, Helen (*see also* Ashington Group) 163, 165, 166, 169
Sweet Pea Productions 176
Swift, Jonathan 45

Tassi, Agostino 88, 89, 189, 191, 194
Tate, Sir Henry 76
Taylor-Wood, Sam 209
Taylor, Marcus 207, 208
Taylor, Paul 176
Thatcher, Margaret 10, 12, 13, 31, 43, 47, 50, 54, 58, 94, 95, 109, 115, 123, 227, 233
theatres
    A Play, a Pie and a Pint, Glasgow 10 n.19
    Almeida Theatre, London 29, 89, 173, 174, 213
    Ambiance Lunch Hour Theatre Club, London 25
    Arcola Theatre, London 9–10, 47, 55, 56, 61, 162
    Barbican Pit Theatre, London 43 n.56, 173, 175, 189 n.72
    Birmingham Repertory Theatre 109, 109 n.48
    Comedy Theatre (now Harold Pinter Theatre), London 109
    Dixon Drama Studio, New York 202
    Donmar Warehouse, London 11, 37, 89, 91, 155, 183, 184, 185, 186, 187,189 n.71
    Drum Theatre, Plimouth 211
    Gate Theatre, London 200
    Globe Theatre, London 18
    Greenwich Theatre, London 159
    Hackney Empire Acorn, London 176
    Hampstead Theatre, London 67
    Kneehigh Asylum Theatre, Truro, Cornwall 157 n.3
    Live Theatre, Newcastle Upon Tyne 35, 66, 167
    Lyric Hammersmith Theatre, London 215, 236
    Long Wharf Theatre, New Haven 113
    Manhattan Theatre Club, New York 98
    Menier Chocolate Factory, London 158
    National Theatre, London 6, 35, 36, 39, 62, 84, 86, 107, 114, 158, 160, 164 n.17, 165, 167, 168, 177, 178, 179, 180, 202, 202 n.99, 203 n.100
    New Diorama Theatre, London 189 n.72
    Old Red Lion, London 25
    Old Vic, Bristol 157 n.3
    Old Vic, London 40, 42
    Opera House, London 52, 54
    Piccolo Teatro, Milan 203 n.99
    Rose Theatre, Kingston upon Thames 43 n.56

Royal Court Theatre, London 20, 31, 47, 48, 49, 54, 54 n.75, 55, 55 n.78, 57, 61, 62, 65, 83, 202, 211, 227, 228, 228 n.13
Royal Exchange Theatre, Manchester 6
Southwark Playhouse, London 10, 66
Swan Theatre, Stratford-upon-Avon 6, 129 n.104
The Hen & Chickens Theatre, London 32
The Other Place Theatre, Stratford-upon-Avon 43, 96 n.12, 97, 124, 128, 131
The Place, London 44
Tobacco Factory Theatres, Bristol 10
Traverse Theatre, Edinburgh 67, 69, 73, 83, 95, 138 n.124, 140, 151, 206, 232, 234
Wyndham's Theatre, London 90, 158
Young Vic, London 6, 124 n.92
Thompson, Don 51
Thompson, Susannah 169, 170
Thornhill (Hogarth), Jane 44
Tillyer, William 48, 49, 83, 155
Tinker, Jack 65, 200
Tintoretto, Jacopo 172, 230
Titian (Tiziano Vecellio) 110, 113, 114, 115, 116, 118, 118 n.77, 119, 121, 162, 225, 230
Treves, Letizia 89, 191
Tulchin, Ted 109
Tulsa, John 58
Turner, Lyndsey 40, 42
Turner, William 5, 9, 60, 85, 162, 166, 186
Turner Prize 52, 62, 68, 203

Uccello, Paolo 21, 230
Ultz 97
Utrillo, Maurice 166

Valadon, Suzanne 5, 9, 55, 56, 57
van Gogh, Vincent 5, 23, 23 n.23, 34, 35, 36, 161, 166, 167
van Meegeren, Han 119, 143
Velázquez, Diego 143 n.135
Velde, Bram and Geer van 21
Vermeer, Johannes 119, 120, 143
Veronese, Paolo 172
Verrocchio, Andrea del 142, 142 n.133
Vicentino, Andrea 171, 171 n.23, 172
Viola, Bill 147, 204

Wainwright, Tom 9
Walker, A. John 233
Walker, Tim 236 n.26
Wallis, Alfred 166
Walmsley, Deka 168
Walpole, Horace 225
Walpole, Robert 44, 98, 224, 224 n.4
Walter, Marie-Thérèse 86, 87
Warhol, Andy 6, 51, 84, 98, 99
Weller, Lucy 176
Wentworth, Richard 233 n.20
Wertenbaker, Timberlake 43 n.54, 54–5, 156, 236
Three Birds Alighting on a Field 2, 12, 16, 31, 32, 43, 47–55, 61, 83, 142, 146, 155, 223, 227–8, 234, 241
The Line 9, 55–7
Whitaker, David 165, 168
Whitelaw, Billie 23
Whiteread, Rachel 3, 60, 82
Whiting, Patsy 87
Whyman, Erica 138
Wieseman, E. Marjorie 120, 122
Wilke, Hannah 201
Wilson, Harry (*see also* Ashington Group) 9, 165, 168, 169, 170
Wilson, Philippa 165
Wilson, Snoo 9 n.18
Windsor, Barbara 193
Woodis, Carole 176
Worth, Irene 107

Wrestling School (*see also* Barker, Howard) 173, 177, 180
Wright, Nicholas
  Vincent in Brixton 161

Yates, A. Frances 18

Yeats, Jack 21
Young British Art (YBA) 3, 12, 16, 47, 48, 50, 57–74, 63 n.96, 75, 83, 146, 169, 179, 207, 236

Zimmermann, Heiner 172

www.ingramcontent.com/pod-product-compliance
Lightning Source LLC
Chambersburg PA
CBHW071809300426
44116CB00009B/1252